2/4/13
$34.95

The Biological
Basis of
Personality

With a new preface by Sybil B. G. Eysenck

Hans J. Eysenck

The Biological Basis of Personality

Transaction Publishers
New Brunswick (U.S.A.) and London (U.K.)

Second printing 2008

New material this edition copyright© 2006 by Transaction Publishers, New Brunswick, New Jersey. Originally published in 1967 by Charles C. Thomas, Publisher.

This book is printed on acid-free paper that meets the American National Standard for Permanence of Paper for Printed Library Materials.

Library of Congress Catalog Number: 2005051414
ISBN: 1-4128-0554-6
Printed in the United States of America

Library of Congress Cataloging-in-Publication Data

Eysenck, H. J. (Hans Jurgen), 1916-
    The biological basis of personality / Hans J. Eysenck ; with a new preface by Sybil B.G. Eysenck.
        p. cm.
    Originally published: Springfield, Ill. : C.C. Thomas, 1967, in series: American lecture series. With a new pref.
    Includes bibliographical references and index.
    ISBN 1-4128-0554-6 (pbk. : alk paper)
    1. Personality. I. Title.

BF698.9.B5E9   2006
155.2—dc22   2005051414

To the Memory of
Ivan Petrovich Pavlov
and
Sir Francis Galton

Nemo Psychologus Nisi Physiologus.

JOHANNES MÜLLER

CONTENTS

PREFACE TO THE TRANSACTION EDITION

THE BIOLOGICAL BASIS OF PERSONALITY is one of the most cited books written by my late husband, H. J. Eysenck. One of the reasons for this is that this was a novel approach to psychology.

There were quite a few personality questionnaires measuring such factors as extraversion, but in addition to postulating the "Big Three" dimensions of extraversion, neuroticism, and psychoticism, Hans was a forerunner of the attempt to align personality theory with physiological concomitants. It was essentially this anchoring of the personality theory in biological measures that distinguishes his approach from all the others.

An analogous situation arose in psychotherapy. While Hans criticized all forms of psychoanalysis, psychotherapy, and counseling, as did other psychologists and even psychiatrists, it was not until the introduction of behavior therapy that psychologists took notice. Why? Because it was based on learning theory and was therefore an alternative that had a scientific basis. Moreover, this therapy cured patients! Similarly, psychology began to take its place as a science when the physiological links could be established with it. So that is what *The Biological Basis of Personality* is all about.

Since this book was first published there has been a plethora of research into the physiological concomitants of personality. Experiments in perception, heart rate, skin conductance, etc. had been carried out in isolation, but with the introduction of individual differences in personality there has been an attempt to link psychology and physiology. This indeed proved to be a very fruitful line of research, which will surely continue for a long time.

However, in the epilogue of this book, the author mentions an experimental problem that has bothered me for some while and is largely unresolved. The introduction of the personality dimensions of extraversion and neuroticism gave rise to many researches but "lamentably," as Hans put it, "so many otherwise well-planned and well-designed studies proved to give uninterpretable results because experimenters failed to keep apart these two dimensions." The problem was that dysthymics, for example, as a group differed from a control group but because the former scored high on both neuroticism and introversion it was impossible to disentangle the contribution of each factor in any differences between the experimental and control groups.

This problem was doubly confounded when the dimension of psychoticism became measurable. Testing an experimental group on say, vigilance, modern day psychologists would hopefully equate a control group for extraversion as vigilance is now known to be superior in introverts; but how about neuroticism or psychoticism? One sample might be comprised of subjects scoring high on neuroticism and the other scoring low on this variable; similarly with psychoticism. Could any differences be partly due to these other dimensions? In my view, samples need to be equated for all personality dimensions except the one under scrutiny in the particular research. Regrettably, this is not the case in all researches even now.

The basic strength of this book is that it paved the way for a "marriage" of the experimental and individual difference approach in personality psychology, a blend that has been very successful in the advancement of psychology as a science. How far this approach has achieved its aim is hard to gauge. Certainly, most psychologists are now aware of the need to anchor personality measurements in physiological terms. Perhaps readers of this book will be able to make up their own minds as to whether progress in psychological research over the years has followed the path suggested in this book.

SYBIL B. G. EYSENCK

PREFACE

"MY NEXT TRICK is impossible!" says the circus acrobat, but the audience knows that he is going to perform it triumphantly nevertheless. Writing a book such as this is an impossible task, and I can only hope that no one will imagine that I am unaware of this fact, or that I am under any illusion that the feat has been performed triumphantly. To straddle the fields of personality research and experimental psychology is in itself quite a demanding task; add to that an attempt to cover also research in psychiatry, genetics, neurology, pharmacology, electrophysiology and several related disciplines, and it will be clear that anyone claiming expertise in all these fields would be either a genius or a charlatan. Nevertheless, evidence had been accumulating in recent years to indicate that personality has a strong biological basis, and the effort had to be made to cover sufficient of the relevant literature to see whether some sort of unified picture would in fact appear. It is my impression that such a picture is indeed beginning to emerge, and that however misconceived some of its proportions and aspects may turn out to be, nevertheless it may serve to direct research into more useful channels, and to pull together existing knowledge from many different sources. Even a bad map is probably better than no map at all, and this book was written in order to provide such a map—as good as I could make it, but of course still very far indeed from anything approaching perfection.

Maps or models of personality exist in rich profusion, and it may be asked why another one should be required. My answer is simply that the field of personality is not an isolated island, lying far from other more civilised countries and continents; personality interacts constantly and inevitably with experimental psychology, pharmacology, neurology, and the various other sciences mentioned earlier.

xi

Personality theorists can only benefit from discovering what light these other sciences may have to shed on their problems, and conversely scientists in these other fields may benefit from knowing something about the ways in which their disciplines interact with personality. Divisions between academic subjects tend to be of administrative convenience, but they may easily obscure the real and much more important links which exist between them and which may provide some of the most exciting fields for fruitful research. I cannot pretend to have uncovered all the suggestive and fruitful relations existing between personality study and surrounding fields, nor can I pretend to have made no errors in dealing with disciplines in which I have not myself had an opportunity of working; in extenuation I can only join Dr. Johnson in pleading "ignorance, sheer ignorance!" This is a pioneering effort, and as such is subject to more possibilities of downright error than most books.

The model of personality which emerges is in fact the third I have tried to construct. My first was presented some twenty years ago; it was a purely descriptive model bringing together psychological experiments, psychiatric assessments, and psychometric methods of analysis, notably factor analysis. The resulting books (*Dimensions of Personality*; *The Experimental Study of Personality*; and a historical account entitled *The Structure of Human Personality*) contained some adumbrations of notions developed later on, but did not essentially go beyond description. The second model took shape ten years ago and tried to supply some form of causal analysis by reference to concepts current in experimental psychology; *Dynamics of Anxiety and Hysteria*, *Experiments in Personality*, and *Experiments with Drugs* embodied much of the experimental and theoretical work done during this period. In this book I have tried to go deeper still and find biological causes underlying the psychological concepts of emotion, excitation, and inhibition which formed the building stones of my earlier efforts. To me, it seems that the causal links postulated between personality variables on the one hand, and neurological and physiological discoveries on the other, make the whole model more realistic and take it out of the field of solipsistic speculation in which the school of the "empty organism" thrives. Such an estimate depends, of course, on the success of the undertaking; if the suggested links should not in fact prove to give rise to verifiable deductions, then nothing would have been gained. However, I believe that even the small amount of evidence already available makes such an outcome unlikely; however wrong the details may be, the main suggestions made are unlikely to be entirely upset by future research—or so I like to think. The reader must of course be the ultimate judge of this.

Theories of personality may have practical applications, and I have tried in various books to suggest such applications to criminology, for instance, or the treatment of neurosis (*Crime and Personality*; *Experiments in Behaviour Therapy*; *The Causes and Cures of Neurosis*[1]). But however enticing such applications may be, they depend for their value on the truth and accuracy of the theory or model from which they are derived. In this book I am not at all concerned with application, but merely with the facts as they appear at the time of writing. It is for this reason that readers may find the ratio of references to text rather large; where so many different specialties are involved it seemed particularly desirable to stick closely to the experimental facts, and to document every statement. This does not make for elegant writing, but it may be more useful for working scientists.

An exception to this rule (if only a limited one) has been made in Chapters II and III. In these I partly recapitulate the major features of models 1 and 2, and it seemed inappropriate to go into details which had already been published *in extenso*. In relation to the descriptive model, in particular, it seemed unnecessary to do so, as a companion volume to the present one, entitled *Description and Measurement of Personality*,[2] has summarized all the evidence, as well as reporting a large amount of new material. In consequence only a very condensed account of this model is here given, and to many readers this will undoubtedly seem dogmatic in the extreme. For further information, discussion of unsolved issues, and qualifications of too explicit statements, these readers must be referred to the above mentioned volume (exact references to this and the other books mentioned will be found in the bibliography).

In Chapter III I have dealt in a similar manner with my second model, but here it was necessary to go into some greater detail as

[1]With Dr. S. Rachman.
[2]With Dr. S. B. G. Eysenck.

the last summary of experimental work had appeared in 1957 (*Dynamics of Anxiety and Hysteria*). I compromised by dealing mainly with material published since then, except when one or other of the older studies was too important to omit. Altogether, here as elsewhere, I attempted to concentrate on essentials and let the less important, more controversial issues go by default; they are interesting and important, but to deal with them in sufficient detail would have meant doubling the length of the book.

Inevitably, in going from one model to the next, hypotheses and theories had to be modified or even jettisoned. It did not seem advisable to burden the book with an elaborate account of the development of the theories that survived, or a necrology of those that died. In a few cases it seemed interesting and important to refer briefly to historical positions now given up or greatly altered; reminiscence in pursuit rotor learning and figural aftereffects are two obvious examples. But on the whole there is sufficient similarity between earlier and later positions to mediate similar predictions, and where that appeared to be true I did not try to trace developments and connections. The theories presented must stand or fall by their ability to give rise to successful predictions; their historical development is irrelevant in this connection. In the same way, criticisms of earlier versions and experiments apparently disproving positions not now maintained have not been dealt with at length; while important to the development of the theories in question, they are no longer relevant.

Some parts of the book first saw the light of day as lectures given to special audiences. Chapter I in part retains the form of the Charles Myers Lecture, given to the British Psychological Society in 1965, and is reprinted with their permission. Chapter IV derives from the Herbert Spencer Lecture given at Oxford in 1964, and Chapter VI from the Thomas Young Lecture given at St. George's Hospital in 1963. To the audiences at these and other lectures, who by their questions and comments indicated where my account was too unclear to be followed easily, I am grateful; and equally I owe much to my colleagues and students with whom I have discussed in detail many of the ideas contained in this book, and who have contributed importantly to the experimental work discussed. It is not too much to say that without their wholehearted cooperation this book would have remained an empty shell of ideas without experimental justification or support.

H. J. Eysenck
Institute of Psychiatry
University of London

THE BIOLOGICAL BASIS
OF PERSONALITY

CHAPTER I

THE TWO FACES OF PSYCHOLOGY

IN THE WRITER'S OFFICE there hang two pictures—one of a Victorian aristocrat, the other of a Russian peasant. Sir Francis Galton symbolises more than anyone else the fundamental concern of psychology with individual differences, with genetic causes of personality development, and with the statistical investigation of systems of classification. Ivan Petrovich Pavlov symbolises more than anyone else the fundamental concern of psychology with general laws, with environmental modification of behaviour, and with the experimental study of functional relationships. It may seem obvious and indeed inevitable that psychology is equally concerned with both these approaches, but this view does not seem to be at all widely held. Experimental psychologists often seem quite unaware of the problems created by individual differences; personality theorists seem equally unconcerned with the lack of relationship between their concepts and those of the experimentalists.

Let us begin by considering the attitude of the experimentalist. He would claim that his method of procedure is modelled exactly on that of the physicist and that it fulfills in every way the requirements of scientific procedure. A functional relation is hypothesized between a and b, such that a $=$ f (b); experiments are carried out to verify the hypothesis and to elucidate the precise nature of the function, preferably in mathematical terms. Such a programme looks inviting, and appears indeed to resemble the physicist's paradigm. But are things really that easy? Consider Köhler's hypothesis that the size of the Müller-Lyer illusion should decrease with massed practice, due to increased satiation inside the angles formed by the arrowheads (Köhler and Fishback, 1950). Opposed to this we have the hypothesis put forward by Eysenck and Slater (1958)

3

that inhibition of attention during massed practice would lead to an increase in the size of the illusion. During forty massed trials, fifty subjects showed an increase in size of illusion from 1.14 through 1.28 and 1.75 to 2.13, which would seem to be in line with the Eysenck and Slater prediction, but this change was found to be insignificant because of the tremendous size of the individual differences. Some subjects showed a strong increase in the size of the illusion, others showed an equally strong decrease, while yet others showed no change at all, or an up-and-down shift. Individual differences accounted for 99 per cent of all the variance observed; systematic "functional" differences only for 1 per cent! Thus adherence to the procedure of the experimentalist, who relegates individual differences to the error term of his analysis of variance, would leave him with only 1 per cent of all the causal factors to study—surely a somewhat excessive price to pay for apparent adherence to the physicist's paradigm![1]

Another example may be taken from learning theory. Hovland (1939) investigated the differential effects of massed and spaced practice on paired-associate learning. He too found an insignificant main effect, primarily due to large individual differences; some 44 per cent of his subjects learned more rapidly under distributed practice, while some 38 per cent learned more rapidly under massed practice; the remainder showed no effect either way. Similar results were found in serial learning. Research since has paid no attention to this problem of individual differences, in spite of the fact that these differences swamp all other effects; we take leave to doubt whether physicists would throw overboard massive and repeated findings for the sake of some putative "pure" model of experimental procedure.

But in actual fact this alleged model exists only in the imagination; physicists do indeed make use of experimental studies of functional relations, but they carefully supplement these with what in biology we would call taxonomic studies. No physicist would dream of assessing the electric conductivity, or the magnetic properties, or the

[1]Parker and Newbigging (1965) have recently brought forward evidence to show that the decrease in magnitude of the illusion is a function of the psychophysical method employed; their data suggest that learning, rather than satiation or inhibition, is responsible for any decline observed.

heat-resisting qualities, of random samples of matter, of "stuff-in-general"; he would insist on being given carefully purified samples of specified elements or of equally carefully prepared alloys. Much energy was spent on the construction of Mendeléev's table of the elements, precisely because one element does not behave like another. Some conduct electricity, others do not, or do so only poorly; we do not throw all these differences into some gigantic error term, and deal only with the average of all substances. But this is what experimental psychologists do, in the cause of imitating physics! It may be suggested that the root of many of the difficulties and disappointments found in psychological research, as well as the cause of the well-known difficulties in duplicating results from one study to another, may lie in this neglect of individual differences.

What sort of an answer would the experimental psychologist make to this argument? In the first place, he would say that physics is in possession of Mendeléev's table but that psychology has nothing of the kind; consequently he has no choice but to pursue the path on which he has embarked. But this argument is patently fallacious; physicists have never neglected differences between one substance and another, even before the notion of an "element" was sufficiently advanced to be practicably useful. Throughout history, classification and experiment were intimately connected, and the table of the elements could never have been constructed if it had not been preceded by much work linking both approaches.

The experimentalist might next argue that individual differences are not his field but that of the psychometrist, or the personality theorist. But insofar as such differences affect his work, they clearly are his concern, and he cannot disembarrass himself of personality variables by handing them over to someone else. Nor can he argue that there are so many theories that he cannot make a choice; it is only by making such choices and embodying them in his experiments, that the experimental psychologist will improve the situation and make future choices easier and more fruitful.

The most usual argument made by the experimental psychologist, however, is probably along these lines. He will say that individual differences are no doubt important, but that they are "unsystematic," and that such forces which cannot be reduced to any form of order cannot *eo ipso* form part of a scientific discipline.

This view is widely held, and if it were in fact true, it would perhaps give strong support to the traditional view. It can be maintained, however, that this view is not in fact true; there is much evidence to show that individual differences are systematic in their effects, and that they are subject to theoretical formulation in terms of general laws. There are two points to this assertion. The first is purely empirical: can we in fact sort people into groups on the basis of an objective procedure, alpha, in such a way that they behave differently in an experiment of the kind a = f (b)? The second is theoretical: can we predict on the basis of some form of personality theory the relationship between alpha and the functional relationship in question? We shall quote a number of investigations which purport to demonstrate that the first part of this assertion is true; we shall also try to show that the second part is true, but this of course is a much more difficult endeavour, and no unequivocal judgment may be possible.

Consider the following problem: does a change in rate of stimulus presentation from four seconds to two seconds affect the subject's error rate in a paired associate learning task? This is a typical experimental problem, with error rate considered as a function of rate of stimulus presentation. A. Jensen (1962) found that for some people the error rate went up, for some it went down, and for some it did not change at all. However, he had also administered the Maudsley Personality Inventory[2] (Eysenck, 1959a) to his subjects; when he plotted the regression lines for subjects high and low respectively on the trait of "neuroticism" or "emotionality," he discovered, as shown in Figure 1, that the change in rate of presentation produced no change in error rate for those low on N, whereas for those high on N the error rate doubled when

[2]The M.P.I. measures the two main dimensions of personality, i.e., emotionality or neuroticism (N) and extraversion-introversion (E). A discussion of these terms and their operational definition will be given in a later chapter (see also Eysenck and Eysenck, 1967). Work there summarised indicates that means, standard deviations, and intercorrelations between these scales are almost identical from one population to another; this has been found to be true with Japanese, Hindi, Scandinavian, South American, Italian, German, and various other groups tested at various times and compared with the English standardisation group. In all these countries N and E are independent (orthogonal) dimensions of personality, and both are in turn independent of intelligence. The M.P.I. has recently been improved in various ways and is now called the E.P.I.

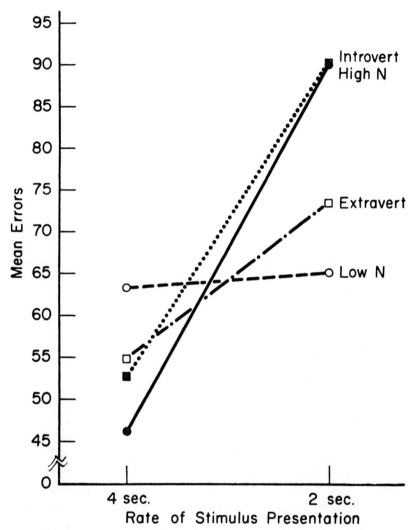

Figure 1. Number of errors in serial learning as a function of rate of stimulus presentation for stable (low N) and emotional (high N) subjects, and for introverts and extraverts. Reprinted with permission from A. Jensen: *Acta Psychol.*, 20:69-77, 1962.

stimulus presentation was speeded up. We thus have an objective measure alpha (in this case the M.P.I.) which sorts out very efficiently two groups of subjects who react very differently to change in stimulus conditions. So much for the empirical demonstration; does this finding also make theoretical sense? On common sense grounds we might regard a speeding up of stimulus presentation as a stressful condition, which would be expected to upset the emotionally labile high N subjects more than the nonemotional low N subjects.

Looking at the problem in a slightly more technical way, we might have recourse to the so-called Yerkes-Dodson Law (Broadhurst, 1959). This law posits a relation between drive or motivation on the one hand and performance on the other, such that optimum performance is achieved at an intermediate drive level, lower degrees of drive failing to promote optimum performance and too high degrees of drive interfering with optimum performance and thus reducing it below its highest level. This relationship is also sometimes known as the inverted U relation between drive and performance (Malmo, 1959; Hebb, 1955). The Yerkes-Dodson Law goes on to state that this optimum drive level is dependent on the complexity and difficulty of the task; easy tasks have a relatively high optimum drive level, whereas difficult and complex tasks have a relatively low optimum drive level. We can now proceed to relate personality differences in "neuroticism" or "emotionality" with different levels of drive or motivation, on the hypothesis explicitly put forward by Spence (1956) that emotion acts as a drive. To put this in a quantitative fashion, we assume that an individual's drive state is a kind of overall activation or arousal level to which emotional upset contributes; this emotional upset is greater in persons high on neuroticism or emotionality, and consequently their drive level is higher than that of people low on neuroticism or emotionality. To illustrate the application of this hypothesis to our example, we might place our groups as indicated in Figure 2, where N_4 and N_2 refer to the high N group under conditions of four-second and two-second presentation while S_4 and S_2 refer to the stable (low N) group. The accuracy of this theory could of course be tested by adding further intervals to the two used in Jensen's actual experiment.

Somewhat related to this experiment is one recently reported by Doerr and Hokanson (1965), in which they studied the change in performance of a timed coding task following frustrating or neutral instructions. Their subjects were children in three age

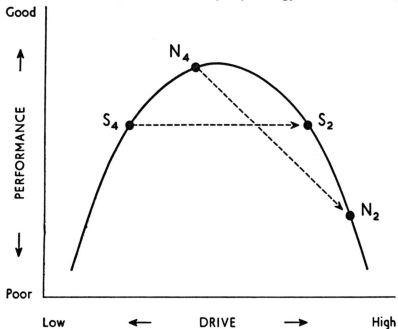

Figure 2. Inverse-U relation between performance and drive, as related to results of experiment shown in Fig. 1. S and N refer to stable and emotional groups; 2 and 4 refer to duration of intertrial interval (in seconds).

groups (seven, nine and eleven), and each group of children was in turn subdivided into low, medium and high heart-rate subjects on the basis of an initial recording under resting conditions. Predictions were made in terms of the Yerkes-Dodson law; i.e., it was predicted "that performance level should increase as general activation increases up to a moderate level, and thereafter decrease as activation increases from moderate to high levels. If the assumption is made that heart rate is an indication of activation level, and that subjects with heart rates falling into the lowest quartile of the distribution of heart rates perform at a low activation level, then their performance level should increase as they are subjected to manipulations (i.e., frustration) that increase heart rate . . . In turn, if the assumption is made that subjects with heart rates falling in the highest quartile of the heart-rate distribution already are performing at or near the optimal level, then an operation increasing heart rate should bring about a decrease in level of performance relative to the practice effects shown by the control subjects." Both effects were in fact observed; low heart-rate subjects improved their performance under frustration, while high heart-rate subjects showed a relative decrease, with medium heart-rate subjects showing no change in either direction. Thus disregard of typological differences would have given results indicative of no effect at all of the independent variable on the dependent variable; proper typological consideration succeeded in demonstrating considerable effects, tending in opposite directions for different subgroups.

The same point can be brought out in quite a different type of experiment, namely one in which we seek to evaluate the effects of drugs on performance. Psychopharmacology has nearly always adopted the simple experimental paradigm based on the assumption that these effects could be traced by comparing group performance under placebo conditions with group performance under drug conditions; failure to find significant effects has usually led to retention of the null hypothesis. In terms of our general personality interaction hypothesis such a procedure is clearly faulty; it is possible, for instance, that a given drug may have a facilitating effect on extraverts and an inhibitory one on introverts. Or, taking psychological effects on mood, a given drug may have a depressing effect on high N subjects, and an elating one on low N subjects. Possibilities such as these will of course complicate very markedly the design of research in this field, but if the underlying hypothesis is correct, then these complications will have to be accepted, and personality differences will have to be taken into account in future work.

As an example of what has been discovered in this connection, consider the work of Munkelt (1965). She administered a battery of tests to male and female subjects under conditions of placebo and drug administration, the drug used being meprobamate, a so-called tranquiliser or depressant (Eysenck, 1963). None of the twelve tests used showed any difference between the two conditions even at the 5 per cent level, and one might have concluded that meprobamate had no effect on performance. However, Munkelt divided her subjects into those high and low on N, and showed that these groups reacted quite differently to the drug; almost half of the tests were now found to differentiate significantly. Figure 3

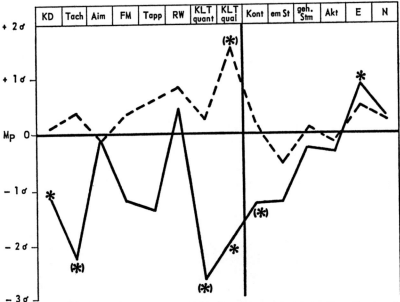

KD	Tach	Aim	FM	Tapp	RW	KLT quant	KLT qual	Kont	em St	geh. Stm	Akt	E	N

Figure 3. Performance of high N (solid line) and low N (broken line) subjects on a variety of tests under drug conditions. The scores plotted are differences between performance under meprobamate and under placebo. Reprinted with permission from P. Munkelt: *Psychol. Beiträge, 8:98-183,* 1965.

gives a diagrammatic representation of her results; the values plotted are the differences between placebo and drug performance for labile (solid line) and stable (broken line) subjects. The tests used are shown at the top; they are a complex reaction-time apparatus (KD, for Kieler Determinationsgerät; see Eysenck, 1964c); a tachistoscopic test (Tach.); an aiming test (Aim.); a tremometer test (FM); a tapping test (Tapp.); a railwalking test (RW); two concentration tests involving mental arithmetic (KLT); four questionnaires relating to momentary emotional reactions; and the E and N scales of the M.P.I.

Munkelt summarizes her findings in this way. "Labile subjects under drug perform below their placebo value in seven of the eight performance tests, in four cases significantly so. In their momentary emotional state they are also influenced in a negative sense. Stable subjects are not at all affected as far as their emotional state is concerned, and in the case of the performance tests

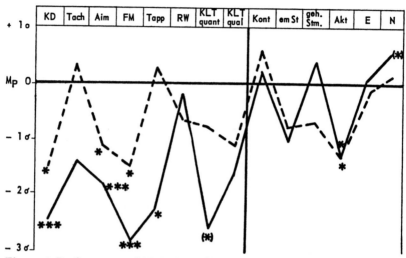

Figure 4. Performance of high N (solid line) and low N (broken line) subjects on a variety of tests under drug conditions. The scores plotted are differences between performance under alcohol and under placebo. Reprinted with permission from P. Munkelt: *Psychol. Beiträge, 8*:98-183, 1965.

their performance under the drug is, if anything, superior." Orthodox analysis, relying on overall comparisons and not paying attention to individual differences in reaction linked with high and low scores on neuroticism, would have failed to discover these important and highly significant effects. It should perhaps be added that Munkelt also subdivided her population according to sex, and found that this variable too produced significant differences, the men showing reactions similar to the stable group, the women reactions similar to the labile group.

The same battery of tests was applied by Munkelt in another study comparing the effects of placebo and alcohol. Here five differences were significant when a simple overall comparison was made, but important conclusions follow from an analysis of the labile and stable subgroups, as shown in Figure 4. It is clear that alcohol has a much stronger effect on labile than on stable subjects as far as performance, particularly motor performance and concentration; there are no differential effects on mood. These results are psychological, but if the view is correct that personality differences reflect differences in underlying innate physiological struc-

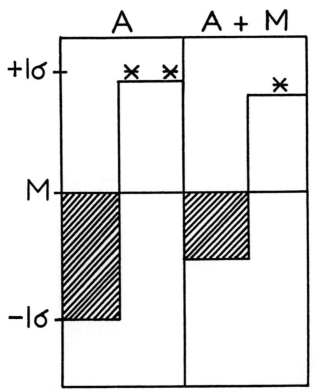

Figure 5. Alcohol concentrations in the blood of high N (shaded column) and low N (white column) subjects after administration of either alcohol alone (A) or alcohol and meprobamate (A and M). Reprinted with permission from P. Munkelt: *Psychol. Beiträge,* 8:98-183, 1965.

tures, then we might perhaps expect similar complex results in measurements of the alcohol concentration in the blood. Figure 5 shows such a result; the comparison is between the effects of a standard dose of alcohol and a standard dose of alcohol administered together with a dose of meprobamate. It will be seen that the labile (shaded column) and stable (white column) subjects react quite differently under both conditions; it is found that the concentration is significantly higher in the stable than in the labile subjects. This difference may be due to the quicker absorption of the alcohol by the stable group; the results fall just short of significance.

Equally convincing is the exhaustive work published in a recent monograph by Janke (1964). He used an experimental arrangement similar to that of Munkelt, but employed four drugs: Ritalin,® meprobamate (Miltown), promazin, and Medomin®, all of them C.N.S. depressants of one kind or another. The drugs were administered in different concentrations. Consider now some drug effects (always scored as the difference between placebo and drug reaction) to various questions regarding the subject's mood. Figure 6 shows drug effects on mood directly; it will be seen that the stable subjects (shaded) show a negative effect, while the labile ones show a positive effect. The same is true of Figure 7, which shows effects on emotional stability. Labile persons benefit; stable ones become less stable. Such differential effects would of course be completely lost if undifferentiated groups were studied; thus the results again emphasize the importance of working with an adequate typology.

Consider next Janke's results with performance tests. He has summarized these in the following words: "Tranquilizers improve performance on psychomotor tests only in subjects who, because of exaggerated emotional tension, perform inadequately under normal conditions." Thus in this field too we again find support for our hypothesis of the vital importance of individual differences, and we may perhaps add that these specific results find good theoretical support in the Yerkes-Dodson law.

A third example comes from the work of Goldman-Eisler *et al* (1965) on chlorpromazine. She used a measure of "resting breath rate" (RBR) to identify individuals high and low on arousal, and found that those with high RBR, and consequently high arousal, "responded to the drug by delaying speech action under intellectual challenge, taking more time and improving their performance"; this result she attributed to reduction of arousal under chlorpromazine. "Specifically this took the form of allowing these subjects a more relaxed disposal of time available in speech. They took more time for pausing and, as emerged, for thinking." Subjects whose RBR was on the low side, and who were therefore operating at lower levels of arousal, "became less circumspect, more impulsive, and intellectually less successful" under the drug. This was attributed by the authors to the effects "of relaxation in an already sufficiently relaxed 'initial tension state,' which is inimical to the

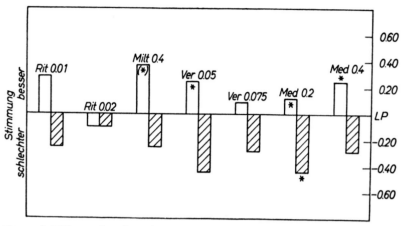

Figure 6. Effects of various depressant drugs on mood ratings of low N subjects (shaded) and high N subjects (white). Reprinted with permission from W. Janke, 1964.

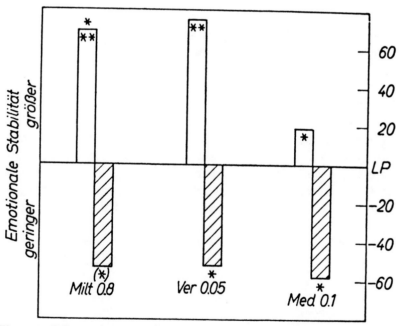

Figure 7. Effects of various depressant drugs on the emotional stability of low N subjects (shaded) and high N subjects (white). Reprinted with permission from W. Janke, 1964.

efficiency of cognitive function." Here again therefore we have contradictory effects of a given drug, depending on choice of subjects tested, and again it seems possible that the results can be explained in terms of an application of the Yerkes-Dodson Law.

Even the structure of personality may change *in different ways* under drugs, depending upon predrug standing on the main dimensions of personality. An interesting paper by Lienert and Huber (1966) may illustrate this effect. They administered amphetamine and placebo to high-N and low-N groups respectively, and tested the four resultant groups on nine intelligence tests. Intercorrelations were calculated and factor analyses carried out on the four groups separately. It was found that among stable subjects, amphetamine produced greater differentiation by *increasing* the number of significant factors from 3 to 4, while *reducing* that of the labile subjects from 4 to 3. In other words, the drug effects were in opposite directions, depending upon the predrug standing of the subject groups. Again, therefore, there is an interaction effect which must be taken into account if drug effects are to be encompassed by the experimental design; omission of individual differences would obliterate the sought effect.

Effects such as those discussed occur not only in human subjects. Does inhalation of alcoholic fumes increase or decrease activity in mice? McClearn (1962) submitted mice of six strains to such an experiment, recording five-minute activity scores for experimental and control animals. The results are given in Figure 8, and it will be seen that in two strains the experimental animals are significantly less active than the controls; in two strains there are no differences; and in two strains the experimental animals are significantly more active. The size and even the direction of the effect of the drug thus depend on the strain of the animals tested; without such typological differentiation the overall results would have been to the effect that alcohol has no effect at all, and that there was a tremendously large error variance. Proper regard to type differences has rescued some of this variance and brought it under experimental control.

Joffe (1965) has submitted another excellent example of the importance of paying attention to typological factors. He studied the very important problem of the influence of prenatal stress on

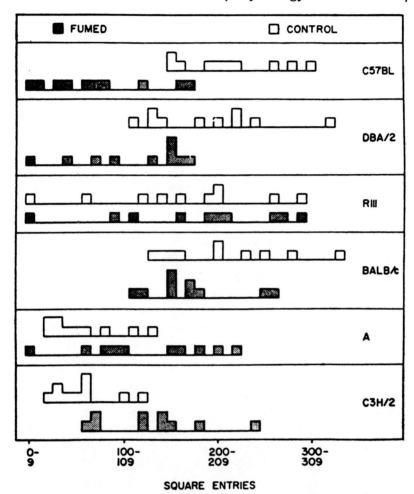

Figure 8. Activity in mice as a function of inhalation of alcohol fumes, as shown by members of six different strains. Reprinted with permission from G. E. McClearn, 1962.

behaviour of offspring, using ambulation scores for his offspring behaviour measure. The stress situation chosen requires females to learn prior to mating to avoid shock on the presentation of a conditioned stimulus. After mating they are returned to the conditioning apparatus and the fear-associated conditioned stimulus is presented without shock and the fear-reducing avoidance response blocked. Joffe subdivided his subjects into emotional and nonemotional animals, choosing these animals from the Maudsley strains, and found that the offspring of emotionally reactive fathers had their ambulation scores raised by the premating treatment, whereas those of the emotionally nonreactive fathers had theirs lowered. Nor is this a solitary finding; Thompson and Olian (1961), Weir and DeFries (1964), and DeFries (1964) all have reported that prenatal strain decreased the ambulation of high active strains and increased that of less active ones. Consideration of typological factors is again essential for an understanding of the effect in question, or even for its very demonstration.

All these findings are of some interest, but they may perhaps be said to have little systematic significance in important areas within modern learning theory. This can hardly be said when we turn to a recent study by Kleban (1965), who studied reversal learning. Using forty-three Sprague-Dawley and forty-three Wistar rats, he gave the animals forty trials of reward training in a Y maze. On the next twenty trials, control groups were continued under the same training procedure, and 50 per cent shock trials were introduced in the training of the experimental animals. This was followed by extinction training, where the reward was shifted to the opposite arm of the maze, and 50 per cent shock continued for a no-delay and a thirty-second delay shock group. This delay helped the Sprague-Dawley rats reverse in a minimum number of trials, whereas it served to establish response stereotypy in the Wistar rats! Kleban comments that "in this experiment, the Wistar albino rats responded to the delay periods as if they had read the experimental hypothesis. The results were consistent with the previous findings on omissions of punishment. But the Sprague-Dawley rats were able to make response reversals following the delay periods without showing evidence of response stereotypy." Clearly the general theoretical system which the author was using applied to one strain but was completely contradicted by the behaviour of the other. It is possible that strain differences in emotionality may be responsible, but in that case theoretical statements must include typological postulates and reference to individual differences as an integral part of any prediction.

Again, this is not the only experiment to demonstrate this point; Storms, Boroczi, and Broen (1963) have drawn attention to the fact that the effects of punishment may be a function of the strain of rats used. Here too it seems likely that differences in emotionality may be the fundamental variable underlying the observed strain differences. The work of Broadhurst (1960) in this field is so well known and so extensive that we have purposely not taken our examples from his publications; many additional experiments to illustrate the point could be taken from his work on the Maudsley strains of emotional and nonemotional rats, and it is also possible to believe that an explanation of many of these somewhat mysterious findings will ultimately be found in terms of the concepts of emotionality, conceived as a congenital, innate quality of the animal associated with his autonomic system (Eysenck and Broadhurst, 1964).

Kleban's experiment suggests that typological differences may be relevant to important theoretical differences; this point has been made most strongly by Marshall B. Jones in a novel and very suggestive context. He starts off by drawing attention to the fact that "no dispute in the history of psychology was more intense or more protracted than the one between Hullians and Tolmanians over the nature of learning. . . . The two schools of thought were strikingly distinct in many ways; in weltanschauung, in their approach to theory, in theory itself, in methodology, and in the kinds of experiments they performed. They were also different in the animals which they studied; Spence and Tolman used two different strains of rats." The derivations of these strains have been carefully traced by Jones, and it appears that the Spence animals were the descendants of C. S. Hall's "nonemotional" strains, while Tolman's, as far as can be ascertained, would be less selected and probably much nearer to the "emotional" strain. (Experimental selection has been found to be largely for nonemotionality; the "emotional" animals are only slightly more emotional than the unselected parental generation, whereas the "nonemotional" animals are far less emotional than the unselected parental generation.) Jones concludes that "inasmuch as these two strains of rats have been separated for over 30 years, have been differently and selectively bred, and have kept such diverse psychological company, the possibility that there may exist genetic differences between them cannot be dismissed; nor can we be sure that hereditary differences

may not have played some role in the great debate between S-R
and S-S theorists."

Let us consider a particular experiment (Jones and Fennell, 1965).
Rats were trained to follow a runway from starting-box to goal-
box, along a U-shaped 8-foot runway which forced them to make
a 180° turn in the middle. Half the rats were hungry, half were
thirsty; reward for each group was appropriate, i.e., food or water.
Latency of emerging from the starting box was measured, and so
was time in the runway. Two strains of rats were tested: a Spence
strain and a Tolman strain. Results are shown in Figure 9; it is
clear that the Tolman strain Long-Evans rats are very much slower
for most of the time; even on the 10th and last day of the experiment the thirsty group is still significantly slower than its Spence
counterpart. These differences appeared both in latency and in
running time; the Figure shows a combination of both. The comments of the authors of this report are very revealing:

> The principal finding of the study was the gross difference in
> level of performance between the two strains. The Long-Evans
> animals were much slower to emerge from the start box and took
> much more time in the runway proper than did the Spence rats.
> . . . The numbers do not do full justice to the contrasting be-
> haviors of the two strains. The Long-Evans animals spent long
> periods of time in exploratory behaviors, sniffing along the walls,
> in the air, along the runway. Even toward the end of testing,
> they would stop, seemingly without reason, and renew their
> explorations. The turn of the maze was a particular common
> point at which the Long-Evans animals would get "stuck." Many
> times they lingered in the turn itself for several minutes. Retrac-
> ing was frequent. The Spence animals behaved very differently.
> After the first two days, the animals popped out of the start box,
> ambled down the runway, around the turn and into the goal box.
> In contrast to the Long-Evans rats they seemed almost oblivious
> to their environment.
>
> These differences between the two strains are strikingly con-
> gruent with the theoretical accounts of the investigators who
> used them. The Spencians maintained that animals learned stimu-
> lus-response connections. The strength of these connections ac-
> cumulated in small increments from trial to trial. Learning was
> a regular, almost mechanical process, in which perception and

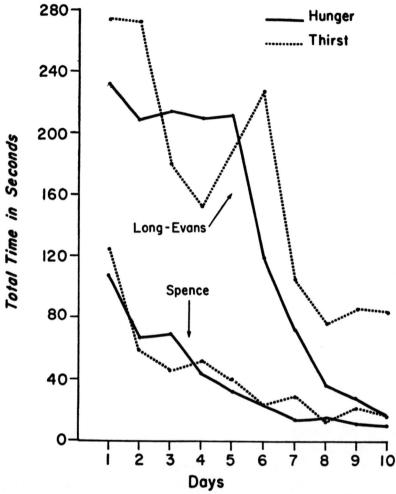

Figure 9. Running speed in U-shaped runway for hungry and thirsty rats respectively, of two strains of animals used by the California and Iowa schools respectively. Reprinted with permission from M. B. Jones and R. S. Fennell: *Quart. J. Florida Acad. Sci.*, 28:289-296, 1965.

cognition played little if any role. The Tolmanians argued that animals learned what leads to what; they acquired expectations and formed "cognitive maps." To the Tolmanians learning was a discontinuous process which depended critically upon perceptual apprehension and organization of the surrounding environment. Exploratory behaviors were central to the Tolmanian argument. The U-maze is a very simple learning situation. Nevertheless, even in it the behaviors of Spence and Long-Evans rats contrast sharply, and in ways which reinforce the theoretical views of the men who studied them.

These behaviour differences, of course, are in line with what one might expect from emotionally reactive and nonreactive animals, respectively. The nonreactive Spence-type animal is not distracted by emotional reactions from his task of learning S-R connections and does so efficiently and quickly. The highly emotional Tolman-type Long-Evans animal is frightened by the novel situation, and his emotional reaction disrupts performance; furthermore, he is slow in settling down and accommodating to the situation. If some such account were even remotely along the right lines, then one would have to conclude that Tolman and his students had been guilty of a simple anthropomorphic fallacy; they interpreted the hesitations and retracings of the animals in human terms as helpful in constructing cognitive maps, furnishing perceptual apprehension, and organizing the environment. In reality, we may simply be dealing with frightened animals looking for a way out or trying to safeguard themselves from the dangers surrounding them on all sides. We are back again with the Yerkes-Dodson law; sedative drugs should improve the performance of the Tolman rats, interfere with that of the Spence rats. Many other ways can of course be devised for testing this general hypothesis, which would rephrase the tremendous theoretical battle between these two schools in terms of simple typological differences.

We have so far discussed typological differences in humans and their effects on the kind of behaviour studied by experimentalists, and we have also been concerned with strain differences in rats. We may go one step further and ask whether we should not also be concerned with phyletic differences in behaviour, i.e., with differences of a fundamental kind which may appear as we ascend the phylogenetic scale. The absence of such differences is almost taken for granted by most experimental psychologists; as Bitterman (1965) has pointed out, "their work has been dominated almost from its inception by the hypothesis that the laws of learning are the same for all animals—that the wide differences in brain structure which occur in the animal series have a purely quantitative significance." Thorndike (1911) put this view very clearly when he wrote: "If my analysis is true, the evolution of behaviour is a rather simple matter. Formally the crab, fish, turtle, dog, cat, monkey, and baby have very similar intellects and characters. All are systems of connections subject to change by the laws of exercise and effect."

Although received with skepticism at first, this view soon became widely accepted, and as a corollary, experimental attention was almost entirely restricted to one or two types of animal—the rat, more recently the pigeon, and very occasionally the monkey. Bitterman (1965) makes clear just how widely accepted this view is, and how uncritically it is accepted; most psychologists will recall, perhaps with some amusement, how Hull, for instance, skips from rat experiments to human experiments, on the explicit assumption that identical laws and even mathematical relationships will be observed! Thus we find that experimental psychologists do not only treat all humans, or all rats, as undifferentiated fodder for their studies, but that they scarcely bother to differentiate one species from another, or even to distinguish between vertebrates and invertebrates, or mammals and fish.

Bitterman has shown that such views are quite erroneous. Consider his work on reversal learning. In order to get food, the hungry animal has to go to the right or left one of two identically illuminated panels; when he has mastered the problem, the correct choice is reversed; i.e., if he learned to obtain food from the right panel, he now has to learn to get it from the left. When this reversal is mastered, the correct choice is changed again to the right, and so on. Figure 10 shows the results of such training for rats and fish respectively; it will be clear that the rats learn to reverse very adequately, while the fish not only do not learn, but show an actual deterioration of performance. Training was in fact continued well beyond the time span illustrated on this diagram, for more than 150 days, without any sign of improvement, suggesting that under no circumstances would fish be able to do what comes quite naturally to rats.

Or consider probability learning. In one experiment, Bitterman, Wodinsky, and Candland (1958) rewarded the correct of two choices 70 per cent of the time, changing later on to a 100 per

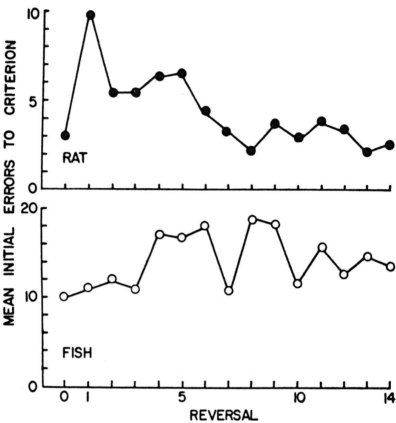

Figure 10. Spatial habit reversal in fish and rats. Reprinted with permission from M. G. Bitterman: *Amer. Psychologist, 20*:396-410, 1965.

cent reward. As Figure 11 shows, rats *maximize* under the 70-30 reward situation; i.e., they tend to go to the rewarded choice on all trials, while fish *match*; i.e., they go to the rewarded choice on 70 of the trials. When the percentage of reward is changed from 70 to 100, their behaviour changes, while that of the rats does not. This is but an example of the now quite strong evidence that fish and rats are characterized quite generally by matching or maximizing behaviour in probability learning situations. It is interesting to note that man resembles the fish more than the rat in this, unless actual money is at stake! We may perhaps conclude that species-specific behaviour can be very marked, and that here too the simple

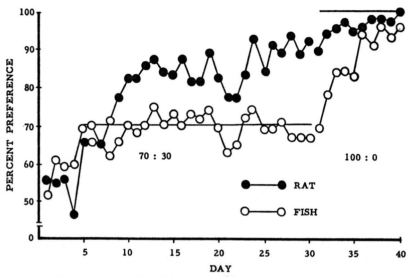

Figure 11. Visual probability learning in fish and rats. Reprinted with permission from M. G. Bitterman: *Amer. Psychologist*, 20:396-410, 1965.

assumption of universal laws obtaining irrespective of individual differences of a phylogenetic nature is untenable.

In stressing the relevance of individual differences, typological considerations, and strain and species variations to experimental psychology, we have no wish to deny that similar considerations apply also to applied psychology. Here also universal assumptions are too frequently made, and here also these assumptions can be shown to be faulty. Educational psychologists seek to determine whether praise or blame motivates children better; yet Thompson and Hunnicutt (1944) have shown that while praise motivates introverted children, blame motivates extraverted children. Psychologists in the field of criminology discuss the relative effects of punishment or counselling *in general*, when there is evidence that for different groups one may be productive of good effects, the other of bad effects, while for other groups these effects are reversed (Eysenck, 1964). Clinical psychologists argue in favour of certain methods of therapy when it is known that the same method may have positive or negative consequences depending on the high or low N score of the patient (Eysenck and Rachman, 1965). In these and all other applied fields, a suitable typology is a *sine qua non* for productive and meaningful research, just as much as this is needed in experimental psychology.

What is true of experimental and applied psychology is equally true of correlational psychology. Where experimental psychology writes a = f(b), correlational psychology, unable to control the independent variable, or even to isolate it, writes $r_{ab} \neq 0$, using this inequality as evidence of causal connection. Cronbach (1957) calls these "the two disciplines of scientific psychology" and suggests that they should pull together, rather than neglect each other, as in the past. Here too it might be suggested that correlational psychology, just like experimental psychology, is subject to typological troubles and erroneously makes the same assumptions of lack of individual differences—even when investigating individual differences! An example will make this apparent confusion clearer. Factor analysis is a correlational device for isolating the main dimensions of individual variability; it has been applied with equal vigour to tests of intelligence and of temperament. Yet in running correlations over random samples of the population, implicitly the assumption is made that the same system of relations obtains in all members of this population; in other words, individual differences in structure of abilities, or temperamental traits, are denied. Yet it can be shown that they exist; the structure of intellectual abilities is different in stable and in labile children, and the structure of personality traits in bright and in dull students (Eysenck and White, 1964).

Ultimately what is being asserted here is that correlations between variables a and b may differ significantly in size and direction when total groups are subdivided according to typological principles and correlations run over these subgroups. A good example is furnished by Venables' (1963) study of level of skin potential and fusion of paired light flashes as measures of arousal. These two indices correlate positively in normal subjects, but negatively in schizophrenics; in fact the two groups are better discriminated by the relation of these two measures than by absolute scores on either or both. Like experimental manipulation, correlational analysis is liable to gross errors unless typological differences are considered in the setting up of the investigation and in the analysis of the data.

Enough has perhaps been said to establish the fact that experimental psychology, either on the theoretical or on the empirical side, cannot afford to leave out of account the consideration of individual differences and typological postulates. Attempts to do so have had very undesirable effects. In the first place, we have in our analyses very large error terms—so large that they frequently swamp our experimental variance. In the second place, even though our main effects may be significant, they only apply to means, and we cannot make predictions in the individual case. In the third place, experimental variables may have opposite effects on different groups of subjects, leading to insignificant results when all are thrown together in the experimental design. In the fourth place, whole systems of theory and interpretation may be built up on the basis of results achieved with one type of subject, whether human or animal; these systems may not survive replication with other types of subject. Lastly, the neglect of individual differences and their systematic consideration on the part of experimentalists has opened wide the door to nonscientific or prescientific theorists and practitioners in the field of personality, leading to the present absurd state of affairs where we have dozens of "schools of personality" but very little in the way of factual support, theoretical rigour, and experimental demonstration.

How then is a personality theorist to proceed? In what way can he integrate the laws of the experimentalists with his typological investigations? An example of this has already been given in our discussion of Jensen's experiment on the effects of changes in the rate of stimulus presentation to the number of errors in serial learning; it will be remembered that an explanation of this finding of increase in error with increase in rate of stimulus presentation for highly emotional subjects and the complete absence of any change in number of errors with rate of stimulus presentation for unemotional subjects was made in terms of the Yerkes-Dodson law. It may be worthwhile to go back to this hypothesis and treat it in more detail.[3]

In experimental psychology we find a large number of studies in which emotion, considered as a drive, is being manipulated experimentally and the resulting behaviour investigated as a function of

[3]The following argument is taken from Savage and Eysenck (1964).

these changes. In the form of a schematic formula we might write this: $B_E = f$ (D_E), where B_E refers to all the forms of behaviour which are affected by changes in the emotional state of the animal, f denotes some specific function (increasing, decreasing, or nonmonotonic) which relates behaviour to the independent variable, and D_E denotes the theoretical concept "emotion-drive" produced by manipulation of such variables as strength of shock, loudness of noise, etc.

To adapt this paradigm to research in personality and individual differences, we can substitute E in the formula for D_E, so that it now reads: $B_E = f(E)$. E in this formula refers to emotionality, i.e., a quality in the animal rather than in the situation, and one which can be evaluated experimentally either by choosing animals respectively high and low on some measure of E, or else by breeding for high and low scores on E. If E (emotionality) is theoretically similar to emotion-drive (D_E), then it would follow that the two can be interchanged in all relevant experimental situations. Thus, if it is found that B_1 is a linearly increasing function of D_E, then it would follow that B_1 should also be a linearly increasing function of differing degrees of emotionality under standard experimental conditions. In effect we postulate that differences in inherited emotionality of different Ss in the same experimental situation should act in the same way as differences in the strength of drive-producing stimuli applied to different groups of Ss equated for emotionality.

A more formal statement of this hypothesis may be in order. We may consider the subject of the experiment in terms of stress and strain as defined in Young's modulus. Consider Hooke's law of elasticity:

$$\text{Stress} = k \text{ x Strain}$$

where k is a constant (the modulus of elasticity) which depends upon the nature of the material and the type of stress used to produce the strain. This constant k, i.e., the ratio $\dfrac{\text{Stress}}{\text{Strain}}$ is called Young's modulus, and is illustrated (with certain simplifications) in Figure 12a. A and B are two metals differing in elasticity; they are stressed by increasing loads, and the elongation corresponding to each load is plotted on the abscissa. It will be seen that identical

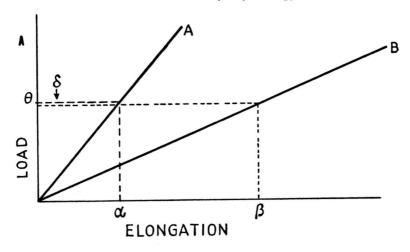

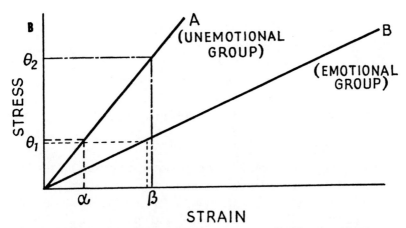

Figure 12. Illustration of Hooke's Law (a) as applied to the measurement of emotionality (b). Reprinted from R. D. Savage and H. J. Eysenck, 1964.

loads θ give rise to quite divergent elongations, α and β. Figure 12b illustrates a similar analysis of rat behaviour in an experimental situation productive of emotion. Again the stress (independent variable) is plotted on the ordinate, and the strain (dependent variable) on the abscissa; A and B represent the unemotional and emotional groups of animals respectively. Identical stress θ_1 gives rise to quite different strains $\propto$ and β. It would require stress θ_2 to make the strain in A animals equal to that produced by θ_1 in B animals. Differences between θ_1 and θ_2 are the kinds of differences traditionally studied by experimental psychologists; differences between A and B are the kinds of differences traditionally studied by personality psychologists, believers in the importance of constitutional factors, and clinical psychologists. Physicists have never attempted to make a choice between these two sets of variables, or to study them in isolation; it seems equally futile for psychologists to do so. Provided the modulus employed is even moderately correct, and more than a mere analogy, the experimental possibilities suggested by this method of approach seem promising.

No assumptions have been made in our experimental work about two important matters which urgently require empirical investigation. Metals have different *elastic limits*; i.e., they differ with respect to the limits of stress within which the strain in a given material completely disappears when the stress is removed. It is not unlikely that animals too have different limits of a similar kind; observation of neurotic and psychotic patients suggests that stress beyond a certain point leaves permanent residues. It is not impossible that this limit may be different for emotional and nonemotional rats, but unfortunately no evidence is available on this point.

The other point relates to the speed of return after stress to the original point of departure. It is possible that emotional animals may require a longer time to return to their prestress level of autonomic tonus than do nonemotional animals. Past work is not a very good guide on this point, because it has traditionally mixed up the two variables concerned, i.e., k (constitution) and stress. Clearly it is impermissible in any such experiment to apply equal stresses to normal and neurotic Ss, or to emotional and nonemotional rats; this would result in dissimilar strains and consequently prejudge the issue. What would be required is indicated in Figure 12, where a stress θ_2 for the unemotional animal is equated with a stress θ_1 for the emotional ones, giving rise to equal strains β. The outcome of such an experiment would be most instructive.

Attempts have been made to define and measure emotionality at the animal level by means of the elimination and ambulation scores on the open field test (Broadhurst, 1960; Hall, 1951). Selective breeding studies and diallel crossing studies have shown that behaviour on this test is indeed genetically determined (Broadhurst, 1960). This, however, is not enough to prove that open field test behaviour is a measure of emotionality. It is possible to argue that behaviour in this situation is quite specific, and that what is inherited is nothing but the reaction (defecation) to this particular situation. Emotionality, if it is to be defined operationally in terms of one single test, could equally well be defined in terms of some other test which might show no correlation with the open field type of measure. Indeed, the identification of an elimination score with emotionality has not gone unchallenged (Bindra and Thompson, 1953; Evans and Hunt, 1942). A full discussion of the work related to this problem can be found in Broadhurst (1960).

If the open field situation is indeed a measure of E, rather than an index of some specific defecation response, then scores on this test may be used as the basis for certain predictions based on theory and general experimental findings. The open field defecation scores may be regarded as an indicator of a hypothetical construct, *emotionality*, which has drive-like properties relating to nonmonotonic increases in performance, interference with the performance of acquired responses, and irrelevant drive functions.

Eysenck and Broadhurst (1964) have reviewed the evidence on this point in considerable detail; they have also reported a variety of physiological and biochemical studies into the precise nature of emotionality in rats. The general consensus of all this work appears to be that emotionality as measured by the open field test does indeed work in the way predicted (see also Broadhurst and Eysenck, 1965). We will return to this point in a later chapter.

Much the same argument can of course be applied to humans except that we must substitute questionnaire scores such as the M.P.I. neuroticism scale for the open field test. Alternatively, we may use physiological measures, as for instance in the Doerr and Hokanson (1965) study already referred to, in which children were grouped according to their heart rate, this recording being used as a measure of emotionality. Many examples of this type of approach will be mentioned in later chapters, but we will quote just one illustration to make the point clearer. Rosenbaum (1953, 1956) found that threat of a strong shock led to greater generalisation of a voluntary response than did threat of weak shock ($B_E = f\ D_E$). He also discovered that anxious subjects showed greater generalisation to identical stimuli than did nonanxious subjects ($B_G = f\ E$). Using this general paradigm then, very much in the manner of Figure 12, provides a strong theoretical link between experimental psychology and the study of personality.

It may be asked how we are to discover the relationships between personality variables and experimental and theoretical variables. There would appear to be three main avenues. The first one would make use of observed individual differences on any particular experimental task, as for instance in the case of the Eysenck and Slater study of the Müller-Lyer illusion already referred to. We can select from our total group of subjects those where the illusion tends to decrease with time, and contrast them with another group where there is a tendency for the illusion to increase in time. Having obtained these extreme groups, we can then experiment with them in various ways to discover consistent differences in personality between them. This mode of procedure is frequently used, but in our opinion it is probably the weakest of the three. There is no guarantee that the particular task chosen and the particular conditions under which it is administered have any great relevance to wide-ranging theories of personality and experimental psychology. Furthermore, the results *per se* do not usually generate any precise hypotheses which can be tested. Last, and worst of all, the number of personality tests which could be administered is so large that choice will usually be made in a random fashion, and it is unlikely that random choice of this type will generate very positive results. For all these reasons we would prefer one of the other two methods of approach.

The second method would begin by analysing the behaviour patterns shown by random samples of people in their everyday life behaviour and next attempt to construct some kind of systematic typology on the basis of such observations and the statistical treatment based upon them. The hypothesis underlying this approach would be that the major dimensions of personality could be identified in this manner and that they would be most likely to be related to important concepts in the experimental and theoretical fields. We will discuss this approach in more detail in the next chapter and will not therefore describe it in greater detail here.

The third approach would take some hypothetical personality trait, such as anxiety or neuroticism or emotionality, conceptualise it in terms of some variable in the experimental field and then carry out experiments to discover whether this identification was feasible and fruitful. This third approach is of course the one advocated here, but we would like to add that it really presupposes that some work has already been done with some measure of success along the lines of our second method; how else could we identify the traits of anxiety or emotionality or neuroticism? We would suggest therefore that the most useful approach to the problem of reuniting the two large areas of psychology which are at present so sadly disjointed would be the one which made use first of the descriptive approach to isolate the main dimensions of personality and then of the hypothetico-deductive approach. In the latter, the main dimensions were tentatively identified with concepts in experimental and general psychology, deductions were made from this identification, and experiments were carried out to test the value of these deductions. In this way we might hope to end up with a unified psychology presenting a single face to the world rather than the present, somewhat schizophrenic, Janus-like apparition.

CHAPTER II

THE STRUCTURE OF PERSONALITY

THEORIES ABOUT THE STRUCTURE of personality go back at least as far as the ancient Greeks, and the theory of the four humours and the four temperaments corresponding to them is of very respectable antiquity. In its most widely accepted form, it is due to the Greek physician Galen who lived in the second century of our era. The famous German philosopher Immanuel Kant accepted this theory in his widely read textbook of psychology which he entitled *Anthropologie*, and his descriptions of the four temperaments have become widely quoted. He followed custom in conceiving of them as being separate categories into one or other of which every person could be sorted, without any possibility of overlap or change (Eysenck, 1960e). This was clearly not in accord with reality, and towards the end of the nineteenth century various psychologists pointed out that a better description of personality could be achieved by using two orthogonal dimensions, along each of which people could be distributed continuously. Wilhelm Wundt postulated that one of these dimensions would segregate the strong from the weak emotions, i.e., the melancholic and choleric temperaments from the phlegmatic and sanguine; as his other dimension he postulated one which divorced the changeable temperaments, the choleric and sanguine, from the unchangeable ones, the melancholic and the phlegmatic (Eysenck and Eysenck, 1967). Figure 13 shows in diagrammatic form this combination of the theories of Kant and Wundt.

The work summarised in this Figure was almost entirely of a subjective character; in other words, what these various philosophers, physicians, and psychologists were doing was to look for uniformities of conduct in the lives of the people whom they were

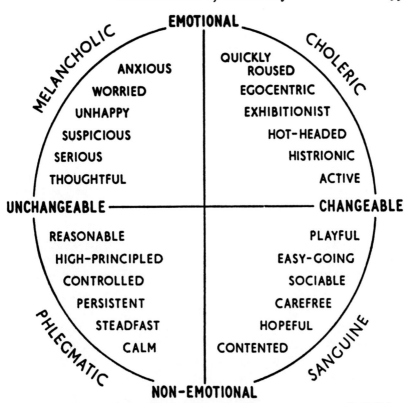

Figure 13. Traits traditionally describing the "four temperaments" of Galen. The actual descriptions are adapted from I. Kant, and the arrangement about the two major axes is as suggested by W. Wundt.

able to observe, and reduce these uniformities to a description of a categorical or a continuous type. They made no attempt to formulate specific theories about the formal structure which was so well described in their word pictures, and they made no attempt to demonstrate by experimental or statistical means the accuracy or otherwise of their hypotheses. Implicitly, however, it is clear that the theories in question were essentially *hierarchical* in nature. The concept of an emotional person depends essentially on the occurrence of a variety of traits in the same person. In other words, we would expect a person who was anxious also to be worried, unhappy, quickly aroused, egocentric, etc.; conversely, we would expect a calm person to be also steadfast, persistent, carefree, hopeful, contented, and so on. Similarly, a changeable person would be active, playful, easygoing, and histrionic; an unchangeable one would be thoughtful, reasonable, serious, and high-principled.

Hypotheses of this kind are, of course, testable. What is implied is, in fact, *correlations between observable traits*, and it is a great contribution of the early psychometrists to have seen the possibility of applying correlational methods to this field and to have carried out a number of studies along these lines. A very detailed discussion has been given of these early efforts elsewhere (Eysenck, 1960e), and there would be little point in duplicating this discussion here. Let us merely note that in all essentials, whether carried out on normal or abnormal subjects, on adults or on children, on male subjects or on females, and making use of ratings, questionnaires, objective tests or other methods, results have very generally verified a two-dimensional system of the kind shown in Figure 13. The dimension labelled there emotional versus nonemotional has variously been called emotionality, neuroticism, stability, ego-strength, anxiety, and so forth, but the identity of the underlying concept has been very clearly demonstrated. With respect to the changeable-unchangeable dimension, the tendency has been to label this trait one of extraversion as opposed to introversion. Figure 14 shows in some detail the conception of extraversion as a personality dimension based upon the intercorrelations between a number

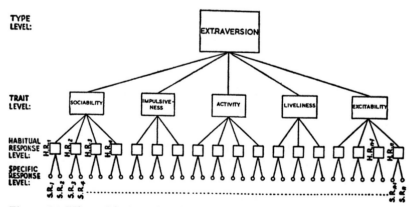

Figure 14. Hierarchical model of personality. Types are supraordinate concepts built up on the observed intercorrelations between traits. Reprinted with slight changes from H. J. Eysenck, 1947.

of different traits, in this case those of sociability, impulsiveness, activity, liveliness, and excitability. It is clearly an empirical question whether in actual fact sociability correlates with impulsiveness, activity with liveliness, and excitability with all the others in a random group of 100 or 1,000 subjects, and as stated before the evidence suggests that the correlations are indeed all positive and reasonably high, however the traits may be assessed. The traits themselves are in turn, of course, based on empirical evidence of a similar kind; in other words, persons who behave in a sociable manner in one situation tend to behave in a sociable manner in other situations, and so forth.

The terms used, such as neuroticism and extraversion-introversion, are immediately suggestive of psychiatric abnormality.[1] This is so partly because, as in the case of neuroticism, they refer directly to emotional illness, and partly it is because terms like extraversion and introversion are often linked with psychiatrists like Jung, who is frequently credited with having invented these terms and having discovered the personality variable denoted by them. In actual fact neither of these two statements is true; as we have noted above, the theory of a personality dimension of this type goes back very many years, and Jung's statement of it is only one among many. Nor is it true that he was the first to suggest the terms extraversion and introversion; these had been in use in Europe for several hundred years before Jung. Jung did, however, make one important contribution, which was to suggest that the two ends of the extraversion-introversion continuum were related respectively to two varieties of neurotic disorders which he labelled the *psychastenic* and *hysteric* respectively. Later work has partly borne out this hypothesis. Psychastenics, or as we would now prefer to call them, *dysthymics* (i.e., neurotic patients suffering from anxiety, reactive depression, phobias, and/or obsessive-compulsive

[1]The connection between "emotionality" as a personality variable of constitutional origin, and proneness to nervous disorders (neuroticism) is already adumbrated in Robert Whytt's famous "observations on the nature, causes, and cure of those disorders which have been commonly called nervous, hypochondriac, or hysteric," published in 1765. On p. 93, for instance, he points out that "those disorders may, peculiarly, deserve the name of *nervous*, which, on account of an unusual delicacy, or unnatural state of the nerves, are produced by causes, which, in people of a sound constitution, would either have no such effects, or at least in a much less degree."

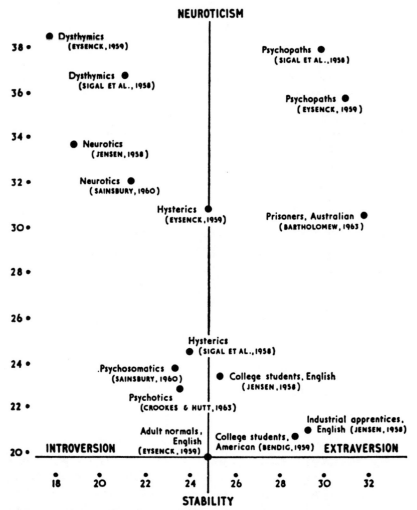

Figure 15. Scores of various neurotic, criminal, and normal groups on the Maudsley Personality Inventory. Reprinted with some additions from the Manual of the American edition (Eysenck, 1959).

symptoms) do indeed tend to combine high neuroticism with a high degree of introversion; and hysterics, while above normal on neuroticism, tend to be much more extraverted than dysthymics. However, they are not more extraverted than normals on the whole, as shown in Figure 15, which quotes some typical studies carried out on a variety of groups by various authors using the Maudsley Personality Inventory (Eysenck, 1959a).[1a] It will also be seen in this Figure that the groups having high extraversion scores in addition to high neuroticism scores are convicts and psychopaths of various kinds. Thus we might say that people of the melancholic temperament, those combining a high degree of emotionality with a high degree of introversion, are apparently predisposed to develop dysthymic reactions; on the other hand, people of a choleric temperament, those highly emotional and highly extraverted, develop psychopathic, criminal, and delinquent behaviour patterns. There would be little point adducing all the evidence available on these relationships; a very detailed account is given in Eysenck and Eysenck (1967), bearing out the general picture shown in Figure 15. Nor are these relationships confined to European or English speaking countries; similar relationships between personality and behaviour patterns have been observed for instance in Australia, India, Japan, and a variety of other countries and cultures.

Strictly speaking, the observed correlation between high N– high E scores and criminality, and between high N–low E scores and neurosis, does not prove that the personality traits predispose the individual to neurosis or crime; it might be argued that the personality traits are a consequence of neurotic breakdown or punishment following criminal activity, or that both personality traits and crime and neurosis are the consequences of some common cause. Something corresponding to this last hypothesis will, in fact, be argued in a later chapter, in which we shall try to show that certain inherited neurophysiological structures affect both personality and social behaviour. Here we will rest content with arguing that some form of "personality predisposition" theory (including the possibility that "personality" itself is in part determined by biological-neurophysiological factors) is in good agreement with the facts. Consider the following study reported by Burt (1965). Seven hundred and sixty-three children, of whom 15 per cent and 18 per cent

[1a]The M.P.I. was constructed by the writer to measure N (neuroticism) and E (extraversion-introversion), and has been widely used. It has since been superseded by the E.P.I. (Eysenck and Eysenck, 1964). Also available is the Junior E.P.I. (S. B. G. Eysenck, 1965), which has been constructed for use with children.

later became habitual offenders or neurotics, respectively, were rated by their teachers for emotionality/neuroticism and for extraversion/introversion. Follow-up of the children disclosed that of those who became habitual offenders, 63 per cent had been rated as high on emotionality; 54 per cent had been rated as high on extraversion, but only 3 per cent on introversion. Of those who became neurotics, 59 per cent had been rated high on emotionality; 44 per cent had been rated as high on introversion, but only 1 per cent on extraversion. Thus we see that even the probably rather unreliable ratings made by teachers of their pupils at school can predict with rather surprising accuracy the later adult behaviour of these children. The concordance is surprising because luck and other unforeseeable circumstances of life must play a large part in determining whether a person prone to crime or neurosis does in fact succumb, and other personality traits such as psychoticism and intelligence obviously also play a part in the social adjustment of the person. However that may be, the figures as they stand argue rather convincingly for the predetermination of later conduct, whether criminal or neurotic, by personality.

The picture that emerges from a great variety of different studies then is a fairly clear and concise one. At the highest and most inclusive level of personality description, we are apparently dealing with two main dimensions, the one ranging from high degrees of emotionality to very low emotional reactivity, the other ranging from high degrees of introversion to high degrees of extraversion. Both of these scales are continuous, and the majority of people have been found to give scores intermediate between the extremes; very high scores in either direction are relatively rare. It is, of course, possible to describe personality in other terms; many American authors have preferred to use descriptive scales at the trait level, that is, to measure sociability, impulsiveness, activity, liveliness, excitability, and so forth directly. There are two reasons why this may not turn out to be a very successful choice.

In the first place, these traits are not independent but quite highly correlated, and a system of description purely in terms of correlated traits leaves out what may be the most important variable of all, namely that which underlies these correlations and gives rise to the higher-order type-level concepts of extraversion and emotionality. In the second place, it has been found that while concepts like extraversion and neuroticism are easily replicable from one investigation to another, concepts at the trait level are very elusive and very difficult to reproduce from one study to another. This is true even when the instruments used are identical; when they differ, then the outcome tends to be one of uttermost confusion. Cattell and Guilford, for instance, have both carried out very extensive investigations using their respective instruments; results from their statistical investigations have demonstrated two separate sets of traits which show hardly any overlap at all. Yet when the intercorrelations between these traits are studied, it is found that quite similar type-level concepts of extraversion and neuroticism emerge (Eysenck and Eysenck, 1967). To say this is not to deny that concepts at the trait level may be very useful under certain circumstances, may have wide practical applicability, and may in due course reach the level of reproducibility which at the moment characterises concepts at the type level. All that is being suggested is that for the time being, trait-level concepts are very much more elusive, and that type-level concepts are of so much wider import that it would seem reasonable to devote considerable energy to an investigation of their psychological meaning and their possible biological background. As far as this book is concerned, at any case, we shall be dealing in the main with extraversion-introversion and neuroticism-stability rather than with the various traits, the intercorrelations between which give rise to these higher order concepts.

How can we relate these two dimensional concepts with theories current in experimental psychology? Let us begin with emotionality or neuroticism; introversion-extraversion will be dealt with in the next chapter. Jones (1960) has put the point very well: "Neuroticism or vulnerability to neurosis implies low tolerance for stress whether it be physical as in painful situations, or psychological as in conflict or 'frustration' situations. In learning theory terms an individual scoring high on the factor of neuroticism would be characterised by a high level of drive in avoidance situations. High appetitive drives are not necessary to the theory and it may be that the high drive of neurotics is aroused only in situations of threat or ego-involvement." This high level of drive must be considered, as we have pointed out before, in relation to the Yerkes-Dodson law. It will be remembered that this law states that too high level of drive exerts a negative influence on performance. There are several theoretical reasons why this should be so; the best known of these is perhaps that associated with the Iowa group (Farber, 1954; Taylor, 1956; Spence, 1956) in which use is made of the Hullian concept of excitatory potential as a multiplicative function of habit and drive strengths. As Jones (1960) points out, "in a situation in which only a single habit is evoked, an increase of drive is expected to improve performance but, where repeating response tendencies are operative, of which only one is scored correct by the experimenter, the effect of changes in drive strength is considered to depend on the number and comparative strength of the competing tendencies. When the correct response is based on a relatively weak habit strength, increased drive is deleterious in that the stronger incorrect tendencies gain relatively more in excitatory potential and have, therefore, an enhanced probability of evocation. During learning, as the relative strength of the correct tendency increases, increased drive becomes progressively less injurious and ultimately advantageous when the correct response is prepotent. In the complex situation, involving competing tendencies, increased drive may also lower efficiency by raising new incorrect competing responses above the threshold value of excitatory potential."

An alternative hypothesis has been put forward by Mandler and Sarason (1952) and by Child (1954). According to these authors, a heightened drive state is linked with a number of previously learned response tendencies, frequently emotional in nature and irrelevant to the task in hand; these response tendencies disrupt performance by competing with the correct response. According to Child, such disruption occurs only when the task already involves competing tendencies, but it is difficult to see why such a limitation should be necessary. An example may make clear the nature of this particular hypothesis. Savage and Eysenck (1964) required emotional and nonemotional rats to learn to escape from a conditioned fear situation by jumping a barrier from one compartment into another. The emotional animals had higher latency scores; that is, they performed this learned task less successfully. The reason appeared to be that they responded to the stimuli with "freezing"; i.e., this previously learned response tendency competed with the correct response of jumping.

The Farber/Taylor/Spence theory concerned itself with the energising effects of emotion; the Mandler/Sarason/Child hypothesis took into account the stimulus aspects of drive. Jones (1960) has considered a third alternative theory which is concerned with the stimulus properties of drive as such. The example he gives is taken from the field of discrimination learning. "Discrimination is most difficult to achieve when the positive and negative stimuli are most nearly alike, i.e., when they have most elements in common. The incidental experimental stimuli contribute to what they have in common and one of these is the drive stimulus. The stronger the drive, the more intense the drive stimulus, the greater its share of the stimulus complex, the greater the similarity between the positive and negative stimuli and, therefore, the greater the difficulty of discrimination. This effect will be opposed to any energising value of increased drive and the interaction of the two effects would determine the optimal level of drive, thus producing a pattern of results similar to those reported by Yerkes and Dodson." Jones has also suggested a fourth possibility, to wit, that increasing task difficulty, irrespective of the degree and nature of response competition, increases drive in a manner analogous to the drive increment postulated as following frustration. These four hypotheses are, of course, not mutually exclusive; and all the postulated effects may conceivably contribute to the interaction between drive and performance.

The results of experimental studies relating to this general theory have been reviewed by Jones (1960), who concludes that "from the review it is abundantly clear that our preceding formulation of theoretical expectations was altogether too flexible for precise validation. Whereas the great majority of the studies reviewed produced results consistent with that formulation, this consistency was only achieved after a post hoc placement of the experimental situation along the stress-difficulty dimension. The relative difficulty of the experimental task is clearly of importance in determining the nature and direction of group differences in learning and may well be the most important single factor. Furthermore it is a factor which can be objectively and quantitatively controlled . . . stress is by contrast a nebulous concept the quantification of which is scarcely possible, but the stress situations derived by many investigators clearly affected the performance and probably the learning efficiency of their subjects, and differentially affected groups selected in terms of personality variables, relevant to abnormal psychology . . . psychological stress, induced by such devices as failure stimulation, generally interacted with personality variables in a manner consistent with our theoretical expectations, but the complexity of the factors contributing to 'psychological stress' was evident in many studies."

Some examples may be useful in making clear the successes as well as the failures of the neuroticism-drive theory combined with the essential features of the Yerkes-Dodson law. To begin with, let us consider eyeblink conditioning as an example of a task where increase in drive might be expected to be related monotonically to improvement in performance. The reasons for this expectation are, of course, (a) that the task is a relatively simple one in that there are no existing habits connected with the conditioned stimulus which might be expected to interfere with the establishment of the new response, and (b) that the strength of the unconditioned stimulus is never such as to trigger off those hypothetical "previously learned response tendencies, frequently emotional in nature and irrelevant to the task in hand" which are posited by Child, Mandler, and Sarason to disrupt performance by competing with the correct response. Willett (1964) has directly manipulated the drive variable and has demonstrated, as shown in Figure 16, that frequency of conditioned responses both during acquisition and during extinction is very significantly greater in the high drive group than in the low drive group.

Making use of a similar argument, Spence and Taylor (1951) have argued for a positive association between eyeblink conditioning and anxiety. Some of the work related to this hypothesis has been reviewed by Spence (1964), who confines himself to work using the Taylor Manifest Anxiety Scale as a measure of the personality variable. Other studies using the M.P.I. neuroticism scale have been reviewed in Eysenck (1965a). At first sight the general picture which emerges is rather confused, as about half the

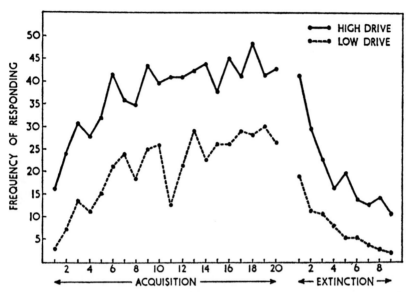

Figure 16. Acquisition and extinction of eyelid conditioned responses in high- and low-drive groups. Reprinted with permission from R. A. Willett, in H. J. Eysenck, 1964.

studies, notably those carried out in Iowa, have positive results, whereas the remainder find low and usually insignificant relationships between anxiety or neuroticism and eyeblink conditioning. One possible way of resolving this impass is by reference to the fact that the theory under consideration is a "process" rather than a "status" theory; in other words, while different individuals are hypothesized to have differential potentials for reacting to emotion-evoking stimuli, these potentials can only be translated into observable behaviour under specified conditions, that is, under emotion-provoking conditions. Unless conditions are such that emotion, anxiety, or fear is in fact evoked, no correlation between behaviour and neuroticism or anxiety will be observed. Spence has suggested that the manner in which the eyeblink conditioning test is carried out in his laboratory is sufficiently threatening and non-reassuring to make it likely that some degree of emotion or anxiety was in fact evoked; most other workers have tended to try and reassure subjects about the situation to such an extent that no emotional reactions were evident. If this explanation be true, and of course there is no direct evidence on this point, then most of the results reported fall into line very neatly.[2]

Our second example is taken from the field of paired associate learning. The study chosen was published by Standish and Champion (1960) and constitutes a direct test of Spence's hypothesis regarding the interaction between drive and correct and incorrect responses. Standish and Champion argue that where task difficulty is determined by such features as "association value" of list elements, the necessary conditions for testing Spence's hypothesis about the interaction of drive level and task difficulty level may well be absent. Spence's hypothesis requires that "correct" responses be dominant in performance if a high drive group is to be superior to a low drive group, and that the obverse conditions prevail if a low drive group is to be superior to a high drive group. Standish and Champion contend that in the case of an "easy" list of nonsense syllables regarded as easy simply by virtue of the high association values of its elements, incorrect responses may still be dominant for much of any learning period. Hence a comparison of the performance of groups of different drive levels on such a task could not necessarily be expected to yield the results predicted on Spence's hypothesis.

Accordingly, Standish and Champion designed an experimental procedure especially relevant to this hypothesis. First they constructed an easy list of stimulus and response words, by using common associates in the Kent/Rosanoff list such as "foot — hand; hungry — food; deep — shallow." A difficult list was then formed by employing the same stimulus words, but this time pairing them with words given rarely in free association according to the Kent/-Rosanoff list. The difficult list was made up of combinations such as "foot — cheese; stem — heavy; sheep — loud."

Since the aim of the experiment was to contrast performance where correct responses were dominant with performance where incorrect responses were dominant, each subject had to learn the easy list first to a criterion of two correct repetitions plus eight

[2]Ominsky and Kimble (1966) have published a paper supporting this view. Spence and Spence (1966) have recently shown that under "masking" condition, i.e., when the subject is confused about the purpose of the experiment, there is no correlation between anxiety and conditioning; this finding is damaging to the Spence hypothesis.

further trials. These ten trials are labelled trials 1 to 10. Having completed the list to this criterion, each subject learned the difficult list also to a criterion of two correct repetitions plus eight further trials. The first ten trials of the difficult list are also labelled trials 1-10 and the last ten trials A-J. It can be seen that trials 1-10 of the easy list and trials 1-10 of the difficult constitute a crucial comparison. In the former case the correct response is clearly dominant; in the latter case the incorrect response is clearly dominant. In trials A-J of the difficult list, the correct response is dominant again, these ten trials being at the same stage of learning as trials 1-10 of the easy list. Exposure time of both stimulus words and pairs was three seconds throughout with eighteen seconds separating trials. The score taken was the latency in tenths of a second of the subject's response to the stimulus words. The results of the experiment are shown in Figure 17, where subjects are di-

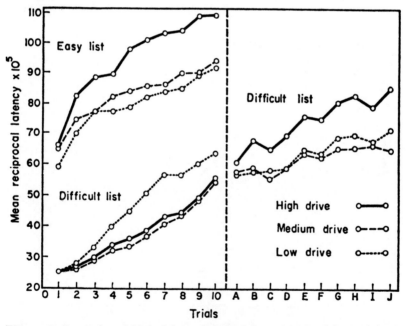

Figure 17. Latencies of high drive, medium drive, and low drive groups in paired-associate learning tasks under different conditions of difficulty. Reprinted with permission from R. R. Standish and R. A. Champion: *J. Exp. Psychol.*, 59:361-365, 1960.

vided in terms of their questionnaire responses into high drive, medium drive, and low drive. It will be seen that on the easy list, as expected, the high drive subjects do best, whereas on the difficult list, again as expected, the low drive subjects do best. On the last ten trials of the difficult list, it is again the high drive subjects who perform best. All these results are in direct conformity with hypothesis.

Willett (1964) repeated the experiment exactly, but substituted groups in whom high and low drive had been induced experimentally for the groups in the Standish and Champion experiment which had been chosen according to questionnaire responses. His results showing mean response latency are shown in Figure 18; there is a superficial dissimilarity from Figure 17 because Standish and Champion recorded reciprocal latency whereas Willett reported

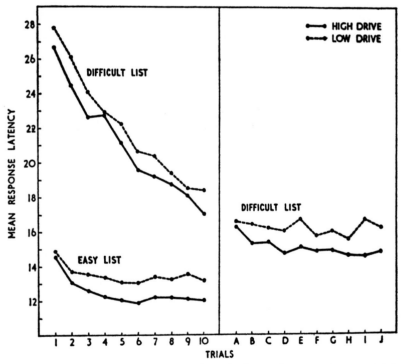

Figure 18. Mean response latencies in paired-associate learning for high-drive and low-drive groups under different conditions of difficulty. Reprinted with permission from R. A. Willett, in H. J. Eysenck, 1964.

direct latency values. However, the crucial feature of the Willett experiment is that under all conditions the high drive group performs better even on the first ten trials of the difficult list. This is completely contrary to the Spence hypothesis and to the Standish and Champion results and is very difficult to explain in their terms. Nor is this the only study of its kind where the relationship between list difficulty level and situation-induced anxiety drive has been studied; Willett and Eysenck (1962) also found no interaction between drive level and difficulty level but rather a simple facilitation by the higher drive condition in an experiment on the serial rote learning of nonsense syllables.

It is, of course, possible to put forward hypotheses to explain the apparent contradiction in this experiment, which is typical of the rather confused literature on this subject. One might postulate that the task itself produces a stress which is itself due to the interaction between rate of stimulus presentation (as we have seen in the Jensen experiment given in Figure 1) and the relative intelligence of the subjects. Standish and Champion used university subjects; Willett and Eysenck used industrial apprentices of a rather lower level of intelligence. Or the explanation may lie in the relatively greater extraversion of these apprentices as compared with students; it has been generally found that students on the whole are more introverted, industrial apprentices more extraverted than the average. These and many other hypotheses can be put up to explain the observed discrepancies; but of course there is no direct evidence to support any of these theories, and until more direct proof is forthcoming we must conclude that the striking confirmation of Spence's results achieved by Standish and Champion cannot be accepted at face value. The same problem arises in connection with most of the evidence that has been put forward in relation to the general hypothesis under consideration. Most of the studies are positive, many of them quite strikingly so; but there are always other studies which give negative results or which are at best inconclusive. To say this is not to deny the importance, relevance, and ingenuity of the theory under consideration; it is merely to draw attention to the very complex ways in which the variables involved are associated and to the difficulty of measuring any of them in isolation.

Some of the variables involved have already been mentioned; we have in mind here emotionality or anxiety, intelligence, degree of arousal, difficulty level, degree of extraversion-introversion, situational stress, and so forth. There is an additional variable which powerfully affects studies involving any form of learning, namely the interaction between stimulus-produced arousal and the consolidation of the memory trace. A very relevant experiment is reported by Kleinsmith and Kaplan (1963) in which subjects were asked to learn a set of paired associates composed of words as stimuli and single digit numbers as responses. The words chosen differed in their arousal value (as measured by galvanic skin response). A differential hypothesis about the learning of words high and low in arousal value was presented somewhat along the following lines. Making use of the consolidation theory of learning, Hebb (1958) had suggested that under conditions of low arousal, relatively little nonspecific neural activity would be available to support the reverberating trace, resulting in little consolidation and poor long term retention. On the other hand, under conditions of high arousal, the increased nonspecific neural activity would result in more reverberation and accordingly better retention. It has also been suggested (Paré, 1961; Eysenck, 1965) that whilst reverberation is taking place, the trace should be expected to be relatively unavailable to the organism, resulting in poor recall of the consolidating material during this interval. Hodgkin (1948) has shown that neurones are sharply limited in their maximum rates of firing repeatedly in a reverberating circuit, and it would seem to follow that memory requiring refiring of such neurones would be impeded. Thus under high arousal conditions consolidation should be effective both in strengthening the memory trace and in making the memory difficult to evoke until after cessation of the consolidation process.

In accordance with this theory, Kleinsmith and Kaplan argued that "word-number pairs of high arousal value should be recalled poorly at first, but should be recalled well at a later time. Low arousal pairs by contrast should be remembered better at first and should show a gradual decay (forgetting) with time." The results of their experiment bear out this hypothesis. Figure 19 shows the differential recall of paired associates as a function of arousal level;

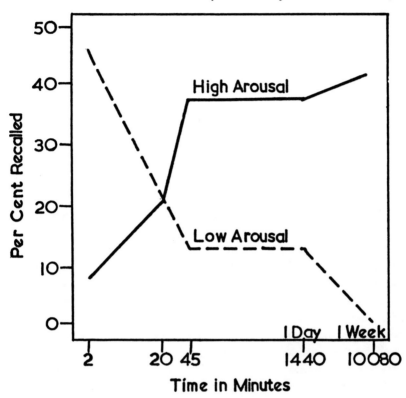

Figure 19. Differential recall of paired associates as a function of arousal level. Reprinted with permission from L. J. Kleinsmith and S. Kaplan: *J. Exp. Psychol.*, *65*:190-193, 1963.

"at immediate recall numbers associated with low arousal words are recalled five times as often as numbers associated with high arousal words. The capacity to recall numbers associated with low arousal words decreases as a function of time in a normal forgetting curve pattern. On the other hand, the capacity to recall numbers associated with high arousal words shows a considerable reminiscence effect. After twenty minutes the increase is more than 100 per cent, after forty-five it has increased 400 per cent. This high capacity for recall of high arousal pairs persists for at least a week — the longest interval employed."

This experiment shows that personality factors associated with arousal may have apparently contradictory effects on learning as assessed by later recall. If recall is shortly after learning, then high arousal subjects may be at a disadvantage, and low arousal subjects may appear to have learned better. After an intermediate length of time (twenty minutes in the case of the Kleinsmith and Kaplan experiment), there may be no distinction between the two groups at all. After longer periods than that (from one hour to one week, for example), the high arousal group would appear to have the advantage. Until much more is known about the relationship between consolidation and personality, it will always be extremely difficult to predict the results of learning experiments and the relationship between learning, memory, and personality.

We may perhaps summarise our evaluation of the general theory of emotionality as a personality trait and its influence on learning and other psychological variables by making the following points: (a) In a very broad sense there is much evidence to support the suggestion that emotion acts as a drive. (b) Emotionality, neuroticism, or anxiety, conceived of as personality variables, are descriptive concepts which refer to a greater emotional arousability of certain people, as compared with others. (c) Emotionality as so conceived is productive of stronger than average drive in emotion-producing situations. (d) Such emotions acting as drives may lead to facilitation of performance or to deterioration of performance depending on complex interactions between amount of drive present, task difficulty, stress experience, and the various other independent variables discussed in this chapter. (e) Proper quantification of all these variables is essential before confident predictions can be made in the individual case. (f) Without such quantification the theory may still be useful in predicting performance at extreme ends of the scale (where there can be little doubt about the precise predictions to be made) and in mediating an understanding of certain everyday life phenomena which otherwise might be difficult to comprehend.

This last point may require some documentation. Consider for example the often noted "rigid" behaviour of neurotic patients. It is reported that certain forms of conduct will persist in patients of this type in spite of the fact that this conduct is not rewarded and may even be severely punished each time it occurs. How can we account for apparently irrational behaviour of this type? In terms of the theory here presented the answer might run as follows. Patients have apparently learned a particular form of response which therefore has a high level of habit strength, very much higher than the appropriate response which we would want them to learn. Such new learning, however, is made very much more difficult by the high emotionality (high drive) under which the subject is working; the drive level in addition is constantly raised or at least kept at a high level by the punishment which the inappropriate response receives. Thus we have the paradoxical situation that environmental pressures which penalise a subject for incorrect responses may in fact only succeed in maintaining these responses. The same argument may, of course, be applied to criminals (Eysenck, 1964a), whose high level of emotionality or neuroticism we have already noted in Figure 15. Here, too, society attempts to alter the behaviour pattern of a person by inflicting punishment, thereby raising an already high level of emotion and making it more likely for the rigid perseverence of that behaviour to be maintained. There is some evidence to show that, unlikely as it may appear on common sense grounds, abandonment of an undesirable set of habits may be achieved more readily by a lowering of drive (nonpunishment) than by an increase of drive level through punishment (Eysenck and Rachman, 1965).

It is, of course, unsatisfactory to deal in this theoretical fashion with facts which are reported only in a clinical and anecdotal setting; the writer has often pointed out the need for making psychiatric observations more objective and quantitative, and it cannot be taken for granted that the alleged observations of neurotic rigidity would in fact be borne out by such more scientific scrutiny. However, there is experimental evidence to support the general line of the argument here presented. Consider for example the work of Kogan and Wallach (1964) on risk taking. These two authors have studied a variety of experimental risk taking situations and have also applied two personality measures to their subjects, namely a test of anxiety and one of defensiveness. Consider the following discussion which is relevant to our hypothetical relationship between neuroticism and rigidity.

> Turning to monetary outcomes and postdecision satisfaction, low defensive-low test anxious males in a skill setting exhibit a

degree of postdecision satisfaction that is proportional to their level of winnings. Interestingly enough, this adaptively appropriate behaviour characterizes only this "least disturbed" of the four personality subgroups. In striking contrast, the male subgroup high on both test anxiety and defensiveness shows exactly the opposite behaviour in a skill setting; the less these individuals win, the more satisfied they are with their bets. Failure seems to confirm them all the more in the rigid continuance of their decision-making strategy. Failure, furthermore, is more likely after risk taking than after conservatism. This finding suggests that the only effect negative environmental outcomes can have for the risk-takers in this subgroup is to push them all the harder into their characteristic high risk taking. Such evidence once again indicates with what single-mindedness the high defensive-high test anxious males are committed to a particular decision-making strategy. Failure makes the risk-takers among them adhere all the more firmly to their risky posture. In contrast, failure leads the subgroup lowest in motivational disturbance to express dissatisfaction with the decision strategy that they have been following—a more appropriate adaptation to environmental outcomes.

In other words, Kogan and Wallach find that subjects high on emotionality-anxiety show a kind of compulsive, rigid risk taking behaviour in which behaviour patterns having high habit strength are preserved in spite of their obvious inefficiency; in persons of low emotionality-anxiety, it is apparently much easier for these faulty habit patterns to be changed.

In animal work, too, there have been many attempts to study rigid behaviour usually under the title "stereotyped" or "fixated" behaviour. Yates (1962) has summarised all this work and quotes a great deal of evidence to show that some such hypothesis as the one here advocated may indeed be along the right lines. It is not, of course, our purpose at the moment to argue that this is indeed the correct explanation of rigid conduct in neurotics and in criminals; our purpose is rather to point out that the general theory we are discussing is not confined to laboratory work but has repercussions outside the laboratory and is, indeed, relevant to quite important life situations such as those giving rise to neurotic behaviour and criminality. Conversely the theory may, of course, be used for the treatment of neurosis (Eysenck and Rachman, 1965) and the reclamation of criminals (Eysenck, 1964). Such interplay between laboratory experimentation and the explanation of behaviour patterns occurring in ordinary life is to the writer one of the main advantages of the attempt to tie together personality variables and experimental psychology (Eysenck, 1957).

Some recent writers have advocated the giving up of the term "emotion" altogether as being unscientific, impossible to define objectively, and difficult to disentangle from other types of "activation" (Duffy, 1962). For reasons to be given later, we shall prefer to continue to use the term emotion, but we would certainly agree that it is desirable to pin this term down and in particular to relate it to neurophysiological mechanisms. There is a great deal of evidence to suggest that what we call "emotion" is strongly related to the activity of the autonomic nervous system (Morgan, 1965; Gellhorn and Loofbourrow, 1963), and we will not here try to recapitulate the evidence on this point. Rather we shall look briefly at the relationship between individual differences in emotionality/neuroticism and try to see whether they are in fact related to individual differences in autonomic and particularly sympathetic activity.

Many indices have, of course, been used for the measurement of autonomic activity; among them are the electric conductivity of the skin, muscular tension as measured by the electromyograph, heart rate, blood pressure, breathing rate, E.E.G., and many others. The principal measures that have been taken are illustrated in Figure 20. Period A in this figure is a resting period preceding the application of a stimulus; we can obtain from this period two measures, one of which is the level of activity, the other the amount of spontaneous activity, i.e., the variability about the mean. The application of a stimulus is indicated by an arrow; stimuli can, of course, be of a great variety, including *physical* stimuli such as immersion of the hand in water, *ideational* stimuli such as questions asked during an interview, *stress* stimuli such as problems posed in an intelligence test, *emotional* stimuli such as the showing of a harrowing film, and so forth. Period B measures the latency of the reaction; C measures the amount of the reaction, and D measures the recovery period, that is, the length of time required to elapse

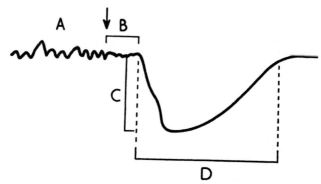

Figure 20. Course of recording of typical autonomic reaction to stimulus indicated by arrow. A indicates resting level, with spontaneous activity; B indicates response latency; C indicates size of response; D indicates recovery period.

before the autonomic index returns to its prestimulation level.

There are, of course, many difficulties attaching to these measures. To take but one example, the so-called base line or resting level preceding stimulation is not in the ordinary case a base line at all, but is in effect the response of the organism to the stimulation associated with attaching electrodes to his body, being given a variety of instructions, being in a strange hospital or laboratory, being left alone or not being left alone, and many other such inevitable stimuli. There is doubt that a true base line can be obtained under these conditions. Consequently, the effect of a new stimulus arbitrarily designated as *the* experimental stimulus can only be evaluated with considerable difficulty.[3] A person who is

[3]The work of Kelly (1966) is probably a good example of the difficulties which arise in this connection. He found that chronic anxiety state patients had a mean "basal" forearm blood flow of 4.8 ml/100 ml/min, which was more than twice as great as that of normal controls (2.2), but that anxiety induced by stressful mental arithmetic produced a mean increase in blood flow of 334 per cent in the group of normal controls, which was at least twice as great as in the chronic anxiety state patients. He argues that "these findings are contrary to the opinion of Eysenck that neurotic patients as a group demonstrate over-reactivity of the autonomic nervous system in response to stressful stimuli." This would be true only if we could be sure that both Kelly's patients and controls did indeed start off from a proper "basal" level; from the published figures one might conclude that the over-reactivity of the patients had already demonstrated itself in their response to the whole situation, hence the marked difference in "basal" flow. A third group on mixed neurotics showed less "basal" flow, but a much greater in-

very responsive to stimuli may have responded so strongly to the stimuli associated with Period A that he has little left with which to respond to the stimulus proper, and consequently will give only a slight change in autonomic activity; it would be erroneous to interpret this as a lack in autonomic reactivity.[4]

Other difficulties are of a more technical kind, relating for instance to the structure of the transducer and its attachment to the organism. Another set of problems is posed by the difficulties associated with measurement itself. For instance, should we take into account in our measurements Wilder's (1957, 1962) "Law of Initial Value," which states, roughly, that given a standard stimulus and a standard period of measurement, the response defined as a change from the initial (prestimulus) value will tend to be smaller when the initial value is higher. The evidence to date seems to suggest that this law operates for some types of autonomic activities such as heart rate and respiration rate responses, that it does not operate for skin temperature responses, and that for GSR responses, expressed in terms of conductance, the converse of the law in fact holds (Hord, Johnson, and Lubin, 1964). A whole book might be written about the problems raised by autonomic measurement, and in our brief review we shall of course not be able to evaluate the various research reports available (Venables and Martin, 1967).

One difficulty, however, is so all pervasive that it must be mentioned here in some detail. Most of the work that has been reported in the literature has compared groups of subjects, usually normals and neurotics, but also sometimes people with and without anxiety. Now we have already found that hospitalised neurotics tend to be characterised by a combination of high neuroticism and high introversion; similarly the main symptom of these dysthymic neurotics tends to be anxiety, so that anxiety, too, is characteristic of high neuroticism and high introversion.

When a comparison is now made between neurotics and normals,

crease due to "stress." This group is so heterogeneous as to make interpretation of their results impossible. It is interesting, particularly in the light of the discussion in the last chapter of this book, that after modified leucotomy, blood flow under "basal" conditions fell in a group of forty patients by 34 per cent (Kelly *et al.*, 1966).

[4]It may even be regarded as doubtful if different stimuli applied simultaneously act in a synergistic manner; Mefferd and Wieland (1965) report evidence in the opposite direction.

or between people high and low on anxiety, then it is very difficult, if not impossible, to interpret any differences that may be found. It is possible that these differences are related to the dimension of neuroticism or emotionality; it is possible that they are related to the dimension of introversion; and finally it is of course possible that they are related to both dimensions simultaneously. It is for this reason that the writer has always advocated the use of direct measures of both personality variables so that differences can be properly interpreted. The failure to make use of a dimensional framework is so widespread and so all-pervasive that hardly any studies would be available for summary if one were to rule out all those which are subject to this particular criticism. The writer has made an attempt to evaluate studies from this point of view, and to interpret the results as well as can be done in terms of the descriptions of populations given, etc.; however, the point remains that this interpretation involves a subjective estimate, and that it is quite possible that errors may creep in unnoticed on the way. The reader is therefore warned that the relationship between emotionality/neuroticism and autonomic factors which emerges from the studies here summarised may in part at least be an artefact due to a confounding of the dimensions of neuroticism and introversion. It is very unlikely that this confounding accounts for all the differences demonstrated, but as a partial influence it is impossible for reasons given to separate it out.

Before turning to autonomic measures proper, we may perhaps concern ourselves with a variety of biochemical differences which have been studied in a similar context. In the early 1920's Ludlum (1918), Starr, (1922), and Rich (1928) found some evidence to suggest that individuals of alkaline saliva and urine were more emotionally unstable than those with more acid excretions (see also Shock, 1944).[5]

[5]It is interesting to note in this connection that lung cancer is known to be associated with acid as compared with alkaline smoke, and also in particular with tobaccos grown in acid soil. Eysenck (1965) has reviewed some evidence showing that there is quite a strong correlation between neuroticism/emotionality and freedom from lung cancer, i.e., demonstrating that neurotics are apparently in some way protected from whatever may be the casual factor in lung cancer. It may be possible that the relationship between neuroticism and greater alkalinity in saliva and urine may be in part responsible for this relationship between neuroticism and absence of lung cancer.

Another variable which has been implicated in neuroticism and anxiety is hippuric acid. Basowitz, Persky, Korchin, and Grinker (1955) related excretion of hippuric acid to degree of anxiety in normal subjects; and Persky, Gamm, and Grinker (1952) found that patients with "free anxiety" showed significantly greater amounts of hippuric acid excretion than normal controls. Other investigators have been concerned with catecholamine excretion, which also appears to be related to stress, and in which people high on neuroticism/emotionality appear to differ from normals (Frankenhaeuser, and Patkai, 1964). Much interest has also centred on the urinary output of adrenaline and noradrenaline (Levi, 1965).

Of autonomic responses proper, one of the most widely used has been the galvanic skin response (GSR), also sometimes called the electrodermal response. Many of these studies were technically imperfect, and even where technique was adequate, the criterion was sometimes faulty. Duffy (1962) reviews several studies in which the Rorschach test was used as a criterion; the recently published book by Zubin, Eron, and Schumer (1965) adequately summarises all the objections which can be made to the reliability and validity of this test. Altschule (1953) reviewed much of the literature and came to the conclusion that measurements of overt palmar sweating in neurotic patients usually showed elevated values but that there was less consistency in reports on skin resistance. Hoch, Kubis, and Rouke (1944) reported greater reactivity of the GSR in neurotics than in normals, but Altschule in the summary already quoted was rather dubious about the generality of this finding. S.B.G. Eysenck (1956) has given a summary of much of the literature and also reported an original experiment comparing normals, neurotics, and psychotics. She also failed to find support for the hypothesis that neurotics could be differentiated from normals in terms of responsiveness. She did find significant differences, however, in "rate of calming down," which was slower for neurotics than for either psychotics or normals (see Figure 21). Katkison (1966) has found similar results with respect to recovery from increased spontaneous autonomic activity.

Rubin (1964) reports a study in which "the tendency of the pupil to constrict in response to light and the dilatation resulting in the absence of light were employed to measure cholinergic and

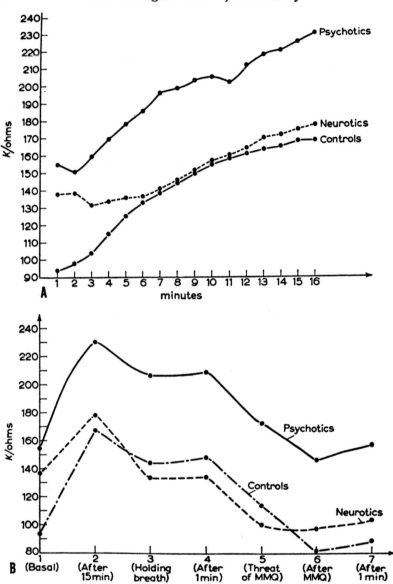

Figure 21. (a) Resistance in kilohms of psychotic, neurotic, and normal groups during a 15-minute rest period.
(b) Resistance in kilohms of psychotic, neurotic, and normal groups during the course of the experiment. Reprinted with permission from S. B. G. Eysenck: *J. Psychosom. Res.*, 1:258-272, 1956.

adrenergic mechanisms respectively." Eleven neurotics and eleven matched normals were examined in detail. "When the subjects were examined at rest, no significant differences in adrenergic or cholinergic activity were found to exist between normals and neurotics. Both groups were also observed to respond in a similar fashion to noxious, painful stimulation. . . . Significant differences between the groups were observed when the homeostatic response curves for adrenergic and cholinergic activity were compared. The homeostatic response curves for adrenergic and cholinergic activity in normal individuals were characterised by a rapid return in the direction of decreased adrenergic and increased cholinergic activity following the termination of the noxious stimulus. In contrast to the normals, the neurotic individuals, following termination of painful stimulation, continued to manifest a sustained pattern of increased adrenergic outflow and decreased cholinergic outflow which was characteristic of their response to noxious stimulation." Figure 22 shows the homeostatic response curves for the two groups; the regular, slow increase in cholinergic outflow in the normal group, following the cessation of the noxious stimulus, is sharply contrasted with the rapid increase in cholinergic outflow in the neurotic group, which is suddenly turned into an even more rapid decrement in cholinergic outflow.

Wing (1965) compared twenty normal and twenty neurotic subjects who were subjected to the stress task of colour naming with delayed feedback. Skin conductance levels for her subjects are given in Figure 23; in her study, too, the only significant differences occurred *after* the task was over, when it will be seen that the normal subjects returned quickly to the resting level whereas the neurotics in fact showed an increase in conductance. Wing also used electromyographic measures, and the results are shown in Figure 24. It will be shown that patients have higher tension levels throughout, except during the stress task when normals rise to the same level as the patients; this indicates a poor adaptation of the neurotics, whose tension level at all times is equal to that of normals under stress. Pulse level rates in the same test are given in Figure 25; they show another pattern again. Here the course of change during the experiment is almost exactly parallel, with the patients always having higher pulse level rates throughout. This

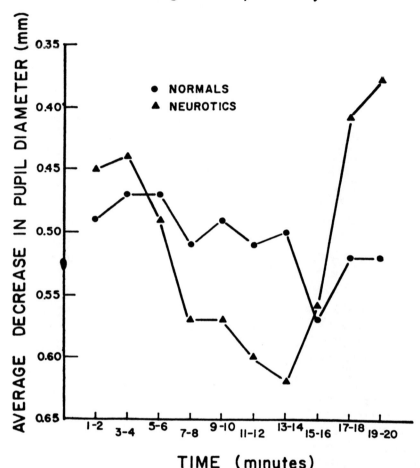

NORMALS

NEUROTICS

AVERAGE DECREASE IN PUPIL DIAMETER (mm)

0.35
0.40
0.45
0.50
0.55
0.60
0.65

1-2 3-4 5-6 7-8 9-10 11-12 13-14 15-16 17-18 19-20

TIME (minutes)

Figure 22. Homeostatic response curves for constriction of pupil in normals and neurotics. Reprinted with permission from L. S. Rubin: *J. Nerv. Ment. Dis.,* *138*:558-574, 1964.

study is interesting because it demonstrates more clearly than most the many possible patterns of differentiation which can be found, and which may characterise one but not another measure of autonomic activity.

One of the first studies of muscle tension was an experiment by Duffy (1930) in which she showed that nursery school children characterised by greater excitability also tended to have greater muscle tension. Freeman and Katzoff (1932) found a correlation

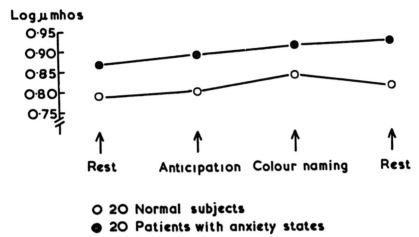

Figure 23. Skin conductance levels of normal and neurotic subjects sub-jected to stress task (colour naming with delayed feedback.) Reprinted with permission from L. Wing, 1965.

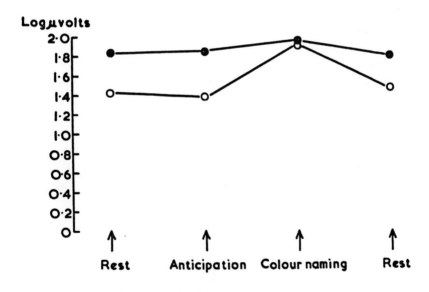

Figure 24. E.M.G. levels of normal and neurotic subjects in stress tasks. Reprinted with permission from L. Wing, 1965.

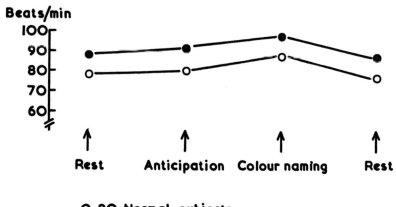

O 20 Normal subjects
● 20 Patients with anxiety states

Figure 25. Pulse level rates of normal and neurotic subjects in stress tasks. Reprinted with permission from L. Wing, 1965.

between grip pressure and irritability, but Martin (1958) failed to confirm any relationship between personality and muscle tension in an experiment of much greater technical sophistication. Studies with normal subjects are therefore fairly inconclusive.

Evidence is much more positive in relation to neurotics, where much work has been done as a follow-up of the early writings of Jacobson (1928, 1938). He concluded from his work that "when individuals are in a state of 'nervous excitement,' action potentials run high in voltage and frequency as a rule in almost any neuromuscular region tested. No shocks or other test stimuli need be employed by the examiner to induce the high voltages; if the patient is in the state mentioned they are present even if he lies down to rest." This has been verified by later writers, including Ruesch and Finesinger (1943) and Lundervold (1952). The extensive work of Malmo and his colleagues (Malmo and Shagass, 1949; Malmo, Shagass, and Davis, 1950; Malmo, Shagass, and Davis, 1951; Malmo, Shagass, Belanger, and Smith, 1951; Malmo and Smith, 1955) has demonstrated very emphatically that there are strong differences in the response to stimulation between neurotics and normals; Sainsbury and Gibson (1954) have succeeded in demonstrating such differences even when the subjects were relaxing and no special stimuli were present. A great number of other studies are summarised by Duffy (1962), who concludes that "a number of investigators have found that psychiatric patients as a group show a higher degree of muscle tension than a normal control group."

Cardiovascular reactivity was used by Armstrong (1938), who reported high relationships between emotional stability and cardiovascular reactivity in 700 air corps candidates. Blood pressure reactivity has often been studied, and the results are summarised by Malmo and Shagass (1952) in the following words. "It would be incorrect to conclude that systolic blood pressure *level* in the clinical sense is generally elevated in psychoneurosis . . . the facts indicate that excessively elevated blood pressure is found in psychoneurotics particularly when they are placed *under stress* and that this elevation may be interpreted as a greater and more prolonged change of blood pressure in response to stress in the psychoneurotic than in normal controls." Malmo, Shagass, and Heslau (1951) found greater adaptation to stress in systolic pressure in control subjects as compared to patients. Psychoneurotics also showed higher systolic blood pressure than normal controls during a rapid discrimination test (Malmo, Shagass, Belanger, and Smith, 1951). Wenger (1948) found both systolic and diastolic blood pressure significantly higher in patients suffering from operational fatigue and in psychoneurotics as compared to aviation students. Duffy (1962) sums up her discussion by saying that "there is fairly general agreement that psychoneurotics show less adaptation in the blood pressure response or slower recovery from the effects of stimulation, than normal subjects. In a number of experimental situations, but not in all, neurotics have shown greater elevation of blood pressure in response to stimulation than were shown by the control groups employed."

Conclusions relating to heart rate are rather similar; Altschule (1953) has concluded that on the whole, heart rate is accelerated in patients with neurotic disorders and shows a rapid increase during stress or exercise. Duffy summarises some later studies and deduces that "in general it may be said that there is some reason to conclude that neurotics have a more rapid heart rate and show greater changes in heart rate than control groups, but the evidence is not very clear." One additional point to be mentioned may be that neurotic subjects tend to have much less *stable* heart rates than normals, a conclusion well in line with Duffy's statement that "spontaneous changes in activation, irregularities in response, and variability in physiological functioning have frequently been found in certain neurotic . . . conditions. Such phenomena may prove to be of greater significance in behaviour pathology than differences in the intensity of response."

This general conclusion has also been borne out by studies of variability in respiration such as those of Finesinger (1944) and Malmo and Shagass (1949). Apart from variability, respiration measures show differences between normals and neurotics in two ways. In the first place, the resting rate of respiration is greater in neurotics, and in the second place, emotional upset tends to increase the rate to an abnormal degree (Altschule, 1953). Some of the studies supporting this conclusion are those of Wenger (1948) and Jurko, Jost, and Hill (1952).

Another measure that has been frequently used in this connection, although not perhaps strictly speaking a measure of autonomic activity, is the EEG. Typical of many studies linking hyperexcitability of behaviour and high frequency EEG patterns is the work of Gastaut (1954, 1957); a good summary is available in the paper by Werre (1957). Similarly, Ulett, Gleser, Winokur, and Lawler (1953) related proneness to develop anxiety under stress to EEG characteristics, finding that the anxiety-prone group showed more fast activity (16-24 cycles per second) or very slow activity (3-7 cycles per second). EEG responses to intermittent photic stimulation were found in these subjects to be least for stimulus frequencies around the alpha range and to be greater for frequencies well above and below it. We shall argue later that departures from the alpha range are indicative of abnormality in the sense that introverts are characterised by faster rhythms, whereas extraverts are characterised by slower rhythms. It is this curvilinear relationship between abnormality and EEG frequency that makes for confusion; and if this general rule is borne in mind, it will be easier to follow the experimental literature.

A very thorough discussion of the EEG in relation to individual differences is given by Duffy (1962) and in the appropriate chapters in the (1964) textbook by Hill and Parr. Only a few of the most relevant works will be mentioned here. Kennard, Rabinovitch, and Fister (1955) have reported a correlation between fast activity in the EEG and anxiety, as have Ulett, Gleser, Winokur, and Lawler (1953), Brockway, Gleser, Winokur, and Ulett (1954), and Shagass (1955). That rapid activity is frequently found in psychoneurotics has been demonstrated by Faure (1950) and Finlay (1954). Ellingson (1954) has suggested that the usual findings of low voltage fast activity on the EEG which characterises psychoneurotics is not abnormal but is a result of the subject's failure to relax during the test, a hypothesis which is well in line with the work on autonomic muscular tension reactions already reviewed.

In contradiction to all the work showing low voltage fast EEG activity in anxiety neurotics are studies showing that theta waves or other slow activity is common in children suffering from behaviour disorders as well as in adult psychopaths. Jasper, Solomon, and Bradley (1938), for instance, found evidence of slow waves ranging in frequency from 2-7 cycles per second (cps) in seventy-one behaviour problem children. Similarly, Lindsley and Cutts (1940) found that children with behaviour disorders differed from normal children in having more slow activity. Other authors reporting similar findings are Solomon, Brown, and Deutscher (1944) and Gottlieb, Knott, and Ashby (1945). Hill (Hill and Parr, 1964) has suggested that these slow waves, especially theta waves, may be evidence of maturational defect. Forssman and Frey (1953) are two more authors to add to this list; they found a significant difference of alpha frequencies below 10 per second in 100 behaviour problem boys in a detention home as compared with 100 boys in a trade school.

Duffy sums up her discussion of the literature by saying that "there is considerable evidence that excited or highly aroused patients tend to have less alpha activity, or a higher frequency of alpha activity, or more fast activity, than control groups, though more of slow activity has also at times been reported. There is some, but less, evidence that depressed patients tend to have more of alpha activity or of lower frequency of alpha activity; and there is considerable evidence that certain patients with behaviour disorders, especially children, tend to have more of slow activity (2-8 cps) than control subjects." Taking these facts in the very broadest fashion, we may perhaps say that they support the generalisation that *introverted neurotics tend to have fast EEG activity* whereas *extraverted neurotics tend to have exceptionally slow EEG activity.* Theoretical justification for this statement will be brought forward in a later chapter when we discuss the relationship between personality and the reticular formation.

Variability of the EEG in neurotics has also often been recognised as a characteristic of these groups when compared with normals. This is in good agreement with the greater variability of neurotics on a great variety of other autonomic measures, some of which have already been mentioned. Perhaps the clearest evidence comes from the work of Van der Werwe and Theron (1947) and Thiesen and Meister (1949). The former found a highly significant correlation between emotional lability and the *rate of change* in finger volume during simple tasks, whereas the latter found greater lability of skin resistance and pulse rate in subjects more disturbed by a frustrating situation. Again a thorough discussion of the subject is given by Duffy (1962).

On the whole the studies reported so far give a definite impression that neurotic and anxious subjects as a whole respond more strongly to stimuli, show greater variability of response, and in particular take much longer to return to their prestimulation base lines (Freeman's "recovery quotient," 1948). Is it possible to talk about a general factor of somatic lability of the autonomic system, individual differences which characterise people who also differ in respect to neuroticism? The great difficulty in the way of postulating such a general factor of autonomic lability is the demonstration by Lacey (1950) and his collaborators (1952, 1953, 1958) of what he called "the principle of autonomic response stereotypy" or more simply, autonomic response specificity. Using a variety of response channels, he found that his subjects "respond with a hierarchy of activation, being relatively overactive in some physiological measures, underactive in others, while exhibiting average reactivity in still other measures. These patterns of response seem to be idiosyncratic; each subject's pattern is different. For a single stressor, patterns of response have been shown to be reproducible, both upon immediate retest and over a period of nine months. Moreover the pattern of response obtained with one stimulus condition tends to be reproduced in other quite different stimulus conditions."

Lacey stated his findings in the form of a general principle which reads as follows: "For a given set of autonomic functions subjects tend to respond with an idiosyncratic pattern of autonomic activation, in which maximal activation is shown by the same physiological function whatever the stress." Lacey also postulated and found "that continuous quantitative variation among subjects exists in the degree to which they exhibit stereotypy (reproducibility) of their pattern of response. There is no doubt that to some extent response specificity is a very relevant factor which must certainly be borne in mind in any critical discussion of the biological basis of emotional response." A detailed discussion of the evidence is given by Eysenck (1960e). That "response specificity" is not the whole answer, however, is indicated by various correlational and factor analytic studies such as those of Darrow and Heath (1932), Sanford *et al.* (1943), Darling (1940), Jost (1947), Wenger (1941, 1942, 1948, 1957, 1966), and many others, who have correlated measures of different aspects of autonomic activity and found meaningful correlations and factors based upon these correlations (but see Terry, 1953).

Of particular interest in this connection are two recent studies, the first of which was carried out by Fahrenberg and Delius (1963). Basing themselves on the intercorrelations between eighteen different measures, two of which were questionnaires dealing with introversion and neuroticism and thirteen of which were measures of autonomic reactivity, the authors found a very clear-cut dysthymic factor with high loadings on neuroticism and introversion which had quite appreciable loadings on six of the autonomic measures. Along similar lines, Wassenaar (1958) has reported a factor analysis in which autonomic factors and questionnaires are combined. He found a strong factor of neuroticism with loadings on three questionnaires and four autonomic measures, including skin conductance, EEG, and peripheral vasomotor reactions. Such results would be impossible if response specificity were really as widespread and absolute as Lacey's writings would lead one to believe.

The argument from correlations and factor analysis is possibly unlikely to satisfy biologists who tend to distrust complex statistical manipulations. There is also available, however, evidence of a more strictly experimental nature deriving from the breeding studies of emotional and nonemotional rats which has been carried on in the Maudsley laboratories for many years. In these breeding studies, which will be discussed in some more detail in a later chapter when we come to deal with the problem of heredity and environment and the causation of individual differences in personality, inbred strains have been established for high and low defecation rate, respectively, in an open field situation; almost thirty generations of these strains have now been bred. On a strict specificity argument, one might be tempted to say that these strains have been bred for defecation rate and will not, therefore, be differentiated with respect to any other autonomic or behavioural characteristics not directly related to defecation. This, however, is not so. Large numbers of studies have been carried out in the Maudsley laboratories comparing emotional and nonemotional rats in a great variety of situations (Eysenck and Broadhurst, 1964), and it has been found that the strains are differentiated in nearly all these situations.

To give just a few examples, the nonreactive strain show a higher ambulation score in the open field situation; the reactives show greater speed in underwater swimming with air deprivation as the stimulus; reactives show a greater decrease in bar pressing in response to a conditional emotional response; nonreactives show lower latency of escape in a conditioned fear situation; nonreactives show greater efficiency of learning in an escape-avoidance situation. Reactives show more grooming than nonreactives, nonreactives more rearing during time sampling of behaviour; reactives show greater response to shock, and are also characterised by greater water consumption; reactives respond to frustration with a greater increase in running speed and to conflict with a greater decrease in running speed. Reactives develop conditioned inhibition more quickly; reactives seem more susceptible to stimulant drugs, nonreactives to depressant drugs.

There are also differences in endocrine status between the two strains; reactives show higher thyroid gland weight and higher water content of the thyroid gland, whereas the nonreactives show more hormone in the gland, greater circulating hormone in the blood, faster uptake of radioactive iodine, and less cholesterol in the blood. There are differences in the recruitment of thalamic stimulations with reactives showing longer time of cortical potentials. Reactives show a heavier corrected adrenal gland weight; nonreactives show greater ascorbic acid depletion. Reactives have greater 17-ketosteroid output and greater thyrotrophic hormone content. These data leave little doubt that strains selected on the basis of one single autonomic reaction are also characterised by differences in a large number of behavioural and endocrine patterns.

In a recent experiment Broadhurst and Eysenck (1965) have tested the generalisation hypothesis directly. Sixty high reactive and sixty nonreactive animals were chosen from the sixteenth generation of the selection experiment and subjected to a whole series of tests. These included escape/avoidance conditioning, a conflict situation of the approach/avoidance sort on a simple runway, underwater swimming, speed, startle responses, water intake. Also ascertained were weight and weight loss during a specified stress period and corrected weight of the pituitary, adrenal, thyroid, and gonad glands. Results are shown in Table I; some of the scores were so abnormally distributed that transformations had to be employed which are shown in the Table. It will be seen that the groups differ with respect to many of the measures taken, and it will also be seen that while on the whole males and females show similar differences, there are also some measures on which the sexes diverge; this is in good agreement with previous observations. These data then seem to give strong support to the argument from generality of autonomic reaction, and suggest that such specificity as occurs must be relatively limited. It would be pointless to extend this discussion to embrace a full review of all animal work, but attention might perhaps be drawn to the recent studies of Scott and Fuller (1965) on the genetics and the social behaviour of the dog; their conclusions are in good agreement with ours.

The true position appears to be this. At one extreme we have a rather simpleminded belief in a general pattern of sympathetic response which is perfectly generalised, similar from one individual to another, and relatively easily measureable. This belief would lead one to expect high correlations between different tests, high discrimination between neurotic and normal groups, and easy replic-

TABLE I
MEANS AND STANDARD DEVIATION FOR THE GROUPS IN THE VARIOUS MEASURES AND THE SIGNIFICANCE OF THE DIFFERENCES BETWEEN THEM

Measure	Trans-formation	Males					Females				
		Reactive		Nonreactive		Signif.	Reactive		Nonreactive		Signif.
		M	SD	M	SD		M	SD	M	SD	
Defecation	log (x + 1)	0.27	0.06	0.07	0.11	***	0.22	0.09	0.02	0.06	***
Ambulation		8.72	1.92	10.28	1.72	**	10.84	2.18	11.33	1.50	n.s.
First Avoidance		6.70	5.48	7.53	5.12	n.s.	9.67	4.44	6.37	4.26	**
Avoidances		4.60	2.90	8.77	4.22	***	6.10	3.76	9.87	4.21	**
Latency	$\sqrt{x}$	1.11	0.26	1.11	0.34	n.s.	1.14	0.23	1.08	0.23	n.s.
Running Speed	log x	0.72	0.23	0.72	0.43	n.s.	0.64	0.25	0.88	0.59	n.s.
Conflict	log (x + 600)	2.82	0.09	2.78	0.01	**	2.81	0.09	2.83	0.10	n.s.
Swimming Speed		6.18	0.66	6.72	0.74	**	7.28	0.67	7.20	1.04	n.s.
Startle		41.7	24.02	57.03	57.58	n.s.	45.23	27.55	83.27	47.00	***
Water Intake		3.34	1.02	2.95	1.16	n.s.	3.57	1.54	2.79	1.43	n.s.
Weight Loss	log (x + 40)	1.61	0.06	1.65	0.04	**	1.60	0.09	1.66	0.03	**
Weight		240.63	19.93	209.33	19.08	***	160.67	13.06	147.93	10.09	***
Pituitary		3.20	0.50	3.27	0.38	n.s.	5.24	0.97	6.25	0.78	***
Adrenal		18.46	2.61	18.29	1.78	n.s.	32.67	4.10	36.95	4.12	***
Thyroid		7.26	1.13	6.20	0.86	***	10.31	1.48	7.58	1.14	***
Gonads		958.06	61.43	1,162.93	128.24	***	32.77	9.65	46.47	5.25	***

Note: * = significant at the 5 per cent level.
      ** = significant at the 1 per cent level.
      *** = significant at the 0.1 per cent level.
      n.s. = not significant.

Means and standard deviations for reactive and nonreactive rats on various tests and measures. Quoted from P. L. Broadhurst and H. J. Eysenck, 1965.

ability of results. At the other extreme we have a belief in complete response specificity, leading to the hypothesis that no correlations exist between different measures, that there is very little differentiation between different clinical groups, and that results from one investigator to another would be very difficult to duplicate. The evidence quoted suggests that the truth lies somewhere in between. There is a considerable degree of response specificity, but there is also a certain amount of response generality. Response generality produces correlations which, while not very large, are definitely above the chance level and require to be taken into account; furthermore, these correlations form consistent and meaningful patterns and are in turn correlated with behaviour and with questionnaire results.

It must be the task of future research to decide which are the optimal conditions for obtaining meaningful, replicable, and consistent results. Clearly measures of resting levels, as used by Wenger in his early work, are not likely to give us very useful results; reaction to stress and return to a base line are more likely to prove useful in this connection. Even so we also have to bear in mind the fact that, as was emphasised in our discussion of Wing's results, different reactor systems do not necessarily react in similar ways to stress. As we found there, some measures show significant differences between normals and neurotics during rest, anticipation, stress, and poststress periods. Some measures show differences during all stages *except* under stress; yet other measures show differences *only* during stress, and, as our discussion has amply shown, others again yield their main differences during poststress periods. Where differences of this type exist, it is of course extraordinarily difficult to come to any generalised conclusions which are not contradicted by certain aspects of the data. It is in further work along very detailed lines, following up the suggestions implicit in the research reviewed, that future progress must lie.[6] However, it will hardly be denied that the evidence already existing is sufficient

[6]In due course, it is to be hoped that investigation will reach an even more molecular, biochemical level; the work of R. J. Williams (1956) on *Biochemical Individuality* is an example of what should be aimed at. It is unfortunate that biochemists and other biologists have hitherto shown comparatively little interest in the sort of joint research which is needed in order to make any headway in such studies.

to conclude that there is a close relationship between the activity and lability of the autonomic system and neuroticism or emotionality, as measured by behavioural indices. We already have some hints as to the nature of these relationships, and no doubt a more quantitative connection will soon be developed.

CHAPTER III

THE EXPERIMENTAL ANALYSIS OF PERSONALITY

THE TERMS excitation and inhibition have a long and honoured history in psychology; they are hypothetical constructs which refer to certain observable phenomena, but they are not themselves observable. Pavlov, who was one of the first to use these terms in the modern sense, assumed that they had a physiological reference point, but his physiological theories have not been widely accepted. It will be simplest to regard his speculations in this respect in the same light as those of other psychologists. We would of course agree that if the concepts of excitation and inhibition are to find any permanent place in psychology then we must ultimately be able to find some physiological reference to them; an attempt to do so will be made in a later chapter. However, for the moment let us merely regard excitation as referring to cortical processes of an unknown character which facilitate learning, conditioning, memory, perception, discrimination, thinking, and mental processes generally, whereas inhibition has the opposite effect of reducing the efficiency of the cortex. Diamond, Balvin, and Diamond (1963) have traced the history of the concept of inhibition in some detail; and we will not attempt to do so here. Rather, our approach will be to indicate the theoretical relevance of the concepts of excitation and inhibition to those of extraversion and introversion.

Consider first the everyday use of the term "excitation" and its adjective "excitable." These terms may be used to describe in a general sort of way the activity pattern of the extravert. A glance at Figure 13 will remind the reader of the changeable, active, playful, hotheaded behaviour of the extravert, as contrasted with the controlled, thoughtful, serious, and indeed inhibited behaviour

75

of the introvert. However, this common sense use of the terms "excitation" and "inhibition" has little scientific value and does not show any definite and simple relation to the psychological use of these terms, whether Pavlovian or otherwise. To the psychologist the situation would rather seem to be one in which the cortex exerts a restraining role on lower structures so that cortical excitation, i.e., an increase in the efficiency of the cortex, would show itself in behaviour as a decrease in excitability and an increase in inhibition. Conversely, inhibition of cortical activity would release the lower centres from control and would therefore show itself in increased excitability and decreased inhibition. This argument may perhaps be clarified by reference to the effects of alcohol; this drug produces its inhibitory action first and foremost on the highest cortical centres, thus releasing lower centres from control and leading to disinhibited, excited behaviour. Magoun (1963) has called this model "geological"; historically it goes back to Hughlings Jackson in neurology, Edinger in comparative anatomy, and Sechenov in physiology.

So far we have used the terms excitation and inhibition in a very inexact and broad sense. One of the first psychologists to attempt the operational definition of the term "inhibition" was E. Ranschburg (1902, 1905). Ranschburg's experiments were of a very simple nature. Series of from two to six digits were exposed tachistoscopically and had to be reproduced by the subject. He noted that certain arrangements of digits were productive of large numbers of errors. He particularly singled out the presence of "homogeneous elements," by which he understood two identical or similar numbers in close proximity. He expressed this fact as a general law: "Heterogeneous stimuli which are presented simultaneously or in quick succession have a lower threshold than do homogeneous stimuli." Elsewhere he put the matter in a slightly different way by saying that the simultaneous production of homogeneous stimuli produced mutual inhibition.

Much work has been done in an attempt to test this hypothesis, to extend it to other varieties of perceptual material, and to relate it to personality variables. Most investigators have found great individual differences in the degree to which subjects are liable to this type of homogeneous inhibition. Bakr (1963) has given a thorough review of the literature and has also furnished us with a table of correlations between different tests of Ranschburg inhibition; these correlations are remarkably high, averaging about .7, and leave little doubt that this phenomenon possesses a certain degree of generality. It is interesting to note that she also found a tendency for various personality tests to correlate with the tests of Ranschburg inhibition. More particularly, she was concerned with the Leipzig typology which opposes a synthetic and an analytic type; the synthetic type corresponds fairly closely to the extravert, the analytic type to the introvert. Her data show a significant tendency for the synthetic (extraverted) type to be more subject to inhibition than the introverted type. (see also Wellek, 1963).

In more recent years psychologists have usually adopted a statement of inhibition theory somewhat broader and more general than that of Ranschburg. The classical statement of modern inhibition theory is probably that of Hull (1943). His statement of the law of inhibition is as follows: "Whenever any reaction is evoked in an organism there is left a condition or state which acts as a primary, negative motivation in that it has an innate capacity to produce a cessation of the activity which produced the state." He goes on to say that "we shall call this state or condition *reactive inhibition* ... The reaction decrements which have been attributed to reactive inhibition obviously bear a striking resemblance to the decrements which are ordinarily attributed to 'fatigue.' It is important to note that 'fatigue' is to be understood in the present context as denoting a decrement in action evocation potentiality, rather than an exhaustion of the energy available to the reacting organ."

For Hull, "the net amount of functioning inhibitory potential resulting from a sequence of reaction evocations is a positively accelerated function of the amount of work (W) involved in the performance of the response in question." He actually expressed the amount of work in terms of foot pounds, "as in ordinary mechanics," but it must be said immediately that this work hypothesis has fared rather ill at the hands of experimentalists—as one might have expected from a simple consideration of Ranschburg inhibition! It is now universally agreed that foot pounds of work done are a very inadequate measure of the reactive inhibition produced in an organism, and it seems appropriate to substitute a central rather than a peripheral theory of inhibition. Accordingly, amount of work (W) will be conceived of not as physical work but rather as mental work, defined in terms of complexity of task, difficulty of task, amount and continuity of attention required, and so forth. The variable (W) in fact cannot at present be identified or defined precisely, but we shall have occasion later on to note some of the characteristics of mental work which give rise to reactive inhibition.

Another characteristic of reactive inhibition noted by Hull is that "each amount of inhibitory potential diminishes progressively with the passage of time according to a simple decay or negative growth function." This formulation extends the notion of inhibition as a fatigue product to the dissipation of inhibition over time, in very much the same way as fatigue is dissipated by rest. These notions do not, of course, exhaust Hull's treatment of inhibition, but they will suffice for our purpose.

The main contention put forward by Hull, then, is that "all responses leave behind in the physical structures involved in the evocation, a state or substance which acts directly to inhibit the evocation of the activity in question. The hypothetical inhibitory condition or substance is observable only through its effect upon positive reaction potentials." Now from the behaviourist point of view, perception is in fact a stimulus-response connection (see Garner *et al.*, 1956); thus this general principle could apply with equal force to the so-called perceptual phenomena. The phenomena investigated by Ranschburg may be considered, in part at least, as perceptual, but more recently Köhler (1940, 1944) has developed a general theory of perceptual inhibition or, as he terms it, "satiation." He postulates that "a specific figure process occurs whenever a figure appears in the visual field. And this process tends to block its own way if the figure remains for some time in the same location . . . continued presence of *any* figure in a given location must change conditions for subsequent figure processes in the same region of the field." As the writer has pointed out (Eysenck, 1957), this statement of the satiation hypothesis in preception is formally identical with Hull's statement of the reactive inhibition hypothesis in learning; both are, in fact, deducible from Spearman's general law of fatigue (1927), which was postulated many years before Hull or Köhler constructed their respective postulate systems: "The occurrence of any cognitive event produces a tendency opposed to its occurrence afterwards." Actually the similarities between reactive inhibition and satiation are not merely formal but extend to experimental details such as rate of growth and rate of decay, as well as to the hypothetical source and locus of the effects in question (Duncan, 1956). In what follows we shall therefore tentatively subsume satiation phenomena under the general heading of inhibition.

The general relationship between personality and inhibition as so conceived was put forward by the present author in two postulates (Eysenck, 1957). The first of these was called the postulate of individual differences: "Human beings differ with respect to the speed with which excitation and inhibition are produced, the strength of the excitation and inhibition produced and the speed with which inhibition is dissipated. These differences are properties of the physical structures involved in making stimulus-response connections." The second postulate was called the typological postulate; it runs as follows: "Individuals in whom excitatory potential is generated slowly and in whom excitatory potentials so generated are relatively weak, are thereby predisposed to develop extraverted patterns of behaviour and to develop hysterical-psychopathic disorders in cases of neurotic breakdown; individuals in whom excitatory potential is generated quickly and in whom excitatory potentials so generated are strong, are thereby predisposed to develop introverted patterns of behaviour and to develop dysthymic disorders in case of neurotic breakdown. Similarly, individuals in whom reactive inhibition is developed quickly, in whom strong reactive inhibitions are generated, and in whom reactive inhibition is dissipated slowly, are thereby predisposed to develop extraverted patterns of behaviour and to develop hysterical-psychopathic disorders in case of neurotic breakdown; conversely, individuals in whom reactive inhibition is developed slowly, in whom weak reactive inhibitions are generated, and in whom reactive inhibition is dissipated quickly, are thereby predisposed to develop introverted patterns of behaviour and to develop dysthymic disorders in case of neurotic breakdown."

Certain points should be noted with respect to these postulates. In the first place they bear some superficial similarity to certain ideas put forward by Pavlov during the last years of his life. Pavlov had always been very much interested in individual differences between his dogs, and he tried to make use of the concepts of excitation and inhibition in a very detailed manner in constructing a system of personality description. Not only was this system extremely complex, but it also changed a large number of times; thus it would not be possible to give any kind of account of it here. Gray (1965) has described in considerable detail the stages through which Pavlov's thinking passed; he has also outlined the more recent experimental work done by Teplov, who attempted to follow up these ideas of Pavlov. Pavlov's final statement seems to call for three relatively independent dimensions of personality, one of which, denoted as strength versus weakness of the central nervous system, appears to the writer to bear some similarity to the excitation-inhibition balance put forth in the typological postulate. Furthermore, there are distinct similarities between the experimental procedures used by Teplov and by the present writer to measure this dimension. However, it would be very difficult to put this identification forward with any high degree of certainty because Russian workers have hitherto omitted to furnish any correlations between their experimental tests and the general behaviour patterns of their subjects; that is, they have not used ratings, self-ratings, or any form of personality test. Without some such external reference, it seems impossible to regard the Pavlov-Teplov system as being at the moment directly relevant to personality study, and it is equally impossible to make any detailed comparisons between the two systems. Certain points of similarity will be noted as appropriate, however.

The second point to be noted is that the theory really deals with an excitation-inhibition balance, i.e., the overall resultant of all the excitatory and inhibitory potentials which are postulated to be active at any given moment. Ideally, no doubt, one would like to measure both excitatory and inhibitory potentials separately, but as long as we are dealing with hypothetical constructs rather than with physiological variables, and can therefore only assess their influence in terms of some other observable variable, it seems impossible to separate out the particular influences of excitation and inhibition with any great efficiency. When, in the studies to be discussed shortly, it is argued that a deficiency in performance is due to reactive inhibition, it is always open to the critic to hypothesize that this deficiency in performance is due rather to a lessening of excitation, and conversely. While admitting this possibility, we shall be more concerned with the actual experimental demonstration of observable performance defects, leaving the detailed attribution of blame to a later chapter.

The third point to be made concerns the scientific status of concepts such as inhibition and excitation. To the purist, hypothetical constructs of this kind may be an anathema because they cannot in their very nature be specifically located in any physiological structure. However, such concepts may nevertheless have a certain heuristic value, provided that they lead to relatively unambiguous predictions of certain experimental outcomes. The rest of this chapter will be concerned with a number of deductions that have been made from our two postulates and with the detailed description of the results which have been achieved. Neither experiments nor discussions are offered as proof of the truth of the particular theories here presented; the available evidence is so large in scope as to make it quite impossible to discuss more than a small proportion within the bounds of a volume such as this. What is presented here has been chosen mainly in order to illustrate the way in which deductions can be made from the postulates stated, and to show some of the difficulties encountered in trying to verify or falsify these predictions. Our choice has been governed entirely by consideration of the aptitude of these examples for this purpose, as well as by the availability of suitable supporting experimental material. In the writer's view there is enough such material now to indicate that, broadly speaking at least, the two postulates under investigation are along the right lines, although he would agree that predictive accuracy is frequently lower than one might have hoped for because of the absence of detailed parametric information about important aspects of the testing situation. Other difficulties exist and will be discussed in due course; there will be a further discussion of the validity of the two postulates in a later chapter when we turn to their translation into physiological terms.

The fourth and last point which we wish to make before turning to a discussion of the experimental evidence relating to our two postulates concerns the point already adumbrated in the preceding chapter. We pointed out there that our aim was to identify a particular factor in the personality field, in that case neuroticism, with a particular concept in the experimental field, in that case emotion and drive. In the case of extraversion-introversion, clearly the concept in experimental and theoretical psychology corresponding to the personality dimension is that of fatigue. This concept, very much like that of emotion itself, is of course in no way as clear-cut, definite, and universally acceptable as one might wish, but there is now considerable agreement on the main facts of the situation (Schmidtke, 1965). And there is ample recognition of the distinction between *physical* and *psychic* fatigue, unsatisfactory as these terms may be from some points of view. The term psychic fatigue does not, of course, imply that there is no physiological change taking place in the central nervous system to correspond to the functional deficit which is used to index this hypothetical state. All that is meant, as Schmidtke points out, is "that there are fatigue functions which can be discovered and quantified with the help of physical or chemical processes of measurement, and that there also exist others which have hitherto proved impossible to measure along these lines." This distinction is, of course, similar to that between Hull's and our own interpretation of reactive inhibition; Hull uses a peripheral, physicalistic interpretation, whereas we have preferred a psychological, central one. No doubt peripheral and central events interact in very complex ways; nevertheless the distinction has a certain heuristic type of validity.

However that might be, there is certainly a very large volume of experimental work on the conditions determining fatigue and the differential effects produced by fatigue, both the peripheral and the central variety; the reader may be referred to Schmitdke's recent introduction to this topic (1965). If this general argument be accepted, then we can say that the extravert as compared to the introvert will behave as a more fatigued person in relation to a less fatigued person, just as previously we argued that a person high on neuroticism when compared with a person low on neuroticism would behave under suitable circumstances like a person high on drive as compared to a person low on drive. Thus the concept of fatigue in relation to extraversion-introversion takes the place of the concept of emotion in relation to neuroticism-stability.

Involuntary Rest Pauses (IRPs) and Blocking

One of the most dramatic consequences of mental fatigue is the complete cessation of performances, however momentary such cessation may be. In the perceptual field such predictable rest pauses following massed practice have been observed particularly in experiments dealing with the stabilisation of the retinal image (Heckenmuller, 1965); when the image of the fixated object is precisely stabilised on the retina, it is found that after a short period of time the object seems to vanish. After a short period of "rest," object-restitution occurs and the object is seen again. Thus there occurs a rapid succession of work (seeing) and rest (not seeing) periods. In ordinary life the incessant movement of the eye, whether voluntary or involuntary, effectively prevents the occurrence of strictly consecutive stimulation of identical retinal elements by identical stimuli. The obvious prediction that extraverts would be more subject to this type of satiation than introverts and would therefore show more frequent and longer rest pauses has not yet been put to the test.

In the field of motor activity also such involuntary rest pauses have been reported in the literature. The first systematic investigations in this field occurred before the turn of the century in the laboratory of Kraepelin in his work on solution times for problems in addition. Voss (1899) discovered that after a period of time, unusually long solution times were returned by his subjects for certain problems, to be followed again by a series of normal solution times. Both the length and frequency of these unusually long times increased over a period. These involuntary rest pauses (IRPs) were studied in considerable detail by Bills (1931) under the title of "blocking." To him blocks represented response-produced inhibitions which allowed the organism to recover from fatigue. To put the matter in Hullian terms, Kimble (1949) has argued that during massed practice, reactive inhibition, which is a negative drive, continues to grow until it equals the positive drive (D) under which the organism is working. When positive and negative drive are equal, the effective drive is zero, and as performance is conceived of as a product of drive x habit, performance ceases. The short involuntary rest pause thus produced allows inhibition to dissipate until positive drive is sufficiently higher than negative drive (reactive inhibition) to allow performance to recommence. Reactive inhibition will again increase until performance ceases again, and in this way there will be a constant series of stops and starts, very much as in the case of perceptual performance with retinal stabilisation.

An experimental study to test the prediction that extraverts would be more susceptible to the accumulation of inhibition and would consequently show more voluntary rest pauses than introverts has been reported by Spielmann (1963). She used as her task simple tapping with a metal stylus on a metal plate. A very complex recording system enabled her to determine with considerable accuracy the exact amount of time the stylus was in touch with the metal plate on each occasion (tap) and the length of time the stylus was away from the plate between two taps (gap). Her analysis was mainly concerned with the gaps because there is an element of artificiality connected with the length of taps, by virtue of the fact that the metal stylus rebounds from the plate to some slight extent. Involuntary rest pauses were scored in terms of discontinuity for any given subject when all his gap times were plotted. These times were arranged in groups according to a predetermined system, and gaps were counted as IRPs when their occurrence was separated from the main body of the data by two empty groups. Ninety working-class subjects in all were tested, and the five most introverted and the five most extraverted selected on the basis of the M.P.I.

Results were very clear-cut, and Figure 26 illustrates them well. It was found that the average frequency of IRPs was significantly higher in extraverts than introverts with a significance level of less than 1 per cent. The total number of IRPs observed was fifteen times as high in the extravert than in the introvert group,

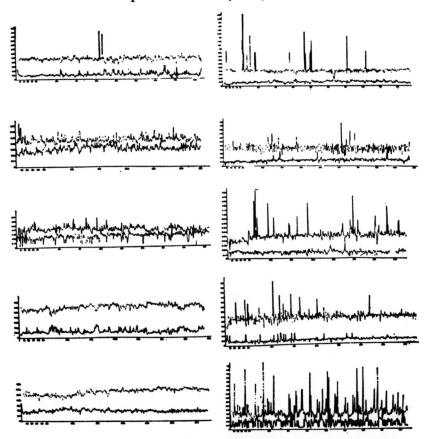

Figure 26. One minute record of 5 introverted (left) and 5 extraverted (right) subjects carrying out tapping task. Recorded are gaps (top line) and taps (bottom line). Ordinate records durations of taps and gaps. Reprinted with permission from I. Spielman, 1963.

there being no overlap whatsoever. The average onset of IRPs was significantly earlier (1 per cent level) in the extravert group than in the introvert group. Furthermore, extraverts showed a decidedly wider range of IRP durations. Testing was done for five minutes on each of five successive days. During this time introverts produced twenty-five IRPs, of which none was longer than .5 seconds; extraverts produced 370 IRPs of which forty-four were longer than .5 seconds. These are only some of the differences observed by Spielmann, and it should be added that they are not due to the fact that the individuals chosen were in any sense extreme. When another four highly extraverted and another four highly introverted subjects were chosen from the same group, their results were very similar to those of the subjects whose scores have already been given; they are represented in Figure 27. We thus have nine highly introverted and nine highly extraverted subjects representing respectively the highest and lowest 10 per cent of scorers on the M.P.I., perfectly normal, average, working-class people adjusted satisfactorily to their life. More extreme groups would undoubtedly have given more extreme results.

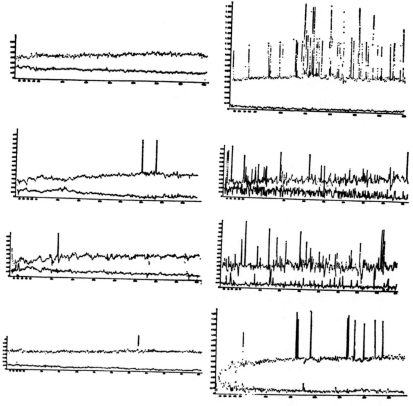

Figure 27. One minute record of 4 introverted (left) and 4 extraverted (right) subjects on tapping task. Reprinted with permission from I. Spielman, 1963.

The results of Spielmann's thesis were verified in a study by Eysenck (1964d), who tested seventy-four industrial apprentices, half under high-drive conditions and the other half under low-drive conditions. Both groups showed a positive correlation between extraversion and the number of involuntary rest pauses; it was also found that when the number of taps was held constant by analysis of covariance, the high-drive group had fewer IRPs, as would be expected in terms of the Hullian hypothesis mentioned above.

A quite different measure of IRPs has been reported by Holland (1965), working with the rotating spiral aftereffect. He found that when the spiral was rotated at a speed above the fusion threshold, there occurred from time to time momentary perceptions of parts of the spiral. These flashes occur with very great reliability (r = 0.93), and Holland accounted for them in terms of eye movements, i.e., IRP interrupting the task of fixation. His argument depends on the synchronisation of the moving stimulus and the moving eye, which has the effect of momentarily suspending differences in relative movement permitting perception of an apparently stationary spiral. If this stroboscopic explanation be accepted, we would expect extraverts to show more of these IRPs than introverts, and indeed a report by Franks (1963) demonstrates a significant correlation between E and number of "flashes" (r = 0.42). This failure of extraverts to fixate consistently may be responsible in part for their generally lower scores on spiral aftereffect tests (Holland, 1965).

A third type of IRP measurement may be found in the extensive work that has recently been done on vigilance. Vigilance has been defined as a state of readiness to detect and respond to certain specified small changes, occurring at random time intervals in the external environment. Operationally defined, the level of vigilance is equated with the performance of the subject in terms of the number of signals not responded to, or the intensity to which signals have to be raised in order to ensure response. Much work has been done in relation to this concept (Buckner and McGrath, 1963), and it seems feasible to regard missed responses on vigilance tasks as very similar in nature to IRPs; according to this view, responses are missed when a stimulus coincides in time with a "block" (IRP). If this be so, then the prediction would follow that extraverts would be more likely to have poor vigilance scores than introverts, just as they have more IRPs in the type of experiment considered above.

Earlier studies on vigilance tended to be carried out under the title of "monotony," and already Muensterberg (1913) suggested that extraverted persons were more prone to monotony, a finding confirmed by Thompson (1929) in the United States and Flechtner (1937) in Germany. Particularly impressive is the work of Bartenwerfer (1957), who used a task involving a simulated car-driving activity; he reports a correlation of 0.44 between extraversion and behavioral effects of monotony, objectively scored. Not all studies have given positive results (Smith, 1955), but those which failed to reveal any correlations were usually based on verbal report, rather than on objective evidence of performance decrement, and used measures of extraversion which were less than perfectly adequate.

One relevant experiment has been reported by Bakan, Belton, and Toth (1963). They used sixty-two extraverted subjects, sixty-two introverted subjects, and an intermediate "normal" group of thirty-one subjects; half of the extreme groups were run under isolation conditions (each person kept in isolation throughout instruction and pretest trials and tested singly), the other half under group conditions. The "normal" subjects were all tested in the isolation condition. The test consisted of a tape, played over earphones, which repeated single digits at 1 second intervals; the task of the subject was to spot and write down any three-digit sequences in the order odd-even-odd, i.e., 963, 347. Figure 28 records the results for the three groups during the 48-minute test, divided into three equivalent 16-minute periods. The relative decline of the extraverts, as compared with the introverts, is obvious. An interesting though nonsignificant finding of this study is that extraverts do better in the "group" condition, introverts in the "isolation" condition.

Similar results have been reported by Claridge (1960). Using a similar task to that employed by Bakan, he tested four groups, all consisting of sixteen subjects; these were (a) a normal control group, (b) a group of hysterics (neurotic extraverts), (c) a group of dysthymics (neurotic introverts), (d) a group of early schizo-

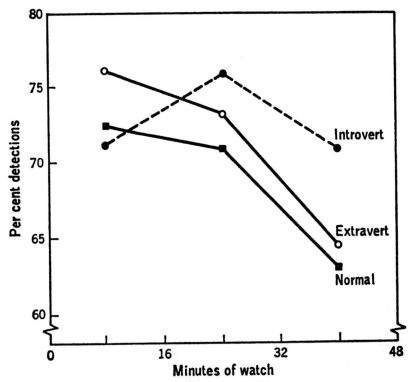

Figure 28. Performance on vigilance task of introverts and extraverts. Reprinted with permission from P. Bakan, J. A. Belton, and J. C. Toth: *Vigilance: A Symposium.* New York, McGraw-Hill, 1963.

phrenics (whose performance is not of interest in this connection). The groups were equated for age and intelligence. The task used was in two parts, the first consisting of a 30-minute tape recording of digits; subjects had to respond to three successive odd numbers. Immediately following the principal part of the test, another series of digits was played, lasting this time for 10 minutes. Here the subject was told to carry on as before, but also to signify the occurrence of any number *six*, this secondary signal occurring much more frequently than the primary signal. The results of the experiment are shown in Figure 29; it will be clear that the introverted dysthymic group show no decrement, but rather an improvement during the principal part of the test, while the extraverted hysteric group show a marked decline. Normals

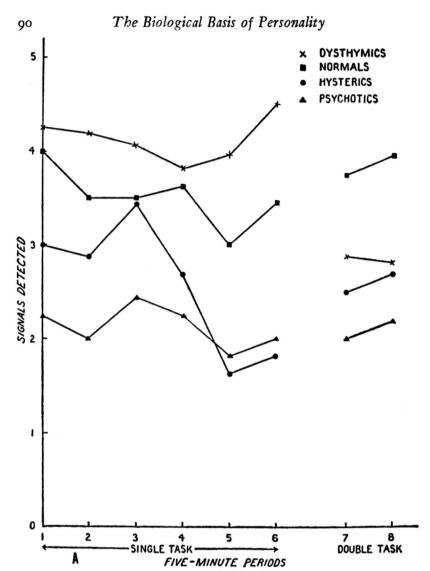

Figure 29. (a) Performance on vigilance task of dysthymics and hysterics. Reprinted with permission from G. Claridge, 1960.

(and psychotics) show only a slight decline.

The figure also shows the effects of introducing a secondary task, the result of which was predicted to be *alerting* in the case of the extraverts, who by this time were hypothesized to be in a state of considerable inhibition, and *distracting* in the case of the introverts, who by this time showed no evidence of any inhibition at all. As expected, the hysteric group showed a significant *increase* in performance, while the dysthymic group showed a significant *decrease*. Neither normals nor psychotics showed any significant change. These results are in good agreement with those reported in another study by Bakan (1959) who found "(a) that the addition of a secondary task, which markedly increases the number of signals to be responded to, results in improved signal detection performance in a primary task, and (b) that extraverts, who do not do as well with the primary task alone, show greater improvement than introverts with the addition of the secondary task."

Among more recent writers, Halcomb and Nirk (1965) have used the California Psychological Inventory on forty subjects who carried out a vigilance task lasting four hours. They found quite high correlations with self-control and "achievement via independence," two scales measuring traits close to introversion; the correlations were in the predicted direction. Intelligence was found to interact with personality. Hogan (1966) found highly significant differences between introverts and extraverts on the Roswold *et al* (1956) Continuous Performance Test (CPI), which may be regarded as a test of vigilance (see Figure 29b). Extraverts performed in an inferior manner, although they were equated with the introverts on the verbal part of the College Entrance Examination Board test.

Results of vigilance tests are not always in line with expectation, nor do scores on them always correlate with extraversion. This may be due to any number of causes. Das (1964), who failed to find any correlation between vigilance and extraversion, used an auditory vigilance task which may have been too easy; he presented digits "at the rate of approximately 20 per minute." Such a slow rate, particularly when used with subjects of above-average intelligence, does not result in proper decrement scores; and indeed Das reports on "the large number of subjects who had zero errors in the last 5-minute period," as well as on a marked decrease, rather than an increase, of errors during the terminal period. Broadbent (1953) has thrown some light on the problem of why decrement sometimes occurs and sometimes fails

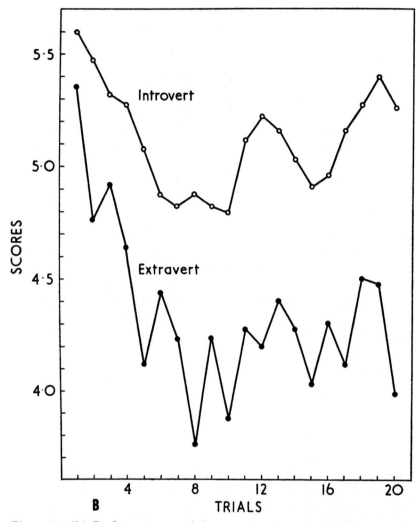

Figure 29. (b) Performance on vigilance task of introverts and extraverts. Drawn with permission from data supplied by M. J. Hogan: *Percept. Mot. Skills,* 22:187-192, 1966.

to occur in vigilance tasks, and his view is relevant to the failure of some experiments to support the extraversion-decrement correlation. He points out that the "small changes, occurring at random time intervals," to which the subject has to respond must occur in their totality during the IRP or blank period if an error is to be recorded by the experimenter. If the IRP lasts for 1 second, and the signal lasts for 2 seconds, then even though signal and IRP coincide, part of the signal is still on view after the IRP is over and can thus be responded to. Fraser (1952) has in fact shown that the same watch-keeping task can be transformed from one which shows "fatigue" decrement to one which does not, by increasing the length of time for which the signal is visible. Great care must therefore be exercised in choosing the correct experimental parameters, having in mind the characteristics of the test in question, the population of subjects, the length of time involved in testing, and even such apparently irrelevant variables as the time of day (Bakan, 1963; Colquhoun, 1960). The latter, for instance, reported that vigilance on a paced inspection task was correlated with extraversion, in the sense that in tests conducted during the morning, good performance was associated with introversion, while during the afternoon the relationship was reversed.

Colquhoun and Corcoran (1964) report an experiment checking on this finding, and also on the relationship between extraversion and group versus isolation conditions of testing already mentioned. They used 122 Royal Navy ratings who were assigned to one of four testing conditions, employing the combinations of morning and afternoon testing and group and isolation testing. The task employed was one of crossing out the letter "e" whenever it occurred in a sample of English prose. Results for these two sets of conditions are shown in Figure 30 for isolation versus group conditions, and in Figure 31 for morning versus afternoon conditions. It will be seen that as before, introverts perform better in isolation, extraverts in groups, and that again introverts perform better in the morning, extraverts in the afternoon.[1] Their explanation of these findings is in terms of excitation-

[1]An interesting study by Th. Ehlers and R. Brickenkamp (unpublished) has reported correlations between personality and success in learning on a teaching machine. For two groups of 30 and 25 Ss respectively, correlations of −0.34 and −0.37 with E were found; both of these are significant statistically. N failed to give consistent or significant correlations. These findings may be relevant to the distinction between group and individual learning, and may suggest important consequences for advocates of the more widespread use of teaching machines. It seems likely that any assessment of the comparative use of this method of teaching, as compared with other methods, would have to use personality measures in order to study the interaction term; it seems unlikely that one method will be found

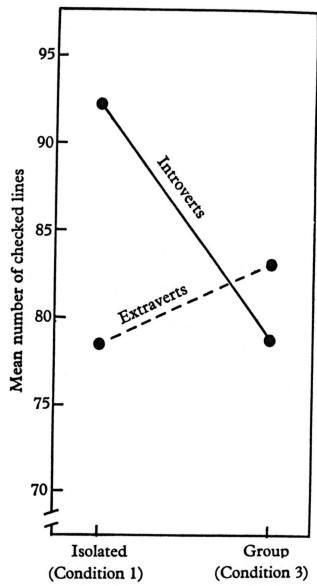

Figure 30. Performance of extraverts and introverts under isolated and group conditions. Reprinted with permission from W. P. Colquhoun and D. W. J. Corcoran: *Brit. J. Soc. Clin. Psychol.,* 3:226-231, 1964.

universally superior to other methods. It is much more likely that children and students will benefit from different methods of teaching, depending on their intelligence, motivation, and personality.

inhibition (they perfer to call the resulting balance between these two cortical states "arousal"), taken in conjunction with the inverse-U relation between arousal and performance which we have already encountered. This hypothesized relationship is shown in Figure 32. They quote Kleitman (1939) as showing that level of arousal is low in the morning, and go on to say that "the first assumption of the model would place introverts in a more favourable (optimal) position at this time, say IM in Figure 32. Extraverts, on the other hand, would be at some position to the left of IM, say EM. A general rise in arousal in the afternoon would shift EM to EA and IM to IA, which would result in poorer performance by introverts and better performance by extraverts. The same kind of model can be applied to the change from isolated to group testing conditions, provided it is assumed that the incentive provided by group testing raises level of arousal."[1a]

Alternative explanations are of course available. It seems likely that social conditions will act as additional drive to extraverts (sociable), but as distraction to introverts (unsociable), thus facilitating the performance of the former and interfering with the performance of the latter. Nor can the evidence for higher arousal during the afternoon be accepted as very strong; most performance curves taken over different times of the day show best performance during the morning, with afternoon performance trailing (Schmidtke, 1965). Whatever may be the explanation of these curious phenomena, they serve to remind us that single, simple experiments to prove or disprove a theory such as that linking extraversion and reactive inhibition are difficult to devise, and that many unsuspected variables have to be carefully controlled before we can regard the evidence as conclusive. Possibly the concurrent polygraph recording of physiological measures of arousal (Eason, Bearshall, and Jaffee, 1965) might throw further light on such complicating features as time of day and socially-produced drive.

Corcoran (1965) presented another attempt to relate the in-

[1a]An alternative hypothesis is that extraverts and introverts differ with respect to diurnal variations in thresholds of arousal. There is good evidence that such individual differences do occur (Walsh and Misiak, 1966), although work along these lines has not hitherto brought personality dimensions into contact with personality variables. A study along these lines might be of considerable interest.

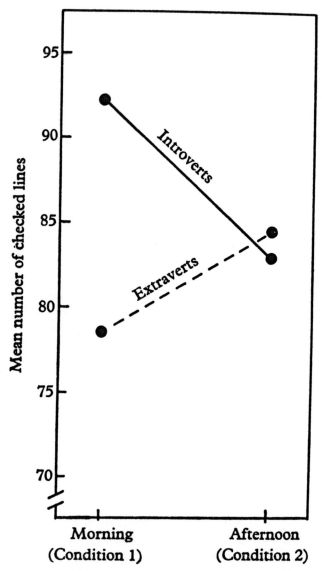

Figure 31. Performance of extraverts and introverts during morning and afternoon testing. Reprinted with permission from W. P. Colquhoun and D. W. J. Corcoran: *Brit. J. Soc. Clin. Psychol.*, 3:226-231, 1964.

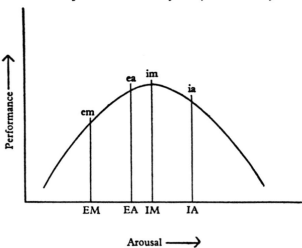

Arousal ———⟶

Figure 32. The "inverted-U" relationship between performance and arousal used as a possible explanation of results quoted in Figs. 30 and 31. Reprinted with permission from W. P. Colquhoun and D. W. J. Corcoran: *Brit. J. Soc. Clin. Psychol.*, 3:226-231, 1964.

verted-U relation to personality. His argument is clearly shown in the captions to Figures 33 and 34; if introverts are higher on excitation/arousal than extraverts, then the two groups should react differently to changes in conditions. Corcoran used sleep deprivation as a de-arousing condition, incentives and loud noise as arousing conditions. Two tasks were used, one easy (multiple reaction time), the other difficult (complex tracking). The results in each case showed differential behaviour by extraverts and introverts; assuming that introverts are in fact more highly aroused than extraverts, Corcoran concludes "(a) that the performance of the less aroused subject deteriorates when the general level of arousal is decreased, (b) that the performance of the more aroused subject is less affected than that of the less aroused subject when arousal generally is decreased and may even improve if the initial level of arousal is past the optimum."

One consequence of the more frequent occurrence of involuntary rest pauses in extraverts should be a more varied output, compared with the more regular output of introverts; the work of Spielmann on tapping has shown very clearly (Figures 26, 27) how in relation to one test the two groups compare with respect

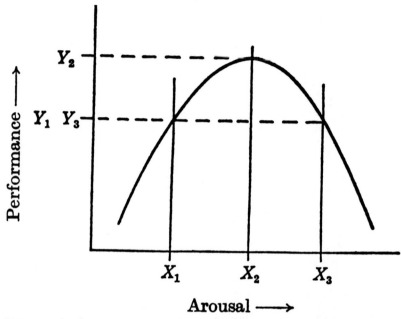

Figure 33. Performance level Y₁, Y₃ would result from arousal levels X_1 or X_3. Given values Y_1, Y_3 it is possible to determine whether arousal level is at X_1 or X_3 by manipulating level of arousal and noting the directional change in performance. Reprinted with permission from D. W. J. Corcoran: *Brit. J. Psychol.*, 56:267-274, 1965.

to this characteristic. In other fields, too, such comparisons have been made; thus Reed (1961) and Reed and Francis (1962) have studied audiometric response consistency in children, demonstrating a tendency for extraverted children to show a less consistent, more depressed set of values on successive tests. Howarth (1963) reported greater variability in line reproduction for extraverts. Ranking (1963a, 1963b) has reported several studies of reading test performance of introverts and extraverts, showing that as predicted, extraverts have significantly lower reliabilities than introverts. He also found that extraverts declined more in performance from the first third of the test to the last two thirds, and in consequence had poorer scores in toto (see also Lynn, 1955). A similar finding has been reported by Eysenck (1959c) in relation to problem solving. School performance (Child, 1964) and university performance (Furneaux, 1962; Lynn, 1959) would on the

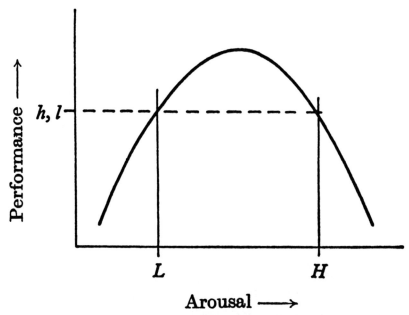

Figure 34. Groups L and H both perform at h, l. By manipulating level of arousal it is possible to determine which group is at H and which at L. Reprinted with permission from D. W. J. Corcoran: *Brit. J. Psychol.*, 56:267-274, 1965.

same grounds be expected to be poorer in extraverts, and the results appear to support this view. Otto (1965) and Otto and Redericks (1963) have shown that poor school achievers have higher reminiscence scores. As will be shown later, reminiscence is higher in extraverts; Child (1964) had also found an inverse correlation between achievement and reminiscence. All these results have only an indirect bearing on the theory under investigation, but on the whole they undoubtedly tend to support it.[2]

Sensory Thresholds

Involuntary rest pauses and the associated decline in vigilance are conceived theoretically as being due to reactive inhibition, although of course the general level of excitation may be invoked

[2]The studies discussed in this section are all concerned in some way with the effects of continuous performance. Bergum (1966) has attempted to make a taxonomic analysis of continuous performance effects; while this was published too late to have an effect on our discussion, it may serve to clarify certain points in it.

to explain certain complex interaction features between vigilance, drive, and time of day. Predictions about sensory thresholds, on the other hand, are made almost entirely in terms of excitation, leading to the prediction that sensory thresholds would be lower for introverts than for extraverts because of the higher efficiency of performance associated with cortical excitation — at least at suboptimal levels. (There is little danger of reaching high levels of excitation in experiments on sensory thresholds as stimulation is by definition at a low level). Even here, however, reactive inhibition cannot be ruled out; the monotonous, low-level stimulation and the repetitive manipulations associated with threshold measurement give the task a character not too far different from that of a vigilance test, and it is certainly not contended here that one might use IRP and vigilance tests as measures of inhibition, threshold tests as measures of excitation. According to our hypothesis, both types of task measure a balance of excitatory and inhibitory potentials which are affected in different ways by the experimental procedures, but which are also at the mercy of many external conditions difficult to specify or to control.

Our hypothesis here agrees well with Teplov's theory, taken from one of Pavlov's two contradictory views about the nature of the weak as opposed to the strong nervous system, to the effect that there exists a negative correlation between strength of the nervous system and sensitivity as measured by absolute sensory thresholds. It will be remembered that there exists a certain similarity on the theoretical level between introversion on the one hand and the Pavlov-Teplov notion of a weak nervous system on the other. Gray (1964) has summarised the evidence adduced by the Russian writers, largely Nebylitsyn (see also Nebylitsyn, Rozhdestvenskaya, and Teplov, 1960); he concludes that "this prediction has since been verified at a high level of confidence."

Work in relation to introversion was begun by Stuart L. Smith (1966), who argued that it would be difficult to test hypotheses about sensitivity by traditional methods of threshold measurement since a failure to find differences might "pertain more to the decision-making habits and risk-taking propensities of the subject groups than to their actual thresholds. In other words extraverts might be predicted to guess more frequently and therefore appear to have thresholds as low as or lower than those of the careful, scrupulous introverts."[3] In his experiment such a tendency was eliminated "by using an ear-choice technique, causing the subject not merely to say whether he heard a tone but to say in which ear the tone was played, the presumption being that when Ss know they can be checked up on they will not be as free with their guessing. Furthermore, a 'guessing correction' was added to the results of testing, and, most importantly, a forced-choice technique was used . . . In a 'choice' technique the question is not 'Did you experience the sensation or fail to do so?' but rather 'If you heard the sound, in which of two or more intervals or places do you think the stimulus was presented?' For *forced choice* the subject must guess on *each* occasion." Forced-choice techniques are known to give stable and useful threshold measures (Blackwell, 1953), and they have been used in the study of decision-making processes and signal detection (Swets, 1959; Zwislocki et al, 1958).

The usual method of forced-choice has been one in which tones were presented singly or in pairs or in one of two or more time intervals, but because this could be claimed to require additional skills, such as memory factors involving the comparison of recent events with past ones, Smith adopted an ear choice method, similar in some ways to that used in certain screening tests (Curry and Kurtzrock, 1951; Nagel, 1957) but not previously used on a forced-choice basis. All tests were conducted in a dark, soundproofed room, with tones played over earphones. A subject was told that a tone would be played after a light was flashed on by the experimenter but that many would be beyond his range of hearing; he was to signal the experimenter as to whether the tone was heard in the right or left ear. In the "Yes-No" technique, subjects did not respond when they did not feel able to hear the tone; in the forced-choice technique they were required to signal on every presentation, even though this represented nothing but a guess.

Four groups of subjects were tested, representing all combinations of high and low extraversion and neuroticism scores; there

[3]Cameron and Myers (1966) have found subjects with extraverted traits much more likely to take risks than subjects with intraverted traits; see also Lynn and Butler (1962).

were three subjects in each group. All subjects were tested under placebo and drug conditions, the two drugs being nicotine (two tablets sublingually, 0.1 mg each) and Seconal® (two capsules orally, 45.0 mg each); this was done as a check on some of the Russian reports on drug effects. Table II shows the main results of this work. Thresholds for the introverted group were considerably lower than those for the extraverted subjects. These results were significant both for the predrug condition mean and for the mean of the drug studies. Differences between groups high and low on neuroticism were not significant, and neither were those between the forced-choice technique and the (corrected) "Yes-No" technique. The drugs had no significant effect, although in some pilot studies nicotine and amphetamine had been found to lower the threshold significantly, while Seconal® had the opposite effect. Why this effect was not observed in the main experiment is not known.

TABLE II

MEAN THRESHOLD: EXTRAVERTS VS INTROVERTS

Condition	Extravert	Introvert	t (one-tailed)	p
Yes-No Technique (Adjusted)	+3.33	−1.75	2.21	<.05
Forced Choice Technique	+1.17	−2.42	1.42	N.S.
Pre-drug Mean	+2.25	−2.08	1.94	<.05
After Seconal®	+0.67	−5.08	3.16	<.01
After Nicotine	−0.17	−3.58	1.71	N.S.
After Placebo	−1.17	−4.92	1.97	<.05
Drug Mean	−0.22	−4.45	2.64	<.025

Results of auditory threshold experiment. Positive values indicate raised thresholds, negative values lowered thresholds. Quoted with permission from S. Smith, 1966.

In another study, Haslam (1966) attempted to relate pain thresholds to personality, using the radiant-heat type of apparatus introduced by Hardy and Wolff (1940, 1952). Twenty-four subjects were used, of whom twelve were extraverts and twelve introverts on the Maudsley Personality Inventory (Eysenck, 1959). The groups were equated for age and mean forehead skin temperature, and they did not differ in sex composition or neuroticism. Mean for head pain thresholds in mc/sec/cm² was 261 for extraverts and 223 for introverts, giving a significant difference in favour of the introverts. Haslam also measured pain thresholds under caffeine and found that thresholds were lowered significantly for both extraverts and introverts; this is in good agreement with the Russian work of Teplov's school (Gray, 1964), who place much importance on drug reaction in their theoretical considerations.

Haslam also reported another, similar experiment, in part replicating the one described above; here the threshold values of the two groups were 251 for the extraverts and 219 for the introverts, supporting the previous result. She then proceeded to argue that while the introverted group was apparently working at or near their optimal excitation level, the extravert was working well below it. An increase in excitation (or possibly a decrement in inhibition) should lead to a considerable improvement in the threshold level of the extraverted group, and either leave the introverted group where it was or produce a slight improvement (or even possibly a slight decrement, if the optimal excitation value were to be exceeded). Using threat of electric shock, she found that both extraverts and introverts now recorded thresholds of 197 mc/sec/cm^2, giving an improvement of 54 points for the extraverts and 22 points for the introverts. These values are well in line with prediction, showing greater improvement for the extraverted group.[4]

Another interesting experiment has been reported by Dunstone *et al* (1964). Using the method of Dzendolet (1963), these writers have related the threshold of electrical vestibular stimulation to personality, employing the M.P.I. for the purpose of assessing personality variables. Low-frequency sinusoidal electrical stimulation of the human vestibular apparatus produces lateral sway, and there are strong individual differences in response. Subjects were divided at the mean into introverts and extraverts; it was found that the absolute threshold for introverts was 0.05 milliamperes at 0.20 cps, while for extraverts it was 0.17 milliamperes. The difference was fully significant statistically, and in line with the prediction derived from our theorem. High scores on the Taylor

[4] It may be queried whether, as the theory would predict, thresholds in one modality correlate with those in others. Ippolotov (1966) has published some data confirming this hypothesis, as well as showing a relationship between low thresholds and "weak nervous system," a term which, as we shall see, is used by Russian investigators to denote a personality dimension in many ways similar to introversion.

M.A.S. also correlated with low threshold values, but at a much lower level of statistical significance; it seems likely that this latter correlation was at least in part due to the fact that manifest anxiety, as measured by this scale, has a significant introversion component (Eysenck, 1960a; Eysenck and Eysenck, 1967).

A related type of investigation is the work of Fischer, Griffin and Rockey (1966) on gustatory chemoreceptors. These workers report a positive correlation between introversion and taste-thresholds for quinine; they also found "that, in general, the extremely sensitive tasters of both quinine and 6-n-propylthiouracil can be classified as Kretschmerian leptosomes or Sheldonian ectomorphs, whereas the extremely insensitive tasters of both compounds conform to the Kretschmerian pyknic or Sheldonian endomorph type." This finding is of interest because of the correlation between extraversion and pyknic body build, to be discussed in a later chapter. The same workers report that "tranquilization increases, whereas excitation decreases, the size of a just noticeable taste difference . . . the jnd and its expression, the Weber ratio, indeed appear to be independent of local receptor phenomena; they reflect individual systemic (re)activity." This result is of interest in view of our own findings with drugs, reviewed in a later chapter; in general stimulant drugs produce introverting changes, depressant drugs extraverting ones.

Do these experiments and that of Smith implicate changes in excitation or inhibition? Ramsey, Utrecht, and Alkema (1966) have studied the effect of massed and spaced practice on auditory thresholds; their results are shown in Figure 35. It will be seen that spaced practice shows no evidence of decrement in performance, and thus of reactive inhibition, fatigue, or lack of vigilance. Under massed practice, however, there is obvious evidence of performance decrement, and it seems permissible to relate this to the growth of reactive inhibition. These results are relevant to our two studies; neither Smith nor Haslam used conditions resembling massing, and it would seem therefore that in these experiments we are concerned with individual differences in the state of excitation, rather than with inhibition.

Thresholds in flicker fusion frequency have also been investigated in relation to personality. Washburn, Hughes, Steward, and

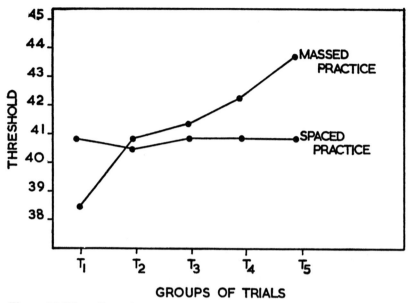

GROUPS OF TRIALS

Figure 35. The effect of massed and spaced practice on auditory thresholds. Reprinted with permission from R. Ramsay *et al.*, 1966.

Sligh (1930) compared two groups of forty-two college students classified as extraverted or introverted on the basis of a personality inventory; extraverts were found to have somewhat lower thresholds (i.e., less efficient cortical resolution of stimuli) than introverts, but the difference was not significant statistically. Madlung (1936) found a similar but much larger difference. Simonson and Brozek (1952) also report a significant difference favouring introverts, who showed a 5 per cent superiority in resolving power. It is also interesting to note that Schmidtke (1961) found persons of leptomatic body build to have higher CFF than pyknics; as pointed out in a later chapter, introversion is associated with leptomorph body build. Simonson and Brozek (1952) also report some data supporting this association between CFF and body build. The suggested constitutional implication is brought out more strongly by Murawski (1960), who found striking similarity in CFF in identical twins. All these data are in good agreement with the hypothesis that CFF thresholds, regarded as evidence of cortical excitation, are higher in introverts.

Further results have been reported by members of the Dutch school of Heymans (1929), who have adopted and adapted the old theory of primary function — secondary function originally put forward by Gross (1902). This theory has been discussed at some length elsewhere (Eysenck, 1960).[5] Reuning (1955) has a correlation between CFF and alpha frequency on the EEG of .55, and there is one of .34 in another study (Shoul and Reuning, 1957). These results make sense if, as we have argued, high EEG frequencies are related to introversion. However, many parameters require to be carefully controlled before experiments with the CFF become properly comparable, and no such control seems to have been exerted. One such variable relates to the psychophysical method used, and the time-arrangements of the experiment; attitudinal factors, such as risk-taking, are difficult to control, unless some form of forced-choice is used, and in lengthy runs reactive inhibition is likely to accumulate and interfere with performance.

In some unpublished work from the Maudsley laboratories, it has been shown that over trials there is a tendency for introverts to show an increase in threshold, while extraverts show a decline; this is as expected from the hypothesis that reactive inhibition attaches to the task if continued for any length of time. As in our discussion of so many other experiments, we can only conclude here that results must depend very much on the appropriate choice of parameter, and that direct comparisons of separate experiments which differ in many respects are useless.[6] Another complication which arises is that neuroticism also appears to be related to CFF; a review of the literature has been given in Eysenck (1957), and the more recent work of Wagoner (1960) and others supports the finding that high N subjects have lower CFF

[5]See also Skawran (1962) and Biesheuvel (1952).
[6]Parameters in question include brightness of test patch, state of dark adaptation of subject, surrounding illumination, area of test patch, light-dark ratio, binocular or monocular presentation, amount of practice, instructions, psychological method used, etc. Most important would appear to be the intensity of stimulation of the eye, as theoretically one would predict that the more introverted the subject, the lower the intensity of stimulation of the eye at which maximum CFF thresholds are reached (see Gray, 1964, p. 314). Many of the parameters listed above are involved in this, and considerable control over all of them is required in order to produce meaningful data.

thresholds, i.e., poorer resolution. What is clearly required is a zone analysis taking both personality dimensions into account and varying experimental parameters in a predetermined fashion so as to test various specific hypotheses.

An interesting application of the set of hypotheses under discussion has been made by Corcoran (1964), who writes: "If introverts are in general more highly aroused than extraverts, then, assuming that arousal is synonymous with a state of high cortical facilitation, it follows that the output of an effector of an introvert should be greater than that of an extravert when both are equally stimulated." The test he used measured the amount of salivation consequent upon placing four drops of lemon juice upon the tongue, as compared with the natural rate of salivation. As predicted, introverts secreted almost twice as much saliva under experimental conditions as did extraverts, Kendall's *tau* coefficient giving a correlation of 0.62 between introversion and secretion. A second group was then tested with citric acid, but no correlation with personality was observed. A third group was tested, using lemon juice again, and the original finding was replicated, with a Spearman *rho* coefficient of 0.70; introverts secreted over twice as much saliva as extraverts under the experimental conditions. It is not clear why the experiment failed when citric acid was used; the theory would not predict any systematic variation in the effects of different stimuli, except in terms of their strength. Until this problem is cleared up by further experimentation, the results of this experiment can only be regarded as weakly supporting the theory, particularly as the number of subjects was rather small. (Results were fully significant statistically, however.) Just prior to publication of this book, S.B.G. Eysenck, in an unpublished study, replicated Corcoran's work on 100 Ss, finding a product-moment correlation of 0.72; she too failed to find any significant correlation when a commercial substitute for lemon juice was used. These correlations are encouragingly high and suggest that this may be a useful physiological index of introverted or extraverted behaviour.

Another application has been made by Lynn (1961), who has shown that the rate of reversal of the Necker cube is a function of stimulus intensity; higher intensities give rise to higher rates of

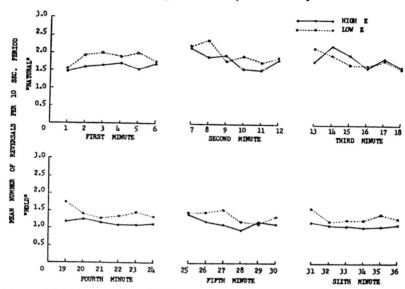

Figure 36. Mean number of Necker cube reversals of 46 introverts and 46 extraverts per 10-sec. period under *natural* and *hold* conditions. Reprinted with permission from C. M. Franks and L. E. H. Lindahl: *Percept. Mot. Skills,* 16:131-137, 1963.

reversal. If this be true, then introverts, having lower sensory thresholds, might be expected to have higher reversal rates than extraverts. Franks and Lindahl (1963) have carried out an experiment along these lines, using forty-six introverts and forty-six extraverts. Results under both *natural* and *hold* conditions are shown in Figure 36; introverts have higher rates under all conditions, but no differences are significant for the second and third minutes. Hold conditions give obviously better differentiation. Blink rates were established but found to be related neither to extraversion nor to reversal rate. As far as they go, these findings are in line with the hypothesis, but until more is known about the nature of the illusion, it would be premature to lay too much stress on the results of this study. It is interesting that McDugall (1929) put forward a similar hypothesis, although his line of argument was quite different to that adopted here.

The theory linking introversion with low sensory thresholds (and small j.n.d.s) has been extended by Eysenck (1963b) to pain tolerance and sensory deprivation tolerance in the following manner. Consider Figure 37; along the abscissa we have plotted degrees of sensory stimulation, from extremely low at the left to extremely high on the right. Along the ordinate we have plotted the hedonic tone associated with these different levels of stimulation, ranging from strongly negative (feelings of displeasure or even pain; desire to escape, to end the stimulation; abience) to strongly positive (feelings of intense pleasure; desire to prolong the stimulation, or even to increase it; adience). Between the positive and negative hedonic tones there is an *indifference level*, indicating that stimulation is neither sought nor avoided but is quite neutral to the subject. The strongly drawn curvilinear line in the centre of the diagram indicates the relationship between hedonic tone and strength of sensory stimulation, as derived from random samples of the population. We find that extremely high levels of stimulation produce pain and discomfort and have consequently a high negative hedonic tone (Beecher, 1959). Extremely low levels of stimulation (sensory deprivation) have also been found to be productive of high negative hedonic tone and to be bearable only for relatively short periods (Solomon *et al.*, 1967; Zubecki, 1964). It is only at intermediate levels of sensory stimulation that positive hedonic tone develops, and this finding is not perhaps entirely out

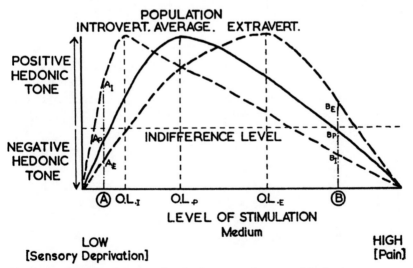

Figure 37. Relation between level of sensory input and hedonic tone as a function of personality. Reprinted from H. J. Eysenck, 1963.

of line with common experience and expectation. In any case, there is ample experimental evidence in the literature for the general correctness of the picture presented in Figure 37 (Berlyne, 1960).

We must now turn to individual differences in excitation and inhibition. Introverts have lower thresholds, and show less adaptation/inhibition to continued stimulation; extraverts have higher thresholds, and show more adaptation/inhibition to continued stimulation. It would seem to follow that any given degree of stimulation would be experienced as effectively higher by introverts than by extraverts. Objectively equal amounts of stimulation, therefore, would not be experienced as equal by extraverts, ambiverts, and introverts; they would appear displaced to the left of the abscissa of Figure 37 for the introvert, and to the right by the extravert. Similarly, if O.L. represents the optimum (or preferred) level of stimulation of a given person, then O.L.$_I$ would lie to the left of O.L.$_P$, and this in turn to the left of O.L.$_E$, where I and E refer to introvert and extravert, respectively, and P to the population average.

Again, consider two points, A and B, on the abscissa, referring to low and high stimulation respectively. If straight lines are drawn through these points, parallel to the ordinate, they will cross the general curve relating level of stimulation to hedonic tone roughly at the indifference level; in other words, for the average person these two stimuli are equally indifferent. For the typical extravert and introvert, however, as already explained, the general curve is not representative and has to be displaced to the left for the introvert and to the right for the extravert. As shown in the diagram, it follows that stimulus A will be positively hedonic for the introvert (A$_I$) and negatively hedonic for the extravert (A$_E$), while B will be negatively hedonic for the introvert (B$_I$) and positively hedonic for the extravert (B$_E$). In other words, we postulate a certain degree of *stimulus hunger* (sensation seeking, arousal seeking) in the extravert, and a certain degree of *stimulus aversion* in the introvert. Conversely, it would seem to follow that extraverts should be more tolerant of pain, introverts of sensory deprivation. What are the facts?

Weisen (1965) has compared groups of introverted and extraverted subjects, selected on the basis of appropriate M.M.P.I.

scales, in an experiment involving essentially behaviour indicative of preference for presence or absence of strong sensory stimulation. Coloured lights and loud music constituted the stimulation in question; silence and darkness constituted its absence. The subject pressed a key against a spring, the strength of his push constituting his selected behaviour for reinforcement. Under "onset" conditions the room was dark and quiet, and a push of predetermined strength produced noise and light for a 3-second period; unless the button was again pushed with predetermined strength, noise and light would then cease. Subjects could therefore ensure continuance of sensory stimulation by constantly pushing the button strongly, or they could ensure absence of stimulation by pushing the button weakly. Under "offset" conditions the opposite state of affairs prevailed; strong pushing was required to produce periods of silence, weak pushing ensured continuance of light and noise. For the first five minutes of the experiment (operant level period) no reinforcement was given; this period established the natural strength of button pushing of members of the various groups. This was followed by a 10-minute conditioning period and finally by a 5-minute extinction period.

Figures 38 and 39 show the frequency of correct (reinforced) responses of extraverts and introverts under "onset" and "offset" conditions respectively. It will be clear that both groups are similar in their behaviour under operant conditions, but that they behave quite differently under experimental conditions. The extraverts increase their rate of correct responses when these are reinforced by stimulation, and decrease their rate when absence of stimulation is the consequence. Introverts increase their rate of correct responses when these are reinforced by absence of stimulation, and decrease their rate when stimulation is the consequence. These results are in good agreement with prediction and may be regarded as replications, as the subjects in the "onset" condition were not the same as those in the "offset" condition. It might be added parenthetically that the choice of personality inventory probably decreased the expected effect; the M.M.P.I. was not designed for the measurement of extraversion-introversion in normal groups and is not well adapted for this purpose.

We must now turn to the question of pain tolerance. Clark and

3.

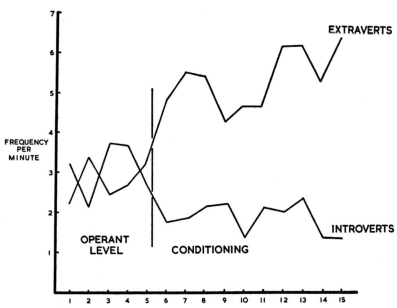

Figure 38. Operant conditioning of extraverts and introverts when noise and light are reinforcement. Reprinted with permission from A. Weisen, 1965.

Bindra (1956) reported high correlations between pain thresholds and tolerance levels, but did not measure personality parameters. Lynn and Eysenck (1961) tested thirty students with the Hardy-Wolff thermo-stimulator for pain tolerance, setting a time limit of 20 seconds for each stimulation because of adaptation effects and also for safety reasons. The subjects were divided into three groups, according to their E scores on the M.P.I., and it was found that pain tolerance scores decreased systematically from high E (17.2 seconds) through average (9.3 seconds) to low E (5.6 seconds). In the most extraverted group 80 per cent reached the time limit of 20 seconds, while in the most introverted group none did. The product-moment correlation between E and pain tolerance was +0.69. A similar correlation was found by Poser (1960), who used eighteen female students subjected to ischemic pain, and correlated tolerance scores with the E scale of the M.P.I.; in his case r= +0.53.

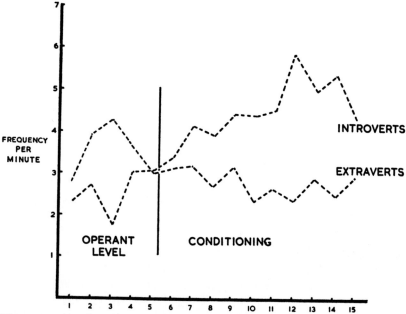

Figure 39. Operant conditioning of extraverts and introverts when silence and darkness are reinforcement. Reprinted with permission from A. Weisen, 1965.

Also relevant is the work of Schalling and Kareby-Levander (1963). They worked with nine dysthymics (introverts) and ten psychopaths (extraverts) so diagnosed clinically. Electric pain stimulation was used, and sensation thresholds, pain thresholds, and tolerance thresholds established. Pain thresholds were measured in units of sensation threshold, "in order to make it possible to compare measurements on various subjects." The three sets of measurements were made eight times at each experimental session; the experiment was repeated on three days. Differences between groups were found to show greater pain tolerance and higher pain thresholds for the "psychopaths"; the majority of these comparisons were statistically significant. Figure 40 shows the results for the dysthymics (Group A) and the psychopaths (Group B); triangles denote first tolerance level of the day, expressed as the ratio of current at tolerance level/current at sensation level, while circles denote first pain threshold of the day, expressed as the ratio of current at pain threshold level/current at sensation level.

Levine, Tursky and Nichols (1966), using electrical stimulation, studied pain tolerance in relation to personality. Working with two samples, one of twenty-nine students, the other of fifty-two housewives, they failed to find significant correlations between pain tolerance and either E or N. The use of a discrete rather than a continuous method of stimulus presentation may have affected the result; "however, the finding that there was no relationship between the discrete electrical measure of pain tolerance and E with two independent samples for a total of eighty-one Ss does weaken the hypothesis that intensity of pain tolerance *per se* is highly related to extraversion."

Slightly more indirect is another method of testing the greater pain tolerance of extraverts. Persistence in a physical task is painful, and consequently greater persistence is expected in extraverts on the basis of this theory. Costello and Eysenck (1961) studied seventy-two children selected as extreme scorers on the E and N scales of the Junior M.P.I.; they found that persistence scores of extraverted children were almost 25 per cent greater than those of introverted children. Singh, Gupta and Manocha (1966) repeated the study with eighty male Indian students and reported correlations of around .4 between persistence and extraversion. In addition they showed that stimulant drugs lowered persistence, while depressant drugs raised it; this is in good accord with the general finding, discussed in a later chapter, that these two types of drugs have introverting and extraverting properties, respectively.

Similarly, positive results are reported by Petrie (1960) and Petrie, Collins, and Solomon (1958, 1960). These writers have also tested the prediction linking sensory deprivation tolerance with introversion, and report positive results in this connection too. They also introduced measures of satiation (kinesthetic figural aftereffect) into their work, following the demonstration by Eysenck (1955) that these were related to introversion, and reported significant correlations with pain tolerance and sensory deprivation tolerance. However, in certain ways their measure of figural aftereffect is unusual and differs from that used by Eysenck; Dinnerstein *et al.* (1962) have suggested, on the basis of a replication of the Petrie studies, that "while the basic results of Petrie, Collins and Solomon are confirmed, their theory requires modification." Fur-

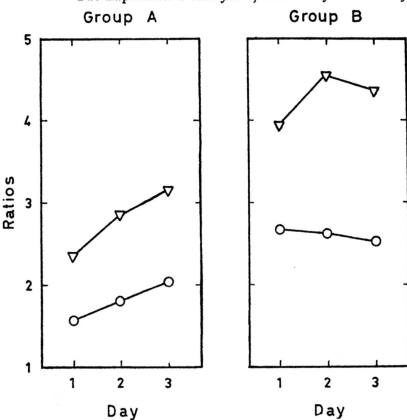

Figure 40. Pain tolerance level (triangles) and pain thresholds (circles) of dysthymics (Group A) and psychopaths (Group B). Reprinted with permission from D. Schalling and S. Levander: *Scand. J. Psychol.*, 5:1-19, 1964.

ther confirmatory data are reported by Blitz *et al.*, 1966. (A discussion of the Petrie technique is given later in this chapter.)

Further predictions of the differential effects of sensory deprivation on extraverts and introverts have been made by Reed and Kenna (1964) and by Reed and Sedman (1964). Along lines similar to those outlined above, the former predict that "both introvert and extravert will tend to judge the duration of a given interval of S.D. as being shorter than it is by clock time, but the extravert's error in estimation will be greater than the introvert's." The latter predict "that under conditions of S.D., feeling of depersonalization will be reported more readily by introverts than by extraverts." Both predictions have been verified at a high level of confidence.

Not all experimenters have been able to confirm the correlation between tolerance of sensory deprivation and introversion. Tranel (1961), for instance, studied twenty extraverts and twenty introverts and found that "as a group extraverts tolerated the isolation conditions significantly better than introverts in terms of time spent in the room." He also, however, discovered the reason for this unexpected result. Subjects had been instructed to lie quietly on their couch, to estimate the time every half hour, and not to go to sleep. "In general, the extraverts reacted by ignoring the instructions . . . while the introverts reacted by attempting to adhere rigidly to instructions." The mean number of movements observed per minute was .38 for the extraverts, 23 for the introverts; the difference would have been much greater if some extraverts had not reacted by going to sleep. "All of the extraverts who spoke during isolation, with one exception, mentioned difficulty in keeping awake. None of the introverts mentioned such a difficulty." Tranel describes the behaviour of the extraverts thus: "Extraverts largely ignored the instruction to lie quietly. They moved about quite freely and this movement was part of their coping behaviour. In other words, extraverts resorted to a form of self-stimulation in the form of tapping, moving, or exploration of the surroundings. They seemed to be much more concerned with devising ways to endure the situation than with following the instructions."

This experiment is of interest for two reasons. In the first place it shows that experimental conditions have to be rigidly standardised and enforced in such a way that deviation from instructions is impossible; the rule-bound behaviour of the introverts and the psychopathic behaviour of the extraverts is in line with our general theory, and has to be taken into account in planning an investigation. In the second place, when rigorous conditions prove impossible to enforce, then it is required of the investigator that he supervise the experiment closely and report all deviations from instructions. Tranel did so, and thus was able to explain the observed deviation of his results from hypothesis; other writers have failed to do so, and leave readers with the unenviable task of evaluating work not reported in sufficient detail, or with an eye to important variables such as obedience to instructions. In this way there may arise many apparently inexplicable differences in experimental outcome between seemingly similar studies.

Before closing this section, it may be interesting to mention two studies using tests of "field dependence and field independence" as measures of extraversion and introversion. Witkin *et al.* (1962) have tried to build up a personality dimension on the basis of perceptual tests which measure degree of perceptual determination by external percepts, and this dimension appears closely related to extraversion-introversion. (Witkin and his colleagues might not agree with this suggestion.) In line with this hypothetical identification, we may note that field-dependent (extraverted) perceivers experienced greater discomfort than field-independent (introverted) perceivers when placed in an environment with low sensory input (Cohen and Silverman, 1963), while they rated pain stimuli as less painful (Sweeney and Fine, 1965). These results are in good agreement with our theory.[7a]

Formation of Conditioned Responses

Eysenck (1957) propsed that the speed with which conditioned responses were formed would provide a good test of the general personality theory under consideration; he specifically argued that introverts would condition better than extraverts. This prediction follows directly from Pavlov's concepts and findings. He has demonstrated that cortical excitation facilitates conditioning, provided that the optimal degree of excitation has not yet been reached. As this provision is doubtful of fulfilment in normal, rested subjects, more stress has been laid on the inhibitory postulate. This would lead us to expect differences between extraverts and introverts to emerge maximally when the conditions of the experiment were arranged in such a manner as to maximize the occurrence of inhibition. The main conditions used in past work have been (a) partial as compared with complete reinforcement, (b) weak as opposed to strong CS and UCS, and (c) discrimination learning as

[7a]Some empirical evidence linking field dependence and extraversion is available in the work of Evans (1167) who administered the embedded figures test to 59 Ss and obtained a correlation with E of 0.39. Franks (1956) failed to obtain a significant correlation with the perception of the upright test.

opposed to single stimulus conditioning. The general point was made by Eysenck (1957) in this form: "Inhibitory potential is expected to be generated during the unreinforced trials interspersed with reinforced trials." This consideration applies to points (a) and (c) above; point (b) relies on the same argument as already mentioned in relation to vigilance experiments, that is, that strong stimuli lead to excitation and disrupt the development of inhibition. These various considerations follow directly from Pavlov's theory, but they also have good experimental backing. Thus Ross and Spence (1960) compared 50 per cent partial with continuous reinforcement under different strengths of the UCS, and concluded that "inhibition of performance is more readily accomplished under conditions of low puff strengths. . . . The large differences between the 100 per cent and 50 per cent reinforcement groups at high levels of puff strength require that considerable 'inhibition' still be present with such puffs." Further evidence for the importance of CS intensity, and even of level of ambient illumination, for the intrasession growth of inhibition comes from the work of Rinquist and Towart (1966).

Franks (1956, 1957) tested the truth or falsity of the hypothesis at the writer's suggestion, using eyeblink conditioning with partial reinforcement on both normal and neurotic subjects. It is feasible to combine the two groups, as no differences due to "neurosis" became apparent in these studies, and the results are shown in Figure 41. The mean values plotted are antilogs, for reasons given elsewhere (Eysenck, 1965); briefly, increments in habit strength nearer the physiological limit must give rise to smaller measured changes in performance, and if a comparison is made between two groups at different points of the habit strength growth curve, direct comparisons of scores are misleading. The data for normal and neurotic groups show very similar and independently significant differences between extraverts and introverts, and Figure 41 makes it clear that the introverts do in fact form conditioned responses more quickly than do extraverts.

Franks' work has at times been criticised, but it does not seem that all the criticisms are well taken. Sloane *et al.* (1965) mention such factors as (a) individual differences in blink rate, which might also relate to personality factors; (b) technical unrealiabil-

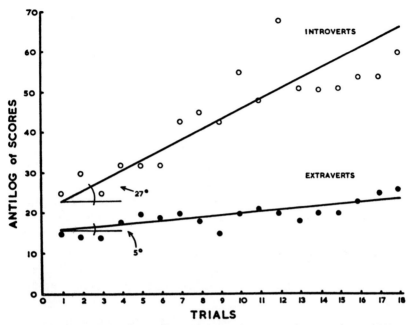

Figure 41. Rate of eyelid conditioning in introverts and extraverts. Drawn from data supplied by C. Franks.

ity of the recordings; (c) the possibility that the eyeblink, being part of a startle response, is often elicited by the tone alone before the experiment begins. These objections do not seem valid. As regards (a), Franks (1963) has shown that there is no significant correlation between blink rate and extraversion, and our own long-continued studies have failed to demonstrate any significant correlations between blink rate and conditioning. As regards (b), the method of measuring reflected light through a light-sensitive cell has been found to be highly reliable, and in any case it is difficult to see how unreliability in the measuring instrument could produce differential effects for extraverts and introverts. As regards (c), Franks was, of course, careful to exclude all subjects "who showed any evidence of pseudo-conditioning or original sensitivity to the tone." Another criticism has been made by Jenkins and Lykken (1957), namely that there is already evidence of differential conditioning on the first trial; they interpret this to mean that differences between the groups cannot be due to the conditioning process. They appear to forget that the method used is one of partial reinforcement, so that the first *test* trial (recorded in Figure 41) is preceded by several *conditioning* (acquisition) trials (not recorded in Figure 41); the difference in performance in the test trial records the differential effects of the acquisition trials. Yet further criticisms have been made by Storms and Sigal (1958), and answered by Eysenck (1959e). In sum, while Frank's studies are no doubt far from perfect, yet it is difficult to see how any of the criticisms advanced can be used to throw doubt on his major conclusion, namely the differentiation between introverts and extraverts in terms of eyeblink conditioning.

Much work has been done in recent years in attempts to test the major prediction using both eyeblink conditioning and GSR conditioning. This work has been reviewed in some detail by the writer (Eysenck, 1965), and no repetition of this review seems necessary. By and large it would seem that when the conditions laid down for the accumulation of inhibitory potential are fulfilled, significant differences between introverts and extraverts appear; when they are not, such differences are absent. There are exceptions; positive results may not appear when populations to whom the questionnaire does not properly apply are tested (coloured groups, youngsters, prisoners), and occasionally positive results are reported even when reinforcement is 100 per cent. This suggests that differences in excitation may not be negligible, even though they may be less important than differences in inhibition. It is interesting in this connection to mention that the most negative studies, showing zero correlation between extraversion and eyeblink conditioning under 100 per cent reinforcement, have been done in Iowa, where, as Spence (1964) has pointed out, conditions are specially arranged to be as arousing as possible, thus presumably wiping out any possible differences in excitation favouring the introverted group.[7b]

[7b] A study investigating specifically the relation between eyeblink conditioning and excitation (arousal) is reported by Spain (1966), who used level of skin potential (Venables, 1963) as her measure of arousal. In both normals and schizophrenics, significant correlations were found between arousal so measured and number of conditioned responses. The size of the correlations is quite respectable, ranging from .63 for normal subjects and .66 for schizophrenic women to .44 for schizophrenic males. Runquist and Ross (1959) and Runquist and Spence (1959) have also provided some evidence for a relation between arousal and conditioning, although they conceptualize arousal in terms of anxiety = neuroticism, rather

An experiment specially designed to test the writer's theories about the importance of controlling various parameters was carried out by A. Levey (1966). The three parameters varied in this experiment were: (a) partial versus continuous reinforcement; (b) weak (3 p.s.i.) versus strong (6 p.s.i.) UCS; and (c) short (400 m/sec) versus long (800 m/sec) CS–UCS interval. According to theory, the first-named condition is in each case favourable to introverts as compared with extraverts, and should demonstrate quicker and stronger conditioning of the eyeblink for them; the last-named condition, in each case, would be unfavourable for introverts (Eysenck, 1957, 1962, 1966a). Figure 42 shows the overall results for 144 male subjects; introverts are somewhat better than extraverts, with ambiverts usually intermediate, but the differences are slight and not significant. This result is of course expected when differences over all conditions are summed. Figures 43 and 44 show the differentiation between introverts and extraverts (a) under conditions favouring introverts, according to theory, and (b) under conditions unfavourable to introverts, ac-

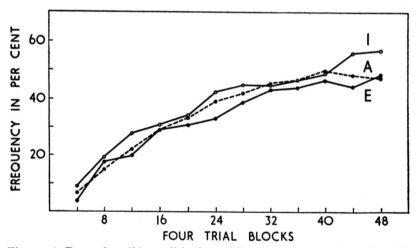

Figure 42. Rate of eyelid conditioning of introverts, extraverts, and ambiverts when conditions of testing are averaged over three parameters. From H. J. Eysenck, 1966.

than in terms of introversion. It is interesting that Spain also took measures of withdrawal on her male patients and found that the more withdrawn (introverted?) showed higher levels of arousal (r = −.47).

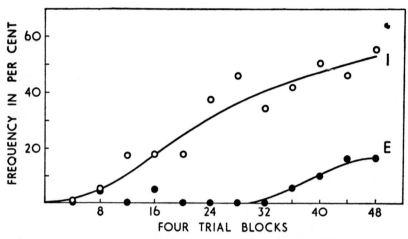

Figure 43. Acquisition of eyeblink conditioned responses of introverts and extraverts under conditions theoretically considered favorable to introverts. From H. J. Eysenck, 1966.

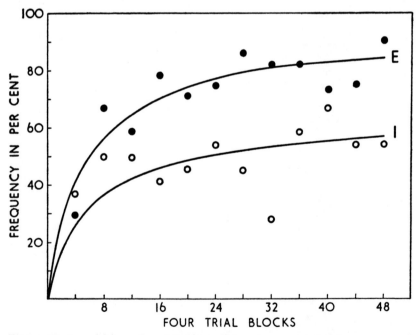

Figure 44. Acquisition of eyeblink conditioned responses of introverts and extraverts under conditions considered theoretically favorable to extraverts. From H. J. Eysenck, 1966.

cording to theory. It will be seen that under (a), introverts condition better than extraverts, while under (b), extraverts condition better than introverts. This difference is well brought out by the correlations between introversion and conditioning under the two sets of parameters: (a) r = 0.40; (b) r = 0.31. This difference is fully significant, and brings out the importance of selecting appropriate parameters for testing the writer's hypothesis; random choice of UCS strength, CS–UCS interval, and schedule of reinforcement can only result in the random kind of result so often found in this field. When an appropriate choice is made, based upon theoretical considerations, meaningful and significant results are found. (A more detailed discussion of the results of this experiment is given by Eysenck, 1966a.)[8]

Eysenck (1959d) suggested the possibility of using verbal conditioning as a test of his theory and found some evidence for the superiority of introverts over extraverts in this field also. Beech and Adler (1963) too found some support for the theory; they reported a tendency for neuroticism to correlate negatively with verbal conditioning, contrary to Spence's hypothesis. McDowell and Inglis (1962) failed to find any significant correlation, while the data reported by Binder and Salop (1961) might be interpreted to support the hypothesis. (They used the M.M.P.I., thus making their findings difficult to compare with those of the other authors cited.)

In the most extensive and best controlled study to date, Jawanda (1966) used subjects at three age levels (21-25, 36-40, and 56-60 years). Within each age level, four groups of subjects were selected such that they were respectively high and low on E and N (N+E+, N+E−, N−E+, and N−E−). Ten replications of this 3 x 4 design were programmed, giving a total of 120 subjects, who were selected on the basis of a Panjabi version of the M.P.I. The technique used was that of "sentence completion"; i.e., a card was exhibited in the centre of which was printed a neutrally toned past tense verb, with the five personal pronouns printed under-

[8]Martin and Levey (1965, 1966) have suggested that the use of simple CR counts does not make use of important sources of information about the efficiency of the CR; it seems likely that the use of the measures pioneered by them will reveal new relations with the personality also.

neath. The task of the subject was that of making up a sentence containing the verb and one of the personal pronouns. No reinforcements were given during trials 1-25; during trials 26-85, the experimenter responded with the word "Good" at the end of any sentence beginning with "I" or "We." Trials 86-110 again omitted any reinforcement. Scores were calculated in terms of an inflection ratio: $\dfrac{B - A}{A}$, where A and B represent a subject's initial and experimental period scores respectively. Positive and negative values of the ratio indicate an increase and decrease respectively of the level of responding with the chosen personal pronouns. An enquiry concerning the subject's awareness of the response-reinforcement contingencies was conducted at the end of the experiment; there was no evidence of awareness in any of the subjects.

Analysis of variance disclosed that personality differences affected the conditioning ratio in a highly significant manner (p< .01); neither age nor interaction effects were significant. Figure 45 shows the values of the ratio for the four groups. Individual

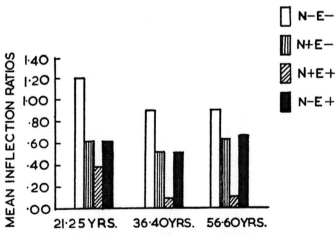

Figure 45. Effects of personality on verbal conditioning at various age levels. Reprinted with permission from J. S. Jawanda, 1966.

statistical comparisons were made between groups; the results are summed up by Jawanda as follows: "Subjects scoring low on extraversion develop verbal conditioning better than their counterparts, scoring high on extraversion. . . . Subjects scoring low on neuroticism develop verbal conditioning better than their counterparts scoring high on neuroticism."

The results thus agree with Eysenck's prediction regarding the greater conditionability of introverts but contradict the Spence-Taylor hypothesis of neuroticism-anxiety facilitating conditioning. The results are particularly impressive because of the similarity of outcome between the three age replications; in each case the N+E+(psychopathic) group shows much the least degree of conditioning, the N−E− (stable introvert) group the greatest, with the other two groups intermediate. The lack of conditionability of psychopaths in tests of this kind has been well demonstrated by Johns and Quay (1962) and Quay and Hunt (1965), working with diagnosed psychopathic subjects. It is also of interest that Jawanda used the same method of verbal conditioning in another experiment to establish the effects of drugs on this type of response; his results will be discussed in a later chapter. Here our concern is merely to draw attention to the fact that in the 100 subjects of this second experiment, personality again emerged as a significant variable at the 1 per cent level, and that again the N−E− group had the highest scores, with the N+E+ group having the lowest scores. Means of these groups were significantly different from each other, and from the other two groups, at the .1 per cent level. This experiment may therefore serve as another, independent replication of the main experiment, giving essentially identical results.

In addition to eyeblink, GSR, and verbal conditioning, other methods have also been used, but the results will not here be reviewed as it is doubtful if they are of any great significance. Willett (1960), who has carried out tests of several methods, including salivary conditioning, has shown the difficulties attending the use of these tests, including the crucial one of knowing whether the observed effects are in fact due to orthodox conditioning. Others have been less cautious in interpreting their results. Thus Davidson *et al.* (1964) used GSR responses contingent upon electric shock leading to finger withdrawal as a measure of "conditioning," in spite of the fact clearly shown in their Figure 1 that there is no change in GSR over test trials, a demonstration that no conditioning had in fact taken place. The results from the finger withdrawal part of the experiment are, of course, irrelevant to our theory in any case, as the strength of the shock used makes the possibility of inhibition developing very small. Too many of the reported experiments purporting to test the excitation-inhibition theory have used experimental parameters which were inconsistent with any proper evaluation of the theory; little would be gained by a detailed criticism of such studies.[9]

Learning

Jensen (1962) attacked the problem of the relation between personality and learning in a study of serial rote learning which has already been mentioned. His hypothesis was based on the assumption that extraverts would build up reactive inhibition more quickly than introverts, so that they would be at a greater disadvantage under a 2-second rate of presentation as compared with a 4-second rate of presentation. He failed to find any significant differences between extraverts and introverts when the effects of neuroticism were eliminated by covariance analysis, "although the extraverts performed somewhat better under the stress of the 2-second rate than did the introverts." His main finding was that "the overall correlation within the High and Low N groups between extraversion and errors in learning was −.31." As is clear from Figure 1, neuroticism interferes with learning at the fast rate, but is if anything of an advantage at the slow rate.

Howarth (1963) has reported superior performance of extraverts on a digit repetition task in which the length of time during which information could be held was the score investigated. Extraverts were found superior in this, giving a mean score of 14.0 seconds, as compared with introverts whose mean score was 11.8 seconds (ambiverts had a score of 13.4 seconds). Howarth states

[9]Purohit (1966) has reported a failure to find a correlation between GSR conditioning and introversion; his UCS was a "500 cps sound 120 decibels above the hearing threshold of the S's better ear." It is difficult to see how inhibition could develop when the subject is periodically blasted out of his chair by this extremely painful onslaught on his eardrums!

that "the direction of these findings was opposite to that antici-pated"; his hypothesis had been based on a statement by Broad-bent (1958) to the effect that extraverts might have a shorter memory span than introverts.

Shanmugan and Santhanam (1964) tested personality differences in serial learning under conditions of no interference and also when competing stimuli were presented at the marginal visual level. They predicted that these interfering stimuli "would affect extraverts less adversely than the introverts." Ten learning trials were al-lowed for the twenty-word list, and the criterion test given after a period of 30 seconds; the number of words correctly anticipated on this trial constituted the subject's score. Under conditions of no interference, a correlation between extraversion and score of .65 was observed; when interference was produced by another ser-ies of words, the correlation was .82, and when interference was produced by letters and numbers, it was .58. These results suggest that (a) extraverts learn and/or remember better than introverts, and (b) interference effects of the kind employed have no, or at best variable, effects. Neuroticism too was found to be posi-tively correlated with scores under these conditions, which can hardly be regarded as stressful. It should be noted that Shanmugan and Santhanam did not make any predictions regarding the relative efficiency of extraverts and introverts on this task; their concern was with the effects of the interfering task.

Jensen (1964) published a large-scale experimental study in-volving many different types of learning and learning tasks, as well as measures of personality; these were then submitted to fac-tor analysis with subsequent oblique rotation. Two third-order factors were obtained, of which the second is of particular interest here; its nature is to be inferred from the loadings which are given below in Table III.

These figures show convincingly that extraversion correlates with *quick* performance on the Matrices intelligence test and with good performance on various learning/memory tasks; the size of the loadings is surprising, as a much less close relation between temperament and learning would perhaps have been expected. Even so, several types of learning task and several scores from those which figure in our Table do not correlate with extraversion,

TABLE III

Variable	Loading
M.P.I. Extraversion	.78
E.P.I., Form A, Extraversion	.68
Serial Retroactive Interference, Oscillation	—.66
Serial Trigram Learning, Errors	—.65
E.P.I., Form B, Extraversion	.61
Time for Progressive Matrices	—.56
Serial Retroactive Interference, Errors (Relearning)	—.54
Serial Retroactive Interference, Errors (Interpolated Learning)	—.46
Delayed Digit Span	.41
Immediate Digit Span	.40
Age	—.40

Factor loadings of personality and learning tests on higher-order factor. Quoted with permission from A. Jensen, 1964.

and form an independent factor of "general learning ability." (Actually, the two factors are not quite independent, but are correlated to the extent of .34; a fourth-order factor was extracted by Jensen which included the majority of learning tasks and scores, as well as extraversion. Neuroticism did not have loadings here or elsewhere in Jensen's data.)

Two more studies require mention. Skanthakumari (1965) used the Brengelmann (1958) type of task to study the learning/memory capacity of his subjects over periods of no waiting, 24 hours, 7 days and 21 days. In this test five geometrical figures are exposed inside a large circle, and the subject has to remember their positions and indicate them after the original stimulus has been withdrawn; errors are scored in terms of degrees of rotation from true. It was found that for the shorter periods extraverts did better, while for the two longer periods there were no differences between extraverts and introverts; these results are of doubtful statistical significance. High N scorers are better throughout than low N scorers. It should be noted that in this study the same group of subjects was tested on all four occasions; it would, of course, have been better if four different groups had been used. The results, showing a relative improvement of performance for introverts over time, might have been more pronounced if the interpolated testing had not interfered with the processes of consolidation postulated below to account for the results of these studies.

In the other study, Gebhardt (1966) applied nine intelligence tests to 400 high school children chosen from a much larger number because of their extreme N and E scores; 100 were chosen from each of the four quadrants. On overall performance, extraverts and introverts were well matched, but on an associative rote learning test of memory, the extraverts were significantly superior. Scores for the four groups were as follows:

	N+	N−	Mean
E+	107	110	109
E−	104	106	105

This difference, which is fully significant, is equal to over one-third of one standard deviation, and is, of course, in the same direction as the differences noted above; apparently group tests too are capable of verifying the general theory linking rote learning and personality.[10]

To the writer it does not seem that the theoretical expectations of Howarth, Broadbent, and others are based on a thoroughgoing exploration of the implications of the excitation-inhibition hypothesis. (Admittedly these writers do not claim to have undertaken such an exploration; they mention theoretical expectations only in passing.) Mention has already been made of the Kleinsmith and Kaplan study of paired-associate learning as a function of arousal (see Figure 19); a similar study, using nonsense syllables instead of words, has recently been reported by the same authors with similar results (Kleinsmith and Kaplan, 1964). In all these studies it became apparent that stimulus words or syllables associated with high excitation/arousal produced short-term interference with the memory process but led to long-term memory of high efficiency; conversely, stimulus words or syllables associated with low excitation/arousal produced no short-term interference with the memory process but led to poor long-term memory. Figure 46 illustrates this course of events; it is taken from the nonsense syllable experiment and shows the decline over time of the memory for low arousal syllables, and the increase over time (reminiscence) for high arousal syllables. (These effects, it will be remembered, are attributed by the authors to the consolidation pro-

[10]Meredith (1966, p. 95) has recently mentioned some data from Cattell's group showing better performance on a learning-memory task for "exuberant" as compared with "restrained" subjects.

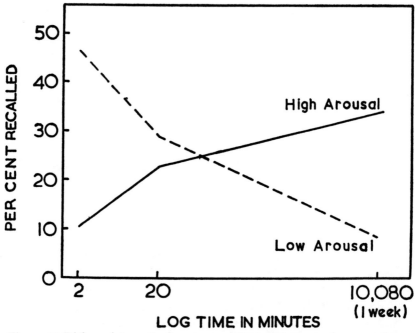

Figure 46. Differential recall of nonsense syllable paired associates as a function of arousal level. Reprinted with permission from L. J. Kleinsmith and S. Kaplan: *J. Exp. Psychol.*, 67:124-126, 1964.

cess which interferes with reproduction, aids the long-term memory effect, and increases monotonically with arousal; Eysenck (1965c, 1966c) has discussed this theory in some detail.

Stimulus-produced arousal may be hypothesized to have similar effects to personality-associated states of excitation/arousal; in other words, introverts would be predicted to react in a fashion analogous to ambiverts confronted with high-arousal words and syllables, whereas extraverts would be predicted to react in a fashion analogous to ambiverts confronted with low-arousal words and syllables. Any predictions for experimental work would consequently be very closely tied to the parameters of the work in question, but in general, and subject to modification as a result of unusual choice of intertrial periods, we would expect extraverts to show better serial learning, paired-associate learning, and digit-span memory than introverts, provided the time interval between learning and testing was relatively short. Conversely, we would expect introverts to show better serial learning, paired-associate learning, and digit-span memory than extraverts, provided the time interval between learning and testing was relatively long. The terms "long" and "short" are to be understood in no absolute sense, of course, but simply in relation to the details of the experiment in question; in the Kleinsmith and Kaplan study, for instance, 2 minutes is short, 20 minutes indeterminate, and 1 hour long. For other types of experiments these times might be quite inappropriate.

These predictions are not made with any great confidence, in view of the fact that they present a considerable extrapolation of existing knowledge. Interest in consolidation has been minimal during the past thirty years, and consequently very little is in fact known about its precise *modus operandi* in these various fields of learning. Also, complications undoubtedly arise because of the possible interference of consolidation for trace A with learning of stimulus B; little is known of the possible interaction of such interference factors with personality. Clearly there is here an extremely interesting and inviting area of research, where theory at the moment can do little more than make some very general predictions along the lines of the statement in the last paragraph. In the absence of more certain knowledge of experimental parameters, more precise predictions are unlikely to find ready verification. Nevertheless, the studies already carried out and quoted above, do in general support the short-term superiority of the extravert predicted by the theory; no studies comparing long-term memory scores of introverts and extraverts have been encountered.[11]

The theory does not deal with the complex role which neuroticism is likely to play, possibly in interaction with extraversion. At first sight, it might appear that arousal could be linked theoretically with N just as easily as with introversion, but we must leave a discussion of this problem until a later chapter. Empirically Jensen (1964) found no relationship between learning and N. Shanmugan and

[11]Crawford and Snyder (1966) have shown that "psychopaths scored significantly higher than psychoneurotics on the Recall test" of the LAIS (Leiter Adult Intelligence Scale); this may also be considered support for our prediction. Similarly, Sherman (1957) has demonstrated that the memories of psychopaths are more retentive than those of either neurotic or normal subjects. Crucial for our hypothesis would of course be an experiment involving long-term recall; no such experiment has to our knowledge been carried out on psycopaths and neurotics.

Santhanam found a positive one, and Jensen (1962) found a negative one under stress conditions and a mildly positive one under no stress conditions. Eysenck (1962) has not reported any marked positive or negative correlations between pursuit rotor learning or reminiscence and N. It may be possible to regard N as a motivational variable, exerting a positive or negative effect on learning/memory in accordance with the Yerkes-Dodson law, but not affecting the consolidation process in the manner characteristic of the cortical excitation associated with introversion. Beyond this rather vague statement we cannot go at this stage, but we will return to this point later.

A very recent study by McLaughlin and Eysenck (1967) shows how complex are the interactions of learning, personality, task difficulty and motivation. Four extreme groups of subjects were tested on either an easy list of paired associates (low stimulus-low response similarity) or a difficult list (low stimulus-high response similarity.) A significant second-order interaction indicated that neurotic extraverts were superior to stable extraverts on the easy list while the reverse was true of the difficult list; neurotic introverts learned faster on the difficult list and more slowly on the easy list than did stable introverts. Intelligence was not correlated with success. The data fit in well with theoretical anticipation, and show otherwise unaccountable paradoxes. Thus stable extraverts actually show fewer errors when learning the difficult task than when learning the easy task, while stable introverts make over three times as many errors! There can be little doubt that personality is closely involved with the lear͏͏͏͏ rocess (much more closely than intelligence in this insta͏͏͏ d that learning experiments should never be carried out v͏͏͏ e inclusion of personality measures.

All the learning stu͏͏͏ ar reviewed are *verbal* in nature; our theory may perhaps͏͏ e used in relation to the learning of skills. The story here is a͏͏ le more complex and may require a rather indirect approach. ͏͏ lance and other performance decrement tests give rise to re͏͏ iscence when a rest pause is programmed at some point aft͏͏ eterioration has set in; this improvement in performance afte͏͏ st is often explained as due to dissipation of inhibition (Kimbl͏͏, 1949). Size of reminiscence effect would on this hypothesis be an acceptable index of degree of in-

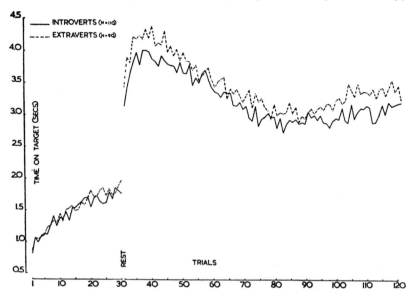

Figure 47. Reminiscence of introverts and extraverts on pursuit rotor after 10-min. rest pause. Reprinted with permission from F. Farley, 1966.

hibition obtaining prior to the rest period, provided the rest pause was long enough to allow all of the inhibition accumulated to dissipate, and on this hypothesis Eysenck (1956) predicted that extraverts would show greater reminiscence effects. The usual instrument of study has been the pursuit rotor, and practice periods of 5 minutes, followed by rest periods of 10 minutes, have usually been employed; postrest practice has varied from a few 10-second trials to 15 minutes or more. A summary of some twenty studies has been published by Eysenck (1962); the results are positive in nearly every case, although not always at a high level of statistical significance. There can be little doubt, therefore, that the prediction is in fact verified; unfortunately a detailed examination of the data shows that the original hypothesis is nevertheless quite untenable.

Figure 47 shows a typical experimental study; as expected, extraverts show significantly higher reminiscence scores, but they differ from introverts, not, as the theory would demand, in having lower prerest scores, but in having higher postrest scores. Eysenck (1965) has discussed in detail the reasons for abandoning an inhibition theory of reminiscence for learning tasks and has proposed instead a consolidation theory; in other words, performance sets up cortical events which, in order to become available to the organism as *learned behaviour*, require a rest period during which they *consolidate* (Eysenck, 1966). This theory does not, of course, apply to well-practised tasks, such as those involved in typical vigilance tests; here reactive inhibition is still theoretically made responsible for deterioration of performance and dissipation of inhibition for recovery (reminiscence). It is quite possible for some tasks to contain elements of both kinds, so that reminiscence could be in variable portion due to consolidation and to dissipation on inhibition; furthermore, these portions could differ from person to person, depending on degree of practice, of ability, of arousal, etc.

Given that the consolidation theory is along the right lines, how can we explain the superiority of extraverts after the rest pause? One possible explanation has been given by Eysenck (1964c) in terms of stronger conditioned inhibition on the part of the introverts, which would interfere with their postrest performance; another explanation might follow the line of argument presented above in relation to verbal learning experiments. It will be recalled that in memory experiments, postrest performance was better for those stimuli producing less arousal, but that delayed postrest performance was better for those words producing high arousal. This was accounted for along the lines of arousal producing lengthy consolidation, and consolidation (a) interfering with postrest performance and (b) leading to better learning and hence to better long-term memory. If we regard extraverts as less aroused than introverts, then, as already pointed out, the postrest performance of the former should resemble that of the less arousing words, of the latter that of the more arousing words. In other words, up to 15 minutes or so after the beginning of the rest pause, extraverts should be superior in performance, but after several hours introverts should be superior, and show higher reminiscence scores. On this hypothesis, then, the almost unanimous support of Eysenck's original hypothesis would have been due to the (arbitrary) choice of a 10-minute rest pause in the experiment reported; and 1 hour or 1 day been chosen instead, introverts would have been found to have higher reminiscence scores. The truth or falsity of this new hypothesis could easily be tested by varying the length of the rest pause; similarly, it should not be impossible to test the alternative theory mentioned above, in terms of conditioned inhibition. Until such tests are carried out, these hypotheses must count merely as *post hoc* attempts to explain some rather puzzling facts. The fact that an obviously erroneous theory can generate factually accurate predictions may serve as a timely warning to the reader that in spite of the strong general support given to the theory linking extraversion with reactive inhibition, the theory may still be wrong in whole or in part and may require change or complete repudiation in the light of further work.

Perceptual Phenomena

In this section a brief discussion will be given of some perceptual phenomena for which predictions can be derived from the general theory of excitation-inhibition. Publications are too numerous to make a detailed consideration possible, but an attempt will be made to give a representative sample of phenomena and to include particularly those which have figured most prominently in the literature.

Figural Aftereffects

In one of the earliest studies to emerge from the theoretical identification of extraversion with inhibition/satiation, Eysenck (1955a) suggested that if figural aftereffects were indeed, as Köhler had suggested, due to satiation, and if satiation built up more strongly and quickly in extraverts, then extraverts should show greater figural aftereffects. Using the kinesthetic modality, he was able to demonstrate differences between hysterics and dysthymics in the predicted direction, and several studies supporting the hypothesis are discussed in Eysenck (1957). Since then several writers (Rechtschaffen, 1958; Rechtschaffen and Bookbinder, 1960; McEwen and Rodger, 1960; Norcross *et al.*, 1961; Howarth and Paul, 1964; and Howarth, 1963) have reported negative results; others (Meier, 1961) results which are difficult to interpret. Broadbent (1961) added a curious complication when he found that results depended very much on the direction of the judgment in relation to the body (movement away from as opposed to movement towards).

Eysenck (1962) has pointed out another complication which

makes valid tests of the hypothesis very difficult. The hypothesis makes predictions which would follow if subjects were exposed to identical sensory stimulation; if these conditions were fulfilled, then greater satiation should be found in extraverts. However, the act of producing the original sensory stimulation (fixation of the stimulus constellation in visual aftereffects experiments; prolonged stroking of wooden block in kinesthetic experiment) must give rise to reactive inhibition and IRPs, which in turn are hypothesized to be more frequent and more pronounced in extraverts. We would thus expect extraverts to obtain in fact less sensory stimulation, and to exhibit less satiation and lower aftereffects. When faced with two such effects which threaten to cancel each other out, we may have recourse to the common finding that satiation effects build up more quickly than reactive inhibition; it would follow that extraverts should show greater figural aftereffects after a short duration of stimulation, while introverts should show greater figural aftereffects after a long duration of stimulation. At some intermediary point there should be a crossing-over point where both groups showed equal aftereffects.

A study to investigate this prediction was carried out by Blakemore (1966), who also varied the direction of judgment in relation to the body as a check on Broadbent's findings. His analysis showed a significant triple interaction, involving period of interpolated inspection, direction of judgment in relation to body, and personality type. Figure 48 demonstrates that the results, when plotted against length of inspection period, show the predicted crossing-over, with extraverts having higher aftereffects with short inspection periods and introverts having higher aftereffects with long inspection periods. However, it is doubtful if these results can be adduced with too much confidence in support of the theory. Only some of the individual comparisons are significant, and such significance as there is is clearly dependent on the direction (towards or away from the body) of the judgment; for this variable there is no very obvious theoretical explanation.

In summary, the position is clearly unsatisfactory. There is too much evidence in favour of the theory to dismiss it outright; on the other hand, there is too much negative evidence to feel that it can be accepted in its present form. Even when it is recognised

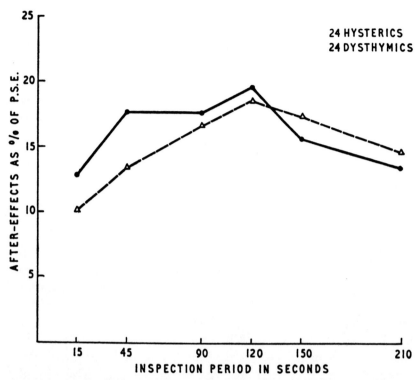

Figure 48. Kinesthetic aftereffects of hysterics and dysthymics for different inspection periods. Reprinted with permission from C. Blakemore, 1967.

that several of the studies reporting negative results have varied conditions in what may be crucial ways from the writer's original experiment, or have used too small samples to give trustworthy results, or have thrown together groups differing in age, sex, or psychiatric classification to an extent which might have affected the results, it is difficult to avoid the conclusion that until the phenomenon of figural aftereffect itself is better understood, it will be difficult or even impossible to design a proper study to test the hypothesis under investigation. In any case, it is already clear that any such study must include variations in several parameters, such as length of inspection period, direction of judgment, pressure on inspection block, etc.; it would also have to take into account recent work on psychophysical judgment formation, which may have crucial consequences for comparisons of this type.[12]

A. Petrie (1966) has taken the problem one step further by her discovery that some people show a general tendency to *increase* the subjective size of the stimulus (augmenters), while others *decrease* it (reducers). Using kinesthetic figural aftereffects, she has followed the usual course of first establishing a preexperimental point of subjective equality; thereafter the subject is again tested after rubbing a stimulus block larger than the test block, and again after rubbing a stimulus block smaller than the test block. Twenty-four hours are required to elapse between the two tests, and in each case several points of subjective equality are established (Figure 49 shows the results from thirty-seven subjects). She points out that "at the end of the period of rubbing, the wooden measuring block is perceived by the extreme augmenter as about doubled in size, by the extreme reducer as about havled—a fourfold difference between the two." (Petrie, Holland, and Wolk, 1965). She goes on: "When palpitation of the block after *any* of the six periods of stimulation led to a reduction in subjective size of 6 mm or more, we classified the subject as a reducer. If he judged it as being 6 mm or more larger, we classified him as an augmenter. The other subjects were called the moderates. These division points were chosen because they separated the nonpathological adult population originally studied into three approximately equal thirds." Scores on this test are highly reliable (Petrie, 1966) and are related

[12]Ganz (1966) has recently advocated a new theory of figural aftereffects which, if true, would lead to a complete rethinking of the interaction of extraversion-introversion and the phenomena in question. Another recent paper (Landauer, Singer and Day, 1966) has suggested that at least one of the usual criticisms of the writer's theory may be misplaced. It has been argued that such a theory demands that FAEs in different modalities should correlate together, but most investigators have in fact been unable to discover such correlations. Landauer *et al.* point out that in these studies adjustment times were not equated, and that without such equation no meaningful results could be expected; when they did equate adjustment times on a visual and a kinesthetic task, significant correlations (although rather low) were in fact obtained. Adjustment times present only one of many different parameters which require to be controlled for proper correlations to appear; intensity of stimulus, $\frac{O}{S \quad R}$, inspection period and I.R.P.s are others which spring to mind immediately. No investigator has in fact tried the experiment of maximizing correlations between different FAEs; only extensive work along the lines of varying presentation and judgment parameters can finally answer the question posed by this theory.

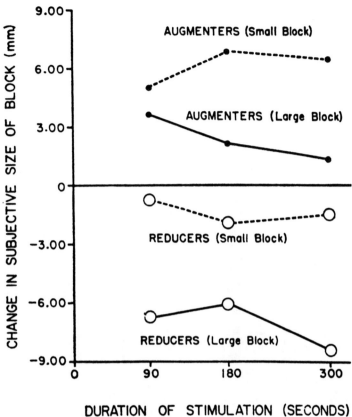

DURATION OF STIMULATION (SECONDS)

Sample of 37. Moderates Excluded

Figure 49. Kinesthetic figural aftereffects according to the method of A. Petrie, contrasting "reducers" and "augmenters." Reprinted with permission from A. Petrie, T. Holland, and I. Walk, 1965.

to extraversion-introversion in a consistent fashion, with reducers more frequently extraverted in personality, and augmenters introverted.

In line with our theory, Petrie and her colleagues had found that augmenters are more tolerant of sensory deprivation, while reducers are more tolerant of pain (Petrie, 1960; Petrie, Collins, and Solomon, 1960). Juvenile delinquents were found to be predominantly reducers rather than augmenters; in this group there was also found another perceptual type rare in the normal population,

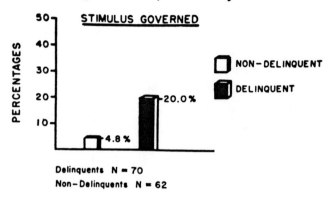

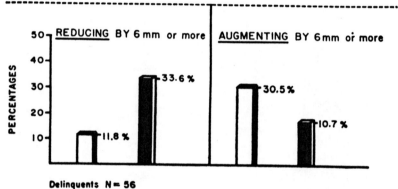

Figure 50. Contrast in percentages showing three different perceptual types in delinquent and nondelinquent groups. Reprinted with permission from A. Petrie, R. McCulloch, and P. Kazdin: *J. Nerv. Ment. Dis., 134*:415-421, 1962.

a type called by Petrie "stimulus governed" (Petrie, McCulloch, and Kazdin, 1962). In this type, there is reduction in the measured block when a larger object is used for stimulation, and augmentation when a smaller object is used for stimulation. Figure 50 shows Petrie's results.

Petrie (with Holland and Wolk, 1963) has also found that augmenters and reducers react quite differently to sensory bombardment, as in audioanalgesia; as shown in Figure 51, augmenters change their response pattern to one of reduction, while reducers remain unaffected. All these, as well as other studies summarized by Petrie (1966), are in good agreement with our theory, but the terms "augmenter" and "reducer" hide considerable conceptual and the-

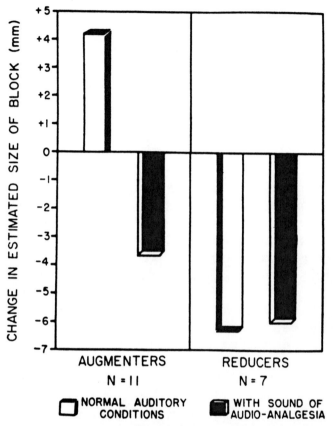

Figure 51. Change in size of figural aftereffect in augmenters and reducers under conditions of audio-analgesia. Reprinted with permission from A. Petrie, T. Holland, and I. Walk: *J. Nerv. Ment. Dis.*, 137:312-321, 1963.

oretical difficulties in the way of explaining the precise manner of action of the forces of inhibition and excitation. Until the experimental findings receive better theoretical underpinning than they have so far, the congruence of experimental findings with predictions from personality theory, while satisfactory from one point of view, must constitute a constant challenge from a more fundamental point of view.

Spiral Aftereffect

A somewhat different aftereffect to that discussed above is the well-known illusion attending the fixation of a rotating spiral;

when the spiral is stopped, it appears to rotate backwards, and the illusion of forward or backward movement attending the rotating figure is reversed. The duration of this phenomenon constitutes the score, which is dependent mainly on the duration of the inducing movement (Holland, 1965). The writer (1957) hypothesized that duration of aftereffect would be shorter in extraverts than in introverts; the reasoning underlying this prediction follows two lines: (a) extraverts receive less effective stimulation than introverts, due to failure to inspect the figure continuously; this failure is in turn due to reactive inhibition, and we have already discussed empirical evidence for this supposition (Franks, 1963). (b) The physiological processes underlying the aftereffect itself are subject to reactive inhibition and will therefore cease earlier in extraverts than in introverts. It will be seen that in this argument we have treated perceptual performance very much like any other type of performance, and it may be asked whether the usual phenomena attending inhibition (differential performance under conditions of massed and spaced practice, reminiscence, disinhibition) can be found in relation to perceptual performance. Holland (1963) has shown that the predicted phenomena actually occur; Figure 52 shows difference between spaced and massed trials, and Figure 53 shows reminiscence after massed practice. He was also successful in inducing disinhibition by means of an external stimulus.

Results relating to personality are on the whole encouraging. Lynn (1960), Eysenck and Eysenck (1960), Eysenck, Willett, and Slater (1962), Eysenck and Claridge (1962), and Holland (1960) have all reported positive findings, as has Mattoon (1962), using the after-contraction effect. Some writers have failed to find the predicted relationship, among them Holland (1962) and Pickersgill and Jeeves (1958). The numerous studies of the Manchester group (summarised by Holland, 1965) give a slightly confused picture, although mainly corroborative, as does a report by Knowles and Krasner (1965). Holland (1965) has discussed all these studies in detail, and his summary suggests that on the whole the hypothesis is supported, although in some more detailed studies discrepancies appear. Thus Holland (1962) predicted, but failed to show, that extraverts would show a greater decrement in persistence scores using intermittent illumination of the inducing disk;

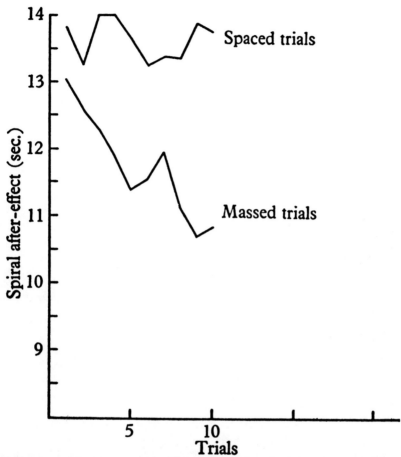

Figure 52. Differences in spiral aftereffects due to massed and spaced practice. Reprinted with permission from H. C. Holland: *Brit. J. Psychol.,* 54:261-272, 1963.

it is possible that by testing complex predictions of this kind, the true mode of action of the illusion and its interaction with personality will be revealed.

Levy and Lang (1966) have reported high negative relationships of aftereffect and a measure of impulsivity, which is, of course, one central trait in the extraversion complex; subjects low on impulsivity had scores almost twice those obtained by subjects high on impulsivity. They also found a rather less marked, and barely significant, correlation with the Taylor Manifest Anxiety

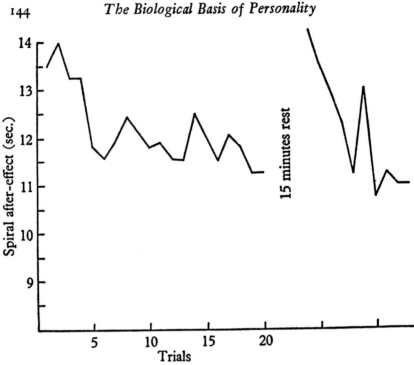

Figure 53. Reminiscence on spiral aftereffect after massed practice. Reprinted with permission from H. C. Holland: *Brit. J. Psychol.*, *54*:261-272, 1963.

Scale, which is possibly due to the contamination of that scale with introversion; no attempt was made to partial out variance due to this variable from the M.A.S. score. Levy and Lang interpret their findings in terms of activation rather than of inhibition, but this seems an arbitrary choice and is not supported by cardiovascular measures taken by them.

Of particular interest is a study by Claridge and Herrington (1963) in which they attempted to link up SAE and EEG recordings, in an endeavour to provide an objective measure of the usually subjectively reported aftereffect. They measured the SAE in the usual way, but then introduced EEG recordings by asking the subject to close his eyes when the rotating spiral stopped; latency of alpha activity return from this moment of time onwards was taken as the score. Several such indices were in fact calculated, all of which correlated with each other and also with the previously ascertained subjective SAE, thus demonstrating the possibility of objective measurement of this highly subjective phenomenon. Alpha latencies were greater for a dysthymic group (20.7 seconds) than for an hysteric group (13.9 seconds), but not significantly so; when obsessionals and psychopaths only were compared, much greater differences were found (26.0 seconds versus 9.5 seconds) with no overlap between groups. SAEs themselves, as subjectively determined, differed significantly for the dysthymics (17.2 seconds) and the hysterics (10.9 seconds), p < .001.

Occasional failures to reproduce the expected effect may be due to departures from the orthodox method of measurement. Thus Becker (1960) used 1 second of light flashes after 3 seconds of darkness to determine length of aftereffect; it is not clear to what extent such sudden on-off stimulation would affect the delicate excitation-inhibition balance and interfere with the correlation between aftereffect and personality. The low intertrial correlations reported suggest that in addition this is not a very reliable method of administering and scoring the test.

A recent study by Dureman (1965) uses a direct measure of excitation/arousal, namely the critical flicker-fusion threshold (CFF). In terms of our general hypothesis, we would expect a positive correlation between CFF and spiral aftereffect. Using fifty-nine subjects, Dureman reports a product-moment correlation of + 0.61, which is highly significant. In view of the many different ways in which CFF thresholds can be determined, and the importance of different parameters, this study might with advantage be repeated, using different variables in the experimental determination of both CFF and aftereffect duration.

Time Errors

It is well known that when two stimuli are compared with respect to size or intensity, the second tends to be overestimated relative to the first (negative time error), and that this tendency towards negative time error increases as the interval between the two stimuli in question increases. Claridge (1960) has suggested that the apparent "fading" of the first stimulus is due to satiation/inhibition effects; arguing along these lines, he suggested that "extraverts, producing more inhibition as a result of the first stimulus, would be expected to show a greater tendency than introverts to over-estimate the intensity of the second of two stimuli." Using pure-tone stimuli, all of a frequency of 1100 cps, on matched groups of dysthymics, normals, hysterics (and psychotics, whose scores are not relevant to our theory), he gave a standard tone of 75 decibels (always presented first) and one of five variable tones ranging from 73 to 77 decibels, with instruction to say which tone was the louder. Intervals between stimuli (S-V intervals) were 1, 2, 4, and 6 seconds. The results are shown in Figure 54; it will be seen that at all intervals hysterics make more negative time errors than normals, and normals more than dysthymics. An overall mean per cent time error measure showed highly significant differences between dysthymics (-0.56), normals (-3.44), and hysterics (-10.78).

Along similar lines, one can predict that if two time intervals are being compared for length, extraverts would underestimate the second one more than would introverts. Claridge (1960) found such a result, using time intervals of 10", 30", 60", and 90"; but the result fell just short of significance, and the normal group was not intermediate between the extreme personality groups. He did, however, report significant correlations with the E scale within the normal group for all except the 90" interval. Eysenck (1959), also using dysthymics and hysterics, repeated the experiment and obtained significant results with short time intervals (5" and 10"), but not with longer times (20" and 30"). Lynn (1961) used the Llewellyn-Thomas (1959) technique in which the judgment of trial one becomes the stimulus for trial two, and so forth, thus snowballing errors; using a standard time interval of 15", he had subjects engage in ten trials in all. On the last trial introverts gave a score of 18.4", extraverts one of 10.2". Differences became significant only towards the last few trials, there being little differences between the groups on the first five trials. Howarth (1963) repeated the Claridge experiment, using time intervals of 5, 10, 15 and 20 seconds, each presented twice in random order. On all four time intervals, and on combined scores, the extraverts tended to underestimate the time interval relation to the instruments, but the results just failed to reach significance.

Not all attempts to test relationships between time estimation and personality have been successful, but again we must note the

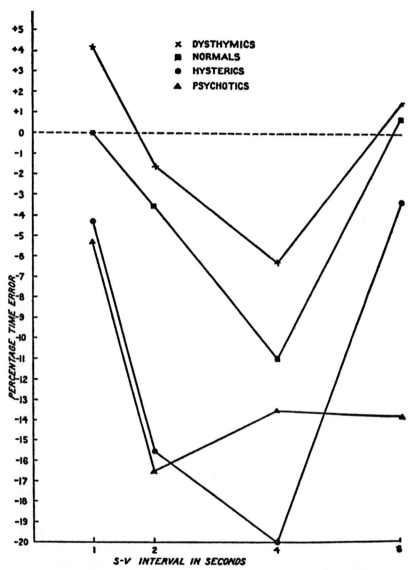

Figure 54. Negative time errors of hysterics and dysthymics on loudness comparison task, after different S-V intervals. Reprinted with permission from G. Claridge, 1960.

failure of some writers to duplicate conditions and time intervals from the successful studies. Thus Orme (1962) used simple estimates of 20 or 30 minutes; no obvious connection between his methodology and the writer's theory springs to mind, and the failure to find any correlations is not unexpected. Du Preez (1964) indicated the time interval to be estimated by means of a tone delivered over earphones, and had the judgment done in various different ways: by means of verbal estimation, by means of horizontal hand movement, and by key pressing. He found that "extraversion correlated significantly and positively with time reproduced by linear movement (contrary to Eysenck's prediction)." It is difficult to follow his argument, however, as the writer never made any prediction to the method of administering the stimulus or of recording the judgment which was used by Du Preez. Both the continuous tone present during the first time interval and the motor movement,[18] which is part of the second time interval, introduce so many sources of error and of interference and confusion that this experiment cannot be regarded as relevant to Claridge's hypothesis or to that of the writer.

Perceptual Defence

There are different conceptions of perceptual defence (Brown, 1961), but essentially we may regard this as a kind of "early warning system" to protect the organism against unwanted or dangerous stimuli. The effects of stimulation may be either response suppression or response sensitization (Bruner and Postman, 1947). Inglis (1960) has given a long discussion of published studies in perceptual defence, and has proposed a general theoretical model linking this with personality. Figure 55 shows Dodwell's (1964) diagrammatic representation of Inglis' model; it will be seen that at low levels of stress introverts show suppression and extraverts sensitization, while at high levels of stress this relation is reversed. Brown (1961) has published a similar hypothesis; Inglis' hypothetical relations (Figure 55) would coincide with the central part of Brown's curves where the two cross. These theories thus generate testable predictions, although there are obvious difficulties in defining level of stress, leading to the danger of *post hoc*

[18]See the section on motor movements below for discussion of differences between extraverts and introverts in this respect.

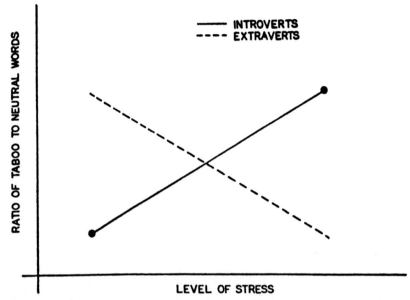

Figure 55. Suppression and sensitization at different stress levels for introverts and extraverts. Reprinted with permission from P. C. Dodwell: *Canad. J. Psychol.*, *18*:72-91, 1964.

rationalization. In any case, both theories implicate extraversion-introversion as an important personality variable in work of this type.[14a]

Some early personality studies, such as those of Kissin, Gottesfeld, and Dickes (1940), Eriksen and Browne (1956), and Osler and Lewisohn (1954), give some vague support to the general theory, but the failure to use appropriate inventories to measure the personality side renders these results relatively inconclusive. Ehlers (1963) has published the first directly relevant research in this field, using the M.P.I. As stimulus material, she used four groups of nonsense syllables, each group being characterised by

[14a]Byrne (1964) and his colleagues have postulated the existence of a personality dimension of repression-sensitization. This is not the place to review the large body of work done in connection with this concept, but it seems likely that this particular trait is one of the many which through their intercorrelations give rise to the higher-order concept of introversion-extraversion. There is no direct proof of this hypothesis, but many of the data furnished by Byrne in his review would seem to give some support to this view. Direct proof would be of some interest in this connection.

containing a particular letter. Three of these groups were paired with (a) painful electric shock, (b) a visual stimulus, (c) an auditory stimulus; the fourth group was not used at all during the association phase. After the association between nonsense syllables and stimuli had been achieved, syllables were presented without being followed by sensory stimuli, and the tachistoscopic reaction times measured which led to correct recognition of the stimuli. It was the general hypothesis of the author that those syllables which had been paired with shock would show "perceptual defence" phenomena and would thus be characterised by longer recognition times; comparison of the four groups did indeed show at a high level of significance that shock-associated stimuli had the highest recognition thresholds.

As regards personality, subjects high on N had lower recognition thresholds for all four groups of stimuli, but did not differ from subjects low on N with respect to the difference between shock and nonshock stimuli. Introverts, as compared with extraverts, showed a significant increase in recognition time for shock stimuli over nonshock stimuli; the extraverts, in fact, showed no increase for shock stimuli at all. Figure 56 shows the differential behaviour of the two groups. If we are willing to agree that the stress produced by the tachistoscopic exposition of nonsense syllables previously associated with shock, or with visual and auditory stimuli, is relatively mild, then this result fits in well with the Inglis-Brown theory. The failure of neuroticism to play any part in this phenomenon may be cited as additional evidence of the relative mildness of the stress produced.

Dodwell (1964) has published several experiments relevant to our hypothesis. He presented two words to his subjects simultaneously, one to the right ear, the other to the left; both words had to be repeated by the subject, and the score was essentially the number of correct recognitions of the experimental words as compared with the control words. In one experiment "good" and "bad" words were paired with neutral words; examples of good words are: truth, church, happy; of bad words: hate, grief, nasty; of neutral words: lofty, mallet, box. "Since both 'good' and 'bad' words appear in the list, each matched against a 'neutral' word, the scoring procedure adopted was to count the number of times a

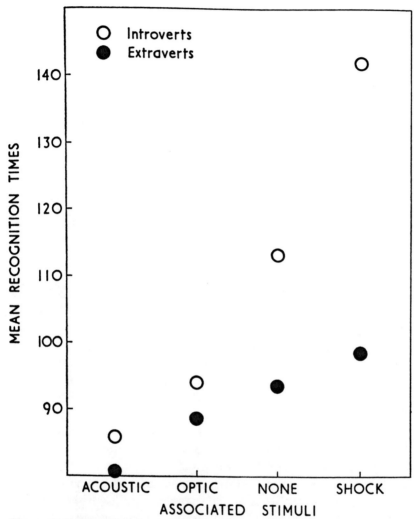

Figure 56. Perceptual defence in extraverts and introverts. Drawn from data supplied by B. Ehlers, 1963.

'good' word was heard, but not its neutral counterpart, and also the number of times a neutral word was heard but not its 'bad' counterpart. Similarly the number of times the opposite effect occurred (the 'better' of the two was not heard, but the 'worse' was) was counted. The final score for a subject was the first of these numbers minus the second, so a positive score indicates that a person tends to hear the 'better' of a pair, a negative score indicates the opposite." Introverts were found to "defend," i.e., not to hear 'bad' words; their mean score was +1.0 while that of the extraverts was −3.7. The result fell just short of significance.

Another, similar experiment also involved dichotic listening; the "bad" words in this case were "taboo" words like vagina and orgasm. Attempt was also made to manipulate "stress" by means of instructions. The details of design and analysis are quite complex, but Dodwell summarises the results by saying that "they confirm Inglis' hypothesis quite clearly." He adds that "it may be noted that the result was obtained in this instance with what can probably be regarded as quite a small change in level of stress, and with subjects who were not extreme types in the sense of displaying clinical symptoms, for example, of hysteria or dysthymia."

A rather indirect but very interesting approach to the problem of perceptual defence was made by Reed (1961), who studied twenty-six hard-of-hearing cases in a child guidance clinic. Fourteen of these presented elevated thresholds for pure tones but were within normal limits for speech (Group A). The other, though normal on pure-tone testing, presented elevated thresholds for all speech (Group B). Clinically, it was found that children in Group A were predominantly "hysteric" (outgoing behaviour problems), while those in Group B were predominantly "anxiety state" (timid, withdrawn, mild phobic symptoms). Reed accounts for these findings in terms of reactive inhibition in the pure-tone testing situation affecting the (presumably extraverted) "hysteric" children more; it is also possible, of course, to subsume this finding under the more general one of extraverts having higher sensory thresholds. The dysthymic children, he points out, are highly reactive and readily conditionable. "They tend to demonstrate strong fear reactions which, linked with oversocialisation, may be triggered off by apparently neutral stimuli in social situations. Heightened thresholds for speech may thus be acquired as an anxiety reducing avoidance mechanism by these children more readily than by hysterics." Whether this be the correct explanation or not, it appears again that under relatively mild stress the introverted children demonstrate more "perceptual defence" than do the extraverted children; it would be interesting to test both groups under more stressful conditions.

Motor Movements

In the preceding section we noted that perceptual inhibition was a function of stress, with Figure 55 showing a crossing-over in the performance of extraverts and introverts as stress increased. The findings of research in the field of motor movements suggest a similar state of affairs, with extraverts showing more rapid and possibly more extensive movements at low levels of stress, and more "inert" responses at high levels of stress. Yates (1960) has given a review of abnormalities of psychomotor functions; here only a few types of response can be discussed.

Davis (1948) carried out a series of experiments on causes of pilot error in which he used a simulated cockpit where instruments on a panel responded realistically to movements of the controls; in other experiments he used an apparatus in which a pointer could be moved to a given position to the right or left, in response to signals. The pointer was controlled through an integrating disc, and movement was to the brighter of two lights. He observed two types of error—overaction and inertia. Subjects who were overactive "obtained large scores on control movements . . . responses to instrument deviations were excessive, the extent and gradient of the movements being greatly increased and over-correcting frequent. Numerous restless movements were observed . . . subjects felt excited and under strain, tense and irritable and sometimes frankly anxious." Subjects who were inert, on the other hand, "made errors which were large and of long duration, whereas activity, represented by scores of control movements, was relatively little . . . The individual responses were less hurried and less disturbed by restless movements than were those of the pilots showing the overactivity reaction, but they were often more extensive than at the beginning of the test . . . Subjects reported that their interest had flagged and that their concentration had failed. A feeling of strain had now given way to one of mild boredom, tedium or tiredness."

From this description one might easily form the impression that overactive responses are characteristic of a high, perhaps over high, state of vigilance, and inert responses characteristic of low vigilance and high cortical inhibition. It is in line with this view that, in general, errors of inertia tended to predominate over errors of overactivity *in all subjects* provided the test was continued for a long enough period. In good accord with this hypothesis, Davis found that dysthymic pilots showed a strong tendency to make overactive responses, whereas pilots of hysterical personality tended to display inert responses. Similar findings were reported by Davis (1946, 1947, 1949) with the apparatus described above, using hospital patients of lower intelligence as subjects.

Venables (1955) has extended this work by adapting the apparatus used by Davis, and by making it possible to alter the difficulty level of the task. The experiment began with an easy period (A), continued with a difficult period (B), and finished with another easy period (C). Venables used dysthymic and hysteric patients as his subjects, as well as groups of what he called "quasi-hysteric" and "quasi-anxious" normals, selected on the basis of personality test responses to resemble the clinical groups. The measure used was response per unit time (R/W), and the results are shown in Figure 57. Venables sums up his work in this way: "If we examine the results . . . it is seen that extravert and quasi-hysteric subjects show a significant tendency to change their performance in the inert direction under increased difficulty. The reverse tendency is show in introvert, quasi-anxious, and anxious subjects. The hospitalised, hysteric patient presents an initially inert type of response. Commencing performance on this level, he does not change his performance in the inert direction under increased difficulty, but maintains a performance which is substantially similar to his starting performance." In other words, for the hysteric it appears that a difficulty level which is relatively easy for the quasi-hysteric is already difficult enough to provoke inert responses which for the quasi-hysteric appear only after the task has been made more difficult and stressful.

Anthony (1960) used the Venables test on large groups of "good" and "bad" R.A.F. apprentices, the method of differentiation being based on the number of convictions and rating of offences committed later on by these apprentices during their Air Force careers. She found that "the *bad* group is found to make a

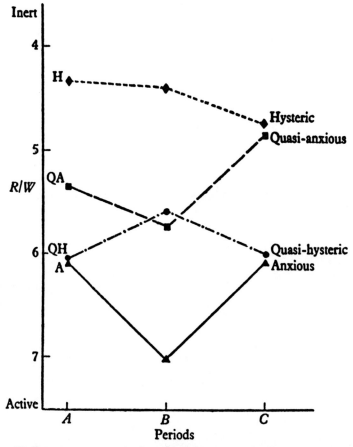

Figure 57. Responses per unit time of different personality types. Reprinted with permission from P. Venables: *Brit. J. Psychol.*, *46*:101-110, 1955.

significantly more active score on the initial series (A); to reduce activity when the task becomes more difficult on (B) series, significantly more than the *good* group; and to revert to approximately the former activity level when the task becomes easier again and the end of the session is in sight." As expected, therefore, the "bad" group behaves in the manner typical of the extravert, the "good" group in the manner typical of the introvert.

Rachman (1961) studied the reactions of 100 normal subjects on a test similar in some ways to the Venables apparatus, but wired to produce "conflict" situations in which incompatible signals were given to the subject whose motor reactions were being measured. He found that extreme extraverts responded more extensively than extreme introverts, a finding which was replicated when twenty-two dysthymics and fourteen hysterics were tested. The extent of activity per unit time (R/W) *increased* under conflict conditions for dysthymics and *decreased* for hysterics, as shown in Figure 58; the results just failed to be significant. However, they are very much in line with those of Venables and Anthony; it seems likely that the "conflict" induced in the subjects was of too mild a form to have a very strong effect. It should also be noted that the experiment, like that of Venables, lasted only for a few minutes, thus making improbable the accumulation of reactive inhibition to any significant extent.

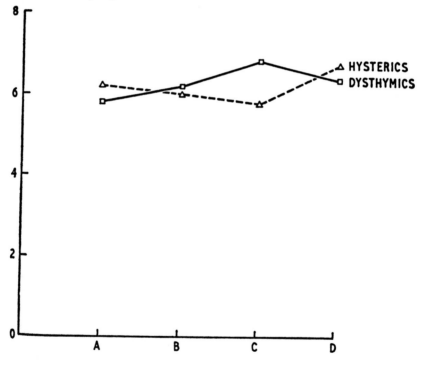

PRACTICE PERIODS

Figure 58. Response per unit time of hysterics and dysthymics under control and conflict conditions. Reprinted with permission from S. Rachman, 1961.

Rachman suggests "that the increased cortical excitation of the introvert facilitates the execution of accurate, economic and confined movements. The increased cortical inhibition of the extravert, however, will hamper the execution of the precise and accurate movements for the task at hand. We might therefore expect that differences in efficiency (of psychomotor performance) between introvert and extravert groups will be inflated in tasks requiring confined and precise movements and diminished in tasks requiring gross movements. Kohlmann's (1958) remarks on this subject are in accord with this expectation." We shall return to a discussion of this point when we turn to a consideration of the physiological effects of reticular system activation. Lynn (1963) has reported that arousal has the effect of decreasing the extent of expressive movements, although his results are somewhat ambiguous in their relation to the present discussion.

In the general field of expressive movements, Wallach and Gahm (1960) (see also Wallach and Thomas, 1963) have published an experiment which gives results similar to those already reviewed. They subdivided their population in terms of neuroticism (anxiety) and introversion-extraversion, and measured an area filled with doodling as a measure of graphic constriction and expansiveness. If we assume that the high N group would be in a state of higher stress than the low N group, we would predict that extraverts high on N would have constrictive scores, extraverts low on N expansive scores, while introverts would reverse this relation. The actual figures bear out this prediction; the crossing-over is shown clearly in Figure 59.[14b]

Howarth (1964) has reported a button-pressing task in which the subject had to press any of five buttons at his preferred rate. On such a very easy task, involving no stress, we would expect extraverts to be more active than introverts, with ambiverts in between, and this Howarth found to be so (see Figure 60). He also

[14b]Some data from Ramsey (1966) may also be relevant here. He studied the non-content aspects of speech, and showed that with different types of tasks there were significant differences in the ratio of length of sound/length of silence, in the sense that tasks requiring higher cognitive activity were characterized by longer silences. He then proceeded to show that extraverts differed very significantly from introverts in showing longer sound and shorter silence periods: "The introvert gives short bursts of speech and long pauses, the extravert long bursts of speech and short pauses."

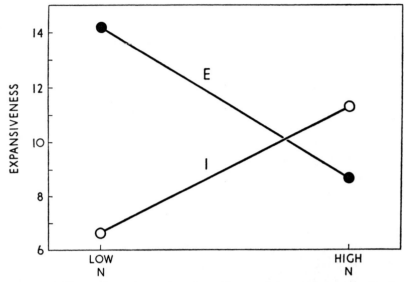

Figure 59. Expansiveness as a function of neuroticism and extraversion-introversion. Drawn from data given in M. A. Wallach and R. C. Gahm: *J. Person., 28*:73-88, 1960.

inserted a period during which subjects had to press two of the buttons alternately; they then returned to the previous task. This "satiation" experience increased the mean number of presses but did not affect the relative ranking of the three groups. Howarth predicted rather different results on the basis that performance would produce "inhibition" and "satiation," but this would only be expected under conditions of *massed* practice. Jensen has shown in some interesting work that under appropriate conditions inhibition can indeed be produced in button-pushing tasks (1966).

Bearing in mind the marked differences in experimental procedures shown in the studies here summarised, it would not be inaccurate to say that agreement is reasonably high on the hypotheses stated at the beginning of this section.[15]

[15]It may seem curious in view of the hypothesis to be advanced presently, linking extraversion with lack of cortical arousal and hypersynchronization of EEG patterns, that extraverts should be characterized by larger movements and more frequent movements, at least in a nonstress state. The answer may lie in some observations made by Kogan (1966) on thresholds of motor movement responses to direct stimulation of the cortex. He found that "during desynchronization an increase of the thresholds of stimulation takes place, and not a decrease. . . . It fol-

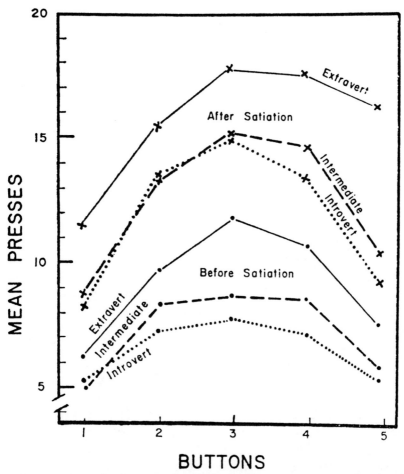

BUTTONS

Figure 60. Rate of button pressing of introverts and extraverts. Reprinted with permission from E. Howarth: *Psychol. Rep.,* *14*:949-950, 1964.

lows that in respect of the cortical nervous elements, at any rate in respect to those which are connected with a motor reaction, desynchronization means a decline, and not an increase in excitability." Conversely, therefore, hypersynchronization signifies an increase in motor reactivity, in contradistinction to sensory reactivity, where it signifies a decrease. These physiological observations are in good theoretical agreement with our experimental observations and may explain the apparent paradox. Kogan attempts to rationalize his findings along evolutionary lines. "It may be assumed that during desynchronization the excitability of the afferent cortical cellular elements increases, while the excitability of the effector ones decreases. This assumption is substantiated by the biological and psychological significance of the attention reaction as an intensification of perception in a situation of retarded movements." This theory thus links this phenomenon closely with the so-called "orienting reflex."

The overactivity-inertia axis is not the only one in the field of motor movements where differences between introverts and extraverts can be expected; equally important is the speed-accuracy continuum. In most motor tasks the subject has a choice between greater speed, bought at the price of reducing accuracy, and greater accuracy, bought at the price of reducing speed. On theoretical grounds one would expect extraverts to choose speed over accuracy, introverts to choose accuracy over speed. There are several reasons for this expectation. It is well known that in most tasks fatigue leads to errors (Schmidtke, 1965,), and this tendency may be due to IRPs arising through reactive inhibition (see the work on vigilance). Extraverts would thus be more likely to make errors. Cortical excitation, leading to greater control over risk-taking behaviour and therefore to a reduction in speed in order to avoid errors, would be expected to be greater in introverts. Last, the social pressure on accuracy which is characteristic of our culture, and which is likely to be acquired through a process of conditioning, would on the grounds of their greater condition-ability be more effective with introverts. An early study by Himmelweit (1946), using five tests on fifty hysterics and fifty dysthymics, and another one by Petrie (1945), using a similar group, gave results in line with this prediction (see the summary by Eysenck, 1947, of work in this field). Mangan (1959) has since demonstrated in a large-scale factor-analytic study that it is impossible "to isolate accuracy as a factor orthogonal to speed, hence it seemed preferable to recognise a bipolar factor contrasting motor speed and tempo with accuracy."

In a series of studies, Foulds (1951, 1952) and Foulds and Caine (1958a,b) have dealt with the speed of response of neurotic patients on the Porteus Maze test; tendencies were found for hysterics, clinically diagnosed, and hysteroids, diagnosed by questionnaire, to be quicker on Mazes and on the Matrices test of intelligence than dysthymics, clinically diagnosed, and "obsessoids," diagnosed by questionnaire. Brierley (1961), using the Nufferno test at two levels of difficulty, demonstrated that "the pattern of speed and accuracy in problem solving is . . . that hysterics are characterised by low accuracy and dysthymics by low speed." In normal university students, Jensen (1966) has found a correlation of .44 between speed of solution for the Matrices test of intelligence and extraversion; extraverts made more errors, but not significantly so.

Farley (1966a) divided his thirty subjects into extravert, ambivert, and introvert on the basis of the M.P.I., and administered to them the Nufferno test, which enables the investigator to obtain an error-free measure of solution time in problem solving

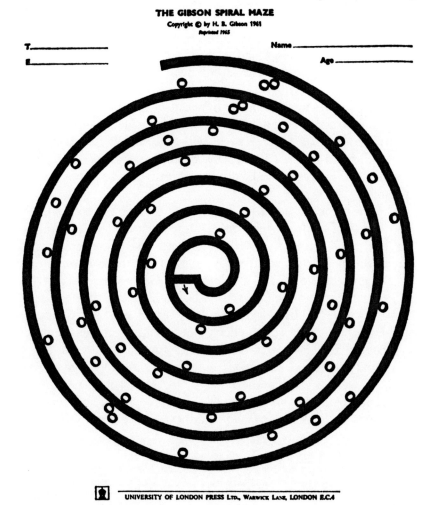

THE GIBSON SPIRAL MAZE

Copyright © by H. B. Gibson 1961

Reprinted 1965

T_____   Name_____

E_____   Age_____

UNIVERSITY OF LONDON PRESS LTD., WARWICK LANE, LONDON E.C.4

Figure 61. The Gibson Spiral Maze. Reprinted with permission from H. B. Gibson, 1965.

(Furneaux, 1955). The groups were significantly differentiated, with the extraverts fastest and the introverts slowest. (The relationship between speed and N was curvilinear, the ambivert group working significantly faster than the high and low N groups; this finding is well in line with the results reported by Lynn and Gordon, 1961, who used the Matrices test.) It should be noted that age, sex, and score on the Mill Hill vocabulary test did not discriminate between the three groups (see also Farley, 1966b).

Shanmugan (1965) reported a reaction-time experiment in which two lines were exposed and a decision had to be made as to which was the longer; the differences between the two lines ranged from .5″ through .3″ and .1″ to .05″. Differences in decision time were nonsignificant between introverts and extraverts for the two size-differences first mentioned, but became significant for the smaller differences, with the introverts giving the slower decision times. (There was, of course, a general trend for slower decision times with smaller objective differences for all groups.)

The most recent work in this field is that of Gibson (1965), who has published a "spiral maze" test illustrated in Figure 61; this has to be traced by the subject, and time taken and errors made (touches or penetrations of sides of the maze or of circular obstacles in the way are calculated). Gibson has shown that delinquent youths are characterised by high error scores and relatively fast work. His test is avowedly based on the "Q" score of the Porteus Maze test, which is essentially a count of errors in this test; this has often been found to correlate with delinquent and criminal behaviour (Eysenck, 1964a). The studies here cited, as well as others not cited,[16] are remarkably unanimous in showing introverts to be slower and more careful and accurate than extraverts; it is also usually found that this tendency is equal-

[16]In a very recent study, Ramsey (1966) examined the noncontent speech behaviour of introverts and extraverts. He found significant differences in the lengths of pauses between utterances, introverts being characterized by *longer* pauses. "If silence is used for higher cortical activity . . . then the results support the idea that the introvert is the thoughtful type, he thinks before acting and weighs his words more than the extravert." These results and interpretations support the general hypothesis according to which the introvert is "slow but sure."

ly pronounced in neurotic extraverts (hysterics) and neurotic introverts (dysthymics). In addition, there is often found an interaction effect, in the sense that neurotics give a worse performance on motor tests, i.e., they are inferior with respect to both speed and accuracy (Yates, 1960).

Achievement and Aspiration

The general tenor of the discussion so far suggests that introverts would be expected to be *achievement* oriented, while extraverts would be *affiliation* oriented, to use the terms of Murray (1938). Affiliation means seeking for people, depending on people, and bears some similarity to the concept of sociability as used hitherto. It has already been shown that extraverts are typically characterised by strong social tendencies, and it seems likely that these tendencies are, at least in part, a consequence of their strong stimulus hunger, which we have already discussed. In civilised societies, most stimulation is mediated by other people, and this would be expected to lead to extraverts (a) seeking out other people in order to receive this stimulation, and (b) becoming conditioned through reinforcement to continue ever more strongly to indulge in this type of behaviour (see the Weisen experiment on a previous page). On the other hand, introverts would react in precisely the opposite manner. Thus the sociable behaviour of extraverts and the withdrawn behaviour of introverts find a ready explanation in terms of previous findings.

As regards achievement and aspiration, we may consider two sources of motivation. In the first place, our type of society places much emphasis, from school through college, on the need for work, achievement, success; individuals who condition more easily (i.e., introverts) would be expected to introject this teaching more effectively than would individuals who condition poorly (Eysenck, 1965). Again, cortical excitation makes possible prolonged periods of complex mental work, and reinforcement provided by society for successful work of this kind may be expected, in line with learning theory, to lead to greater and greater indulgence in this type of work, together with high evaluation of activities of this kind. Is there any evidence of an experimental kind to support these views?

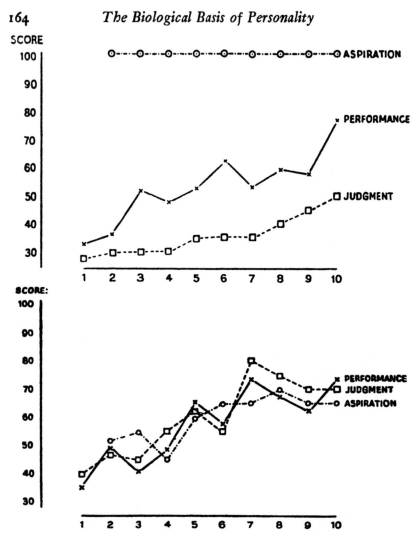

Figure 62. Typical level of aspiration scores of (a) introvert and (b) extravert. From H. J. Eysenck, 1947.

Eysenck and Himmelweit (1946) and Eysenck (1947) have reported work on levels of aspiration tests with hysterics and dysthymics. It was found that dysthymics have high, relatively rigid levels of aspiration, and that they underrate their achievements; hysterics have low, flexible levels of aspiration geared closely to their performance, and they tend not to underrate their achievements. Figure 62 gives typical response patterns from a dysthymic and a hysteric patient; Figure 63 gives mean values for fifty hysterics and fifty dysthymics. Miller (1951) has reported very similar results from a study of psychiatric patients, and Himmelweit (1947) and Broadbent (1958) have provided some support from normal subjects. The evidence certainly suggests a greater concern of introverts with achievement.[17]

A more applied study has recently been reported by Sevransky

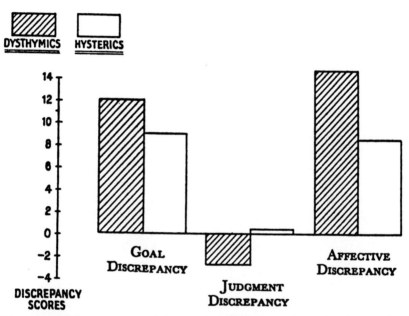

Figure 63. Differential scores of hysterics and dysthymics on level of aspiration test. From H. J. Eysenck, 1947.

[17]It should be noted that Broadbent, while experimentally substantiating many of the experimental findings involved with the differentiation between introverts and extraverts, prefers a theoretical account different from that concerned with the notion of inhibition. He posits differences in length of time over which the organism samples information; introverts on this view are "long time samplers," extraverts "short time samplers." The writer does not wish to quarrel with this ingenious contention; he would merely point out that there must be a causal substratum to account for these differences in length of time sampling, which are purely descriptive in nature. It does not seem farfetched to suggest that it is the action of reactive inhibition which is responsible for the relatively short time samples used by the extravert; conversely it may be the high state of cortical excitation which enables the introvert to make use of relatively long time samples. On such an assumption there is no real difference between the two views.

(1965). He chose eighty extreme scorers on the M.P.I. from 475 senior class boys in two New York city schools, and administered the boys the General Aptitude Test Battery and a questionnaire about their parents' occupation. Three vocational goal discrepancy scores (intellectual, aptitude, and socio-economic) were computed for each of the subjects in the four criterion groups. Sevransky's stated hypothesis was "that the ordering of vocational goal discrepancy scores for Eysenck's four criterion groups (neurotic introverts, stable introverts, stable extraverts, and neurotic introverts) would be the same as that of his experimental studies. In addition to the ordering of criterion groups, the following hypotheses were tested: (1) introverts have higher goal discrepancy scores than extraverts; (2) neurotic introverts have higher goal discrepancy scores than stable introverts; and (3) stable extraverts have higher goal discrepancy scores than neurotic extraverts." Analysis of the results "indicates that the ordering of vocational goal discrepancy scores for the four criterion groups was correctly predicted for the intellectual and aptitude discrepancy scores, but not for the socio-economic discrepancy scores . . . Introverts tended to aspire to occupations above their intellectual level while extraverts tended to aspire to occupations below their intellectual level." The data for the aptitude and socio-economic discrepancy scores did not support Sevransky's *specific* hypotheses.

Experimental work on the need for achievement has been well summarised by Atkinson (1964); most of the measurement of individual differences in this field has been carried out by the use of the Thematic Apperception Test (T.A.T.). Unfortunately the various workers involved have not systematically correlated scores on this test with inventories and other personality measures, so that one has to rely on more subjective descriptions of high-achievers and low-achievers on the T.A.T.; these tend to agree in finding the former characterised by introverted traits, the latter by extraverted traits. Olley (1964) has reported a study in which she compared matched pairs of introverts and extraverts on n. Ach. and n. Affil.; her results show a tendency for extraverts to give more affiliative and fewer achievement responses when the general level of responding for the two groups is equated. Unfortunately the number of cases reported on is too small to place much confidence in the findings.

Concepts such as "n. Ach." are closely related to attitudes, and one might expect introverts and extraverts to show marked differences in social attitudes. The writer has pursued this line of thought in *Psychology of Politics* (Eysenck, 1954), and has demonstrated that introverts are characterised by tender-minded attitudes, extraverts by tough-minded attitudes; interesting though this line of enquiry may be, it is not germane to the main purpose of this book, and will therefore not be pursued here.

In some unpublished work, F. H. Farley has correlated extraversion and the n.Ach. scale of the Edwards Personal Preference Scale, demonstrating a significant but small correlation in the predicted direction; in another study he found a loading of -0.34 for the n.Ach. scale on a factor of extraversion. Young industrial apprentices were used in the first study, university students in the second. These results suggest a positive relation between introversion and achievement motivation.

Autonomic Reactions

In an earlier chapter we have reviewed autonomic reactivity as related to individual differences in emotionality or neuroticism; this point of view is implicit in most writing on the subject (Reymert, 1950; Duffy, 1963). Yet it would appear that this connection is not as firmly based in all its aspects as might at first appear. We have already noted that the experimental connections between neuroticism and autonomic activity are in places surprisingly tenuous; examples are the GSR and the EEG. We have also noted that much of the experimental work is deficient on the personality side because comparisons between groups have confounded the two dimensions of neuroticism and introversion by using *anxiety* as the variable under examination, in spite of the well-documented fact that anxiety is not a unidimensional variable but a combination of neuroticism and introversion. It seems desirable to see whether it is possible to find any evidence clarifying this issue by relating extraversion and introversion to autonomic measures.

One of the first writers to do this in a systematic fashion was van der Merwe (1948), following up some work done by Theron

(1948). Theron had carried out a factor-analytic study of autonomic responses made by fifty normal students. He found evidence for two autonomic factors, the first of which he labelled "emotional stability"; this is clearly similar to neuroticism, as shown by the fact that a questionnaire test of neuroticism has a very high loading on this factor. The second factor was labelled "basic emotional tension," and was found to discriminate between hysteric and dysthymic patients, whose mean scores fell on opposite sides of the scores made by a normal group; on the "emotional stability" factor both hysterics and dysthymics were found to have higher scores than normals. These findings could be interpreted to mean that hysterics (extraverts) show a shift to parasympathetic predominance, while dysthymics (introverts) show a shift to sympathetic dominance, although such interpretations of laboratory tests of considerable complexity are of doubtful value. In any case these studies establish the existence of two independent autonomic reaction patterns, related respectively to neuroticism and extraversion-introversion; apparently a single factor conception of "anxiety" is inappropriate, even in the physiological field (Figure 64).[18a]

We may now turn to a more detailed discussion of some experimental findings. A good beginning for such a discussion, linking it up with our work on vigilance, is provided by Davies and Krkovic (1965), who studied the relation between skin conductance, alpha activity, and vigilance decrement during a prolonged auditory task similar to those described in an earlier part of this chapter. Figure 65 shows a marked congruence of the three measures; as vigilance declines, so *pari passu* do skin conductance and alpha activity on the EEG. (Skin conductance and alpha activity measures were converted to working-rest ratios for each sub-

[18a]An early, if highly speculative, adumbration of the view that introversion and extraversion may be linked with the preponderant activity of the antagonistic parts of the autonomic nervous system is contained in Kempf's book on *The Autonomic Functions and the Personality* (1921.) He observes that "the extroversion mechanism is essentially healthful and conducive to robustness, because the autonomic disturbance is more promptly neutralized; whereas the introversion mechanism tends to a prolonged increase of affective sensitiveness. With introversion a lowering of the threshold of the autonomic reactions occurs so that ordinary, subliminal stimuli may cause vigorous, autonomic reactions which are usually distressing."

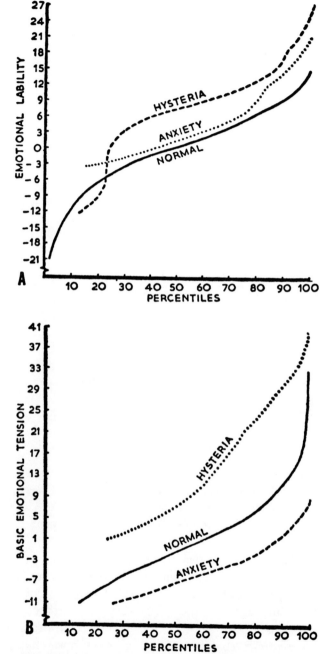

Figure 64. Percentile curves showing emotional lability scores (a) and basic emotional tension scores (b) of hysterics and anxiety patients. Reprinted with permission from S. B. van der Merwe: *Psychosom. Med.,* 10:347-354, 1948.

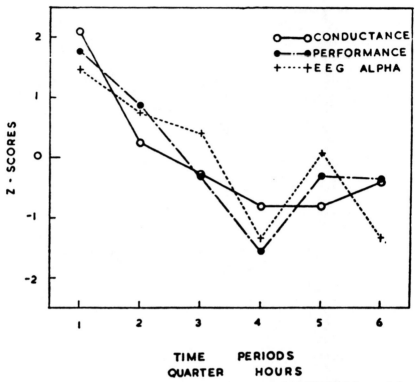

Figure 65. Z scores for conductance, performance, and EEG alpha activity over the six quarter-hour periods of vigilance task. Reprinted with permission from D. R. Davies and A. Krkovic: *Amer. J. Psychol.*, 78:304-306, 1965.

ject, and the values averaged for all subjects for each of the six 15-minute periods of the task. All scores were converted into z values, to make direct comparison possible.) A trend analysis revealed no significant difference among the trend-lines of the three measures.

We would appear justified in arguing as follows: (a) Degree of vigilance decline is a function of extraversion, not of neuroticism. (b) Skin conductance and alpha activity are measures of vigilance decline. Consequently, (c) skin conductance and alpha activity are measures of extraversion, not of neuroticism. Is there any direct evidence to support such a conclusion? Jones (1950) was one of the first to point out evidence contrary to the well-established assumption that GSR and skin conductance were measures of neuroticism. He quotes Landis (1932) as noting that in 100 delinquents those boys who appeared to be the most emotional gave the smallest frequency of galvanic response, and he also refers to Darrow and Solomon (1934) as showing that a lower than normal galvanic reactivity "may often be a sign not of unusual emotional poise, but of some basic disturbance or deficiency in emotional organisation." In his own work Jones compared a high reactive (N = 20) and a low reactive (N = 10) group chosen from 100 adolescent boys and girls; reactivity was measured in terms of mean resistance change in ohms, as well as in terms of log conductance change. Figures 66 and 67 show the social behaviour of these two groups, as mirrored in psychologists' ratings and in peer ratings; it will be seen that the "high reactives" are introverted, the "low reactives" extraverted. There is no trace here of any relationship with neuroticism.

Bronzaft *et al.* (1960) attempted to relate personality and GSR reactions in forty-six female college students; they found negative correlation with E and positive correlation with N, but neither were significant. The multiple correlation with anxiety (high N, low E) would be significant on any reasonable assumption about the correlation between N and E in this group. Burdick (1965) also obtained correlations in a similar direction between spontaneous activity on the GSR, neuroticism, and extraversion; he obtained correlations of .23 with N and −.24 with E on twenty-seven male college students. Again the multiple correlation with anxiety would probably have been significant. Mundy-Castle and McKiever (1953) had already established a correlation between spontaneous activity of the GSR and adaptation to stimuli; high spontaneous activity was found to go with poor adaptation. It was also found that in those subjects showing no spontaneous activity, there was a significant correlation between adaptation and alpha frequency (tau = .40).[22] These facts are of some interest because Scott and Wilkinson (1962) have shown a very significant correlation between adaptation on the GSR and

[22]McDonald *et al.* (1964) have shown that there is less spontaneous GSR activity in drowsy subjects as compared with alert ones, when EEG criteria are used. Lader (1964) has demonstrated on normal subjects that slow habituation is correlated with number of spontaneous fluctuations in GSR and with high skin conductance. He failed to find correlation between any of these variables and E or N.

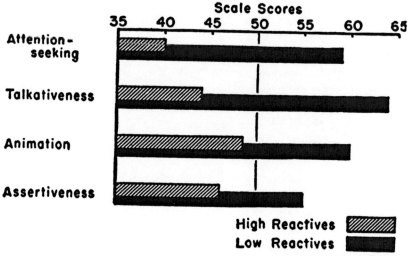

Figure 66. A comparison of high and low reactives (GSR) in social behavior (psychologists' ratings). Reprinted with permission from H. G. Jones: *Feelings and Emotions*. New York, McGraw-Hill, 1950.

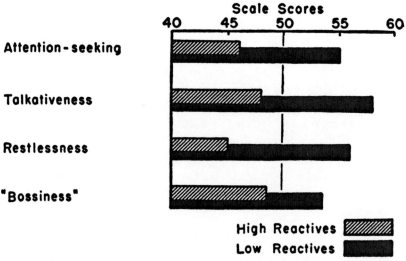

Figure 67. A comparison of high and low reactives (GSR) in reputation traits. Reprinted with permission from H. G. Jones, 1950.

extraversion (rho = .75). During twenty adaptation trials, the two most introverted subjects did not adapt at all, while the two most extraverted ones adapted in three and five trials respectively. This experiment was carried out on only seventeen subjects, and would repay repetition and extension.

Another report relating to spontaneous GSR activity (Fox and Lippert, 1963) compared ten sociopaths with ten inadequate personalities. No differences were found on basal skin conductance, but the sociopathic (extraverted?) group exhibited a significantly smaller frequency of spontaneous reactions (8.5 as compared with 14.7 on an average; p < .05). The results again are not conclusive because of the obvious contamination with anxiety, but they are in the expected direction. Certainly spontaneous autonomic activity is a reliable and consistent human characteristic (Wilson and Dykman, 1960), and it appears to be related to some form of arousal or activation (Burch and Greiner, 1960). The data reviewed are generally in line with an assumption that this arousal or activation partakes of the nature of introversion rather than of that of neuroticism. Possibly both hypotheses are true; discussion of this point must be postponed to a later chapter.

Hare (1965) has reported a study similar in some ways to that of Fox and Lippert. He worked on three groups of eleven subjects each; P (psychopaths), NP (nonpsychopathic prisoners), and C (normal controls). Skin conductance was measured, and subjects were conditioned to receive shock whenever number 8 came up on a memory drum; one no-shock presentation of the numbers was followed by five shock presentations. Results for the first and last shock trials are shown in Figure 68. It will be seen that (a) psychopaths show less conductance throughout, (b) psychopaths show less evidence of *anticipation* of shock (numbers 4 to 7), (c) psychopaths show less overall effects of shock. These results are in good agreement with Lindner's (1942) finding that "constitutional psychopathic inferiors" were less responsive on GSR than other criminals, prior to noxious stimulation. Lindner also found that psychopaths recovered more rapidly from the effects of stimulation, and he, Schachter, and Latane (1964) found psychopaths more responsive to noxious stimulation. All these results are in part made difficult to compare because of differences in

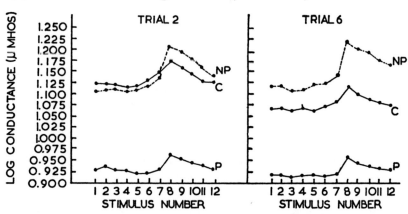

Figure 68. Log conductance as a function of anticipated shock (shock at stimulus number 8) for psychopaths (P), nonpsychopathic prisoners (NP), and normal controls (C). Reprinted with permission from R. D. Hare: *J. Abnorm. Psychol.*, 70:442-445, 1965.

definition of experimental and criterion groups, and because different GSR measures and experimental tests were used. On the whole, if we agree to regard psychopaths as extraverted neurotics (high E, high N), Hare's data suggest that it is extraversion-introversion, rather than N, which is related to GSR measures which differentiate his P group from the NP and C groups. It is unfortunate that no personality inventories were applied to the subjects of these experiments; in the absence of such direct evidence interpretation must remain hazardous.

Lader and Wing (1964) have reported an important study of GSR adaptation in twenty patients with anxiety state (dysthymics) and twenty normal subjects. Figure 69 shows skin conductance of the two groups during rest, and adaptation to twenty auditory stimuli; each point represents the mean of four log conductance readings. Patients show higher conductance at rest; they show less reaction to the first stimuli; and they do not habituate. Furthermore, during rest the patients increase slightly in conductance, while the normals decrease substantially. The differential rates of adaptation are shown even better in Figure 70, where regression lines have been fitted to the data. As habituation of the GSR follows an exponential course, the mean GSR values have been plotted against the logarithm of the stimulus number. Spontaneous skin conductance fluctuations were also measured; both groups responded similarly to the experimental changes but retained quite different levels of responding, with patients showing much higher rates. Unfortunately, again, no personality inventories were applied, but if we regard dysthymics as introverted neurotics (high N, low E), then the results agree well with our view that GSR habituation and spontaneous activity[23] are related to introversion rather than to neuroticism/emotionality. Lader and Wing, too, regard these phenomena "as indicants of the level of general cerebral vigilance (level of arousal)."

Of particular interest in relation to the question of whether such measures as basal conductance are connected with E or N is a

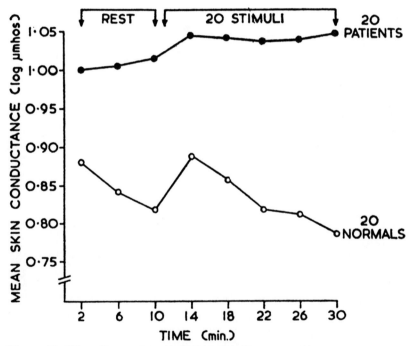

Figure 69. The effects of 20 auditory stimuli on the skin conductance of normals and dysthymics. Reprinted with permission from M. H. Lader and L. Wing: *J. Neurol., Neurosurg. and Psychiat.*, 27:210-218, 1964.

[23]Habituation in this context is regarded as similar to, if not identical with, reactive inhibition. This point will be taken up in a later chapter. Similarly, spontaneous activity may be regarded as a measure of "excitation" or vigilance.

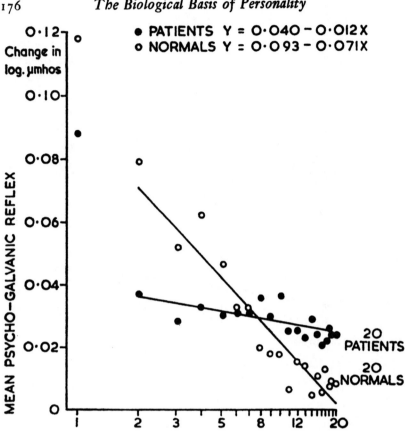

Figure 70. Habituation regression lines (for normals and dysthymics) of the psychogalvanic reflex. Reprinted with permission from M. W. Lader and L. Wing: *J. Neurol., Neurosurg. and Psychiat.*, 27:210-218, 1964.

report by McReynolds, Acker and Brackbill (1966); these authors found no association between conductance and palmar sweating, on the one hand, and subjective indices of anxiety, on the other; this failure was equally apparent when comparison was between subjects, tested on the same occasion, as it was when the same subjects were tested repeatedly and correlations run over time. It seems unfortunate that the authors did not include a measure of E in their study; it would seem from our present point of view that high conductance would have correlated negatively with E. Some indirect evidence for this proposition comes from the recent work of Andreassi (1966) who correlated reaction times in a vigilance task with skin conductance; he showed that as conductance declined, reaction times increased. As we have shown, vigilance in connected (inversely) with E, not with N, and the correlation between conductance and vigilance is therefore likely to indicate a relation with E. Again it is unfortunate that no measures of E were applied in this study, so that our argument must remain indirect and circumstantial.

In all discussions of arousal, the EEG emerges as one of the most widely accepted criteria, and we must enquire about the relationship between EEG, extraversion, and neuroticism. We have already noted, in Chapter II, a tendency for high frequency, low amplitude responses to be characteristic of dysthymic subjects, and for high amplitude, low frequency responses to be characteristic of psychopathic subjects. Does a similar relationship obtain in the normal field? Early studies by Gottlober (1938), Henry and Knott (1941), and Knott (1941) were contradictory, Gottlober finding extraverts to have greater alpha index, while the latter investigators found introverts to have great alpha index. McAdam and Orme (1954) reported a tendency for high frequency activity, low alpha index, and little sign of low frequency activity to go together, but their personality data in relation to these indices were derived from alcholics, and are difficult to evaluate. The work of Mundy-Castle (1955) suggests a relationship between high alpha frequency and "primary function," both as rated and as measured experimentally by Biesheuvel and Pitt (1955); the correlation obtained between ratings and EEG was .46.

None of these studies was satisfactory from the point of view of personality criteria, and in most cases there was also lacking any kind of theoretical rationale. Savage (1964) argued "that the relative differences in inhibition between extraverts and introverts should be measurable in terms of electro-cerebral activity," and put forward the hypothesis "that extraversion resulting from high cortical inhibition will result in significantly higher alpha rhythm amplitude than that recorded from introverts whose cortical inhibition is low." As his measure of personality, Savage used the M.P.I., selecting subjects high and low respectively on extraversion and neuroticism, thus giving four groups. EEG data were collected over twenty-four 10-second periods, with subjects resting quietly with eyes closed. The average amplitude of each alpha frequency recorded over the 240 seconds was calculated for each subject; this score was taken as an index of cortical activity.

Mean scores for extraverts and introverts respectively, together with their S.D.s, were 81.0 ± 14.9 and 28.7 ± 8.55; those or neuroticism were 61.5 ± 16.9 and 50.2 ± 11.08. Analysis of variance disclosed highly significant differences between the extraverted and introverted subjects (p. < .01), but no significant differences between subjects scoring high and low respectively on N. These results support the hypothesis as stated by Savage; we will resume discussion of their theoretical import in a later chapter.[24]

This completes our brief account of experimental studies carried out in an attempt to test the extraversion-inhibition theory; as mentioned earlier, it is by no means complete, and in particular, studies already reviewed in *Dynamics of Anxiety and Hysteria* (Eysenck, 1957) have usually been omitted in favour of later ones. Certain types of study have been omitted because it is not clear what kind of prediction can in fact be made from our hypotheses. In some cases results of specially designed experiments turned out positive, but in the absence of confirmation it seemed better to wait; examples are work on alternation behaviour (Eysenck and Levey, 1965), the constancy effect (Ardis and Fraser, 1957; Howarth, 1963), probability learning (Wallach and Gahm, 1960), verbal fluency (Foulds, 1953; Siegman and Pape, 1965), perceptual "sharpening" (Forrest, 1963), Rorschach responses (Allen et al., 1964; Böcher, 1965), group decisions (Rim, 1964) and persuasiveness (Carment et al., 1965), free association (Dunn et al., 1958), autokinesis (Voth, 1941, 1947; Schwartz and Shagass, 1960); extra-sensory preception (Eysenck, 1967); dark-vision (Granger, 1957) and many more.

[24]Marton and Urban (1966) have quite recently published data on a comparison of 20 extraverted and 20 introverted subjects, using EEG and GSR recordings of habituation responses to weak sound stimuli. They found that habituation occurred more quickly in extraverts (12-15 trials) than in introverts (28-45 trials), and that the average alpha frequencies at rest were lower for extraverts (9.15 c/sec) than for introverts (11.1 c/sec); both differences were significant at a level below $p = .01$. They conclude that "our data confirmed the thesis according to which the 'inhibitory potential' develops faster in persons with traits of extraversion."

In some cases a deduction was disproved only to be followed by evidence that this disproof did not in fact negative the theory. This is an important point, and may be worthy of brief discussion. Any deduction from a theory such as that under discussion requires a minor premise before logical conclusions can be drawn. Consider the writer's prediction that extraverts would show greater bowing effects in serial learning experiments (Eysenck, 1955). Formally this prediction is mediated by two premises. The major one states that extraverts develop inhibitory potential more readily and strongly; the minor one asserts (Lepley, 1934; Hull, 1943) that bowing effects are due to inhibition. Failure to observe the predicted effect may be due to the fact that the major premise is erroneous, or to the fact that the minor premise is erroneous, or to the fact that the "inhibitions" referred to in the two premises are not in fact identical. In an unpublished study, Carpenter failed to find any differences in bowing in the serial learning position effects of extraverts and introverts, and Eysenck (1959) was able to show that certain experimental effects observed in a study specially designed to test the inhibition theory of bowing were incompatible with this theory, which has now been widely given up and replaced by more efficient ones (e.g., Jensen, 1962). In the chains of deduction used in this volume, the minor premises present possibilities of error which should not be overlooked; if they are in fact in error, then disproof of the deduction does not damage the major premise or the theory incorporated in it. Also, studies dealing with this particular deduction automatically lose all interest from the point of view of testing the major theory.

One method of approaching the testing of the hypothesis of a general trait of "inhibition" as characteristic of certain individuals is factor analysis; several attempts have indeed been made to use this method (Becker, 1960; Honigfeld, 1962). These writers conclude from their studies that there is no evidence for a general factor of the kind postulated, but this conclusion is in part at least dependent on the method of rotation of axes ("varimax") employed. The postulated "inhibition" factor would be expected to be a second-order factor, emerging from the intercorrelations of oblique primary factors. However, the use of varimax as the criterion of rotation precludes the emergence of obliqueness between primaries and forces these into an orthogonal pattern. In other words, these studies merely illustrate the well-known fact that orthogonal rotations, superimposed on the data regardless of their intrinsic nature, beg the only question of interest in this connection, i.e., the true relationship among factors of the first order. Some such method of rotation as "promax" (Hendrickson and White, 1964) should have been employed; this allows oblique or orthogonal relations among factors, depending entirely on the intrinsic relations among variables, and not begging the question by a prior decision as to the angular relations to be accepted. No proper study following these lines of rotation would appear to have been carried out so far. An alternative method would be to use the first principal components without rotation. There are several successful factorial studies (Hildebrand, 1958; Eysenck and Claridge, 1962) in the Anglo-American literature, and recently similar studies have begun to appear in the Russian literature (see Gray, 1964).

In this connection it should also be pointed out that among the variables to be controlled must be the sampling of subjects employed. To replicate an experiment conducted with neurotic patients by using sophomores is not to take one's scientific duties very seriously. We have often pointed out the interaction effects of drive, stress, and emotionality with introversion/extraversion; all these variables are changed in a completely uncontrolled fashion when populations so very different from those originally used are employed. Again, considered as parametric studies, such experiments are of course perfectly admissible, and extend our understanding and our ability to quantify our variables, but they do not constitute proper replications; if findings differ, that is not to be construed as disproof of the theory in question or of the study so "replicated." As we have seen, even such aspects of the testing programme as whether the testing was done in the morning or in the afternoon can profoundly alter results, and to imagine that the much more serious changes in procedure, choice of experimental subjects, instructions, etc., would not affect the result is to disregard a very large body of evidence. It would not be necessary to repeat such very obvious home truths were it not that in the past such considerations have been almost universally disregarded. In a number of cases quite extreme departures from the original design have been presented as "replications"; it would be a waste of paper discussing these here in detail.

A related source of error is the use of personality scales other than the M.P.I. or E.P.I.; some authors have used the Hy and Pt scales of the M.M.P.I., for instance, as measures of extraversion and introversion. In a study comparing these and other inventories and tests, the writer (Eysenck, 1960) found the Pt scale to be an excellent measure, not of introversion, but of neuroticism; the Hy scale also had a higher correlation with neuroticism (negative) than with extraversion. (The Cattell extraversion and anxiety scales, however, had loadings quite similar to those of the M.P.I. E and N scales; they might be used with good justification instead of the M.P.I.)

A number of studies have given negative results for reasons which suggest that they are not very relevant to the theory under discussion; a few of these have already been mentioned. Consider the writer's prediction that introverts will condition more readily under conditions of partial reinforcement. Several writers have in fact tested this hypothesis by using 100 per cent reinforcement, with negative results; it is difficult to see why such studies should be regarded as relevant to the theory in question. Others have replicated experiments giving positive results, but with vital changes in procedure which rule them out as valid tests of the theory; in spite of this the writers in question have often given the impression that their results did in fact invalidate the general theory (examples have already been given). It will be clear from our discussion so far that experiments in this field are very sensitive to changes in test parameters, and replications of published studies should duplicate all important parameters if they are to be taken seriously as tests of the theory. Investigations which test changes in performance with changes in test parameters are of course not only desirable but vital for a more quantitative working out of the theory, but they are not to be confused with replications of published studies.

The interaction effects between N and E mentioned in the previous paragraph should always be examined in detail, particularly when direct correlations between N or E and the experimental variable are nonsignificant.

This type of analysis has been designated "zone analysis" by Furneaux (1961) and "moderator variable" analysis by Ghiselli (1963); it may be interesting to discuss briefly the procedures involved. Furneaux (1961) found little correlation between Body Sway Suggestibility, on the one hand, and extraversion/introversion or neuroticism/stability, on the other. Instead of resting content with this finding, he put forward the following hypothesis, which is illustrated in Figure 71. On the basis of the Yerkes-Dodson law, we would expect a curvilinear relation between Drive and Performance on the Body-Sway test. Neuroticism may be regarded as an indirect measure of drive, but we must also bear in mind the differential motivation which is produced in extraverts and introverts by identical stimuli, as demonstrated in the Weisner experiment. As Furneaux points out, "it is entirely con-

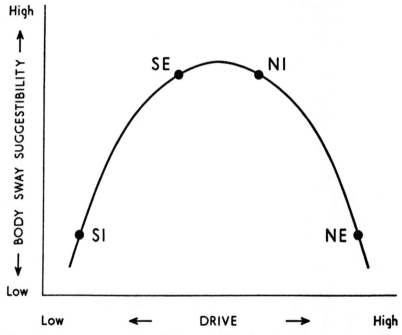

Figure 71. Body-sway suggestibility as a function of drive and personality. Reprinted with permission from H. J. Eysenck: *Bull. Brit. Psychol. Soc.,* *19*:1-28, 1966.

sistent with the known characteristics of the extravert to assert that he has a strong and continuing set to attend to stimuli associated with the activities of other people, and that the situations which lead him to enter states of high drive are predominantly interpersonal in character." This combination of high N and strong drive production in extraverts through the interpersonal relation involved in suggestibility tests would put the neurotic extravert beyond the optimum drive level and thus make him little suggestible. Similarly the stable introvert, being low in drive and not motivated highly by interpersonal stimuli, would be below the optimal drive level. Stable extraverts and neurotic introverts would on the same argument be expected to be intermediate with respect to drive, and consequently also with respect to body sway. These results have indeed been found empirically by Furneaux, and the relations discovered in his original paper have been duplicated since in an unpublished study by Lindahl. Furneaux and Gibson (1961) have also observed similar results in a hypnosis test procedure.

Without wishing to give the impression that these results and hypotheses necessarily represent the truth, and without going into a detailed discussion of certain apparently contrary findings (Hilgard, 1965; Furneaux, 1963; Gibson, 1962), it does seem reasonable to maintain that zone analysis may sometimes be an appropriate technique of analysis when linear correlations with single personality dimensions cannot be found. Even when such correlations are significant, zone analysis may nevertheless give rise to unexpected and important findings, suggesting new and worthwhile relationships and theories.

The notion of zone analysis is based on the hypothesis that various combinations of traits produce different types of behaviour, so that means on tests of behaviour differ in the divergent zones produced by combining two or more traits. The notion of moderator variables (Ghiselli, 1956, 1963; Saunders, 1956) is based on the hypothesis that correlations between variables may be different in different zones similarly created. In the simplest case, there may be only two zones, say high and low scorers in a questionnaire on anxiety; and we may be interested in the correlation between two variables, such as age and risk taking. Kogan and

Wallach (1961) have shown that among subjects who scored low in anxiety, there was a significant (negative) correlation between subjective (felt) age and risk taking, whereas among high-scoring subjects there was no correlation at all. This relationship could of course be translated into a zone analysis, with high and low anxiety and high and low apparent age the two variables making up four zones, and amount of risk taken as the dependent variable. Thus the two types of analysis are only nominally different; mathematically they can be rendered equivalent.

In their book on *Risk Taking*, Kogan and Wallach (1964) have used two personality variables to "moderate" the observed correlations with risk taking measures, namely anxiety and defensiveness. Their results agree well with the arguments and theories put forward in *Crime and Personality* (Eysenck, 1964), and they certainly support the value of zone or "moderator" analysis —without some such device no significant correlations would have been discovered. As Kogan and Wallach state in summary:

> It is evident that the consideration of personality dispositions of test anxiety and defensiveness as moderator variables has rendered clear a psychological picture that otherwise would have been totally ambiguous. Overall sample correlations that were nonsignificant or, although statistically significant, so low as to be of doubtful psychological value have been found to be substantial in one moderator subgroup, negligible in another. In some cases, these overall correlations have been found to be significant in a positive direction in one moderator subgroup, significant in a negative direction in another. Such findings require the conclusion that consideration of potential moderator variables is nothing less than essential in psychological research involving the study of correlations. In most of the authors' present work, the assumption of linearity that has typically been made in previous studies of the overall relationship between two psychological variables simply does not hold. The present authors found that correlation coefficients depicting overall relationships often conceal more psychological truth than they reveal. Time and again, consideration of one or the other of our two moderator variables has considerably clarified the correlational picture in comparison with what the state of affairs seemed to be when neither moderator was considered. And consideration of the joint effect

of both moderator variables operating simultaneously has provided a sizeable further clarification of the correlational picture in comparison with the results obtained by considering the effect of either moderator alone.

One interesting consequence of the adoption of the notion of zone analysis may be that psychologists will recognize the superiority, for certain purposes at least, of the use of *polar coordinates* as compared with Cartesian coordinates, which are almost universally used. Figure 72 illustrates the difference between these two methods, which are of course mathematically exactly convertible into each other. The position of subject A is normally shown in the two-dimensional space generated by the two per-

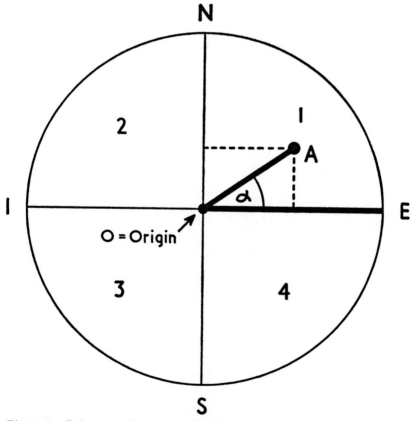

Figure 72. Polar coordinates as referents for personality types. Reprinted with permission from H. J. Eysenck: *Bull. Brit. Psychol. Soc.*, *19*:1-28, 1966.

sonality variables Neuroticism-Stability (N-S) and Extraversion-Introversion (E-I) in terms of the projection of this position on the two dimensions, as shown by the broken lines. This individual would be in zone number one (N;E). Using polar coordinates, we would characterize his position by the angle alpha and the length of the line O-A. Given such a system, we could plot results such as those reported by Furneaux as in Figure 73, where the ordinate shows degree of suggestibility, and the abscissa the angle alpha, from 0° to 360°. The regular wave-form of the suggestibility scores clearly indicates the relationship obtaining in a manner which would not easily be duplicated by Cartesian analysis. Regular use of polar coordinates would probably reveal many complex relationships which now remain undiscovered through failure to use this method of analysis.

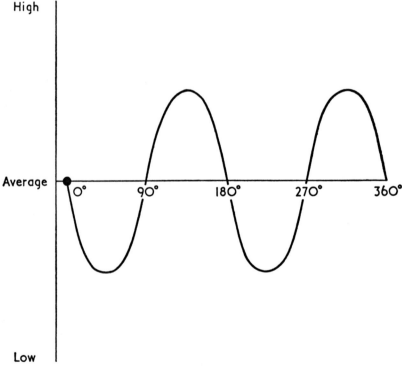

Figure 73. Application of principle of polar coordinates to data shown in Fig. 71. Reprinted with permission from H. J. Eysenck: *Bull. Brit. Psychol. Soc.*, *19*:1-28, 1966.

CHAPTER IV

HEREDITY AND PERSONALITY

THERE HAS BEEN MUCH DISCUSSION among psychologists about the relative influence of environment and heredity on intelligence and personality; unfortunately much of this discussion has been conducted in the absence of a sufficient grasp of modern principles of genetics, particularly biometric genetics (Mather, 1949). As is well known, modern biometrical genetics has developed from the foundations laid by Fisher (1918), who reconciled the views of the early biometricians, such as Weldon, and those of the Mendelians, such as Morgan. "The original discordance seems to have arisen because neither side understood the full implications of Mendel's fundamental separation of determinant and effect, of genotype and phenotype. The biometricians seem to have regarded continuous somatic variation as implying continuous genetic variation, and the Mendelians seem to have considered discontinuous genetic variation as incompatible with anything but obviously discontinuous somatic variation. Indeed, de Vries took continuity of variation in the phenotype as a criterion of nonheritability" (Mather, 1949).

Fisher's main contribution consisted in showing that the familial correlations which were found by the biometricians could be predicted on the hypothesis of multiple genetic factors. As Burt and Howard (1956) have pointed out, "at that time, however, Fisher's methods of handling statistical problems were too new and too technical to attract much attention; and it was for long widely supposed that Pearson's results had conclusively shown the 'utter inapplicability of any Mendelian hypothesis to continuous variation in man.' Thus for the next fifteen years it was generally agreed by both Mendelians and biometricians that whichever hypothesis

187

came nearer to the truth, the hereditary determination of graded traits was quite incompatible with the segregation of discontinuous units postulated by the Mendelian theory. This view still seems to survive in the arguments adduced by many psychological writers. Nevertheless, as the recent advances of genetics have amply shown, on the one point over which the two disputants happen to agree, both, strange to say, were utterly wrong." Figure 74 shows how the normal distribution of phenotypes in an F_2 can result from a segregation in the F_1 mating of two genes of equal and additive effect, each having two degrees of expression but without dominance of the one over the other. A more detailed discussion of the application of biometrical genetics to psychology is given by Broadhurst (1960), and there is a more recent discussion by Jinks (1965).[1]

Most work in psychology relevant to the question of heredity and environment has been concerned with the differences between identical and fraternal twins. The distinction between one-egg and two-egg twins was pointed out by Galton in 1875, and since his time the degree of divergence in form or behaviour between one-egg twins has been supposed to be a satisfactory measure of the effect of differences in the environment, particularly as compared to differences between two-egg twins. The argument stated in its simplest form maintains that all differences between identical twins must be due to environmental influences, but that differences between fraternal twins may be due either to genetic or to

[1]It is rather odd that this dispute should ever have arisen, because Mendel himself did not by any means hold the view later advocated by the self-styled "Mendelians." Having based his theories on studies of *pisus*, Mendel experimented with other plants, e.g., he crossed Phaseolus nanus L, which has white flowers and white seed-coats, with Phaseolus multiflorus W, which has scarlet flowers while the seed-coats are spotted black on a peach-bloom coloured ground. In the almost infertile hybrids of the F_1 generation the flowers showed the most varied shades ranging from scarlet to pale violet, while the colours of the seed-coats also ranged through various shades of brown and black. "Still, even these enigmatic phenomena could probably be explained in accordance with the laws found valid in the case of Pisum if we could assume that the colour of the flowers and the colour of the seed-coat of *Phaseolus multiflorus* is composed of two or of several completely independent colours each of which behaves individually like any other constant character of the plant" (Mendel, 1866, 34-35; see also Iltis, 1966, 156-157). In other words, Mendel himself advocated an hypothesis similar to that of modern biometrical genetics.

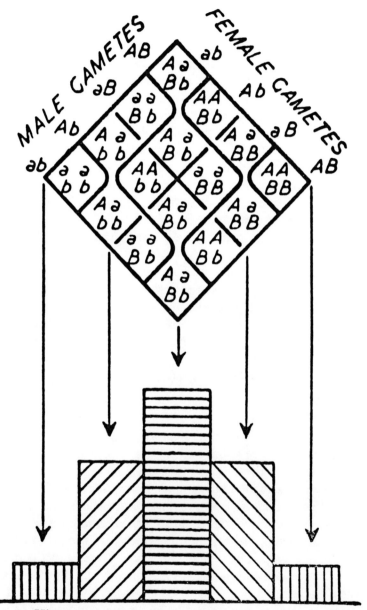

Figure 74. Histogram at bottom illustrates the polygenic theory of heritable variation. It shows the distribution of phenotypes in an F_2 resulting from the segregation in the F_1 mating—shown at the top—of two genes of equal and additive effect, each having two degrees of expression but without dominance of the one over the other. The phenotypic expression is proportional to the number of capital letters, nonheritable variation being neglected. Reprinted with permission from K. Mather, 1949.

environmental differences; if on any particular test of an ability or temperamental trait, identical twins are more alike than fraternal twins, then to that extent the influence of heredity has been demonstrated. Holzinger (in Newman, Freeman, and Holzinger, 1937) has suggested a statistic (h^2) which actually gives an estimate of the proportion of the variance contributed by heredity; this, although it has many obvious weaknesses, has been widely used. May (1957) has succinctly discussed the dependence of h^2 on certain unlikely assumptions.

Newman, Freeman, and Holzinger, like almost all other writers on the subject, assume "that the members of a pair of identical twins are genetically identical." As Darlington (1954) points out, "this assumption can be justified by authority, by axiomatic authority; but it cannot be justified by experimental evidence assisted by the usual processes of inference. Various situations are known in which it is groundless and indeed positively false. The two one-egg twins must differ on genetic grounds; that is to say they must differ internally at the beginning." Such cases may be arranged fairly neatly in three classes, as follows: a) nuclear differences, b) nucleocytoplasmic differences, and c) cytoplasmic differences.

Nuclear Differences

Individuals may be asymmetrical as a result of genetic changes in the chromosomes. Darlington suggests two main kinds: a) gene mutations, such as those which give differences of colour between the two eyes of an individual, and b) chromosome errors at mitosis, such as those which give various mosaic markings and occasional structural asymmetries, either small or large, within individuals. He also suggests a third situation in which two sperms fertilize the halves of one egg. This could also cause asymmetry in one-egg twins whose classification might seem uncertain. "The occurrence of these nuclear causes of discordance is largely overlooked. For example, one-egg twins are said to be always concordant in blood groups, but it would be more correct for an author to say that twins which are not concordant in blood groups are not regarded as one-egg twins."

Nucleocytoplasmic Differences

It is known that there are certain new unadaptive and deleterious genes like those affecting ptosis (Renssen, 1942) and perhaps hip articulation and a pleiotropic form of harelip (Grebe, 1952) which act asymmetrically in development, and, as Darlington points out, "presumably they react asymmetrically with the asymmetrical cytoplasm of the egg. However that may be, such genes are bound to react differently in two one-egg twins; one shows the defect and the other shows it less or not at all. The basis of this difference, although it arises from the action of specific genes, is cytoplasmic."

Cytoplasmic Differences

The division of the ovum into two is itself inherently liable to asymmetry, and it is now clear that two kinds of unlikeness arise from the splitting of one embryo into two. "One of these unlikenesses is due to the cytoplasm which determines the normal asymmetry of development. It appears as a regular mirror imaging. We may call it a primary or cytoplasmic asymmetry, related in this case to the whole genotype. The other is less regular. It is probably due to errors or inequalities of splitting, or to migrations of cells, errors which we may refer to as due to a secondary or *embryological* asymmetry. It includes gross defects of one partner such as those which lead to its death or in less extreme cases to such abnormalities as a local gigantism or asymmetry of one twin as described by Liebenam (1938)." Darlington goes on to point out that differences between one-egg twins are partly like differences between two sides of an individual; they may be due to a reaction, either of an incorrect gene or genotype with a correct asymmetry of the cytoplasm, or of a correct genotype with an incorrect asymmetry of the cytoplasm. "Neither of these types of difference arise between two-egg twins and it is for this reason that two-egg twins are more alike in birth weight than one-egg, or so called identical, twins. In every cytoplasmic reaction, one-egg twins are bound to be, not more but less alike than two-egg twins. And likewise of course in every defect due to errors of splitting." Darlington concludes that "discordances from all three sources no doubt affect only a minority of one-egg twins. But the total effect, I believe, is sufficient to lead to a gross underestimate, as well as to specific misunderstandings, of the force of genetic determination in all twin studies." And in another publication (Darlington, 1963) he writes: "We have to admit that comparisons of one-egg and two-egg twins do not give us the uncontaminated separation of heredity and environment which Galton and his successors have hoped for. The measure they give is an estimate: but it must always be an *underestimate* of the effects of heredity."

With this caution in mind we may now turn to some empirical determinations. The first and still the most widely quoted study is that by Newman, Freeman, and Holzinger (1937), in which one hundred pairs of twins, fifty identical and fifty fraternal, were compared with respect to a number of physical measurements and mental and educational tests. Their conclusion was that "the physical characteristics are least affected by the environment, that intelligence is affected more; educational achievement still more; and personality or temperament, if our tests can be relied upon, the most. This finding is significant, regardless of the absolute amount of the environmental influence." This conclusion has been widely quoted, but unfortunately it rests on a very uncertain foundation as far as personality or temperament is concerned. There are two main criticisms. In the first place, the measures used would not now be regarded as either reliable or valid. They included the Woodworth-Mathews Personality Inventory, the Kent-Rosanoff Scale, the Pressey Cross-Out Test, and the Downey Will/Temperament Test. It is doubtful whether any psychologist would nowadays wish to make very strong claims for these measures; even if they could be regarded as reliable and valid, the question would still have to be asked: valid for what? The Woodworth-Mathews Inventory is the only one for which detailed statistics are presented, and we discover that for identical twins the intraclass correlation is .562, for fraternal twins it is .371, and for identical twins brought up in separation it is .583. If we regard, as the original authors certainly did, this questionnaire as an inventory of neurotic tendency, then we would here seem to have some mild indication of the importance of heredity, seeing that identical twins are distinctly superior in point of intraclass correlation to fraternals. Moreover, and this is a particularly interesting feature of this table, identical twins brought up in separation are more alike than are identical twins brought up together; this is the only test used, including physical measurements, where this is true. The authors comment that "the Woodworth-Mathews Test appears to show no very definite trend in correlations, possibly because of the nature of the trait and also because of the unreliability of the measure." It is not quite clear to the present writer why there is this denial of a definite trend; it seems fairly clear that identical twins, whether brought up in separation or together, are more alike than are fraternal twins, and as we shall see, later modern work has amply justified such a conclusion.

We must now turn to our second criticism, which has curiously enough not to our knowledge been made before. The personality tests used by Newman, Freeman, and Holzinger were essentially tests for adults; the Woodworth-Mathews Inventory for instance was constructed specifically for selection purposes in the army and in hospitals. It is quite inadmissible to use tests of this kind on children, and as is made clear on page 106 of the twin study, the average age of the whole group of identical and fraternal twins is only about thirteen years. No details are given, but it is clear that there must have been children as young as eight or even younger in this group, and it is doubtful whether a large proportion of the children were in a position to understand the terms used in the tests or to give meaningful replies to them. Our own work in questionnaire construction (S.B.G. Eysenck, 1965) has clearly shown the difficulties attending the construction of personality inventories for children, and the difficulties which children may encounter in answering questions even when these are specifically constructed for them. Taking together these two criticisms of the Newman, Freeman, and Holzinger study, it is perhaps justifiable to say that the data do not support their conclusions. Identical twins whether brought up together or in separation are clearly more alike than are fraternal twins, thus suggesting the importance of heredity in contributing to the temperamental differences studied; the poor reliability and inappropriate nature of the test used suggest that the differences found would have been larger and possibly much larger had more suitable tests been employed. We shall indeed find in our examination of the evidence that later studies using more appropriate methods of examination have resulted in much better discrimination between identical and fraternal twins. It must of course be remembered that the Newman, Freeman, and Holzinger study was a pioneering venture and that at the time few if any personality tests existed, particularly as far as children were concerned. More to blame perhaps are later writers who have cited their work as support for the proposition that heredity is a relatively unimportant factor in the causation of individual differences in temperament and personality, without a closer look at the details of the evidence offered.

Carter's early work (1933) gave similar results to that of Newman, Freeman, and Holzinger; he used Bernreuter's Personality Inventory on a group including high school students as well as more mature subjects. Results for fifty-five pairs of identical twins and forty-three pairs of like-sex twins are available for the four traits (allegedly) measured by the Bernreuter test: neurotic tendency, introversion, self-sufficiency, and dominance. The intraclass correlations for identical and fraternal twins are, respectively: .63 and .32 for neuroticism; .50 and .40 for introversion; .44 and −.14 for self-sufficiency; and .71 and .34 for dominance. The interpretation of these results must be subject to the proviso that the scales are by no means independent, as indeed emerges quite clearly from a table of intercorrelations given by Carter himself. For various reasons it seems that Bernreuter's arbitrary and subjective naming of his scores is misleading; what he has called "self-sufficiency" is probably nearest to our concept of introversion, with neurotic tendency, introversion (so called), and lack of dominance all forming part of our conception of neuroticism. Whether this be the correct interpretation or not, Carter's results certainly support the view that heredity plays some part in the genesis of the individual differences measured by the four scales of the Bernreuter Personality Inventory.

Gottesman (1963) studied thirty-four pairs each of identical and fraternal same-sex adolescent twins, using the Minnesota Multiphasic Personality Inventory and Cattell's Highschool Personality Questionnaire. He summarised his results as follows: "Within the limits of the assumptions, the attempt at quantification of the proportion of scale variance accounted for by heredity gave positive results for six of the HSPQ factors. Factors E, Submissiveness versus Dominance; H, Shy, Sensitive versus Adventurous; and J, Liking Group Action versus Fastidiously Individualistic, showed appreciable variance accounted for by heredity but with environment predominating. Factors F, Q$_2$, and O, Confident Adequacy versus Guilt Proneness, showed about equal contributions of heredity and environment. The same kind of analysis of the MMPI gave positive results for five of the ten scales. Scales 7 (Psychasthenia) and 8 (Schizophrenia) showed appreciable variance accounted for by heredity but with environment predominating. Scales 2 (Depression) and 4 (Psychopathic Deviate) showed about equal contributions of heredity and environment. Scale O (Social Introversion) showed a predominance of variance ($H = .71$) accounted for by heredity. The value H for the Otis IQ in this study was .62." Table IV shows the results in some detail.

TABLE IV

MINNESOTA STUDY MMPI SCALE HERITABILITY INDICES
FOR TOTAL GROUP, FEMALES AND MALES

Scale	Total Group		Females		Males	
	H	F[a]	H	F[a]	H	F[a]
1 Hypochondriasis	.16	1.19	.25	1.33	.01	1.01
2 Depression	.45	1.81	.22	1.28	.65	2.83
3 Hysteria	.00	.86	.00	.56	.43	1.74
4 Psychopathic Deviate	.50	2.01	.37	1.60	.77	4.35
5 Masculinity-Femininity	.15	1.18	.00	.99	.45	1.83
6 Paranoia	.05	1.05	.00	.70	.52	2.09
7 Psychasthenia	.37	1.58	.47	1.89	.24	1.31
8 Schizophrenia	.42	1.71	.36	1.56	.50	2.00
9 Hypomania	.24	1.32	.33	1.50	.00	.81
0 Social Introversion	.71	3.42	.60	2.49	.84	6.14

[a]The three values of F required for significance at the .05 level are 1.78, 2.04, and 2.72 for the total group, the females, and males. Quoted with permission from I. I. Gottesman, 1965.

In a second study Gottesman (1965) reports on results from another twin experiment using eighty-two pairs of MZ twins and sixty-eight pairs of DZ twins. The detailed figures of a preliminary analysis are given in Table V. It will be seen in both

TABLE V

HARVARD TWIN STUDY MMPI SCALE HERITABILITY INDICES
FOR TOTAL GROUP, FEMALES, AND MALES

Scale	Total Group		Females		Males	
	H	F[a]	H	F[a]	H	F[a]
1 Hypochondriasis	.01	1.01	.00	.89	.09	1.10
2 Depression	.45	1.82	.48	1.91	.37	1.58
3 Hysteria	.30	1.43	.44	1.79	.11	1.12
4 Psychopathic Deviate	.39	1.63	.46	1.47	.46	1.84
5 Masculinity-Femininity	.29	1.41	.30	1.43	.29	1.42
6 Paranoia	.38	1.61	.40	1.67	.40	1.67
7 Psychasthenia	.31	1.46	.60	2.53	.00	.99
8 Schizophrenia	.33	1.49	.37	1.58	.29	1.41
9 Hypomania	.13	1.15	.19	1.23	.04	1.04
0 Social Introversion	.33	1.49	.35	1.53	.29	1.40

[a]The three values of F required for significance at the .05 level are 1.47, 1.66, and 1.78 (preliminary analysis). Quoted with permission from I. I. Gottesman, 1965.

Tables IV and V that the highest heritability values relate to extraversion-introversion variables (social introversion, psychopathic deviate, psychasthenia, and to a lesser degree hysteria). The psychotic scales (schizophrenia and depression) also reach satisfactory levels, but in this book we are not concerned with psychotic deviations. It is unfortunate that Gottesman used the MMPI scales as they stood; it is well known that these scales are far from univocal (Eysenck, 1960). A factor-analytic study might have revealed much more clear-cut results by relating heritability to more meaningful dimensions of personality (Eysenck and Eysenck, 1963). Even as they stand, however, the figures are of some interest.

Another interesting recent study is by Wilde (1964), who administered a personality questionnaire to eighty-eight monozygotic and forty-two dyzygotic twin pairs. He obtained scores for the following variables: (a) neurotic instability or neuroticism (N); (b) neurotic instability as manifested by the presence of functional bodily complaints (NS); (c) extraversion score (E); (d) lie score (L); (e) masculinity/femininity scale (MF). Wilde divided his twin pairs into those who had been living separately for five years or more and those who had been living in the same home or who had been separated for less than five years. His results are reproduced in Table VI. It will be seen that as far as neuroticism is concerned we again find little in the way of difference between

TABLE VI

INTRAPAIRCORRELATIONS OF 88 MZ AND 42 DZ TWIN PAIRS*

	N	NS	E	T	MF**
1 MZ-cohab. $n = 50$	0.55	0.46	0.58	0.48	0.45
2 MZ-separ. $n = 38$	0.52	0.75	0.19	0.46	0.44
3 MZ-all $n = 88$	0.53	0.67	0.37	0.46	0.44
4 DZ-cohab. $n = 21$	−0.14	−0.05	0.19	0.33	−0.34
5 DZ-separ. $n = 21$	0.28	0.64	0.36	0.49	0.30
6 DZ-all $n = 42$	0.11	0.34	0.35	0.54	0.02

*Double underlining refers to a significance of 01; single underlining refers to a significance of 05; assuming normality of distributions. Quoted with permission from G. Wilde, 1964.

monozygotic twins brought up together or brought up in separation, but a great difference between monozygotic twins and dyzygotic twins. Findings for the NS score, i.e., neurotic instability as shown by functional bodily complaints, show the same pattern, but here we find that both monozygotic and dyzygotic twins brought up in separation have much greater intraclass correlations than do twins brought up together. The pattern for extraversion is rather curious. Monozygotic and dyzygotic twins brought up together show the usual greater intraclass correlation among the monozygotic twins as compared to the dyzygotic twins. When we turn, however, to twins brought up in separation, we find that dyzygotic twins show greater intraclass correlations. The L score (lie score) shows no evidence of hereditary determination, but the masculinity/femininity scale does so very clearly. We may perhaps summarise Wilde's results by saying that except for the curious finding relation to extraversion scores in twins brought up in separation, the results are very similar to those discussed previously.

Partanen, Bruun and Markkanen (1966) studied 902 male twins of twenty-eight to thirty-seven years of age from all over Finland; among the instruments used by them was a set of questionnaires covering sociability, need of achievement, neuroticism and agressiveness; of these unfortunately only one (sociability) would appear to be sufficiently reliable and valid to give worthwhile data; the others are too short, arbitrarily selected and unvalidated to an extent which makes it impossible to draw any serious conclusions from them. Sociability "shows evidence of the presence of hereditary influences"; a canonical variate abstracted from the questionnaire and representing largely this variable, showed an index of heritability of .47. This canonical variate may be regarded as an approximation to extraversion, which thus again shows itself to be determined to a marked extent by hereditary influences.

Of particular interest and importance is a recent monograph by Shields (1962) in which he used a self-rating questionnaire devised by the writer which is very similar to the M.P.I., sharing a number of items in common with it; this questionnaire provides scores for extraversion and neuroticism. Shields applied it and a test of intelligence to a collection of pairs of twins who had been separated from one another in childhood; he also had a control group of twins who had been brought up together. There were forty-four separated MZ, forty-four nonseparated MZ control pairs, and thirty-two pairs of DZ twins of which eleven had been brought up apart. His findings with the questionnaire are given in Table VII. It will be seen that identical twins are much more alike than fraternal twins, regardless of whether they are brought up together or in separation; it will also be seen that in each case the twins brought up separately are more alike than twins brought up together. These results are therefore in good accord with those originally reported by Newman, Freeman, and Holzinger as well as with those of later writers. They are rather

TABLE VII

INTRA-CLASS CORRELATION COEFFICIENTS

	C	S	DZ
Height	+0.94	+0.82	+0.44
Weight	+0.81	+0.37	+0.56
Dominoes	+0.71	+0.76	−0.05
Mill Hill	+0.74	+0.74	+0.38
Combined Intelligence	+0.76	+0.77	+0.51
Extraversion	+0.42	+0.61	−0.17
Neuroticism	+0.38	+0.53	+0.11

Intra-class correlation coefficients for MZ twins brought up together (C), MZ twins brought up apart (S), and DZ twins brought up together (DZ). Quoted with permission from J. Shields, 1962 (Oxford University Press).

more clear-cut perhaps, due to two possible causes: (a) the subjects of the experiment were adults rather than children, and consequently the questionnaires applied to them much more readily than they would apply to children; and (b) the questionnaires used had been elaborated for many years on the basis of factor analytic studies of personality and were consequently perhaps more reliable and valid than those used earlier. It is of some interest that in the above table the fraternal twins have a negative intraclass correlation for extraversion, very much as in the study by Eysenck (1956a) cited below. Again this intercorrelation is not significantly different from zero, but the coincidence is certainly striking, although the writer cannot present any reasonable hypothesis which would account for such a negative correlation.

Before turning to studies using objective performance tests, we must note one more twin study employing personality inventories. Gottesman (1965) has tested school children from grades nine through twelve with the Gough California Psychological Inventory; it would seem likely that the results would be attenuated through the use of an adult-centered inventory with school children, but in spite of this flaw the data are well worth reporting. There were seventy-nine pairs of MZ twins and sixty-eight pairs of DZ twins. Heritability was established by the formula;

$$H' = \frac{\text{DZ within-pair Variance} - \text{MZ within-pair Variance}}{\text{DZ within-pair Variance}}$$

Relying on previous factor analyses of the scales which make up this inventory, Gottesman reported results in two clusters. One of these, labelled "person orientation" or extraversion-introversion, is made up of scales relating to sociability, self-acceptance, social presence, and dominance; the other, labelled value orientation or dependable-undependable, bears some superficial resemblance to neuroticism but cannot be identified with confidence in the absence of direct correlational evidence linking the C.P.I. scales with the M.P.I. Table VIII shows the H' values of these scales, as well as the $F = \frac{V\ DZ}{V\ MZ}$ values and significance levels. On the whole the data agree with those already examined in providing evidence for the importance of genetic factors; out of eighteen traits measured

TABLE VIII

Factor	C.P.I. Scale	H'	F
	Sociability	.49	1.97**
Extraversion-	Self-acceptance	.46	1.85**
Introversion	Social presence	.35	1.55*
	Dominance	.49	1.95**
	Responsibility	.26	1.35
	Socialization	.32	1.48*
Dependable-	Self-control	.27	1.38
Undependable	Tolerance	.27	1.37
	Good impression	.38	1.60*
	Communality	.19	1.23

Heritability indices of C.P.I. Scales constituting two higher-order factors. Quoted with permission from I. I. Gottesman, 1965.

by the inventory, seven had one-third or more of the within-family variance significantly associated with genetic factors, and a further five traits had H' values greater than 25 per cent. When the fact is borne in mind that the inventory used is not entirely appropriate to the population, which in addition was nonhomogeneous in age, these values must be regarded as surprisingly high.

Eysenck and Prell (1951) have reported another twin study purporting to assess the contribution of heredity to individual differences in this trait; they made two new contributions. In the first place, they argued that objective tests of behaviour are superior to personality questionnaires, particularly when used on children, and are in any case less liable to faking. In the second place, they argued that conceptions such as neuroticism are essentially based on the notion of intercorrelated traits and measurements, and that twin studies carried out on single measures confound the issue by mixing up variance due to the trait under investigation and specific variance relative to the test in question. They suggest, therefore, that a whole battery of tests should be given and factor analysed and that a score based on a combination of tests having the highest saturations with the factor in question should be used. In addition they suggest that these factor scores should be validated against some form of external control; in their own work they have done so by comparing an experimental group of children under treatment at a child guidance clinic with normal children in school, demonstrating significant differences between

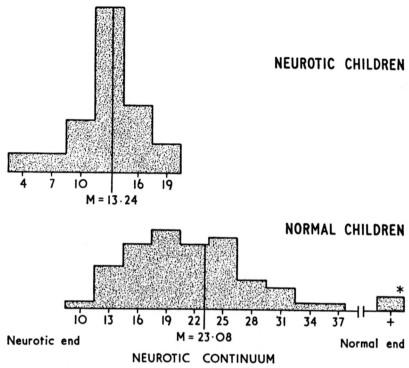

NEUROTIC CHILDREN

4 7 10   16 19
M = 13·24

NORMAL CHILDREN

*

10   13   16   19   22 │ 25   28   31   34   37   +
Neurotic end   M = 23·08   Normal end
NEUROTIC CONTINUUM

Figure 75. Factor scores on "neuroticism," as measured by objective tests, of groups of normal and neurotic children. The asterisk indicates that some normal children were too far removed from the mean in the normal direction to fit on the diagram. Reprinted in slightly changed form from H. J. Eysenck and D. Prell: *J. Clin. Psychol.*, 8:202-204, 1952.

the two groups of children (Eysenck and Prell, 1952). The results of this comparison are shown in Figure 75.

Using this approach, Eysenck and Prell found that the factor score derived from all the tests gave an intraclass correlation of .851 for identical twins and of .217 for fraternal twins; this factor score showed a greater difference between identical and fraternal twins than any single constituent test, thus suggesting that it was indeed a general factor of neuroticism which was inherited rather than specific variance for any single test. The Holzinger h^2 coefficient showed a hereditary determination of .810 if we are willing to assume that this coefficient can indeed be used to measure hereditary determination in this manner.

In another similar study, Eysenck (1956a) has reported results on a battery of tests of intelligence, extraversion, and autonomic activity. Again intraclass correlations for identical and fraternal twins were calculated for three factors corresponding to these concepts rather than individual tests. For extraversion the correlation for identical twins was .50, for fraternal ones -.33; for the autonomic factor the two correlations were respectively .93 and .72. For intelligence the values were .82 and .38. Holzinger's h^2 statistic was calculated for all three factors, giving very similar results in the neighbourhood of .7 for all three. The appearance of a negative intraclass correlation for the fraternal twins is unusual, and Eysenck concluded that it seems "likely that this value represents a chance deviation from a true correlation of zero, or of some slight positive value, an assumption strengthened by the fact that a correlation of the observed size is not statistically significant. Under the circumstances, however, we cannot regard the h^2 statistic derived for the factor of extraversion as having very much meaning . . . much more reliance fortunately can be placed on the significance of the differences between identical and fraternal twins for this factor which . . . is fully significant."

The results of the Eysenck studies give values indicating a greater influence of hereditary causes than would be true of the other studies quoted so far. Apart from the possibility of chance deviations, it may be suggested that the following causes have possibly been operative: (a) behavioural tests are more likely than questionnaires to reveal deep-seated constitutional features of the personality; (b) factor scores are more reliable and valid than single tests; (c) the measures selected have been chosen on the basis of a theory of personality which has perhaps more experimental and theoretical backing than that which gave rise to the measures used by the earlier workers. It is possible that any or all of these causes may have been operative, and it must be left to future investigation to discover to what extent these hypotheses can be upheld.

One frequently made criticism of twin studies may with advantage be taken up at this point. Jones (1955), Smith (1965), and Scarr (1964) have shown that MZ co-twins are more similar in the treatment they receive from their parents than are DZ co-twins, and it seems fairly well established that the home environment of MZ twins is in general more similar as far as the two children are concerned than is the home environment of DZ twins. Such findings have sometimes been interpreted as throwing doubt on the results of twin work, because it is alleged that the excess MZ intraclass correlation so frequently found may be due to more similar environmental treatment of MZ twins rather than to hereditary causes. Such criticism of course fails to touch such studies as those of Shields, which made use of twins brought up in separation; but it may be considered quite cogent in relation to the majority of other studies quoted so far or to be mentioned later.

Scarr (1966) has pointed out that the facts are not in dispute, but that their interpretation is by no means obvious. When parents are correct about their twins' zygocity, two important factors are confounded: (a) the greater genetic differences of DZ co-twins, with accompanying physical, intellectual, and behavioural differences; and (b) the greater differences of parental treatment of DZ pairs, which might create additional intrapair dissimilarities. "If parents are simply reacting to the existing differences between their DZ twins' behavior, then no bias is introduced into twin studies. But, if they effectively train differences, then these environmentally determined differences would bias the comparisons of intraclass correlations in favour of genetic hypotheses, by reducing the possible similarities of DZ co-twins. By the same token, the parents of MZ twins who know their twins are identical may react to existing similarities or seek to train greater similarities than would otherwise exist. When parents are correct about their twins' zygocity, it is impossible to distinguish between parental behavior that is a reaction to the phenotypic behavior of their twins and parental treatment that seeks to train greater differences or similarities."

Scarr goes on to point out that fortunately not all parents are correct about their twins' zygocity and that these parents offer a critical test of environmental bias in twin studies. "By examining the cases of parents who are *wrong* about their twins' zygocity, it is possible to separate parental reactions to similarities and differences based on *genetic relatedness* from parental behaviors which arise from their *belief* that their twins should or should not be similar." She found that in fact something like 20 per cent of twins in a group of 164 twin pairs were misclassified by their mothers; twelve MZ pairs and twenty-one DZ pairs were misclassified. Using various rating scales, check lists, and other devices, she came to the conclusion that "differences in the parental treatment that twins receive are much more a function of the degree of their genetic relatedness than of parental beliefs about 'identicalness' and 'fraternalness' . . . The comparisons of parental behavior for correctly and incorrectly classified pairs suggest that environmental determinants of similarities and differences between MZ and DZ co-twins are not as potent as the critics charge." The number of twin pairs about whom mothers were mistaken is of course not very large, and the study should be repeated with larger numbers, but the direction of the results is quite definitely contrary to that expected from the point of view of the environmentalistic hypothesis, and the data thus support the results from studies carried out on MZ twins brought up in isolation from each other. If this criticism is to be taken seriously, then it will have to be supported by stronger evidence than seems at hand at the moment.[2]

A somewhat different approach to the problem of genetic causes of individual differences in personality has been that of studying the concordance rate of known neurotics and criminals. Here in a sense we are confounding our two personality dimensions, in that criminals may be supposed to be emotional and extraverted, whereas neurotics may be supposed to be high on emotionality as well as introverted. Nevertheless, the prediction would follow from any theory of genetic determination that criminals and neurotics should both have concordant twins in greater pro-

[2]Scarr (1965) has also reported an empirical study of the inheritance of sociability which is relevant to our general discussion, but which arrived too late for proper inclusion. Twenty-eight pairs of DZ twins and twenty-four pairs of MZ twins were studied with the Gough Adjective Check List and the Fels Child Behavior Scales, and other rating scales created for the study. Intraclass correlations were reported for the following variables; in each case the correlations given refer to the MZ group, then the DZ group. Friendliness: .83; .56 (H' = .78). Social apprehension: .88; .28 (H' = .83). Likeableness: .93; .82 (H' = .61). Affiliation: .83; .56 (H' = .61). These values all indicate considerable heritability for the traits rated.

TABLE IX

CONCORDANCE OF IDENTICAL AND FRATERNAL TWINS
RESPECTIVELY FOR VARIOUS TYPES OF CRIMINAL,
ANTISOCIAL, AND ASOCIAL BEHAVIOUR

	Number of Twin Pairs	Identical	Fraternal	Proportion Concordant Identical	Fraternal
Adult Crime	225	107	118	71	34
Juvenile Delinquency	67	42	25	85	75
Childhood Behaviour Disorder	107	47	60	87	43
Homosexuality	63	37	26	100	12
Alcoholism	82	26	56	65	30

From H. J. Eysenck, 1964.

portion for identical as compared to fraternal twins. Table IX is taken from Eysenck (1964a), who has given a discussion of the literature as far as criminal, antisocial, and asocial behaviour are concerned; and it will be seen that identical twins show concordance in roughly twice as many cases as do fraternal twins. Much the same is true in relation to neurotic complaints and emotional disorders, as can be seen from a table given by Shields and Slater (1960, p. 327).

A study by Shields (1954) is very relevant here. Working with thirty-six identical and twenty fraternal twins aged between twelve and fifteen years, he evaluated concordance for psychiatric maladjustment both quantitatively and qualitatively. Along both lines he found much higher concordance rates among the identical twins, values over twice as high being found among them as compared with those of the fraternal twins. He also made a check on the degree of closeness of social relationship, finding that as expected identical twins were much closer to each other socially. This degree of closeness, however, was not related to degree of concordance, thus disproving an hypothesis frequently voiced to discount the value of twin studies, *viz.* that identical twins, being closer to each other, are growing up in an environment which is in fact more alike than that provided for fraternal twins who are less close. This hypothesis cannot account for Shields's data, and of course it cannot account for the finding already mentioned, that identical twins brought up apart are if anything more alike than are identical twins brought up together.

In a very recent study Slater and Shields (unpublished) have compared monozygotic and dyzygotic twins for concordance on a number of ratings derived from their case histories; they attempted to show that concordance differences became greater the more specific the diagnosis. Table X shows the results of this work; in the first line we have the simple notation of psychiatric abnormality, leading to greater and greater specificity until at the end we arrive at a quite specific diagnosis. It will be seen that the ratio of concordance rates for monozygotic and dyzygotic twins increases from the first to the last line. However we may interpret this change in ratios, there is no doubt that the results as a whole support the notion that monozygotic twins show greater concordance for neurosis than do dyzygotic twins, roughly to the same

TABLE X

NUMBER AND PERCENTAGE OF PAIRS ALIKE IN INDEPENDENT
PSYCHIATRIC DIAGNOSIS, AND MZ:DZ RATIO, ACCORDING
TO SPECIFICITY OF DIAGNOSIS*

	MZ	DZ	MZ:DZ Ratio
Number of Pairs	80	112	
Diagnostic Resemblance			
Any Coded Psychiatric Abnormality in Co-twin	40 (50.0%)	33 (29.46%)	1.7
Both Twins Neurosis or Personality Disorder (310-326) *or* Both Psychiatric Disorder Outside 310-326	30 (37.5%)	16 (14.3%)	2.6
Both Twins Psychotic (30−), Neurotic (31−) or Personality Disorder (32−)	25 (31.3%)	10 (8.9%)	3.5
Both Twins Same Diagnostic Code (whole number)	23 (28.8%)	4 (3.6%)	8.1
Both Twins Same Diagnostic Code (smallest subdivision used)	20 (25.0%)	3 (2.7%)	9.3

Concordance of DZ and MZ twins for neurotic disorders, grouped according to different degrees of generality and specificity of diagnosis. Quoted with permission from J. Shields and E. Slater, 1966, and personal communication.

*The twins studied are a consecutive series of 192 pairs in which the index case was diagnosed at the Maudsley Hospital (IP or OP) as having a nonpsychotic, nonorganic psychiatric disorder. The diagnoses used in the table are based on follow-up information. They were all made by Dr. Slater, who in making them was deprived of information about the zygosity of the pair and the psychiatric history of the co-twin. They were coded according to the International Classification of Diseases (psychiatric codes 320-326).

or an even greater degree than do criminals and antisocial and psychopathic people.

Intraclass correlation comparisons between groups of identical and fraternal twins furnish us with one method of assessing the importance of hereditary influences, and differential concordance rates furnish us with another. A third method relies on the assessment of intrafamilial resemblances (Burt and Howard, 1957; Cattell, 1953, 1960, 1961, 1963). Mathematically these methods are rather more complex than the simple twin methods discussed so far, although these too have their difficulties which are not resolved by having recourse to Holzinger's h^2 statistic. This is not the place to describe in detail the many complexities involved, and the reader is referred to Cattel's (1963) paper on the subject. Cattell, Blewitt, and Beloff (1955) and Cattell, Stice, and Kristy (1957) have reported a number of investigations using the Cattell design. Unfortunately the results are not at all easy to summarise and in any case suffer from one great disadvantage. Cattell and his colleagues have throughout used factor scores on a large number of primary factors, the very existence of which is still rather doubtful (Eysenck and Eysenck, 1967). As valuable as Cattell's theoretical analysis has certainly been in this field, it is doubtful whether we can follow him in any of his conclusions derived from factors so precariously based.

More recently Lienert and Reisse (1961) have used the writer's Maudsley Medical Questionnaire, a measure of neuroticism, on 721 members of 200 German families; the relations considered were those between father, mother, and children above fourteen years of age. Statistical methods used were those advocated by Burt and Howard (1956). It was found that the correlation between parents was 0.17, that between father and child 0.13, and that between mother and child 0.31. Calculation from these figures suggests that heredity contributed something like 50 per cent to individual differences in relation to MMQ test scores. This estimate is of course very much influenced by assumptions regarding incomplete dominance. If we choose to exclude the possibility of dominance in the inheritance of neuroticism, the proportion contributed by heredity would fall to 37 per cent, whereas an assumption of complete dominance would raise it to 75 per cent. In the absence of empirical data no rational choice can be made, although it seems unlikely on *a priori* grounds that either of these extreme assumptions could be justified. The values given by Lienert and Reisse are similar to those found by other authors such as Hoffeditz (1934), Crook and Thomas (1934), Sward and Friedman (1935), and Crook (1937). A good review of all this work is given by Fuller and Thompson (1960).

More recently Coppen, Cowie, and Slater (1965) have extended work on familial aspects of personality to the relatives of neurotic patients; they used the Maudsley Personality Inventory in their studies. Assortative mating was found for neuroticism but not for extraversion, and significant correlation coefficients were found between various groups of relatives for both N and E. Contrary to expectation, mean neuroticism scores in different classes of relatives were not found to be raised when compared with the general population. Again contrary to what had been expected, correlation coefficients within classes of relatives were generally low. Omitting spouses, correlation coefficients in ungrouped relationships were significantly positive only in the families of the male patients, and in them solely for the relationship between the mother and her children and between the patient and his male siblings. All these findings were thought by the authors to be incapable of explanation along genetical lines. It is possible, and the literature on the M.P.I. (Eysenck and Eysenck, 1967) supports this, that the scores of neurotic patients are raised over their average level at the time that they are under treatment, and that the proper scores to have taken would have been those recorded after treatment had been completed. Even if this suggestion should not be acceptable, it would seem prudent to have available scores on patients both during and after treatment so that comparative studies could be undertaken. Questionnaire scores are obviously phenotypic and not genotypic measures, and care must be taken in dealing with them to rule out unusual and exceptionally strong environmental influences if a genetic analysis is to be made.

One strong reason for believing that the study just discussed may lead to erroneous conclusions lies in the fact that other well-controlled studies have given rather different results. Brown (1942) has published an important review of the incidence of neurosis

TABLE XI

	Anxiety Neurotics		Hysterics		Obsessionals	
	Parents	*Sibs*	*Parents*	*Sibs*	*Parents*	*Sibs*
Anxiety Neurotics	21.4	12.3	1.6	2.2	0.0	0.9
Hysterics	9.5	4.6	19.0	6.2	0.0	0.0
Obsessionals	0.0	5.4	0.0	0.0	7.5	7.1

Intra-familial concordance for three different types of neurosis. Quoted with permission from F. W. Brown, 1942.

among parents and sibs of three groups of neurotic patients diagnosed as anxiety neurotics, hysterics, and obsessionals. His results are shown in Table XI; these figures should be seen against a normal expectancy rate of about 2 per cent (Fremming, 1947). It seems clear that close relatives of neurotics are themselves neurotic more frequently than chance would allow, and it also appears that the form of neurosis manifested is rather closely related to that shown by the proband, indicating a certain degree of genetic specificity. Fuller and Thompson (1960) comment that "since from these data no correlation can be made between expectancy rate and closeness of kinship, and since there is no control for environment, the results cannot be regarded as very decisive evidence for the operation of genetic factors. At least, however, they are compatible with the hypothesis that neuroses are heritable." To this it might perhaps be added that the figures almost certainly underestimate to a considerable extent the true relationship; this follows from the well-known low reliability of psychiatric diagnoses (Eysenck, 1960e). Any appropriate correction for attenuation would probably more than double the published degree of concordance and decrease the overlap between categories. A combination of the approaches through questionnaire and through psychiatric diagnosis would seem to give a better chance of obtaining convincing data than does either approach by itself.

There is no doubt that the study of familial resemblances has a great future, as far as an understanding of genetic processes in personality is concerned. However, at the moment preference for this kind of study as opposed to twin studies seems to be somewhat premature and unsupported by evidence. The difficulties of obtaining samples of all the required degrees of relationships present at the moment considerable sampling difficulties which also extend of course to the statistical treatment. Furthermore, Cattell's statistics are not directly related to genetic concepts, and until such a relationship is established it must remain doubtful to what extent conclusions from such calculations are acceptable. On the whole, estimates from familial studies seem to give lower values for hereditary influence than do results from twin studies; why this should be so is not clear at the moment. In part it may be due to the direct estimation of heredity-environment interaction effects, which can be estimated in Cattell's method of calculation but which cannot at the moment be properly calculated in the twin study type of design.

Furthermore, it seems on statistical grounds that Holzinger's h^2 statistic overestimates the influence of heredity. On the other side, as we have already seen, there is a built-in tendency to underestimate the contribution of heredity in twin studies because of the underlying assumption that the heredity of identical twins is indeed identical. Taking all these considerations into account, it would seem to the writer that the evidence suggests fairly strongly that something like 50 per cent of individual differences in neuroticism and extraversion, as measured by current inventory tests, is accountable for in terms of hereditary influences. For types of tests other than questionnaires, where the assumption may be made that phenotypic behaviour is more closely related to genotypic determination, this proportion may go up to 75 per cent.[3]

Statements such as these have of course fairly wide margins of error, as we have already pointed out. They are also, moreover, frequently misunderstood. Psychiatrists and psychologists often quote individual case histories where some outstandingly traumatic event has clearly had disastrous consequences for the mental health of a patient, and claim that an estimate of environmental influences which reduces these to a contribution of 50 per cent or 25 per cent is patently absurd. Such criticisms are of course not relevant to statements of averages; what is said is that in a particular cultural group, such as the British or the American, *overall* differences in neuroticism or extraversion are largely inherited. It is

[3]Loehlin (1965) has suggested an interesting method for separating out more phenotypic clusters of items from more genotypic ones in inventories, using a mixture of factor-analysis and twin studies.

not stated that the percentage of hereditary determination which is estimated to be roughly applicable to the population as a whole is equally applicable to every single person in it, just as a statement that the average height of Englishmen is 5'10" is not intended to mean that every Englishman is 5'10", and that none will be found who are 6'2" or 5'4". In the same way, therefore, it is perfectly possible that in *individual* cases behaviour is determined very largely by environmental influences, provided that we are prepared to admit that in other cases there is a compensatory lack of environmental determination, giving a rough average for the whole population. There are of course dangers in using average estimates of this kind which are similar to those attending the use of averages in other fields; nevertheless, a quantitative estimate, however wide its margin of error, is of some use in considering both research and practical problems that arise.

To the three methods of investigation so far mentioned we must add a fourth, the relevance of which will be more apparent to biologists than to many nonbiologically oriented psychologists. Work with human subjects suffers inevitably from the fact that all our studies have to be done *a posteriori*; in other words, we cannot manipulate conditions to suit our experimental design but have to make do with whatever conditions are produced by the haphazard circumstances of everyday life. It is only when dealing with animals that we can enter into a proper experimental design, and consequently much work has been done in an effort to make use of animals in throwing light on genetic determinants of personality. A comprehensive survey of this work is offered by Fuller and Thompson (1960), and no effort will be made here to cite even a sample of the many studies quoted there. We would just like to draw attention to one series of experiments which have already been mentioned in an earlier chapter.

Work on emotionality in rats was started at the Maudsley laboratories by Eysenck and Broadhurst (1965), specifically in order to aid in an understanding of the hereditary mechanism of emotionality; and the most modern methods of genetic analysis, particularly that of diallel crosses, have been used (Broadhurst, 1960). It proved feasible to apply these rather technical methods to behavioural problems, which had not previously been done, and to demonstrate for instance that ambulation scores in the open field are characterised by low dominance with high heritability. Defecation scores, on the other hand, showed higher dominance and less marked heritability. We have already pointed out in an earlier chapter that single scores of this kind are not merely specific behaviour patterns but are complexly related to autonomic functioning as a whole, and that consequently we are dealing with problems in the total inheritance of emotionality or autonomic imbalance. It is not claimed of course that more than a beginning has been made with this work, but it is encouraging that the main results of animal and human work are essentially in good accord, and that even the most recent and recondite of genetic mathematical techniques can be applied in the field of behavioural genetics.

More recently, attempts have been made to extend animal work from the area of emotionality and neuroticism to that of extraversion. It may seem inappropriate to use this term in connection with rats, and of course from one point of view this objection is perfectly justified. However, if it is true that extraverts condition less well, say, than introverts under certain circumstances, then it seems reasonable to measure conditionability in rats and proceed on the hypothesis that less conditionable rats resemble in respect to their inhibition-excitation balance the less conditionable humans, i.e., the extraverts. As so stated this hypothesis has very little *a priori* validity, but it is possible to check on it along two rather separate lines of research. One is indicated in a study of Eysenck (1963a). In this experiment rats were required to learn a "rule" that food in a trough must not be eaten for three seconds after delivery under pain of being shocked; after this period, the food could be eaten without any punishment being incurred. Eating without punishment was called the "normal" reaction; eating with shock was called the "psychopathic" reaction; and not eating even when safe was called the "dysthymic" reaction. These terms were applied because of an explicit analogy with human behaviour along the lines of the writer's general theory of personality. It was predicted on the basis of this theory that nonemotional rats should show more "normal" reactions and emotional rats more "abnormal" reactions, under both levels of shock used in the experiment. It was found that emotional rats did show more "dysthymic" and more "psychopathic" reactions than did nonemotional rats. Thus a two-dimensional theory of behaviour is requisite in the case of "dysthymic" and "psychopathic" behaviour with rats just as much as with humans, and the second factor in this case also is independent of emotionality. Results of this kind support the hypothesis that individual differences in conditioning are related to the second factor, which therefore has certain similarities with human extraversion and introversion.

Another line of argument is followed by Broadhurst and Bignami (1965), who developed strains of rats selectively bred for speed of acquisition of conditioned avoidance responses. If conditioning, as the writer maintains, is related to extraversion and relatively independent of emotionality, then it would follow that the two strains should not be differentiated with respect to open field defecation measures. This is precisely what was found by Broadhurst and Bignami. A similar finding, but in reverse, was reported by Savage (1965); he attempted to condition reactive and nonreactive rats and demonstrated that rate of conditioning was independent of strain. Experiments along these two lines do not of course prove the hypothesis that it is possible to breed strains of extraverted and introverted rats which show analogies with human behaviour, but they do show that predictions can be made from a general conception of animal behaviour which bears striking similarity to the conceptions of human behaviour outlined in an earlier chapter.

A fifth line of evidence which has frequently been used to support the view that constitutional differences are important in personality development is the argument for physical habitus or bodybuild. This twin studies of Verschuer (1952) and of Vogel and Wendt (1956) leave little doubt that heredity plays a strong part in the determination of human physique; and if physique could be shown to be related to personality, then we would have here an additional argument to support the case for partial hereditary determination of human personality and conduct. Rees (1960) and Eysenck (1960) have made a thorough review of the literature; it would appear that there is a distinct relationship between introversion and leptosomatic bodybuild, i.e., predominance of length as opposed to width and thickness, and between extraversion and pyknic bodybuild, i.e., width and thickness as opposed to length. Correlations in representative studies range from .3 to .4, with occasional values above or below these. These are raw correlations which, when corrected for attenuation, become somewhat more respectable, but which in any case do not reach very high levels. There is a relationship between bodybuild and personality, but this relationship is obviously not very close.

Some writers such as Kretschmer and Sheldon have advocated a rather curious triangular scheme of description in which they add a third type of bodybuild which Kretschmer calls "athletic." Ekman (1951) has shown very clearly that a two-dimensional scheme is sufficient to incorporate all the observed relationships between different parts of the body, and factorial studies (Rees and Eysenck, 1945) support this view. Zerssen (1964) has discussed the literature in detail as well as giving his results, and has made out a good case for admitting a second factor, orthogonal to the leptosomatic/pyknic one, which he labels gynaecomorphy as opposed to endromorphy, i.e., femininity as opposed to masculinity of bodybuild. This second factor is no doubt of interest in itself, but it does not concern us very much here.[4]

A rather different point which is relevant to our discussion has been made by Conrad (1963). If we contrast the general behaviour of the extravert with that of the introvert, we might agree that a general term to describe it is immaturity; in a similar way the EEG patterns of extraverts, as we shall see later, tend to be rather immature, i.e., similar to those of younger age groups. Conrad has tried to show that the pyknic habitus which characterises the extravert is also characteristic of younger age groups and may therefore be said to be a sign of immaturity. Figure 76, taken from his book, shows the change in bodily proportions as a person grows up. Thus, for instance, the infant has proportionately a much larger head than the adolescent or adult. Figure 77 illustrates a decrease in proportion of size of head to body with advancing years. It will be

[4]This factor opposes fat to muscle, and may correspond to Sheldon's (1940, 1942) division of the thick-set type into endomorph and mesomorph. This subdivision also agrees with the "dual nature of extraversion" (Eysenck and Eysenck, 1963), in that mesomorphs are characterised by impulsiveness, endomorphs by sociability. This also agrees with Sheldon's own subdivision of extraversion into somatotonia and viscerotonia.

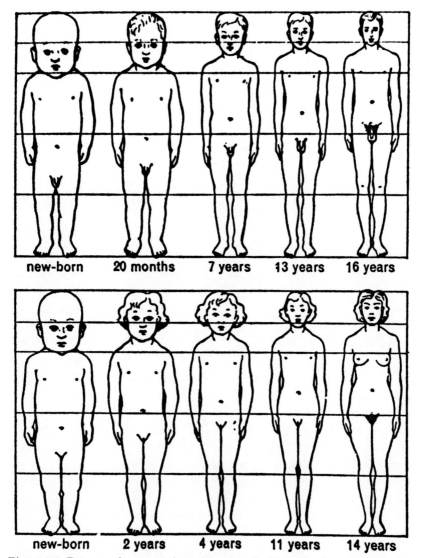

Figure 76. Decrease in proportion of head to body with advancing age, for boys and girls. Reprinted with permission from K. Conrad, 1963.

percentages

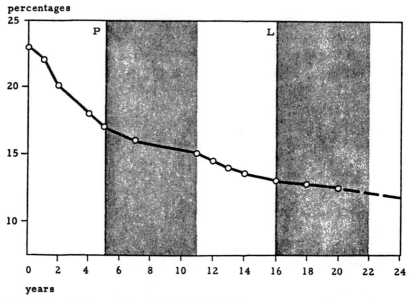

years

Figure 77. Adults with pyknic bodybuild (P) resemble children of eight years old in respect of the proportion of size of head to body, whereas adults with leptosomatic bodybuild (L) resemble grown-ups. Reprinted with permission from K. Conrad, 1963.

seen that the newborn has a head which is about 23 per cent of the total size of the child, whereas the adult has a head which is only 13 or 14 per cent of the body. Conrad has shown that adults with pyknic bodybuild resemble the child rather than the grownup with respect to this proportion, whereas adults with leptosomatic bodybuild do not resemble children in this way. The column headed P shows the proportions observed in a group of pyknic subjects, whereas the column headed L shows the proportions observed in a group of leptosomatic adults. It will be seen in this respect that the adult pyknic resembles an eight-year-old child. Figure 78 shows an index dividing the size of the chest by the width of the shoulder; this also shows a considerable change with age as indicated by the curve in the diagram. Here also grown-ups with pyknic bodybuild resemble children, in this case a four-year-old, whereas adults with leptosomatic bodybuild are displaced towards the values of typical of older groups.

Conrad has published a large number of similar figures and comes

percentages

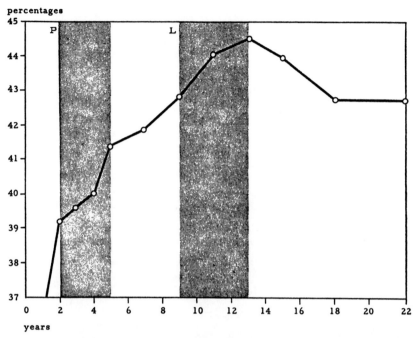

years

Figure 78. Adults with pyknic bodybuild (P) resemble children of four years old in respect of index dividing size of chest by width of shoulder, whereas adults of leptosomatic bodybuild (L) resemble older children. Reprinted with permission from K. Conrad, 1963.

to the general conclusion that "with respect to its morphological proportion, the pyknic bodybuild is related to the leptosomatic bodybuild as is an ontonogenetically early compared with an ontonogenetically later stage. In other words, these proportions in which there are marked differences between pyknics and leptosomatics will also be different for young as compared with older children." Conrad also demonstrated the corollary of this; to wit, that where there were no changes with age and bodily proportions, there were also no differences between pyknics and leptosomatics. He went on to demonstrate a similar principle in the physiological field, where he studied a variety of autonomic and other reactions, and in the psychological field, where he came to the conclusion that here too the pyknic, as compared to the leptosomatic, is characterised by behaviour patterns which distinguish the child from the adult, or the younger from the older person. Altogether the summary of his findings may be interpreted to mean that pyknics tend to be more immature in personality, behaviour, and bodily functioning than are the leptosomatics. This conclusion, which has a good deal of empirical research to support it, could be of very great importance indeed; but until Conrad's finding has been repeated by other investigators it may be best to regard his theory as challenging, supported by certain experimental results, but not fully proven as yet. If it could be demonstrated to be true, then we would have here a means of measuring and quantifying the concept of "immaturity" which has hitherto always been too subjective to be of much scientific value.

The outcome of this brief discussion of work on physique appears to be that bodybuild is indeed largely determined by heredity and is also related to temperament, particularly extraversion/introversion. It does not of course necessarily follow that there is a direct relationship between heredity and personality; bodybuild may intervene through interaction with the environment, in the sense that a person born with an athletic body is more likely to engage in certain adventurous and aggressive types of activity than a person born with a leptosomatic body. Furthermore, the athletic person is more likely to be rewarded by the environment for his activity and receive positive reinforcement, whereas the leptosomatic person is more likely to receive negative reinforcement for such types of behaviour. It is also possible of course that exactly the opposite may happen. Thus Adler for instance has argued that small people tend to be more aggressive as a kind of compensation for inadequate body size. Eysenck (1947) has submitted this hypothesis to some empirical testing but with completely negative results; the correlations which were observed went counter to Adler's hypothesis.

Unfortunately little is in fact known about the way in which environment and body-type interact, and therefore we are reduced to speculation. It is for this reason that the writer is not convinced that Kretschmer, Sheldon, and other investigators in this field are right in using the observed relationships between bodybuild and personality as evidence for direct constitutional determination of behaviour; it seems likely that in part at least the observed correlations are mediated by physique-environment interactions of a complex type. It is perhaps unlikely that this interaction should account for all the observed correlations, but as long as this possibility exists we must be extremely cautious in interpreting the observed data.[5]

There is a sixth and last line of argument which leads to an emphasis on the importance of constitutional factors in personality development. When we contrast expectations deriving from a typological and constitutional theory with those which derive from an environment-reactive outlook, we may say that consistency of conduct observed at a very early age argues for the former, while lack of consistency would argue for the latter. Thomas *et al.* (1964) have discussed the reasoning underlying this proposition in detail, and have also furnished strong evidence to suggest that even in the first two years of life infants show consistent behaviour patterns. Of the eighty children studied, for instance, 92 per cent maintained a consistent pattern of responses in mood, 88 per cent in intensity, 83 per cent in adaptability, 81 per cent in approach, and so on down to 28 per cent in activity. Using methods of co-twin control, Rutter, Korn, and Birch (1966) have demonstrated that in part at least these consistent patterns of response have a genetic basis. Prenatal, paranatal, and early life experiences cannot of course be entirely ruled out, but the evidence so far available is certainly consistent with a genetic-constitutional point of view.[6]

It may be useful to pull together the general conclusions and hypotheses dealt with in this chapter. Figure 79 shows in diagrammatic form the kind of hypothesis here presented. We are dealing with three levels of which the lowest (L_1) deals with the theoretical construct of the excitation-inhibition balance, i.e., the relative predominance of excitatory or inhibitory potential in different people. From this hypothetical conception we can make certain deductions

[5]The fact that Walker (1962) and Kagan (1966) found bodybuild related to the aggressive and impulsive components of extraversion at quite young ages in childhood suggests that genetic factors are perhaps more likely than environmental ones to be decisive in causing these relations; if environment were all-important, one would expect a growth in the strength of the observed relationships with increasing age, but there is no clear-cut evidence of any change with age in the relations found. This appears to be an interesting field of research.

[6]It seems possible that blood groups may be associated with personality (Cattell, Young, and Hundleby, 1964; Hanley, 1964), but the evidence to date is too inconclusive to warrant detailed exposition.

PERSONALITY PHENOTYPE

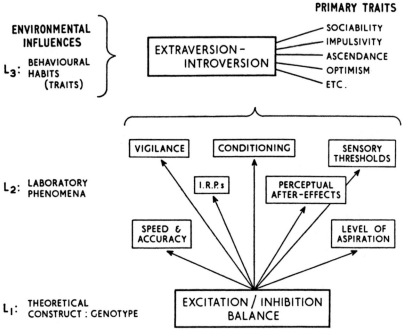

Figure 79. Relation of personality phenotype to genotype and environment.

on behaviour in laboratory situations, and these are listed on the second level (L_2); i.e., we are dealing here with hypotheses regarding conditioning, vigilance, sensory thresholds, level of aspiration, perceptual aftereffects; involuntary rest pauses, speed versus accuracy, and so on as observed in different people. If and when the hypotheses underlying this connection between L_1 and L_2 are satisfied, then we may regard the laboratory phenomena as measures of the excitation-inhibition balance or, if the terms be preferred, of the weak or strong nervous system (Gray, 1965). The tests on the second level are of course not direct measures of the genotype, but they are probably closer to it than the measures to be discussed at the third level, and if suitable precautions are observed may be regarded as an approximation to genotypic measurements.

Primary traits, such as sociability, impulsivity, ascendance, optimism, and so on, which combine to make up our phenotypic concept of extraversion, arise through the confluence of a person's genotype, i.e., his excitation/inhibition balance, with a great variety of environmental influences. These primary traits and type-level concepts of extraversion/introversion are therefore listed under L_3. It will be clear that there is no intention in this conception of personality and behaviour to rule out the influence of environment and to give a purely hereditary account. The relative importance of heredity and environment and the interaction between the two are experimental problems which cannot be solved on any *a priori* basis; all that we may be certain of is that no complex pattern of behaviour, such as is subsumed under conceptions of personality, is likely to be exclusively the product of environment or of heredity.[7] Equally, we may be certain that the combination of influences is unlikely to be identical in different people; for some heredity will play a greater part, for others environment. All these points are perhaps obvious; but any reader of the research literature on personality, social psychology, and abnormal psychology which has appeared during the last twenty or thirty years will be aware that the influence of heredity has usually been played down and that of environmental forces has been given much greater weight than the evidence suggests is a reasonable estimate. Human behaviour is rightly said to be bio-social in nature, i.e., to have both biological and social causes; it is time the pendulum started swinging back from an exclusive preoccupation with social causes to an appropriate appreciation and understanding of biological causes.

It is not the purpose of this chapter, or indeed of this book, to make the pendulum swing too far in the other direction; biological causes are important, but they are not all-important. If this book seems to deal exclusively with biological rather than with social causes, the reason is obvious: there are many other books stressing the environmental as opposed to the genetic and biological influ-

[7]The failure of questionnaire answers on such instruments as the M.P.I. to give direct and unambiguous measures of genotypic personality status is well illustrated by Ingham's (1966) follow-up study of 119 patients who had done the inventory while in hospital, and who were retested after three years. Patients who had improved most had N score which had declined most, and were now virtually the same as those of a random normal sample; similarly their E scores had increased. Patients showing no clinical change also showed no change in inventory scores. M.P.I. scores give an indication of phenotype, and can only be related to genotype indirectly and by independent experimental procedures, such as twin studies.

ences, and the time seemed ripe to redress this balance. There is no implication in our relative neglect of social and environmental causes that these are of little importance or may safely be left aside. Any such assertion would be foolish in the extreme. It must be clear, for instance, from our discussion of conditioning, that considerable importance is placed on environmental conditions. Individual differences in the speed and strength of formation of conditioned responses are clearly unimportant if the environment is arranged in such a way that no conditioned and unconditioned stimuli are presented at appropriate time intervals. Equally a facility for forming conditioned responses says nothing about the type and nature of the responses which shall be conditioned; these depend on the specific unconditioned and conditioned stimuli which are presented in contiguity, and this presentation is of course the task of the environment. Biological causes act in such a way as to predispose an individual to respond in certain ways to stimulation; this stimulation may or may not occur, depending on circumstances which are entirely under environmental control. Psychological textbooks written from an exclusively environmental point of view often accuse biologists and others who are concerned with hereditary influences of neglecting environment and of attributing too great an influence to heredity. Such accusations are usually directed at a man of straw; the author knows of no responsible biological writers who have expressed any such extreme and unlikely views. Nevertheless, however unrealistic a man of straw may be, his existence makes necessary a recapitulation of facts and views which should be perfectly obvious.

Before closing this chapter, one further problem requires at least a short discussion. Our descriptive theory of personality has dealt with two main dimensions; it has not said anything about the psychotic disorders or about possible normal variants of these. Yet we have seen in such studies as those of Gottesman (1965) that psychotic scales on the M.M.P.I. give rise to intraclass correlations for MZ and DZ twins, which indicate that heredity plays some important part in these personality variables, even in normal subjects. Similarly, the evidence is strongly in favour of hereditary determination of schizophrenia and manic depression when concordance studies are considered (Shields and Slater, 1960; Gottesman and

Shields, 1966). These facts would not present any great problem were it not true that multifactorial inheritance is not considered to be a likely basis for psychotic disorders. Manic-depressive disorders are believed to be determined to a considerable degree by a dominant gene with reduced manifestation, and schizophrenic disorders are sometimes explained along similar lines, or else by reference to a recessive gene whose effects are influenced by modifying genes. If either of these hypotheses, or any other similar one, were to be accepted, then it would be difficult to explain the demonstrated contribution of heredity to the manifestation of psychotic personality traits in normal subjects; this would seem to require either some form of polygenic inheritance or else a much greater degree of pervasiveness of specific genes than has ever been postulated by responsible writers.

The writer has suggested that *psychoticism* may be regarded as a third general personality dimension, independent of neuroticism and inherited according to some form of polygenic model, very much as are the other two main personality dimensions (Eysenck, 1952b); experimental studies of this hypothesis have on the whole supported this proposal (S.B.G. Eysenck, 1956; Eysenck, 1952a, 1955c; Trouton and Maxwell, 1956; Cattell and Tatro, 1966). Experimental work with psychotic subjects certainly finds it easier to measure what all psychotics have in common (psychoticism) than what differentiates one type of psychotic from another (Payne and Hewlett, 1960). Furthermore, the evidence just cited makes it seem likely that psychoticism and neuroticism are indeed quite separate dimensions of personality, and not, as is sometimes suggested, one and the same dimension, with neurotic disorders merely psychotic disorders writ small. Evidence in respect to this point is not only statistical but also genetic; Cowie (1961) for instance has shown that the children of psychotic patients do not show any elevation of scores on personality inventories of neuroticism. This whole issue has been reviewed in Eysenck and Rachman (1965), and no further discussion would seem required.

How can we reconcile the requirements of a polygenic theory of psychoticism as a major dimension of personality with the genetic hypotheses of single gene transmission of schizophrenia and manic-depressive psychosis? One possible explanation may lie in the postulation of a more complex scheme which recognizes the existence both of a polygenic factor of psychotic predispostion and also of separate single genes determining the precise nature of psychotic breakdown encountered. Such a scheme would serve to solve many problems which at present plague the investigator, such as the excessive rarity of clear-cut "textbook" cases of schizophrenia and particularly of manic-depressive illness; when the writer inaugurated one of his research schemes and tried to locate relatively "pure" cases of these two types of psychotic illness, he found that not one case in ten could be said to be clear-cut and indisputable. In terms of our scheme, therefore, we would postulate that a large proportion of psychiatrically diagnosed psychotics are high on psychoticism but lack the specific genes making for either manic-depressive illness or schizophrenia; they are accommodated only with difficulty in our diagnostic categories, which are based on the presence of such single genes. Persons with somewhat lower loadings on this factor, in the absence of specific genes, would be regarded as odd and unusual but might get by without special difficulties unless put under stress. Conversely, persons with the special manic-depressive or schizophrenic genes would show certain schizoid and cycloid personality patterns in their everyday lives, but would not be certified unless they also had high loadings on psychoticism.

There is no direct evidence in favour of this hypothesis; all that can be said in its favour is that it serves to reconcile well-established phenomena otherwise difficult to bring together in one theory. We will not in this book deal any further with psychoticism, both because it would extend the scope of the book unduly to do so, and because what is in fact known about the subject does not justify any extended treatment. Nevertheless it seemed desirable to refer to the subject briefly in order to clarify the situation to some extent at least. It is hoped that within the next few years the picture will clarify sufficiently to make possible the inclusion of psychoticism in a later edition of this book.

In conclusion, we may perhaps point out one implication of the findings discussed in this chapter for our general conception of personality. We have shown that certain behaviour patterns, i.e., those related to extraversion/introversion and to neuroticism-emotionality, have a substantial hereditary basis. Such a statement makes sense only if we assume some kind of structural intermediary between the two concepts involved, i.e., heredity (genes, chromosomes, etc.) and outwardly observable behaviour; it is clear that behaviour as such cannot be inherited and that only structures, i.e., glands, neurones, nerve cells, etc., can be inherited in any meaningful ways. As T. H. Huxley once put it, there is "no psychosis without a neurosis," i.e., no psychic or behavioural event without some underlying neurological event. It follows from these considerations that it is not only sensible but obligatory for us to search for underlying neurological, physiological, biochemical, and other causes for the observed behaviour patterns, insofar as these are not due entirely to environmental influences. It is a task of the next chapter to take up this search.

CHAPTER V

ACTIVATION, AROUSAL, AND EMOTION

THERE HAS IN RECENT YEARS been a considerable stress in psychological writing on some general "activation" or "arousal" theory of emotion and motivation. One of the earliest exponents of this theory was Duffy (1962), who talked about "degree of excitation" and "energy mobilization" as early as 1934 and 1941 respectively. Similarly Freeman (1948) was concerned early with the "energetics of behavior." Duffy (1952) makes it clear that terms such as activation and arousal "do not refer specifically to the activation pattern of the EEG. On the contrary, they refer to variations in the excitation of the individual as a whole, as indicated roughly by any one of a number of physiological measures (e.g., skin resistance, muscle tension, EEG, cardiovascular measures, and others). The degree of activation appears to be best indicated by a combination of measures." And in an earlier article Duffy (1934) defined excitation as "the extent to which the organism as a whole is activated or aroused, not as measured by overt behavior but as measured by the activity of those processes which supply the energy for overt behavior." Changes in the degree of activation, so considered, "are found in studies of sleep, of 'fatigue,' and of various psychiatric conditions. . . . A unifying concept which covers the range of physiological changes from deep sleep to extreme excitement would appear to offer hope of dealing with these phenomena more effectively. Such a concept would not only permit economy in the treatment of this subject matter but would no doubt serve also to reveal relationships now obscured by traditional categories." And these traditional categories, forthwith to be discarded, include drives, emotions, and motives.

This general way of looking at the energetics of human behaviour probably dates back at least to Cannon's theory of the emotions, in which he suggested that certain emotions, like rage and fear, serve an emergency function by preparing the organism for action; "emotion serves the purpose of mobilizing the resources of the organism to meet a situation that might endanger it" (Morgan, 1965). Activation theory, as Cofer and Appley (1964) have pointed out, has arisen "in relation to two main bodies of fact. . . . These are, first, that behavioral efficiency varies as a function of energy mobilization and muscular involvement; and, second, that recent neurophysiological discoveries have suggested that cortical function is related to activity in an arousal system of the brain stem." These facts are related to the concepts of emotion and drive for two reasons: "First, emotion and motivation are concepts designed partly for the purpose of dealing with variations in behavioral vigor or arousal, and, second, some of the physiological indicators of arousal have figured, also, historically, as methods of expression in the study of emotion, stress, and conflict."

Among the first to use the term "activation" was Schlosberg (1954), who also realized a point often forgotten by later writers, *viz.* that the activation dimension does not represent all the aspects of emotion; we will return to this problem. Malmo (1958, 1959), whose extensive experimental studies we have already noted, was another pioneer who urged the identification of arousal and the notion of generalized or nondirective drive (*D* in Hull's notation). Hebb (1955, 1958) is another influential writer who accepted some form of activation theory and facilitated its acceptance. Many others have also played a part, and their contributions are well reviewed in Cofer and Appley (1964).

These authors also point out, however, that activation theory is in fact hardly a theory. "Its major tenet, aside from the assertion that emotion means arousal, is that there is a curvilinear relationship between behavioral efficiency and measures of physiological arousal—a tenet of high theoretical neutrality. The redefinition of emotion is also hardly theoretical." They then go on to attribute the appeal of activation theory to recent physiological discoveries associated with the ascending reticular activating system and with the theoretical links between this system and emotion which have been pointed out particularly by Lindsley (1951), who actually coined the phrase "activation theory of emotions." His argument, to which we shall return later, is premised upon the fact that emotional arousal produces an "activation pattern on the EEG, characterized by reduction or abolition of synchronized (alpha) rhythms and the induction of low amplitude fast activity"; this pattern, as he points out, is very similar to that produced by sensory stimulation and by problem solving and other mental activities. His main concern is with the neural mechanism which mediates this arousal, i.e., the reticular activating system.

Before turning to a discussion of the physiological basis of emotion, drive, arousal, activation, motivation, or D, we may ask some questions relating to individual differences as they mirror these various concepts. Duffy (1962) discusses such differences with the implicit (and sometimes explicit) hypothesis in mind that we can get along with just one single dimension of activation along which persons suffering from functional psychiatric disorders can be located, and on which they will be differentiated from persons not so afflicted. "In spite of some conflicting evidence, there appears to be considerable support for the conclusion that individuals with various forms of behaviour pathology differ from 'normal' subjects in various aspects of activation, as well as in the directional aspect of their behavior." Furthermore, she appears to believe that "activation is an organismic phenomenon, and that it is recognized as such when we speak of an individual's being relaxed or being excited rather than of a particular system's showing this condition." And she concludes a survey of experimental studies by saying that these studies "give support to the conclusion that differences between individuals in activation are basically differences in responsiveness or excitability. These differences appear to be associated with differences in certain other characteristics which might be regarded as derived from a basic difference in responsiveness."

Such a theory produces considerable difficulties when viewed in the light of the experimental evidence presented in previous chapters. It would seem possible to identify Duffy's "activation-responsiveness" factor as underlying neuroticism or emotionality; much of the material in her book lends support to such an hypothesis. But it would be equally easy to identify her factor with introversion; again, as we have seen, there is much material in her book which can be interpreted along these lines. But there is an obvious difficulty here, in that introversion and neuroticism are in fact uncorrelated; it is difficult to see how one and the same dimension of activation-responsiveness can underly two orthogonal behavioural factors.

One way out of this difficulty would perhaps be to locate the activation-responsiveness factor at a 45° angle to both introversion and neuroticism, so that both can be said to be correlated with this factor. Indeed, as we have pointed out several times, much of the evidence has been collected in studies which have used as criterion groups dysthymics, i.e., neurotics high on both introversion and neuroticism; when these are compared with normal subjects on measures of activation, the usual finding is that the patients are indeed found to be in a higher state of activation. We have interpreted this as a weakness in the design of the experiment, because the choice of the experimental group makes it impossible to relate observed differences unambiguously to either neuroticism or introversion; the same criticism was made when subjects were chosen on the basis of anxiety questionnaires such as the M.A.S., which has loadings on both the personality axes. If we changed our major axis position and located it in such a way that it coincided with the anxiety-dysthymic quadrant, then would perhaps all the data fall into place?

The data do not suggest that such a rotation would be advisable. In the first place, such a choice of position for the "activation" axis would be completely arbitrary; practically all the studies reported in the literature emerge with two factors closely corresponding to N and E (Eysenck, 1960e; Eysenck and Eysenck, 1967). In the second place, these experimental and statistical results agree well with psychiatric experience and nomenclature, in that the term "neurotic" is applied not only to dysthymics, but also to hysterics, mixed neurotics, and psychopaths; in other words, it is universally recognized that there is something common to all types of neurotics, and it is this "something" which comes out as a common factor in statistical studies. In the third place, if the factor structure were to be rotated in this fashion to coincide with theory, how would the second, orthogonal factor be identified? This factor would contrast the choleric and the phlegmatic types; i.e., its two ends would be characterized by high N—high E persons at one end and low N—low E people at the other. There is nothing in the literature even remotely resembling such a factor.

In addition to these objections, there are many detailed findings, noted in the preceding chapters, which speak against any such hypothesis. Frequently it is only one dimension or the other which is involved significantly with an experimental parameter; such cases in fact are more frequent than those involving both. Even when both dimensions are involved, it is usually not under identical conditions; in other words, those parameters which are relevant to one dimension of personality are not relevant to the other. While it would be premature to rule out completely the possibility that a rotation of the factorial structure through 45° would give a better fit to reality, the evidence at present available does not encourage the expectation that such a change would make for an easier understanding of the position or lead to better predictions in the future.

The position which will be argued in this chapter accepts as a fundamental reality the existence of two major, independent dimensions of personality, E and N. It identifies differences in behaviour related to the former with differential thresholds in the various parts of the ascending reticular activating system, and differences in behavior related to the latter with differential thresholds of arousal in the visceral brain (MacLean, 1958, 1960), i.e., the hippocampus, amygdala, cingulum, septum, and hypothalamus. It does not postulate complete independence of these structures but only relative and partial independence; as Gellhorn and Loofbourrow (1963) have pointed out, "it is obvious, since ascending and descending pathways connect the reticular formation with the hypothalamus, that under experimental conditions similar effects may be produced by stimulation of either structure, but this fact should not obscure the fundamental functional difference between the two structures." Similarly, we may say that, depending upon external stimulation, similar or different effects may be produced by these two structures. It seems very unlikely that they could in any sense be identified and regarded as a single structure, which would seem to be the logical outcome of the argument presented by Duffy.

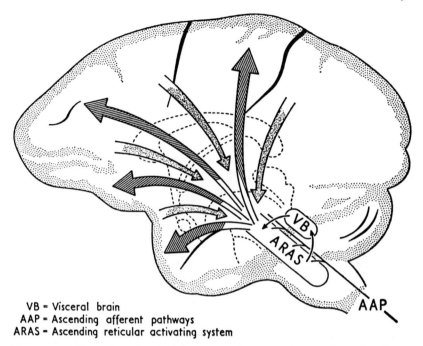

VB = Visceral brain
AAP = Ascending afferent pathways
ARAS = Ascending reticular activating system

Figure 80. Diagrammatic representation of mutual interaction of reticular formation, visceral brain, and cortex. Direct arousing effects of V.B. stimulation are not indicated in this Figure.

Figure 80 presents the scheme sketched above in a very preliminary and diagrammatic form. We have two sets of loops, which are in turn connected with each other. The first of these is the cortico-reticular loop. Neural messages ("sensations") going along the classical ascending afferent pathways relay to the particular projection areas involved in the cortex; they also send collaterals into the reticular formation, which in turn sends "arousal" messages to the cortex to keep it in a state of functional tonus. Depending on the nature of the information transmitted, the cortex in turn instructs the reticular formation to continue sending "arousal" messages or else to switch to "inhibition." This loop then is concerned with information processing, with cortical arousal and inhibition, and in its application to personality differences with introversion and extraversion.

The second loop involved concerns the visceral brain and the reticular formation. Messages from the visceral brain also reach the reticular formation via collaterals and have arousing effects on the cortex in a manner very similar to that produced by information received via the ascending afferent pathways. It is this loop that is concerned with emotion, and in its application to personality differences, with neuroticism/emotionality. It follows that cortical arousal can be produced along two quite distinct and separate pathways.[1] It can be produced by sensory stimulation or by problem-solving activity of the brain, without necessarily involving the visceral brain at all; in this case we have no autonomic arousal, but possibly quite high cortical arousal. A scientist sitting quite immobile and to all appearances asleep, but thinking profoundly about some professional problems, might illustrate this state of affairs; there is considerable cortical arousal but little autonomic activity.

Cortical arousal can also be produced by emotion, in which case the reticular formation is involved through the ascending and descending pathways connecting it with the hypothalamus.[2] In this case we have both autonomic arousal and cortical arousal. The fact that cortical arousal is concerned in both types of loops does not mean that these loops are identical, and it certainly is dangerous to assume, as Duffy and many others have done, that indices of cortical arousal can be used as measures of emotional involvement. It might be true to say that emotional arousal can be indexed in terms of cortical arousal, but this proposition cannot be inverted; cortical arousal can take place without any marked degree of autonomic-emotional arousal. Thus it is not sufficient to prove that a given change in EEG, GSR, or EMG follows upon the presentation of an emotion-producing stimulus in order to argue that these

[1]This general suggestion is supported by such studies as those of Bernhaut *et al.* (1953), in which two kinds of cortical activation patterns were found in response to stimulation. Nociceptive and proprioceptive stimuli gave rise to generalized arousal throughout all areas of the cortex, accompanied by excitation of the hypothalamic portion of the brain stem reticular formation; visual and auditory stimuli gave rise to a more specific arousal pattern, confined for the most part to the specific sensory projection areas and *not accompanied by hypothalamic excitation.*
[2]It is possible that the role of the reticular formation has been over-emphasized in relation to the arousal aspects of emotion. As Gellhorn (1961) points out, the hypothalamus has its own activating functions by direct connection with the cerebral cortex and also through autonomic activities which in their turn activate the reticular system.

manifestations are pure measures of emotional activation. They may be measures of cortical arousal accompanying many other types of stimuli which are not emotional in nature, and which do not in any way involve the hypothalamus, the visceral brain, or the autonomic system as a whole. There is thus some degree of partial independence between autonomic activation and cortical arousal; activation always leads to arousal, but arousal very frequently arises from types of stimulation which do not involve activation. For ease of discussion we will use the terms "activation" and "arousal" in this specialized sense, as referring to autonomic and reticular activity respectively; to use them as synonyms, as is the custom, seems to invite confusion between two clearly distinct types of excitation.

The distinction made above may seem relatively unimportant, in view of the partial dependence of arousal on activation. In our opinion such a view would be mistaken. Strong emotions are aroused relatively rarely in our type of society, and a person may go through days, weeks, or even months without ever reaching a state of "fight or flight," in the meaning of that phrase given to it by Cannon. For something like 90 per cent of our lives, or perhaps even 99 per cent in many cases, cortical arousal is dependent on mild sensory stimulation rather than on emotional activation; and for most of our lives, therefore, the distinction between the two concepts is meaningful and useful. It is only when strong emotions are involved frequently and for long periods that activation and arousal tend to become synonymous, thus giving a semblance of sense to the hypothesis of an "anxiety" dimension discussed above. This confluence of the two concepts under extreme conditions has in fact been documented even in the questionnaire field; while E and N are quite independent in the normal population, they tend to be negatively correlated in neurotic populations and among subjects with very high N scores (Eysenck, 1959). In other words, when highly emotional people are involved, i.e., people for whom even quite mild stimuli are emotionally activating, then the distinction tends to break down, and activation=arousal. But this occurs only in a very small proportion of the population, and under unusual circumstances, e.g., in war; for most people, and under most circumstances, the distinction is worth retaining.

So far we have given only a very general overview of the theory to be advanced in this chapter; we must now turn to a more detailed examination of this theory. We will deal with emotion and activation first and then turn to arousal and the reticular formation. Our account of emotion-activation will be quite short, primarily because this area has been well served by summaries and discussions in psychological and physiological journals and books; our account of arousal will be more detailed because it is in this area that much of the original contribution of this book lies.

Currently the most widely accepted theory of emotion is that of Papez (1937) and MacLean (1958, 1960). Papez, in his very original formulation, grouped together structures like the hippocampus, fornix, cingular gyrus, and the mamillary bodies of the hypothalamus and made them responsible for emotional expression, organization, and experience. As Morgan (1965) points out, "the Papez–MacLean theory is now much more than a theory. It is a general description of what experiment has established, namely, that the limbic system is the central system in emotion." Of particular importance, for both Papez and MacLean, is the hypothalamus; to quote Morgan again, "if there is a 'seat of emotion,' it is the hypothalamus . . . the hypothalamus is the principal center in which the various components of emotional reaction are organized into definite patterns." The various components, as such, are separately activated at lower points of the brain stem. Furthermore, the hypothalamus is subject to cortical influences on the one hand and to excitatory and inhibitory ones from the reticular formation on the other. It thus becomes "the focal, organizing structure in emotional behavior" This function, of course, must be seen in perspective; as Herrick (1956) has pointed out, "it is very important to recognize that all levels of integration interpenetrate, and one never operates independently of the others. Each higher level is derived from the lower and can work only with the instrumentation provided by the lower levels. Nonetheless, each level has its own distinctive qualities and the laws of its operation are peculiar to it."

The limbic system serves the organism as a "visceral brain"; it interprets experience in terms of *feeling* rather than in terms of intellectual, symbolized constructs. As Gellhorn and Loofbourrow (1963) put it, "whereas intellectual expression may be carried out by the use of verbal symbols which require a well-developed neocortex, emotional expression can be achieved by the more primitive neural mechanisms of the limbic system, using a sort of 'organ language' instead of words." Thus the limbic system is of special importance in emotional phenomena, while the neocortex is essential to mental operations involving verbal symbols.

The reticular formation (with which we will be concerned in more detail later) supplies the tonic impulses without which the neocortex could not function, and it also acts to establish the functioning level of the visceral brain. But although the reticular formation thus plays a dominant role in hypothalamic activity, Gellhorn and Loofbourrow (1963) emphasize "that the hypothalamus should be separated conceptually from the reticular formation." The hypothalamus, as they point out, controls hypophyseal functions, regulates certain instinctual drives, integrates sympathetic and somatic activity into the characteristic patterns of the ergotropic system, and is responsible for the maintenance of the balance between the parasympathetic functions of the anterior lobe and the sympathetic functions of the posterior lobe. "These are functions which are not mediated by the more basic but less differentiated reticular formation." In view of the close anatomical and physiological relationship between hypothalamus and reticular formation, it is not surprising that stimulation causes arousal and activation whereas lesions produce somnolence and coma, irrespective of whether it is the posterior hypothalamus or the reticular formation being experimented with. "Yet, there is some evidence which suggests that the prevalent tendency in modern neurophysiology and psychology to attribute arousal and emotion to the reticular formation has gone too far."

Particularly impressive in this connection are the work of Bradley and Key (1958) and the studies of Wikler (1952) and of Bradley and Elkes (1957), in which these writers demonstrated a "pharmacological dissociation" between behavioural and EEG patterns of arousal. Thus for instance Bradley and Key showed that increasing doses of atropine sulfate raised the threshold of the reticular formation for the evocation of cortical arousal, as registered on the EEG, but failed to change the state of alertness ("behavioural arousal"). Physostigmine produces cortical asynchrony, and atropine produces synchrony; yet neither wakefulness nor threshold of behavioural arousal is altered by these drugs. Evidence of this kind, as well as anatomical studies (Scheibel and Scheibel, 1961), has led Starzl, Taylor, and Magoun (1951a, 1951b) to offer the hypothesis that arousal is primarily due to excitation of the hypothalamus directly and reflexly, so that arousal and emotion would appear chiefly as the result of an activation of the visceral brain. This suggestion agrees well with the proposal made earlier that arousal and activation should be considered as relatively separate functions of anatomically separate structures. Further evidence is cited by Gellhorn and Loofbourrow (1963).

The integration of autonomic functions produced by the "visceral brain" is perhaps more effective with sympathetic than with parasympathic stimulation. "The sympathetic system is, in general, more diffuse in its effects than the parasympathetic; certain parasympathetic reflexes may occur without the involvement of other parts of the parasympathetic system, whereas the sympathetic system tends to discharge as a whole" (Morgan, 1965). In part, at least, this tendency to "discharge as a whole" is almost certainly connected with the *level* of activation, higher levels of activation giving rise to greater diffuseness of discharge. It is possible that the low correlations often reported between different autonomic responses are merely a reflection of the low level of emotional stimulation employed; it is of course realized that for experimental purposes it would be difficult if not impossible to raise this level, at least in human subjects. On the other hand, the antagonistic activity of the two systems is often seen more clearly under conditions of not-too-strong emotional activation; when stimuli are too strong, swings from sympathetic to parasympathetic activity may be seen, or even a raising or lowering of activity of both systems simultaneously. Altogether, the antagonism of these two systems is often exaggerated; defecation, for instance, which has provided the classical index of emotional reactivity in rat experiments of the "open field" variety, is due to *parasympathetic* outflow. Facts like these make one less surprised that observed correlations between experimentally produced autonomic reactions are rather low; it is on the whole remarkable that they seem to provide a rough-and-ready pattern not too unlike what might have been expected from a consideration of physiological factors.

The (partial) antagonism of the two branches of the autonomic system has often been suggested as underlying, at least in part, the qualitative differences in the emotions. Allport (1924), for instance, related pleasurable and unpleasurable emotions to the parasympathetic and sympathetic systems respectively, a suggestion which would fit in well with the tentative one made in an earlier chapter that hysteric and dysthymic reactions are related to easy activation of these two systems respectively. For emotions of moderate intensity (such as are produced in the laboratory), such a correlation is probably not far from the truth, but as emotional excitement increases, whether pleasurable or unpleasurable, the downward discharge from the hypothalamus fails to confine itself to one or other division of the autonomic system. Experimentally, there is much evidence that "stimulation or lesions of certain parts of the limbic system alter emotional behaviour through a change in the balance of the hypothalamus" (Gellhorn and Loofbourrow, 1963), and that "pathological processes in man which lead to increased sympathetic or parasympathetic discharges (are) accompanied by different emotional states." "Different emotions cannot be explained by considering only the factor of intensity as the activation theory does."

When we turn to strong emotions, i.e., conditions where we have suggested a breakdown of the distinction between the cortico-reticular and the cortico-hypothalamic system to occur, Gellhorn and Loofbourrow come to a rather similar conclusion. Under these circumstances, they suggest, the hypothalamus "starts firing nearly maximally under the combined influence of discharges from the reticular formation and the sense organs, the latter impinging on the reticular formation and hypothalamus not only directly but also via the neocortex and limbic cortex. Under these circumstances the differentiation in activation pattern and function which exists between various cortical areas under strictly physiological conditions is lessened (Lindsley, 1960). The resulting 'functional' decortication is not the result of a 'cortical conflict' . . . but is due to an *excessive excitation of the hypothalamic system which is incompatible with the differentiated action of the cortex neces-*

sary for attention and the higher nervous process." This general
statement may be regarded as furnishing us with a physiological
basis for the Yerkes-Dodson Law.[3] Furthermore, it allows us to
interpret behavioural differences between high N and low N subjects in terms of differential thresholds for hypothalamic activity.
While many of the details discussed above are still *sub judice*, it
seems possible to the writer that in general outline the picture given
may not be too impressionistic to be useful in directing research
activities along promising channels.

In turning now to a more detailed discussion of our theoretical
alignment of extraversion-introversion and reticular activity, it
should perhaps be pointed out at the beginning that we are concerned, not so much with the reticular formation alone, but with
a cortico-reticular loop in which it is often difficult to ascertain
the primogeniture of hen or egg. Potentials induced in the reticular
system (both brain stem and thalamic) by cortical projections are
larger, more widespread, and have *a shorter latency* than those
evoked through collaterals from afferent sensory tracts (Her-
nandez-Péon and Hagbarth, 1955). Transmission latencies in the
specific and nonspecific systems show clearly that impulse veloc-
ities are faster in the former than in the latter (e.g., French, Ver-

[3]It is possible that a more precise statement of this relation can be made in terms
of the two parts of the reticular formation. It has been shown (Gauthier *et al.,*
1965; Gellhorn *et al.,* 1954; Jasper *et al.,* 1955) that strong arousal responses orig-
inating in the brain stem reticular formation may block the cortical recruiting
responses evoked by the diffuse thalamic nuclei; thus strong activation would appear to be "inimical to the optimal functioning of the regulatory effects mediated
by the thalamic reticular system. This overshadowing of the more differentiated
functions of the thalamic nuclei by the diffuse arousal response of the brain stem
may have its behavioral counterpart in the many failures of discrimination which
occur under high emotion and excitement" (Samuels, 1959). Similarly, the work
of Sharpless and Jasper (1956) on habituation concluded that this occurs within
"the brain stem reticular and the unspecific thalamic systems with their associated
collateral pathways"; adaptation remained frequency-specific despite cortical re-
moval for cats with intact medial geniculate bodies sending collaterals into the
diffuse thalamic nucleus, but was specific only for intensity and sensory mode for
animals whose specific sensory pathways above the colliculi had been transected,
thus leaving them only with functional collaterals to the brain stem reticular formation. "If finer discriminations are indeed related to thalamic mechanisms, then
the prepotence of brain stem reticular arousal over thalamic activity under conditions of high activation would suggest a possible neural mechanism underlying the
failure of discrimination which occur under conditions of high drive" (Samuels,
1959).

experimental procedures to cortical arousal. Not all the experiments noted in Chapter III will be so dealt with, partly because results in them may follow logically from more fundamental ones, and partly because in some cases there is simply not enough evidence to justify any lengthy discussion. In a number of cases Gray (1964) has already surveyed the field in connection with his work on the weak-strong nervous system dichotomy, and reference will be made to this discussion in preference to repeating what has been said there. The sequence of topics is not the same as that in Chapter III, for reasons which will become readily apparent.

Sensory thresholds provide a good beginning for our discussion. While there is no direct evidence that stimulation of the reticular formation reduces sensory thresholds, there is much circumstantial evidence showing that in general reticular stimulation enhances the efficiency of the sensory systems; we have already discussed the manner in which the reticular formation can affect the strength of sensory impulses prior to the point where they give off collaterals to the R.F. Fuster (1958) has been able to show that stimulation of the R.F. increased the accuracy of visual choices made by monkeys, and although improved visual discrimination is unlikely to be the only effect of such stimulation, some direct effect is not unlikely. In spite of its only partial relevancy, this would appear to be the only behavioural study cited. The electrophysiological evidence (Bremer and Stoupel, 1958, 1959) appears at first paradoxical, because cortical arousal patterns in the EEG are accompanied by decreased amplitudes of evoked potentials following photic stimulation. However, as Gray explains, "in recent years the evidence has accumulated that reticular activation of the cortex is accompanied by a *facilitation* of the potentials evoked by stimulation of the visual system which is, under certain conditions, masked by the influence of reticular activation on the intrinsic activity of the cortex. It seems that, under certain conditions . . . stimulation of the reticular system can enhance the potentials evoked by sensory stimulation."

Another line of indirect evidence relates to the fact that the generalized EEG arousal response is a component of Pavlov's orienting reflex (Voronin and Sokolov, 1960; Lynn, 1965); other components of this reflex, too, are controlled by the brain stem reticular formation (Gastaut and Roger, 1960; Rossi and Zanchetti, 1957). Now recent Russian work surveyed by Gray (1964) has shown "that the orienting reflex is accompanied by an overall increase in the organism's sensory capacities, including a fall in absolute sensory thresholds. It would seem reasonable to implicate the same mechanism in the production of this increase in sensory capacities as is involved in the control of the other aspects of the orienting reflex—namely, the brain stem reticular formation."

Gray also reviews the literature relating to CFF thresholds and summarises his discussion "by saying that the frequency at which the evoked potentials of the cortex are able to follow flicker is increased: (1) under conditions in which the EEG shows a shift to patterns characteristic of more alert states; (2) under conditions in which an orienting reflex, as indicated by the GSR and alpha-depression responses, is displayed; (3) by an increase in background stimulation (additional auditory stimulation, light instead of darkness and, possibly, induced muscle tension when the subject is instructed to clench the hand upon presentation of flicker); (4) by conditions which demand that the subject pay more attention to the intermittent stimulation (instructions to differentiate between two different frequencies of flicker, or instructions which confer a signal value on the flicker); (5) by the administration of caffeine; (6) in individuals with relatively high-frequency resting alpha rhythms. It will be seen that all these conditions represent either circumstances which can be thought of as increasing arousal level (presentation of additional, especially novel, stimulation, administration of a stimulant drug, need to pay attention, induced muscle tension) or indices that arousal level has in fact risen (acceleration and desynchronization of resting EEG waves, GSR, high-frequency resting alpha waves)." Further direct evidence of the effects of reticular formation stimulation is available from the work of Lindsley (1957), Jung (1957), and Steriade and Demetrescu (1962). "All these findings, then, support the hypothesis that stimulation of the reticular system increases the organism's ability to respond to high-frequency trains of stimuli."

In Chapter III we linked our discussion of sensory thresholds with that of tolerance for pain and sensory deprivation. The application of the reticular model to pain is perhaps obvious, but sensory deprivation presents a rather more complex problem. Hebb (1955) has suggested that conditions which make for boredom also produce unusually low arousal, and that low arousal as well as high arousal has negative hedonic tone and is aversive in character. Berlyne (1960) has argued against this interpretation, advancing good reasons for assuming "that the torments of boredom are associated with an upsurge of arousal" and that "diminutions of arousal are rewarding." An answer to this problem is not crucial for our purpose, and no point would be served if we were to duplicate Berlyne's extensive and well-considered discussion; while persuasive, this discussion leans to a considerable extent on indirect and circumstantial evidence. Berlyne recognizes this by entitling the section concerned "A Hypothesis," and until more direct evidence is available we may perhaps put this whole problem aside as unsolved.

When we come to conditioning, we find that most of the Russian work has dealt with "transmarginal inhibition" rather than with the more orthodox kind involving stimuli below the level at which such inhibition sets in (Gray, 1964). "From the point of view of the *behavioural theory of arousability*, Pavlovian transmarginal inhibition is simply an instance of impairment in the efficiency of performance of a learned response at high levels of arousal, whether a high level of arousal is induced by the presentation of an 'ultrastrong stimulus,' by the protracted application of a stimulus of moderate intensity, or, as in the case of the method of 'extinction with reinforcement' which has been used in Teplov's laboratory, by the frequent presentation of a stimulus of moderate intensity at intervals of time short enough to allow summation of excitation. Clearly, then, this theory predicts that individuals high on the dimension of arousability should show greater decrements in response, or show a decrement in response at lower intensities, durations or frequencies of stimulation, than individuals low on this dimension. On the identification of weak individuals with highly arousable ones, this is exactly what is found." Under the experimental paramenters mentioned, therefore, introverts would be expected to condition less well than extraverts; conversely, we have already noted that under certain other parametric conditions the opposite prediction follows. The results of the Russian work, surveyed by Gray, and those from our work, surveyed in a previous chapter, are broadly in line with the general tenor of the above quotation from Gray (1964).

Possible reticular mechanisms for "transmarginal inhibition" phenomena have been discussed by Dell, Bonvallet, and Hugelin (1961); the most likely explanation is perhaps that this type of inhibition is the result of the operation of a reticulo-cortico-reticular feedback-loop of the kind described by Hugelin, Bonvallet, and Dell (1959) and by Bonvallet and Hugelin (1961). This hypothesis furnishes us with a means of accounting for the inverse-U shaped relation between arousal and performance, comparable to the already discussed theory relating activation and performance in the shape of an inverse U. As Gray puts it, "arousability and the degree of reticular cortical bombardment of the cortex can only be considered to be monotonically and positively related to one another *up to the point at which transmarginal inhibition is induced in the weak nervous system; beyond that point, level of arousal is (paradoxically) higher in individuals low on the dimension of arousability*."

Most of the Anglo-American work in this field has been carried out at levels which are well below that at which transmarginal inhibition is likely to arise; we have seen that under these conditions, simple and direct predictions based upon monotonic relations between arousal and conditioning are sufficient to generate testable hypotheses which can be shown to be along the right lines by actual experiment. The same is true of experiments in rote learning; here too we have already discussed the support which the findings receive from arousal theory and the complications which arise through the intervention of consolidation processes which in turn interfere with immediate memory, and which also serve to facilitate long-term memory. There is no need here to repeat this discussion.

It may, however, be of some interest to point out that several studies have given direct evidence of a relation between arousal and learning and conditioning. While habituation phenomena in the EEG confound the interpretation of many findings (Stern *et al.*, 1961), some clear relationships have nevertheless emerged. Thompson and Obrist (1964) summarise these as follows: "A common finding in conditioning experiments is the occurrence of EEG desynchronization, which undergoes systematic changes during the acquisition of a response. In early trials desynchronization is generalized, but after repeated pairings of the CS and UCS it becomes localized to specific sensory and/or motor areas . . . Conditioned EEG changes typically occur before the appearance of a conditioned motor response when both are elicited . . ." In their own researches (Thompson and Obrist, 1964; Thompson and Thompson, 1965), they have extended this type of work to verbal learning, but without proper control over habituation. This was achieved by Freedman *et al.* (1966); whose findings on the relation between behavioural and EEG (alpha) changes as a function of trials before and after the last error are shown in Figure 82. There is a clear shift in alpha activity preceding the first correct response. When the experimental group was compared with a yoked

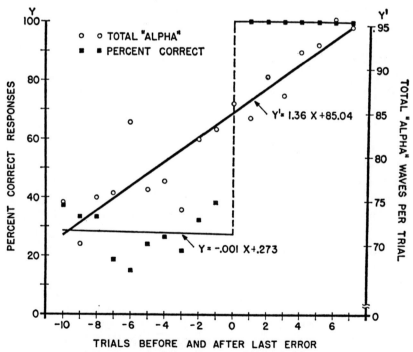

Figure 82. Comparison of behavioral (Y) and EEG alpha (Y′) changes as a function of trials before and after last error. Reprinted with permission from N. L. Freedman *et al*: *J. Comp. Physiol. Psychol., 61*:15-19, 1966.

control group, in order to rule out EEG habituation as a factor, it was found that "the experimental group became less aroused as learning progressed . . . this effect may be a consequence of effective information feedback or an antecedent of correct response . . . Under exposure to the same stimulus-response complex, the yoked control group became more aroused." This group also showed a significant rise in low frequency waves of 6–8 cps, a band which contains theta waves. Mundy-Castle has suggested that increases in these waves are related to heightened emotionality, stress, and frustration, and Freedman *et al.* apply the same interpretation to their data; "the control group might be expected to be progressively more frustrated as a consequence of no information feedback." Here clearly is an important area where only a beginning has been made; it is hoped that in future research the importance of individual differences will be recognized.

It will have been noted that in terms of our excitation-inhibition theory, most stress in accounting for extravert-introvert differences had been laid on inhibition ("reactive inhibition" or "internal inhibition"); in linking up this theory with neurophysiology, stress seems to have shifted to arousal, differences in arousal level, and high arousal thresholds. This would still leave many phenomena to be explained, particularly those associated with involuntary rest pauses, with vigilance decrement, and with adaptation. Here a theory of inhibition would seem to be required by the facts; a simple account in terms of arousal is clearly not sufficient (Diamond, Balvin and Diamond, 1963). Fortunately work on the reticular formation has thrown up concepts and findings which fit the role of causal agents for these inhibitory processes very well (Roitback, 1958; Hernandez-Peón, 1960; Gluck and Rowland, 1959; Kogan, 1960). Magoun (1963) has summarised much of the work done in this field:

> . . . many contributions point to the existence of a nonspecific, thalamo-cortical system, the low-frequency excitation of which evokes large slow waves as well as recruiting responses and spindle bursts in the EEG. These characteristically bear a close relation to internal inhibition, behavioral drowsiness and sleep, although they can display dissociation from such behavior. Differentiable components exist in this thalamo-cortical system and are

capable of being driven more or less independently by inputs from a number of other parts of the brain. Involvement of this mechanism from bulbo-pontile sources may be designed to affect a general reduction of visceral processes. Its excitation from hypothalamic and limbic structures appears to serve a feedback control of pituitary secretion and provide a means of terminating innate behavior by satiety. When activated from the basal ganglia and cerebral cortex, this system appears to manage all the Pavlovian categories of internal inhibition of higher nervous activity, including that of sleep itself. . . . It is now possible to identify a thalamo-cortical mechanism for internal inhibition, capable of modifying activity of the brain partially or globally, so that its sensory, motor and higher functions become reduced and cease. The consequences of the action of this mechanism are the opposite of those of the ascending reticular activating system for internal excitation. The principle of reciprocal innervation proposed by Sherrington to account for spinal-reflex integration would appear relevant to the manner in which these two higher antagonistic neural mechanisms determine the alternating patterns of brain activity manifested as wakefulness and light sleep.

It is one thing to have available neural substrata for arousal and inhibition, but it is quite another to integrate these into some form of model adequate for the explanation of the behavioural phenomena relating to extraversion and introversion. Perhaps the model suggested by Sokolov (1960) (and Voronin and Sokolov, 1960) for the orienting reflex may serve as a more general theoretical structure for the integration of physiological and psychological effects. The model is shown in Figure 83. We have already seen how, in the case of novel or significant stimuli, the cortex sends down to the brain stem excitatory impulses, whereas in the case of repeated or familiar stimuli, inhibitory impulses are sent down. The cortex clearly acts as an analysing mechanism to determine the kind of message which has been received and the kind of impulse to be passed down to the reticular formation. "In developing this part of the theory, Sokolov advances the concept of the 'nervous model.' According to this conception, incoming stimuli leave traces of all their characteristics within the nervous system and especially in the cortex. These traces are the nervous models. They preserve information about the intensity

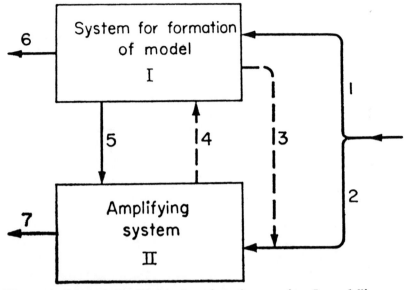

Figure 83. Sokolov's model for the orientation reaction. I: modelling system. II: amplifying system. 1: specific pathway from sense organs to cortical level of modelling system. 2: collateral to reticular formation (represented here as amplifying device). 3: negative feedback from modelling system to synaptic connections between collaterals from specific pathway and reticular formation (RF) to block input in the case of habituated stimuli. 4: ascending activating influences from the RF to the modelling system (cortex). 5: pathway from modelling system to amplifying system (this is the pathway through which the impulses signifying nonconcordance between input and existing neuronal models are transmitted from cortex to RF). 6: to specific responses caused by coincidence between the external stimulus and the neuronal model (habitual responses). 7: to the vegetative and somatic components arising from the stimulation of the RF. From Sokolov, 1960.

and duration of the stimulus as well as other more obvious stimulus dimensions" (Lynn, 1965). As Sokolov (1960) himself puts it, "the model postulates a chain of neural cells which preserve information about the intensity, the quality, the duration, and the order of presentation of the stimuli." This conception clearly resembles very closely Helson's notion of the "adaptation level" (Helson, 1964).

Sokolov makes the assumption that incoming stimuli are compared with the neural models existing in the cortex; if the stimulus does not match any existing (recent ?) model, the orienting reflex occurs and if it does match, the reflex is blocked. We have already seen that the speeds of nervous conduction involved in the various structures are such that direct cortical reaction to incoming sensory stimuli is capable of stimulating or suppressing arousal activity in the reticular formation before the reticular formation is able to act in response to the original stimuli sent to it directly via collaterals. The physical possibility for something of the kind posited by Sokolov to occur thus definitely exists. Furthermore, there is good evidence that cortico-reticular connections of the kind envisaged in this model do exist, and that stimulation of the cortex can elicit the orienting reflex via these pathways (French, 1957; Lagutina, 1955). The most important cortical areas from which connections to the reticular formation project are in the sensorimotor cortex, superior temporal gyrus and tip, paraoccipital region, and entorhinal cortex (see also Thompson and Welker, 1963).

The Sokolov model is able to handle both the elicitation of the orienting reflex and the blocking of it with habituated stimuli, but it cannot be accepted without modification. Furthermore, there are several other models, such as those of Roitbak (1960), Moruzzi (1960), Grastyan (1959), Jouvet (1961), Hernandez-Peón (1960), and others which, while similar in certain ways to the Sokolov model, differ from it in important directions. It is not necessary here to advocate any particular model, even if the evidence could be said to be conclusive, which it certainly is not at this stage. A good discussion of the whole problem is given by Lynn (1965), who devotes several pages to a detailed description of the various models and impartially cites the arguments in favour and against each author. His final conclusion is "that afferent neuronal habituation is a mechanism that comes into play after habituation of the orientation reaction has been accomplished by some other mechanism. Its purpose is presumably to block or attenuate unimportant stimuli peripherally and thus free the higher centres of the brain for more important functions."

Experimental work linking the orienting reflex with individual differences is curiously lacking, particularly in view of Pavlov's frequent observations and statements that the weak nervous system is particularly liable to display persistent orienting reflexes. Work in Teplov's laboratory (Gray, 1965) has been ambiguous at best, largely due to imperfections in design, and the little American work that has been reported (Maltzman and Raskin, 1965), while on the whole in line with expectation, failed to include measures of introversion which alone could have made it directly relevant. The work on habituation reported in Chapter III is well in line with expectation but is not on a large enough scale to support by itself such an important point. Here would seem to be an area where further research would be particularly welcome and worthwhile.

The Sokolov model or something resembling it may also serve to integrate our findings with respect to perceptual defence. Attention has already been drawn to the ability of the cortex to respond with corticifugal impulses (to the reticular formation) to input before this has time to arouse the reticular formation directly, and this mechanism, whether or not we envisage its action precisely as depicted in the Sokolov model, would admirably serve to mediate perceptual defence. As Samuels (1959) has pointed out, "if the perception of complex stimuli requires extensive supportive elaboration from nonspecific sources in order to be retained as conscious memory, and if reticular input can be blocked during this period of consolidation by a discriminative center which is capable of monitoring its own input, then theoretical constructs such as 'subception,' 'perceptual defence,' and 'repression' may have more validity than their critics have yet been prepared to admit." This type of blocking would serve to explain one type of perceptual defence, *viz.* the *suppression* of sensory input; it is equally possible to look to the model to explain the other type of perceptual defence, in which *sensitization* is found. If we attribute the effects to cortically triggered activity of the thalamo-cortical inhibition system and the brain stem arousal system respectively, then we may also deduce that the lower thresholds of these two systems, postulated to characterize extraverts and introverts respectively, are responsible for the greater frequency of sensitization in introverts or of repression in extraverts. (The term "repression" is used in a purely operational sense, to refer to observed instances of sensory suppression; no suggestion is intended regarding the existence or possible mode of functioning of psychoanalytic mechanisms.) There is little experimental evidence regarding this suggestion, but what there is has been reviewed in Chapter III and tends on the whole to support the hypothesis.

It is also possible that we may have here the explanation of two rather distinct phenomena. In the clinical field, hysteria has often been associated with inhibitory phenomena, such as fugues (inhibition of memory), muscular paralysis (inhibition of motor function), and sensory suppression (functional blindness, deafness, etc.). As we have seen, hysterics tend to be more extraverted than dysthymic neurotics (although less extraverted than psychopaths and no more so than normal subjects); it is conceivable that the mechanism under discussion may be responsible for these symptoms and for the fact that it is the (relatively extraverted) hysterics who more frequently suffer from them rather than the (introverted) dysthymics, whose troubles are more frequently associated with sensitization. The nature of the clinical evidence makes any test of this hypothesis rather difficult, and no great confidence is felt in its correctness; all that can be claimed for it is that here we seem to have a physiological and neurological mechanism which may possibly be useful in explaining these very odd and unusual phenomena. Direct evidence would of course be needed before any more could be claimed for this hypothesis.

The other phenomenon to be discussed is the so-called "masking effect," also known as "meta-contrast." If a disc is presented for a period of from 15 milliseconds upwards, it can be seen clearly by human subjects. If an annulus is presented some time after the disc has been withdrawn, then the annulus may wipe out the percept of the disc so that the subject is unaware that he had in fact been presented with a disc before being presented with the annulus, which is all he reports as perceiving. (The inner contour of the annulus is presented in precisely the same position as the outer contour of the disc.) It has been shown that the extinction period (i.e., the period elapsing from the beginning of the exposure of the disc to the end of the interval, and the beginning of the exposure of the annulus) is a constant; i.e., in order for the masking phenomenon to be seen, there is a threshold value of about 86 milliseconds for the extinction period. If the period is longer, the disc is seen. (This law breaks down for exposure periods of 5 milliseconds and less, probably because such short periods are critical durations for the summation of i x t.) A good account of the phenomenon and of the precise experimental details of procedures used in our laboratories is given by Holland (1963). This writer discusses in some detail the various theories advanced to account for this phenomenon; he favours a central over a peripheral hypothesis but agrees that no final decision can be made.

It may be possible to account for the experimental facts in terms of a model not too dissimilar to that used for our discussion of sensitization and repression. Let us call the image of the disc S_1, that of the annulus S_2, and the interval between exposures I. We may postulate that S_1 is transmitted to the cortex and also goes, via collaterals, into the reticular formation. If, within a critical period, no further stimuli are received in the cortex in a position adjacent to S_1, then an impulse is passed down to the reticular formation producing arousal, and S_1 is "perceived." If, however, S_2 is received by the cortex within the critical ("extinction") period, then an impulse is transmitted to the thalamo-cortical inhibition system suppressing S_1, and the image is not "perceived."[4] If this theory be at all along the right lines, then we would expect the critical period to be longer in extraverts and shorter in introverts; in other words, our prediction would be that introverts have lower thresholds of arousal for S_1, i.e., their ability to resolve the two percepts is better. Extraverts, on the other hand, have lower thresholds of inhibition and consequently poorer ability for resolving the two percepts.

This account is of course highly speculative, but experimental data do bear out the prediction. Holland (1964) found consistent, though statistically insignificant, correlations with extraversion in the predicted direction; and more recently MacLoughlin and Eysenck (1967) reported a correlation of 0.36 between extinction period and extraversion, which is statistically significant. The fact appears to be that inhibition, as indexed by the extinction period, is greater in extraverts; whether or not this inhibition is caused along the lines suggested here must remain a moot point

[4]This may be identical with Granit's "pre-excitatory inhibition."

until more direct methods of testing such hypotheses are available.[5]

A similar statement may perhaps be made in summary of all the theoretical discussions offered in this chapter. The psychological data quoted in Chapters II and III demand certain neurophysiological structures as explanatory concepts; neurophysiologists have discovered structures of the requisite type which fit surprisingly well the requirements of the psychologists. One might almost say that if the hypothalamus and the reticular formation had not been discovered, psychologists would have had to invent them—and up to a point, as Hebb forcefully pointed out in his allusion to the "conceptual nervous system," that is precisely what they did. The fact that the needs of psychological data and the findings of the neurophysiologists agree so well is not of course proof of the propositions advanced in this chapter; it is conceivable, although perhaps not altogether very likely, that different and as yet unknown structures might exist in the brain stem and the midbrain which served the function of mediating the personality features associated with neuroticism and extraversion. Until methods of obtaining direct evidence of the postulated association are worked out, one can only acknowledge the weaknesses of the theory presented, while pointing out at the same time that even in its existing state it has enabled many investigators to make testable predictions and to verify these predictions experimentally; this of course is one of the main functions of a good theory. Similarly, the theory has enabled us to give a unified account of the experimental facts as they are known to date; this is the other main function of a good theory. Only future work will tell whether much or any of the theory will survive further testing, particularly the direct kind of neurophysiological study which so needs to be done. What little work has already been undertaken (particularly in relation to the EEG) has certainly supported rather than disproved the general outlines

[5]One interesting method has recently been suggested by O'Hanlon (1966). He took regular blood samples during a vigilance task and analysed these for adrenaline concentration; he found that a lowering of adrenaline levels went with a failure to register signals. The correspondence was quite close ($r = 0.84$), and subjects who showed no deterioration in vigilance also failed to show a decline in adrenaline level. O'Hanlon relates vigilance and adrenaline level to reticular formation functioning, and of course we have seen that vigilance is correlated with introversion, failure of vigilance with extraversion. Thus this study supports our general thesis, as well as suggesting an interesting technique for investigating it.

of our theory, but that cannot, in this very complex field, be taken as a firm promise of further success.[6]

One promising source of information has only recently become accessible to neurophysiologists, *viz.* the study of somatosensory cerebral evoked potentials (Dawson, 1954). Using an averaging technique to eliminate spontaneous brain rhythms, Shagass (1955) recorded EEG from the left sensorimotor area during periodic stimulation of the right ulnar nerve through electrodes placed over the skin of the wrist. The averaging was confined to a brief period of about 250 milliseconds following the stimulus whose duration was 0.1 millisecond. The usual sequence of events consists of an initial, downward-going, negative component of the somatosensory evoked potential (T), followed by an initial, upward-going, positive component (P), followed by a series of later components which alternate between negative and positive. In responses to visual stimuli there has also been observed a so-called "ringing" phenomenon (Walter, 1962), which consists of rhythmic oscillations, starting some 300 milliseconds after the light flash and sometimes continuing for long periods; this response seems to be particularly associated with visual phenomena and suggests that later evoked activity is strongly modality specific. Amplitude of response increases with intensity, and the first evidence of an evoked response is usually obtained with a stimulus intensity corresponding to sensory threshold (Dawson, 1956; Shagass and Schwartz, 1963).

Considerable variation can be observed between subjects in the relationship between stimulus intensity and amplitude of the somatosensory cortical response. "In some subjects response amplitude rose sharply as stimulus intensity increased, whereas in others the rise was much more gradual and amplitude was low even at the highest intensities available to us" (Shagass, 1965). Using sensory threshold as a physiological "zero point" for the intensity scale, curves were plotted relating stimulus voltage increments above threshold to the amplitude of the primary component (defined as T + P,i.e., by measuring the distance from lowest decline during T to highest peak reached during P). Typical curves for dysthy-

[6]It would seem to be particularly desirable to quantify the complex EEG indications of arousal, perhaps in the manner suggested by Daniel (1966) when assessing differences between extraverts and introverts.

mics and psychopaths are given in Figure 84; it will be seen that amplitudes are lower throughout for dysthymics. (In actual fact, the groups graphed are made up in a rather complex manner. Dysthymics are grouped together with nonpatients because no differences were observed between these two groups. Similarly, psychopaths, sociopaths, hysterics, and behaviour problem cases were grouped together with psychotic patients, again because the mean regressions did not differ between these groups. As we are not here interested in the normal and the psychotic groups, we will not go into detail regarding their performance, except to draw attention

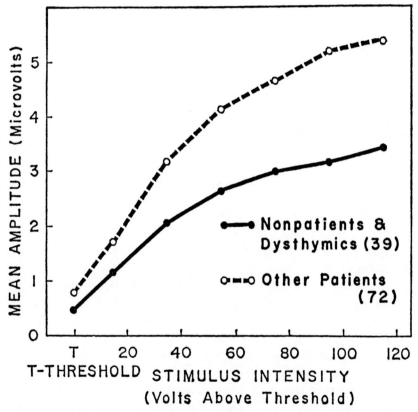

Figure 84. Mean curves comparing intensity-response function in nonpatients and dysthymics with that of all other patients. Reprinted with permission from C. Shagass and M. Schwartz: *Psychiatric Res. Rep.,* 17:130-152, 1963.

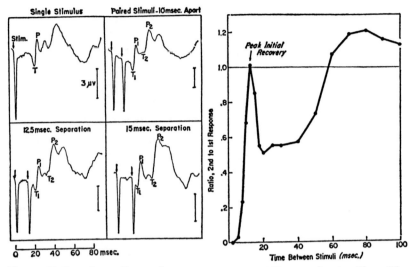

Figure 85. Sample tracing and recovery curve to 100 msec for 1 subject. Upward deflection indicates relative positivity of electrode over somatosensory area, amplitudes measured from T, maximum negativity (trough) to P. maximum positivity (peak). Reprinted with permission from C. Shagass and M. Schwartz: *Arch. Gen. Psychiat.*, 8:177-189, 1963.

to the alignments observed.) "All intensity points, even those at threshold, were statistically significantly different." In his interpretation of the results, Shagass suggests that "some mechanism, which normally operates to restrict the amplitude of response in aggregates of cortical neurones, is impaired in a large variety of psychiatric disorders," but, interestingly enough, not in dysthymic disorders.

Another measure of cerebral responsiveness used by Shagass involves the administration of paired stimuli, thus making it possible to plot the cycle of recovery of responsiveness. Figure 85 illustrates the kinds of recovery cycles found in normal individuals. As shown in the curve on the right, the early portion of the recovery cycle for the primary somatosensory response tends to be biphasic in form. The first phase of recovery occurs very early, the amplitude of the second response equalling that of the first, or exceeding it, before 20 milliseconds. There is then a phase of diminished responsiveness, followed by a longer phase of full recovery, usually reaching a peak at about 100 to 130 milliseconds. Shagass and

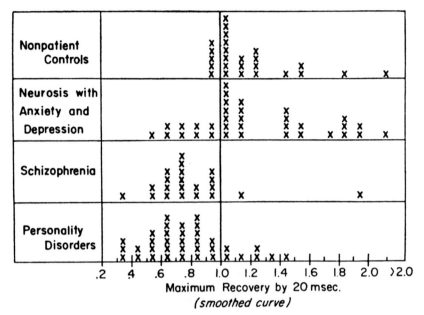

Figure 86. Distribution of ratios representing maximum recovery by 20 msec in 4 subject groups. Each X is one subject. Vertical line at 1.0 indicates full recovery level. Reprinted with permission from C. Shagass and M. Schwartz: *J. Nerv. Ment. Dis., 135*:44-51, 1962.

Schwartz (1963) have plotted the distribution of ratios representing maximum recovery by 20 milliseconds in four subject groups, and their findings are reproduced in Figure 86. Each X represents one subject. It is apparent that dysthymics have higher recovery ratios than psychopaths (personality disorders); in this they again resemble the normal group, whereas the psychopaths resemble the psychotics. The theoretical interpretation of these data is still very much in doubt, but it may be possible to link them with our findings on meta-contrast (masking), where too "recovery" was faster in introverts than in extraverts. (Douchin and Lindsley, 1966, have provided experimental evidence linking masking and visually evoked responses in a manner which gives support to this notion.)

In these studies personality was inferred from diagnosis, which is perhaps a dangerous path to follow; fortunately results are also available from work done on normal subjects with the M.P.I., both using electric stimulation (Shagass, 1965) and visual stimulation

(Shagass, Schwartz, and Krishnamoorti, 1965). The main findings can be summarised by saying that evoked cerebral responses are related to extraversion, but not to neuroticism. They are related to age; age and personality interact in a rather complex fashion. Figure 87 shows mean amplitude values by age groups in subjects with high and low E scores respectively. "The data suggest that, if it were extrapolated to infancy, the overall curve relating age to amplitude would probably be U-shaped. The ascending limb of the U is demonstrated by our older subjects. The descending limb is shown only by those subjects which had high E scores in the youngest group; they had significantly higher amplitudes than the 20-38 group. Should the true curve be U-shaped, desceasing am-

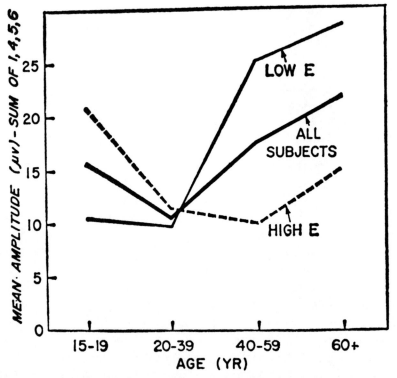

Figure 87. Mean amplitudes by age groups of peaks 1, 4, 5 and 6 summed without regard to sign, in high and low extraversion subjects, and in both groups together. Reprinted with permission from C. Shagass and M. Schwartz: *Science, 148*:1359-1361, 1965.

plitude in early years would be associated with maturation and increasing amplitude in late life with neuronal degeneration. A further implication would be that neurophysiological maturation and aging both tend to occur later in more 'extraverted' individuals." There is here an interesting echo of the point made in an earlier chapter, in relation to Conrad's work, regarding the greater immaturity of extraverted persons as compared with introverted ones.

These studies are cited, not so much because their relevance has been established, but because they present us with a challenging task for the future. There are suggestions implicating the reticular formation in these phenomena (Goff *et al.*, 1962), but the theory of somatosensory evoked potentials is not at the moment sufficiently advanced to have much faith in any particular interpretation. There is, however, a fairly definite relationship between these potentials and personality, particularly extraversion-introversion, and it seems reasonable to infer that further study will throw a much needed light on the role which the central determinants of individual differences in these phenomena have to play in personality development.

Direct support for our hypothesis then is limited, and we have to rely to a large extent on what has sometimes been called a "nomological network" of hypothesis, deductions, and experimental findings. As A. von Haller (1768) put it, *"natura in reticulum sua genera connexit, non in catenam; homines non possunt nisi catenam sequi, cum non plura simul sermone exponere."* There is one field of study, however, which promises to furnish us with a more direct experimental approach to the testing of our theory. Some limited knowledge is available about the site of action of various chemical agents, and also about the general effects which these drugs have on the structures with which they interact. It seems possible that direct deductions could be made from our theory, taken in conjunction with what is known about pharmacological effects, and that the verification or disproof of these predictions could furnish us with a method of direct testing of our theory. The next chapter is devoted to a brief review of work carried out along these lines. Another field of study which promises to be of use in this connection is that of brain damage, whether accidentally sustained or whether inflicted as a therapeutic measure; a survey of relevant information will be undertaken in the Chapter VII. It is hoped that the data surveyed in these two chapters will be accepted as relevant to our theory, and that they will go some way towards making the theory somewhat less unlikely as a true, if not as a sufficient, account of the physiological basis of personality.

CHAPTER VI

PERSONALITY AND DRUGS

Studies of personality, such as those reviewed in Chapters II and III are not strictly experimental, in the sense that conditions are held constant except for changes in the independent variable, while results are noted for the dependent variable. Instead of varying experimentally the degree of extraversion or of neuroticism, we select groups of people occupying different positions on the continuum in question. This type of experimental design has many weaknesses as compared with the classical design; ineluctable though these may be, they still make conclusions drawn from such "experiments" rather doubtful. Thus two groups selected to differ only on the relevant variable may in fact differ on many others as well, and although some of these other variables may be irrelevant, others may not. Complete matching is in principle unattainable, and even reasonable degrees of matching are not usually achieved in many studies. Selection assumes prior knowledge of the appropriate principles of selection, as well as possession of a reliable and valid means of selection; the former is only too frequently missing in personality research, or else merely assumed without sufficient proof, while the latter is difficult to come by. Even if all these difficulties could be overcome, still large numbers of cases would be required in order to cancel out chance errors; even then, there are still many experimenter-subject and situation-subject interaction errors which cannot be eliminated. All these problems are inherent in the failure to manipulate the independent variable except by selection, and the use of physiological and biochemical methods of testing and measuring personality variables is equally subject to difficulties of the kind described as are psychological tests. It follows that interpretations of empirical findings must always be regarded with extreme suspicion, and that alternative hypotheses should always be canvassed with more than usual eagerness.

It is difficulties of this kind which have caused many experimental psychologists to look with disfavour upon personality research as a whole and to disregard the problem presented by the indisputable existence of individual differences. Yet psychology is not the only science which upon occasion has to jettison the full use of the experimental method and rest content with empirical studies of less exalted status; astronomy and meteorology, to give but two examples, are in much the same boat, and geology, hydrography, and many others share this defect. Personality theory in its broadest aspect cannot escape from this limitation, but specific theories may do so, and in this chapter an attempt is made to use psychopharmacological investigations as a direct experimental method for verifying or disproving certain deductions from the personality theory outlined in previous chapters. The mediating link, without which such an effort would not be very convincing, has been provided in the previous chapter; if personality differences are dependent, in the ultimate analysis, upon such factors as threshold differences in the reticular formation arousal system and the thalamic synchronising system, then we can use drugs known to act in stimulating or depressing ways upon these systems to produce temporary changes in the experimental subject's position on the excitation-inhibition continuum. These changes should produce predictable alterations in behaviour, both on the level of outwardly observable activity and also in relation to laboratory investigations of conditioning, perception, learning, and the like. It is these latter changes with which we shall primarily be concerned in this chapter.

This line of argument, which will be presented in much more detail later, gives rise to two paradigms which differ in important respects; these two alternatives are presented in Figure 88 (Eysenck, 1957). According to paradigm A, we take a random sample of the population and compare their performances under the particular experimental conditions in which we are interested. Predictions can be made either on the basis of our general theory of cortical arousal or else from previous knowledge of the respec-

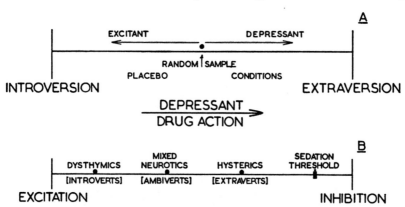

Figure 88. Two paradigms for studying the effects of drugs on human personality. Reprinted from H. J. Eysenck, 1963.

tive behaviour on the test of known extraverts and introverts, or both. In general, the prediction would be that stimulant drugs lead to greater arousal and hence to more introverted behaviour, while depressant drugs lead to greater inhibition and hence to more extraverted behaviour. (The terms "stimulant" and "depressant," as applied to drugs, require much more careful specification, of course; we will return to this point later.)

Paradigm B takes into account the preexisting differences in state of arousal between extraverts and introverts and deduces that introverts, being in a comparatively high state of cortical arousal, would require less stimulant drug than extraverts to reach a specified state of excitation, but would require more of a depressant drug to reach a specified state of inhibition. In other words, introverts have higher sedation thresholds than extraverts, but extraverts have higher excitation thresholds. Average, ambiverted people would be expected to be intermediate between introverts and extraverts. One essential feature of paradigm B, i.e., the fact that individual differences between subjects are taken into account, can of course also be incorporated in paradigm A, either by correlating position on the experimental continuum with amount of drug-induced change, or by the calculation of an interaction term in the analysis of variance. It is possible that such interactions may arise from two causes. In the first place, the scales of measurement used for the experimental test in use may not (and probably do not) have equal units of measurement, or, to put it in another way, the regression lines may be monotonic but not linear; quite possibly slopes become steeper as extreme values are approached, so that extraverts would seem (or be) more susceptible to depressant drugs, introverts to stimulant drugs. In the second place, it is conceivable that reticular formation thresholds are not independent of drug sensitivity. These are empirical matters with respect to which speculation would be idle.

Before we can turn to a more precise delineation of the theory proposed, or discuss the experimental evidence, we must turn to face several objections which will immediately occur to the reader, and which indicate that the suggested types of investigation may run into severe difficulties. The first difficulty which arises stems from the large number of variables which influence drug effects. A list, by no means complete, is given of some of these variables (Table 12); it will be seen that control of all of these, or even of a majority, poses difficulties no less serious than those encountered in connection with the use of personality-type groups instead of proper independent variables. Some simplification can be produced by excluding psychiatric patients, using only small doses of drugs, avoiding too-frequent repetition of administration, taking into account all the latest knowledge about the effects of the drug in question, and generally designing the experiment with a mind open to all the multifarious difficulties presented by this formidable list. A more detailed discussion of some of the points raised is given by Trouton and Eysenck (1960); here we have space only to note them in passing.

The second problem is if anything an even more forbidding one. Stimulants and depressants are both very heterogeneous groups of drugs (Goodman and Gilman, 1955). Depressants, for instance, include general anaesthetics, sedatives-hypnotics-soporifics, antiepileptics, narcotics, analgesics and antipyretics, and centrally acting skeletal muscle relaxants, while among the central nervous stimulants the diversity is even greater, and, besides the differences in the mode and site of action, there is apt to be a multitude of side effects. Toman (1952) concluded that "so diverse in chemical structure are the many substances which produce central depression or complete anaesthesia that it is hard to imagine any single

TABLE XII

THE MAIN VARIABLES INFLUENCING DRUG EFFECTS

1. *Nature of the Drug*
   Preparation (including concentration, vehicle of administration and whether disguised).
   Mode (oral, intravenous injection, etc.) and rate of administration, absorption and excretion.
   Dosage (according to body weight, or the same for all).
   Interval before testing.

2. *The Subject*
   Personality (including intelligence, extraversion-introversion, neuroticism, suggestibility, etc.).
   Familiarity with the situation and the amount of stress occasioned by it.
   Practice; fatigue; motivation.
   Tendency to react to *placebos*.
   Psychiatric state, and its duration.
   Age, sex, physique, height and weight.
   Present state—
   General state of health, nutritional status, sleep.
   Conditions of work, e.g., temperature, humidity, oxygen lack.
   Diseases, disabilities (e.g., fever, thyrotoxicosis, liver or kidney damage) or effects of operations, etc. (e.g., leucotomy, concussion).
   Time of day.
   Interval since last meal (if drug given orally).
   Recent medication with other drugs (e.g., sedation) or ingestion of drinks containing stimulants or depressants.
   Previous experience of drugs—
   Cumulative effect of some drugs (e.g., bromides).
   Habituation, tolerance (including cross-tolerance).
   Addiction.
   Idiosyncracy or hypersensitivity.

3. *The Social Environment*
   Interaction with other subjects.
   Activities required or permitted after administration of the drug.
   Suggestion.
   Reinforcement of responses by the experimenter.

From D. Trouton and H. J. Eysenck, 1961.

mechanism of action common to all. Indeed, there is no reason to believe that a common action is essential, since there must be as many different ways of blocking central nervous activity as there are independent parameters necessary for the normal maintenance of function in the central nervous system." Furthermore, "although stimulants and depressants have actions which are opposed in some respects, the antagonism is usually not perfect, because each drug tends to have not just one effect but a whole range of effects which are unlikely to correspond exactly with those of the antagonist. Some effects of stimulants and depressants are even synergic (e.g., the effects of amphetamine and amylobarbitone on mood)" (Trouton and Eysenck, 1960). Some drugs which stimulate the nervous system in small doses cause depression if larger doses are given, and depression commonly follows the stimulant effect.[1]

Domino *et al.* (1955) have discussed the difficulties of classifying the actions of a drug into stimulant and depressant on the basis of "gross observation." They say: "The usual definition of a 'stimulant' is an agent that increases a functional activity, and that of a 'depressant' an agent that decreases functional activity. In the complex organization of the central nervous system it is difficult to determine whether a compound is a true 'stimulant' or 'depressant' on the basis of gross observations in the intact animal. A drug may exert its effects at a variety of central sites. It may act at the neuronal level either to excite or depress; it may act at the synapse or other portions of the neuronal arc, or it may influence facilitatory or inhibitory neurons which feed into the common nervous pathway. Thus a pharmacological agent that stimulates inhibitory neurons might be an overt depressant, whereas an agent that selectively depresses inhibitory neurons may cause an overt excitatory response." We are here encountering terminological difficulties which should never be allowed to arise; "the use of terminology borrowed from pharmacology or neurophysiology such as 'stimulation,' 'depression,' 'facilitation' and

[1]One cause for the differential action of certain drugs when administered in different doses may lie in the differentiation between *direct* and *indirect* effects. Consider adrenaline, which is often called a stimulant drug, yet which was classed by Dewhurst (1965) with the depressant amines. Small doses of the drug had typically depressant effects on brain and behaviour and none on *blood pressure*. "If the amounts given are increased small rises in blood pressure are also seen and at this stage the animal's response is a mixture of drowsiness with spells of alert behaviour. When the dose is increased still further marked rises in blood pressure occur, and alerting is the sole reaction with complete masking of depressant responses. It seems clear, therefore, that the alerting produced by adrenaline is secondary to a peripheral blood pressure effect and is not a primary cerebral action. Indeed, only the blood pressure effect is possible in most species with intact blood-brain barriers" (see also Dewhurst and Marley, 1965). It is important to know something about the site and mode of action of a drug if it is to be used in meaningful psychopharmacological work.

'inhibition' to describe phenomena concerned with total adaptive behaviour is not only unjustified, but actually misleading" (Wikler, 1950; see also Wikler, 1952).

We have in an earlier chapter pointed out a similar possible confusion between *inhibited behaviour* and *cortical inhibition*; the dual use of the term "inhibition" easily leads to identification when in actual fact cortical inhibition is, if anything, related to *uninhibited* behaviour. Altogether, the difficulties here described arise less from real complexities than from the confusion attending verbal habits; depression of mood or emotional tone, depression of outward behaviour, and depressant action in the nervous system are entirely different and separate universes of discourse which should not under any circumstances be identified with each other or be taken as indicative one of the presence of the other without specific proof.

Fortunately it is possible to give a more operational meaning to the terms "stimulant" and "depressive" by identifying them theoretically with arousal-excitation and inhibition as defined in the last chapter; this also gives us experimental methods of measuring the predicted effects of both types of drugs, along the lines of the studies described in Chapter III. In addition to anchoring the terms and concepts thus more securely than was possible before, we now also have the added advantage of being able to account for the curious fact, mentioned above, that "stimulant" drugs may have "depressant" effects and vice versa. In many cases this is clearly an artefact due to a mistaken idea of whether observable phenomena are in fact due to cortical depression or arousal, but where the observation is genuine, it may be possible to account for it in terms of the inverse-U relation between arousal and performance which we have encountered so frequently in previous chapters. Last, we may be able to account for a frequent finding in psychopharmacological work, i.e., that it is easier to produce decremental results through depressant drugs than incremental results through stimulant drugs. If, as seems likely, most people are working at or near their optimum level of cortical arousal, then the administration of even small amounts of depressant drugs would be expected to lower performance, while small amounts of stimulant drugs would be relatively ineffective. Large amounts of stimulant drugs, by pushing the individual on to the descending branch of the inverse-U, would have decremental effects, although this effect would be very dependent on the precise shape of the (nonlinear) regression obtaining between arousal and performance. The ideal conditions for demonstrating the arousing effects of stimulant drugs would consequently appear to involve a state of lowered initial arousal (suboptimal), whether induced through fatigue, depressant drugs, or some other means.

Even though physiological and pharmacological evidence may pinpoint the effects of a certain drug in affecting the reticular formation, and through it the arousal state of the cortex, many problems clearly remain. Many drugs have side effects, and our experimental measures may be affected by these rather than by the main effects. This objection is perhaps less serious when very small doses of the drugs involved are taken, but it must always be guarded against. More interesting is the possibility that drugs less crucially related to the reticular formation in their action may produce effects similar to, or identical with, those of "true" stimulant and depressive drugs as defined above. Obviously the cortico-reticular loop may be affected in other places than the reticular formation, and the various other loops involving the R.F. which we have described in the last chapter are equally vulnerable. It would seem that, pending the proper exploration of the exact site of action and mode of action of all the drugs on which experimentation is proceeding at the moment, a method would be useful which could purely from the experimental-behaviour side tell us to what extent the effects of n drugs on m tests involve more than one putative causal agency. A mathematical method for carrying out such a programme has been suggested by Eysenck and Eysenck (1960), who also provide a worked-out example. The method used derives from Fisher's discriminant function analysis, generalized to n variables; it is too technical to be described here, but in view of its potential usefulness in solving a very important problem in psychopharmacological research it seemed appropriate to mention it here.

Wikler (1957), Baker (1961), and Killam (1962) have published surveys of drug actions on the reticular formation, and it would take us well out of our way to retrace these intricate and complex relations and experiments. Furthermore, many of the drugs studied pharmacologically, and frequently also clinically, have not been used much in experimental work, and therefore do not require evaluation here. Space will be given only to drugs which have been used sufficiently to make discussion, however brief, worthwhile, and which have been shown to be reasonable choices for the roles of "core stimulant" and "core depressant" agents according to our definition.

"On the depressant side, the sedative and anesthetic agents were the first compounds the actions of which on the R.F. were clearly demonstrated" (Killam, 1962), and in particular, "considerable evidence has accumulated that reticular influences on cortical poentials, on spinal reflex activity, on recovery cycles in the thalamic relay, and on the conduction through the cochlear and geniculate relays are reduced or blocked by barbiturates . . . So repeatable has the barbiturate depression of reticular activity been from species to species that in numerous studies pentobarbital, and, less often, thiopental have become the standards of comparison for the study of other depressant drugs." The phenothiazines and Rauwolfia alkaloids have a much more complex and occasionally paradoxical action; thus small doses of chlorpromazine have been reported to depress reticular mechanisms, while higher doses have opposite effects. Biochemical explanations of reserpine action "have not been localized in the brain to a specific area such as the R.F."; doubts about the "core" quality of these drugs suggest that experimental work with them might for the moment be left out of account with some advantage. Meprobamate, which has been used quite widely in our own researches, possesses certain clinical resemblances to the barbiturates, but, particularly at small doses, "there is little evidence of a selective reticular depression like that produced by barbiturates" (Killam, 1962). The possibility of a thalamic locus of action for meprobamate has been suggested.

As regards the stimulants, the amphetamine-like compounds appear to have a position analogous to that of the barbiturates in the depressant field; amphetamine itself, pipradrol, methylphenidate (Ritalin®), and caffeine have probably been more widely used experimentally than most (Trouton and Eysenck, 1960). Even with these substances there are still many problems and complexities in the way of making clear-cut and unambiguous predictions, but at least the general line of argument is reasonably clear. In any case, as the writer suggested elsewhere (Eysenck, 1963b), pharmacological work and experimental-behavioural studies act like the two working parties which seek to construct a tunnel under a mountain; the most conclusive proof that their combined efforts are going along the right lines lies in their actual meeting in the middle. In the same way, empirical findings mediated by hypotheses deriving from probable assumptions in the pharmacological field and equally probable assumptions in the psychological field tend to support both sets of assumptions and lay at least a foundation for that nomological network which will ultimately constitute the science of psychopharmacology; if we were to wait until both sides had certainties rather than probable assumptions to offer, then little work along empirical lines would be done at all.

In turning now to the experimental literature, we must make it clear that no complete or even partially complete account of this vast and fast-growing body of data will be attempted; readers interested in such a review must be referred elsewhere (Eysenck, 1960c; Herz, 1960; Trouton and Eysenck, 1960; Lippert, 1959; Weiss and Laties, 1962). In this chapter we shall concentrate entirely on those studies which are directly relevant to our general theory, those which can thus be said to manipulate personality along the introversion-extraversion axis. Mostly our account will be restricted to human subjects, but occasionally animal experiments also will be referred to. In view of the often held belief that animal experiment cannot in the nature of the case be relevant to theories of human personality, an example may perhaps be given to make clear the nature of our approach.

Alternation behaviour is frequently observed in human and animal subjects and is theoretically ascribed to cortical inhibition, which may affect motor aspects, perceptual aspects, or both. If this is so, then depressant drugs should increase alternation behaviour, while stimulant drugs should decrease it. Figure 89 shows the results of an experiment in which alternation was induced in rats by forcing them to make 0, 1, 2, or 3 turns in one direction before choosing whether to turn right or left to obtain a reward present in both directions (Sinha *et al.*, 1958). The placebo group shows the

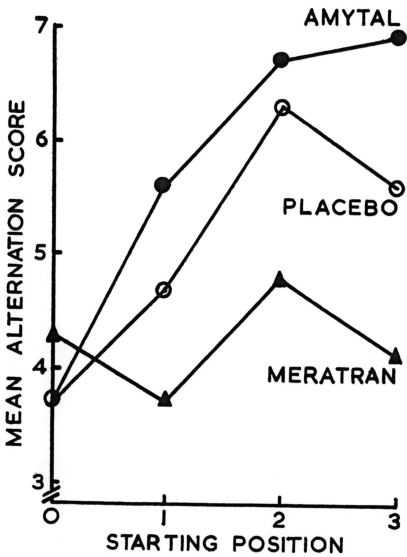

Figure 89. Alternation behavior in rats as a function of stimulant and depressant drugs. Reprinted with permission from S. N. Sinha *et al.*: *J. Exp. Psychol.*, 56:349-354, 1958.

amount of alternation produced by the experimental condition; it will be seen that the animals given Amytal® alternate more in all positions, while those given meratran do not alternate at all (see also Sinha, 1964). No comparable drug experiments have been done with human subjects to complete the findings that introverts alternate less than extraverts (Eysenck and Levey, 1965); in the absence of such studies not too much should, of course, be claimed for the experiment reported; nevertheless, it does illustrate the way in which animal behaviour may be used to test predictions derived from theory.

We must now turn to an examination of the evidence concerning paradigm B (Figure 88), i.e., mainly the work on sedation thresholds begun some twelve years ago by Shagass (1954), and continued by him and his collaborators (Shagass, 1956, 1957, 1958; Shagass and Jones, 1958; Shagass and Kerenyi, 1958; Shagass and Naiman, 1955, 1956; Shagass, Naiman, and Mihalik, 1956). This threshold is defined as "that amount of Sodium Amytal® (in mg per kg body weight) required to produce an inflection point in the amplitude curve of frontal 15 to 30 c/s activity, within one injection interval of onset of slurred speech. The inflexion point was defined as that point which followed an abrupt rise in the curve and preceded a tendency to flatten, or the point just preceding a clear plateau in the curve." A clearer understanding of the defi-

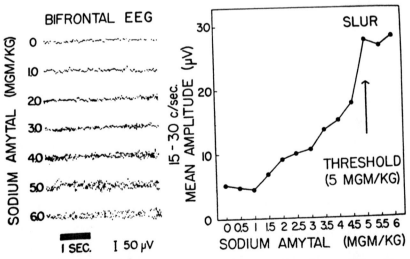

Figure 90. Effect of increasing amounts of amobarbital (Amytal®) sodium on bifrontal EEG. Reprinted with permission from C. Shagass: *Psychosom. Med.*, *18*:410-419, 1956.

nition of the sedation threshold can be gained from Figure 90, which illustrates the measures taken. Some authors (e.g., Ackner and Pampiglione, 1959) have found difficulties in discovering a clear-cut interval defined in this manner, and in our own laboratories a rather simpler type of measure has been used (Eysenck, 1963). In the hands of its originators, however, the test as described has certainly proved both reliable and valid, and we may now summarise briefly some of the empirical correlates discovered by them in relation to personality differences. According to our theory, we would expect extraverts (and neurotics diagnosed as hysterics, psychopaths, personality disorders) to show *low* thresholds and introverts (and dysthymic neurotics) to show *high* thresholds. The facts are in good agreement with theory, as shown in Figure 91.

Figure 92 shows results from over 300 neurotic patients; it will be seen that as expected hysterics have the lowest thresholds, anxiety states the highest, with other diagnostic categories intermediate. The sequence of diagnostic groups is very similar to that found by Hildebrand (1958) in a factor-analytic study of personality using a variety of questionnaires and objective tests. Less than 5 per cent of the hysterics had sedation thresholds of 4mgm/kg or more, as compared with over 90 per cent of anxiety states, or just under 90 per cent of neurotic depressions. It would be most interesting to know what thresholds might be found in psychopaths; by our theory they should be even more extreme than hysterics.

The inclusion of neurotic (reactive) depressions raises the old problem of whether these patients can in fact be regarded as fundamentally different from psychotic (endogenous) depressions (Eysenck, 1960). The writer, in summing up the evidence, has concluded that this is indeed a true and fundamental distinction, and Shagass, Naiman, and Mihalik (1956) provide evidence from their data on sedation thresholds that this is indeed so. Figure 93 shows thresholds for various psychotic depression groups, as compared with neurotic depressions; it will be clear that the psychotic depressions resemble the hysterics, while the neurotic depressions resemble the anxiety states. The discrimination is very clear and almost without overlap. The same authors also report that short-term response to ECT is significantly better in "typical" psychotic

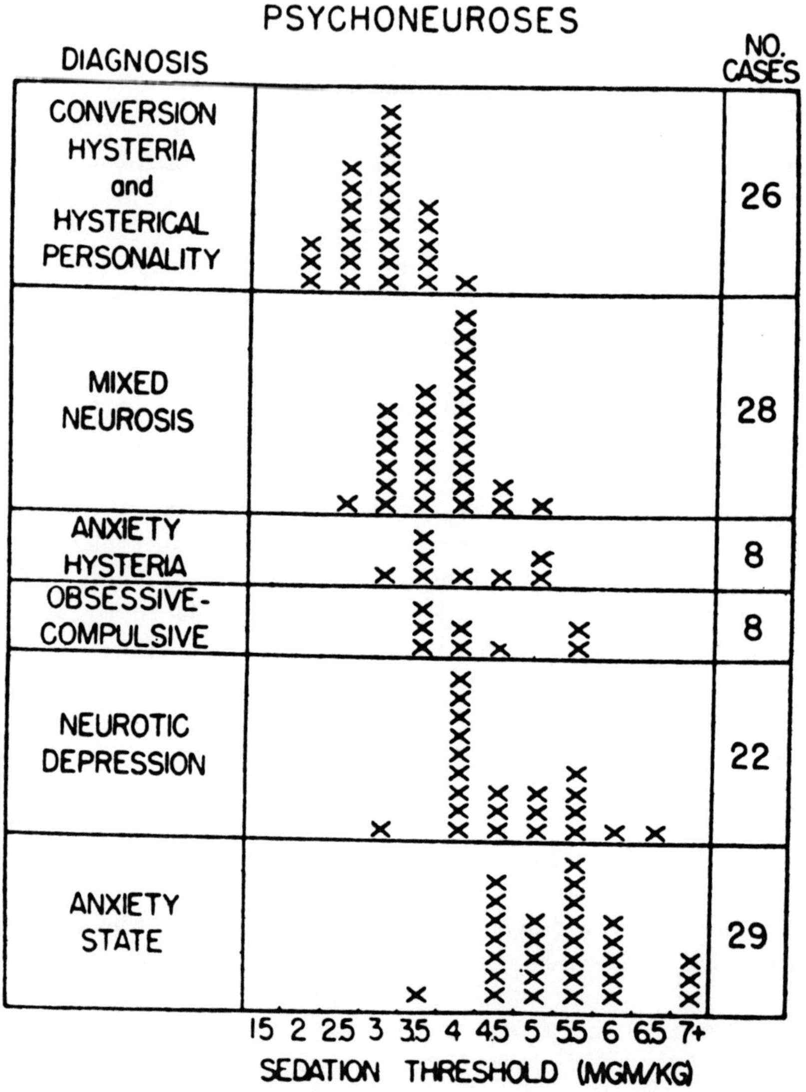

PSYCHONEUROSES

Figure 91. Sedation threshold distribution for various neurotic groups. Reprinted with permission from C. Shagass and J. Naiman: *J. Psychosom. Res.,* 1:49-57, 1956.

depressives, i.e., those with low sedation thresholds. This suggests that perhaps the slight amount of overlap remaining may have been due to errors in diagnosis.[2]

[2]Kretschmer has always maintained that manic-depressive patients were prototypes of the cyclothymic (extraverted) personality type, while schizophrenics were

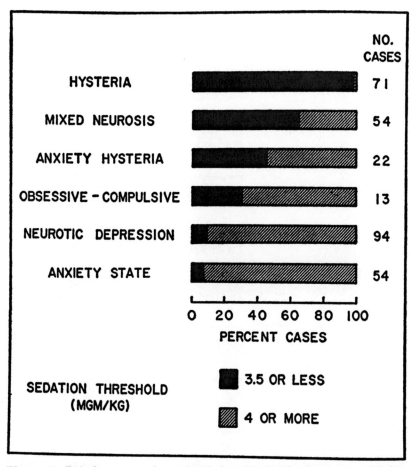

Figure 92. Relative proportions of sedation thresholds above 3.5 and below 4 mgm/Kg in various psychoneurotic groups. Hysteria includes conversion hysteric and hysterical personality. Reprinted with permission from C. Shagass and A. L. Jones: *Amer. J. Psychiat.,* *114*:1002-1009, 1958.

prototypes of the schizothymic (introverted) personality type. The data quoted above lend some support to this theory: neurotic, reactive depressives are *intro-verted* and have *high* sedation thresholds, while psychotic, endogenous depressives are *extraverted* and have *low* sedation thresholds. If this dual nature of the symptom "depression" is accepted, Kretschmer's personality theory falls into good alignment with that proposed here, at the same time as extending the extravert-introvert dimension into the psychotic field. Bodybuild data also support such an interpretation. The position of paranoid patients is left somewhat unclear; they may be intermediate on the schizoid-cycloid continuum, and therefore ambivert as regards personality. These suggestions are of course highly speculative, but may repay experimental study.

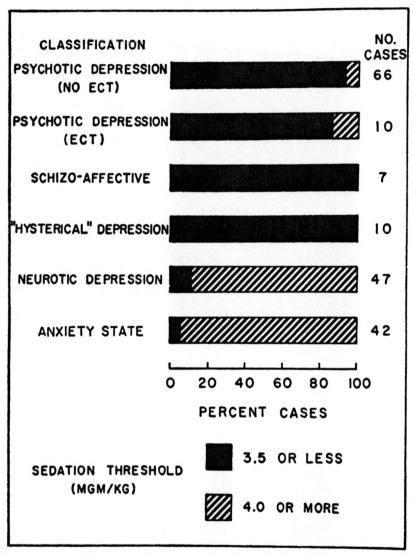

Figure 93. Sedation thresholds for various psychotic depression groups, as compared with neurotic depressions. Reprinted with permission from C. Shagass *et al.*: *A.M.A. Arch. Neurol. Psychiat.*, 75:461-471, 1956.

In addition to their sedation threshold, Shagass and Kerenyi (1958) have pioneered the concept of a "sleep threshold," in which the test is continued until the subject becomes totally unresponsive. The writers report that this test gives rather similar results; as an example they quote Figure 94, in which psychotic and neurotic

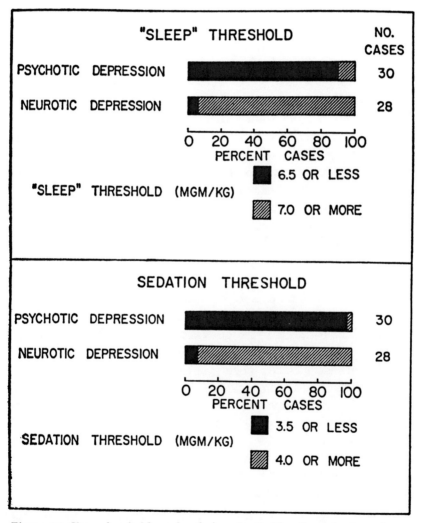

Figure 94. Sleep thresholds and sedation thresholds of psychotic and neurotic depressions. Reprinted with permission from C. Shagass and A. Kerenyi: *Canad. Psychiat. J.*, 3:101-109, 1958.

depressives have been subjected to both the sleep and the sedation threshold test. In addition, they found that "the gradient of increasing thresholds from hysteria to the mixed neuroses to the dysthymic groups . . . which has been consistently noted with the sedation threshold, was also present with the 'sleep' threshold, and was statistically significant." The correlation between the two thresholds was found to be 0.66 in ninety-one patients; the writers feel that the sleep threshold is probably less reliable and accurate than the sedation threshold.

The studies discussed so far were undertaken in such a way that psychiatric diagnosis constituted the main criterion. Figures 95 and 96 show results from studies using (a) an "hysterical-obsessional rating" for 224 patients, each patient being rated by two psychiatrists for his position on this personality continuum which closely resembles the extravert-introvert one (see Foulds, 1965), and (b) scores on the Guilford personality scales R and S combined, which provide a close approximation to an introversion score (Shagass and Kerenyi, 1958). It will be seen that the use of those two different criteria also provides good evidence for the postulated relationship between sedation threshold and personality. The bi-serial correlation coefficient for the rating versus threshold data was 0.84 when considered were only those cases to whom both psychiatrists assigned H or O ratings. For the inventory data, the correlation was 0.60. The former correlation was considered inflated, the latter too small because of restriction of range; the true (but uncorrected) correlation was probably in the neighbourhood of .7.[3]

As already mentioned, some authors have failed to replicate Shagass's findings because of difficulties with the method used for determining the sedation threshold (Ackner and Pampiglione, 1958; Thorpe and Baker, 1957; Moffat and Levine, 1964), while others (Laverty, 1958) were more successful and succeeded in discriminating extraverted and introverted neurotics and normals; Laverty, too, however, comments on the difficulty in many cases

[3]Sloane *et al.* have reported a correlation of −.57 between sedation threshold and extraversion on forty female neurotics, which is not too different from this estimate. They found a completely insignificant correlation of .04 with neuroticism. Sedation threshold also correlated significantly with GSR fluctuation' (r = 0.33), but not with basal GSR.

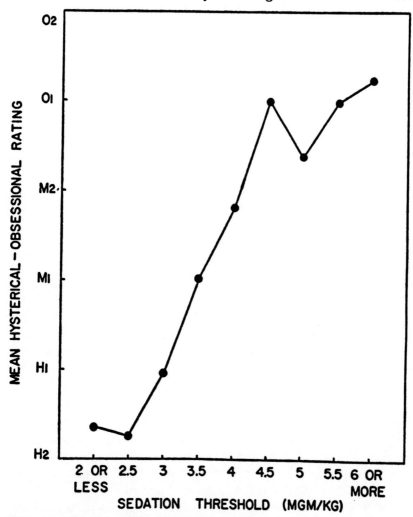

Figure 95. Mean hysterical-obsessional rating plotted against sedation threshold for 224 patients. Reprinted with permission from C. Shagass and A. Kerenyi: *J. Nerv. Ment. Dis.*, *126*:141-147, 1959.

in assessing sedation thresholds from slurred speech.[4] In order to get over this difficulty, Claridge and Herrington (1960) have developed a different, much simpler criterion than the EEG + slur

[4]Some writers, e.g., Martin and Davies (1962), have failed to replicate Shagass's findings although using the more easily duplicated "sleep threshold" method. It is difficult to see why such failure has occurred in these instances.

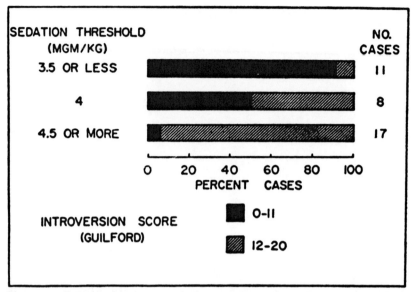

Figure 96. Relationship between sedation threshold and introversion (Guilford combined C score for R and S scales). Reprinted with permission from C. Shagass and A. Kerenyi: *J. Nerv. Ment. Dis., 126*:141-147, 1958.

one used by Shagass. In their work "the sedation threshold was assessed in terms of the effect of Sodium Amytal® on a simple task of attention. The stimulus material consisted of a tape-recording of random digits relayed to the subject through earphones. While receiving a continuous intravenous infusion of Sodium Amytal® at the rate of 0.1 G/min, the subject was required to respond by doubling the digits, which occurred regularly at intervals of two seconds. The digits were grouped on a score sheet into blocks of five and the errors recorded were then plotted against blocks, giving graphs of the form shown in Figure 97. The threshold was taken as the point midway between the last two blocks with less than 50 per cent error and the first two blocks in which errors exceeded 50 per cent. In the majority of cases these blocks were consecutive. The amount of drug administered at this point was determined from a chart relating blocks to drug received and this dosage corrected for the weight of the patient, giving the threshold in terms of mg. Kg." Krishnamoorti and Shagass (1963) found this threshold to correlate very highly with their "sleep threshold" (rko = 0.91).

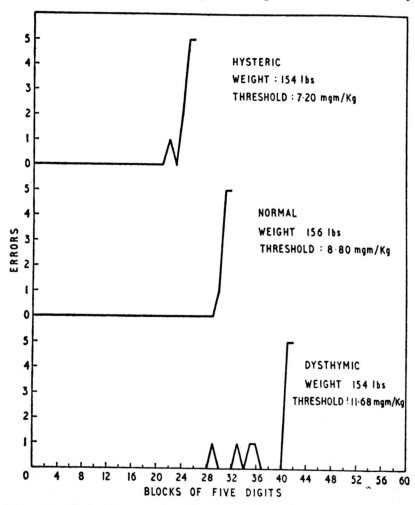

Figure 97. Typical hysteric and dysthymic performances on Claridge-Herrington sedation threshold test. Reprinted with permission from G. S. Claridge and R. N. Herrington: *J. Ment. Sci., 106*:1568-1583, 1960.

The group of subjects tested included dysthymics, hysterics, and normals, and the sedation threshold scores were as expected highest for the dysthymics (10.18, S.D. 1.61), lowest for the hysterics (6.43, S.D. 1.77), with the normals in between (7.86, S.D. 1.31.) Within the normal group introversion correlated significantly with thresholds (r = 0.52), but this value dropped to an insignificant

0.27 when all groups were included. Neuroticism was found to be positively correlated with sedation thresholds. The writers suggest on the basis of these and numerous other experimental findings too detailed to discuss here "that a shift occurs in the excitation-inhibition balance of dysthymics and hysterics" due to "changes in neurotics in the level of arousal"; this would appear to be the first suggestion relating personality dimensions to the reticulo-cortical system. Claridge (1961) applied this notion to a vigilance task (five choice serial reaction time), arguing that while differential fall-off in performance might be due to reactive inhibition, initial differences in performance were more likely to be due to differences in arousal; his results demonstrate this point very well. Claridge then extended his work on the five choice serial reaction time task by testing the effects of administering a depressant drug (meprobamate). The effects of this drug were identical with those of taking a placebo; both depressed the starting level of performance (Figure 98). The effects of the drug were seen only at the end of the performance period, when the placebo group showed improved performance.

Claridge, Wawman, and Davies (1963), in a series of three papers in which the name of the senior author is sequentially rotated, have followed up this general idea of an interaction between autonomic and reticular activities by measuring the effects of various physiological and pharmacological stressors in neurotics and normals, while also administering the sedation threshold test. Among the tests used were the cold pressor test, the Mecholyl® test, and blood pressure response to an adrenaline antagonist. The final conclusion arrived at was "that central nervous excitability was the result of at least two processes. First, cortical excitation is maintained by the level of afferent input into the nervous system, a process corresponding to what Eysenck refers to when he talks of an excitation-inhibition balance underlying introversion-extraversion. A second process, however, that affects the overall level of excitability is the degree of autonomic, specifically sympathetic, responsiveness to stimuli. This may be roughly identifiable with Eysenck's neuroticism factor, in the sense that extreme lack of autonomic equilibrium is essentially pathological." These views are

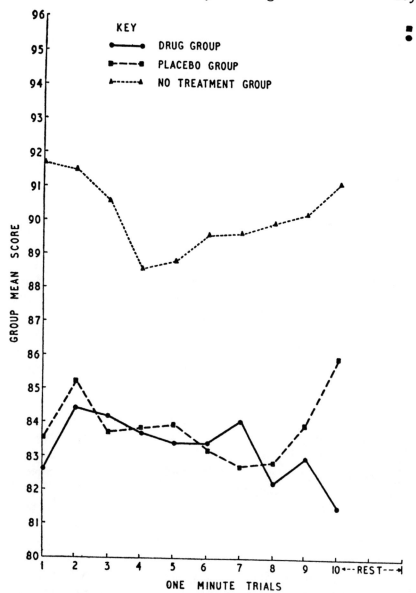

Figure 98. Mean score for each group on each trial. Reprinted with permission from G. S. Claridge: *J. Ment. Sci.*, 107:590-601, 1961.

in good agreement with those expressed in this volume.[5] They are further amplified, and further evidence relating to the sedation threshold and various psychological and physiological given, in a chapter by Claridge and Herrington (in Eysenck, 1963b). One study reported there may be cited, as it supports the view that introverts, at the beginning of a vigilance task, have higher state of arousal than extraverts; Figure 99 shows mean sleeping pulse and mean change in waking pulse during vigilance performance; the marked differences at the beginning of the task will be apparent. They agree well with the performance figures shown in Figure 29.

Claridge's view about the importance of taking into account neuroticism as well as extraversion in relating personality and sedation thresholds is borne out strikingly in a study by Rodnight and Gooch (1963). These writers used nitrous oxide in oxygen mixture as a suitable general central nervous system depressant (Haugen and Melzak, 1957, have provided evidence for the action of this gas on the reticular formation). The main test for indexing the effect of the gas was a finger dexterity test; it was found that when the values of the percentage concentrations of nitrous oxide were transposed into units based on an inverse log scale, and plotted against the raw scores, the relationship between performance and drug dosage became linear, different individuals showing different slopes.

An arithmetical task was also used, similar to that already described in connection with Claridge's work. Figure 100 shows the outcome, susceptibility to the drug being plotted against E and N. The relationship was shown to be highly significant, a correlation of .59 being obtained with the joint personality scores. It will be seen from the Figure that without zone analysis no statement is possible relating susceptibility to one dimension only; stable extraverts show the lowest degree of susceptibility, neurotic ones the highest. The small number of cases used makes generalization difficult, and it is of course quite possible that the paraphernalia attending the continuous administration of the gas mixture may

[5]Claridge's recent book on *Personality and Arousal* (1967) should be consulted in this connection; unfortunately it came to our attention too late for a discussion of its contents to be possible. It contains much interesting experimental material relating to sedation thresholds in normal, neurotic, and psychotic groups, as well as other psychological and physiological tests.

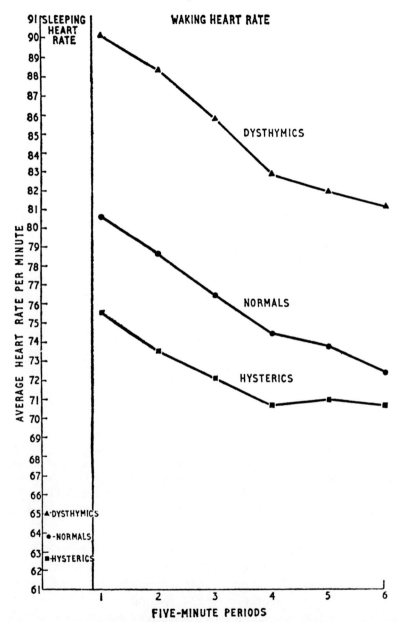

Figure 99. Mean sleeping pulse and mean change in waking pulse during vigilance performance. Reprinted with permission from G. S. Claridge and R. N. Herrington, in H. J. Eysenck, 1963.

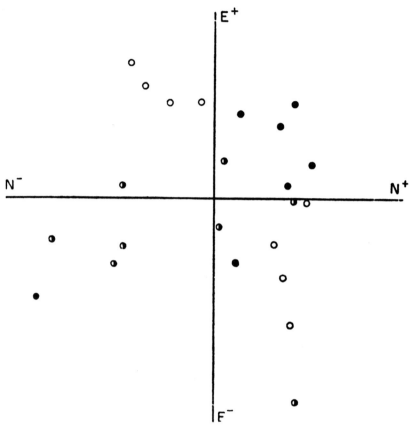

Figure 100. A diagrammatic representation of the distribution of the total sample with respect to the personality variables of extraversion (E) and neuroticism (N), showing the interrelationship between these and degree of susceptibility to N_2O. Black circles indicate high susceptibility, half-shaded circles moderate susceptibility and white circles insusceptibility. Reprinted with permission from E. Rodnight and R. N. Gooch, in H. J. Eysenck, 1963.

have raised the activation level of predisposed subjects in ways which might have interfered in the determination of deterioration scores. Nevertheless, the results should stand as a warning not to underestimate the complexity of the relations involved or to regard sedation thresholds as a *pure* measure of extraversion. It will be remembered that most of Shagass's work was done with *neurotic* extraverts and introverts, and when we look at the N+

groups in Figure 100 we see that there, as expected, it is the extra-verts who show susceptibility, while the introverts do not. With the stable groups this relationship is confounded, and clearly what is required is much further work with normal groups before a proper understanding of these relationships can be said to have been achieved.

At the opposite end of the scale, we would expect that intro-verts would have a lower "arousal threshold" as compared with extraverts. The only relevant work to have been done in this field comes from Russia and has been well summarised by Gray (1964); the methods used are rather dissimilar to those used in the West, and the drug used (caffeine) is one which has not frequently figured in Anglo-American research along these lines. Therefore, instead of going into an inevitably overlong and over-detailed ac-count of the experimental data, we shall quote Gray's summary of the experimental evidence. He lists three main findings, of which the second is particularly relevant here: "(a) The administration of caffeine tends to produce behaviour characteristics of individuals with a weak nervous system. (b) The effects of caffeine tend to be greater, the weaker the nervous system. (c) Caffeine alters ab-solute sensory thresholds (usually lowering them) in the weak nervous system, but leaves them unchanged in the strong ner-vous system." This third conclusion too would seem to be anal-ogous to the sensory threshold findings, in that the stimulant drug effects are stronger and more easily elicited from introverted subjects. (It must of course be remembered here that in the Russian work individuals are identified as having a "strong" or "weak" nervous system, not in terms of self-ratings or observed behaviour patterns, or even of clinical diagnosis, but in terms of experimental findings. This makes the argument more circular and also precludes absolute identification of the Russian work with our own.)

In addition to these experimental data, there is ample clinical evidence to suggest that extraverts, and particularly psychopaths, are much more tolerant of amphetamine than are ambiverts and introverts, and that stimulant drugs of this kind have an ameliorating effect on their behaviour. Conversely, they do not seem to tolerate depressant drugs as well and are affected for the worse by them. A detailed discussion of this type of work has been given by the writer elsewhere (Eysenck, 1965); in view of its nonexperimental nature there would seem to be little point in digressing here sufficiently to cite all the evidence in detail. On the whole, however, the clinical evidence is in good agreement with the experimental evidence to suggest that introverts have higher sedation thresholds and lower excitation thresholds than do extraverts. The evidence also suggests that neuroticism may interfere in complex ways with this simple generalization, but in the absence of proper zone analyses it is difficult to go beyond this statement.

Some further experimental evidence regarding "arousal thresholds" is also available from studies using "paradigm A," to a discussion of which we now turn; clearly here the crucial point is the interaction term. Paradigm A, it will be remembered, simply involves testing groups of subjects under placebo, stimulant, and depressant conditions respectively, predicting the direction of change on suitably chosen tests in terms of greater arousal or greater inhibition. If the personality scores on subjects in these groups are known, then an interaction might be expected between extraversion/introversion and amount of change; i.e., extraverts would change more when given an introverting drug (stimulant), and introverts would change more when given an extraverting drug (depressant). Such a simple prediction cannot of course be expected to apply to all types of tests and situations, nor to all doses of drugs; it is unlikely that relations involved are linear or even monotonic. However, subject to the many considerations we have discussed on previous pages, both as regards the pharmacological and the psychological sides, it may be possible to look for such interaction effects as interesting corollaries to the main predictions being tested.

Our discussion will begin with the relatively unexplored area of perception, particularly sensory thresholds. There is some evidence that depressant drugs raise sensory thresholds (e.g., Burns *et al.*, 1960; Wolff *et al.*, 1941), but this effect might be mediated by so many factors that it is not of very great interest. Of much more interest would be the discovery of a positive effect of stimulant drugs on sensory thresholds, and such findings have indeed been published by Russian workers (see Gray, 1964). However, American workers have been unable to duplicate these results (Mandelbaum, 1941), and Granger (1960) concludes that the "results of the more recent and carefully controlled experiments are almost entirely negative." He adds, however, that "the amount of well-controlled experimentation in this field is not yet large enough for final conclusions to be drawn." This is particularly unfortunate, as some of the most interesting Russian work has in fact compared the effects of stimulant drugs on introverts and extraverts (weak and strong nervous system) respectively, and claims that effects are greater in the former than in the latter. Clearly much work remains to be done in this area before any definite conclusions can be drawn.

Positive results have been reported in the field of pain sensitivity by Haslam, whose work we have referred to before. She found that caffeine significantly lowered pain thresholds in her (normal) subjects; her account does not make it clear whether there might have been any interaction effects. The difficulties of arriving at definitive results in the field of pain threshold measurements are of course very great (Beecher, 1959), but there are no obvious sources of error in her work to make one doubt the general validity of her conclusion.

One area alone has received more adequate attention, *viz.* that of CFF. Here the work of Aiba (1963), Landis and Zubin (1951), Mücker and Wendt (1951), Roback *et al.* (1952), Schmidtke (1951), and Simonson *et al.* (1941, 1952) leaves little doubt that stimulant drugs raise the threshold (i.e., improve ability to discriminate separate stimuli), while depressant drugs lower it. A more recent study by Shagass and Lipowski (1958) is of particular interest in this connection as they have studied the effect of a stimulant drug on different groups of subjects. Figure 101 shows the results of their study; it will be seen that the dysthymic group shows the least improvement, the hysterics the most, with the mixed group intermediate. Psychotic depressions are clearly separated from the dysthymic group and react more like the hysterics. If we may regard the dysthymics and hysterics respectively as representative of introverted and extraverted groups, then we have here evidence, not only of the general introverting effect of the stimulant drug used (Methedrine®), but also of the predicted greater effect of such a

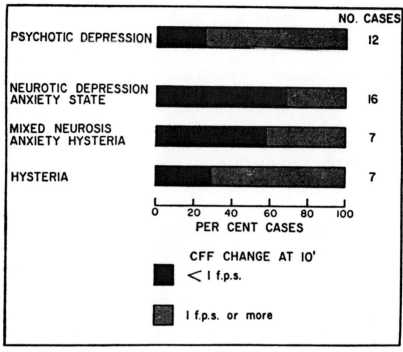

Figure 101. Effects of stimulant drugs on CFF for different psychiatric groups. Reprinted with permission from C. Shagass and Z. J. Lipowski: *J. Nerv. Ment. Dis.*, 127:407-416, 1958.

drug on extraverted persons. It must of course be remembered that in this study we are dealing exclusively with neurotics, not with normal extraverts and introverts, and that the possibility exists that in a normal group no such interaction might be found. Nevertheless, the finding is interesting and important in its own right and deserves to be replicated and extended to normal subjects. (It should perhaps be added that Shagass and Lipowski failed to find any relation between CFF change and sedation threshold in a group of fifty-six patients tested with both measures. Both tests showed the predicted relation with personality, and their failure to correlate together suggests (a) that a multiple correlation would have given a very high degree of diagnostic accuracy, and (b) that the effects in question may be mediated by partly independent systems.)

Auditory flutter fusion might be expected to give similar re-

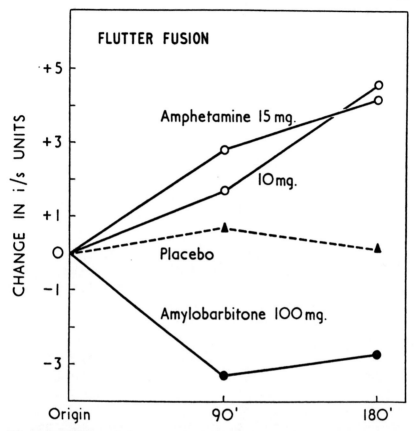

Figure 102. Flutter fusion as a function of stimulant and depressant drugs. Redrawn and reprinted with permission from G. M. Besser, 1966.

sults as CFF, but the results of an experiment by Eysenck and Easterbrook (1960d) were essentially negative. G. M. Besser (1966) used a more refined apparatus in which the interruption rate could be varied in steps of 1 i/s. Using doses of 10 mg and 15 mg of amphetamine, as well as a placebo, and testing both 90 minutes and 180 minutes after administration, Besser obtained the results shown in Figure 102; differences between doses are not significant, but those between drug and placebo are (p < .01). Using a dose of 100 mg of amylobarbitone, Besser found a significant decrease (p < .001) as compared with a placebo; the drug effect is included in Figure 102, but not this placebo group, as it would have made the crucial differences less easy to see. The mean shift for the stimulant drug, as compared with the placebo, is about $+4$ i/s; for the depressant drug it is about -5 i/s. These values, while fully significant, are small enough to lend plausibility to the argument that the Eysenck and Easterbrook study failed because of too large i/s steps being used.

Other perceptual phenomena have been studied in a variety of experiments which are not very conclusive, largely because the theoretical position is rather confused as regards appropriate predictions and because experimental studies, as reviewed in Chapter III, have failed to give clear-cut evidence on differential performance of introverts and extraverts. Furthermore, many of these studies were done on small groups of subjects in an exploratory way. For this reason we will not discuss in detail work on figural aftereffects (Eysenck and Easterbrook, 1960a, 1960b; Costello, 1962; Holland and Gomez, 1963), visual constancy (Sylvester, 1963), apparent movement (Costello, 1963; Sylvester, 1963), reversible perspective (Eysenck, Holland, and Trouton, 1952), or time estimation (Goldstone *et al.*, 1958; Costello, 1961). Drug effects on after-images (Costello, 1963) and spiral aftereffects (Eysenck, Holland, and Trouton, 1957b; Eysenck and Easterbrook, 1960c; Costello, 1963) are rather more clear-cut, and as the theory is more definite these experiments may perhaps be counted in favour of the general position taken. Depressant drugs definitely cut down the length of the aftereffects, and there is some evidence that the amount of decrement is negatively correlated with extraversion; this too is in line with expectation. However, of rather more interest from the theoretical point of view is the slightly more extensive work that has been done on visual masking (Eysenck and Aiba, 1957; Aiba, 1963; Holland, 1963). Here the prediction of more intensive masking effect in extraverts has been well substantiated, and the deduction of greater masking effects with depressant drugs, less masking with stimulant drugs, is relatively obvious and less dependent on a variety of parameters than in the case of figural aftereffects, say, or some of the other perceptual phenomena mentioned.

The original work of Eysenck and Aiba was concerned with the so-called Bidwell effect. In this experiment Bidwell demonstrated

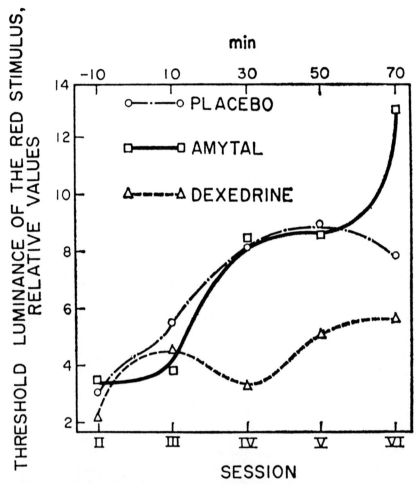

Figure 103. Effects of stimulant and depressant drugs on visual masking (Bidwell effect). Reprinted with permission from S. Aiba, in H. J. Eysenck, 1963.

the suppression of the primary visual stimulus and the simultaneous production of the negative after-image of the stimulus suppressed. If a brief exposure of a red stimulus is followed by a brief exposure of a white stimulus, then (assuming suitable time intervals have been chosen) the subject does not see the red stimulus (suppression of the primary stimulus) but only the green after-image. Durations for the primary stimulus vary from 5 to 50 milli-

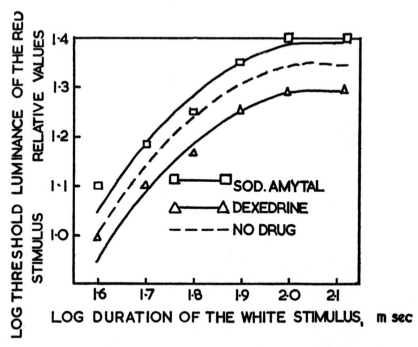

Figure 104. Effects of stimulant and depressant drugs on visual masking (Bidwell effect) with various durations of white stimulus. Reprinted with permission from S. Aiba, in H. J. Eysenck, 1963.

seconds, while the white stimulus varies from 50 to 100 milliseconds. This phenomenon represents a special case of visual masking. The effects of amylobarbitone and Dexedrine® at various times from the administration of the drug are shown in Figure 103, when the duration of the white stimulus was fixed; it will be seen that with the depressant drug a primary stimulus of greater luminance is masked than when a placebo is used (sixth session only), while with the stimulant drug the opposite effect is produced (fourth, fifth, and sixth sessions). These effects are in line with expectation. Figure 104 shows results from a similar experiment in which the duration of the white stimulus was varied; results are clearly similar. In these experiments, therefore, stimulant drugs have an introverting effect, depressant drugs an extraverting one.

Holland (1963) used the more widely known procedure outlined in Chapter V, in which a disc is presented tachistoscopically,

followed by an annulus after a short period of 40 to 80 milliseconds; at appropriate intervals the disc is masked (not seen). The
effects of Sodium Amytal® and Dexedrine® are shown in Figure
105 for various durations of disc exposure (primary stimulus)
and interval; it will be noted that the stimulant effects of the Dex-
edrine® are marked, while the depressant effects of the Amytal®
are not apparent. Another experiment, using meprobamate, gave
more clear-cut results (Figure 106). Other experiments using nitrous oxide and oxygen as depressant and stimulant substances respectively also gave results in line with expectation (Figure 107).
Therefore, on the whole Holland's results too are in agreement
with expectation, except for the puzzling failure of Sodium Amy-
tal® in the first experiment to show a stronger masking effect.

Turning now to motor movements, we may note that Rachman
(1961) has followed up his work on the relation between person-

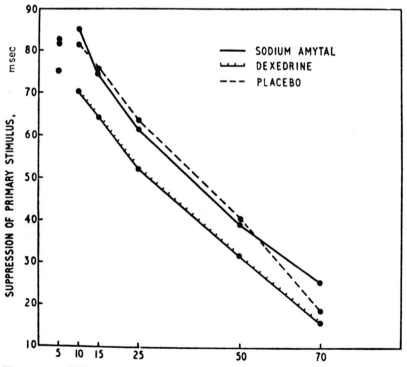

Figure 105. Effects of stimulant and depressant drugs on the masking interval. Reprinted with permission from H. C. Holland, in H. J. Eysenck, 1963.

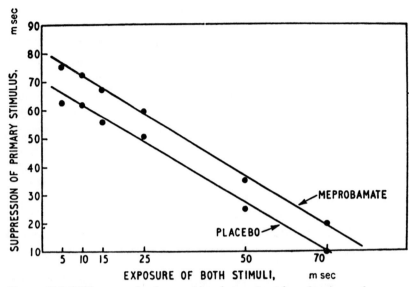

Figure 106. Differences in the masking interval under placebo and mepro-bamate conditions. Reprinted with permission from H. C. Holland, in H. J. Eysenck, 1963.

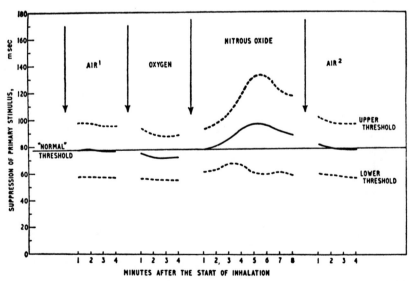

Figure 107. Course of four treatments on visual masking. Reprinted with permission from H. C. Holland, in H. J. Eysenck, 1963.

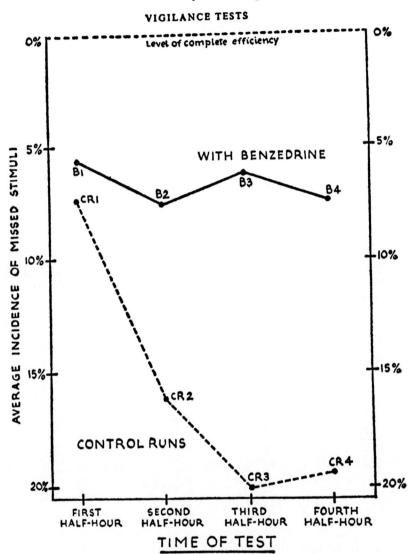

Figure 108. Course of vigilance test with and without Benzedrine®. Reprinted with permission from H. Mackworth: M.R.C. Special Rep. No. 268. London, H.M.S.O., 1948.

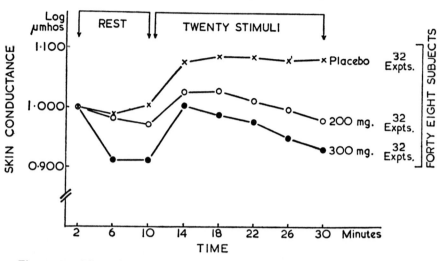

Figure 109. The effect of cyclobarbitone on skin conductance. Each point represents the mean of four log conductance readings. Reprinted with permission from M. H. Lader: *Brain,* 87:321-340, 1964.

ality and motor movements, noted in Chapter III, by an experiment in which the effects of two doses of dexamphetamine sulphate were studied and compared with responses under placebo. It was expected that extent of movement would be reduced by the stimulant drug, and the results for the three conditions were as follows: Placebo—20.3; 5 mg dose—20.0; 10 mg dose—14.5. "Thus the stimulant drug reduced the extent of motor movements, which is consistent with Eysenck's postulate. It is possible that the smaller movements made under the influence of amphetamine indicate that greater accuracy and economy of action are produced by this additional cortical stimulation." It must be noted, of course, that the task used was not an emotionally arousing one; had it been, the opposite effects would have been predicted. An experiment along these lines remains to be carried out. Legge (1965) has reported results with a depressant drug which are also in line with prediction; he found that this drug induced an increase in size of handwriting.

The effects of stimulant drugs on vigilance tests are very much as expected; Figure 108, taken from Mackworth (1948), is typical of the remainder. The drug succeeds in averting the decline in

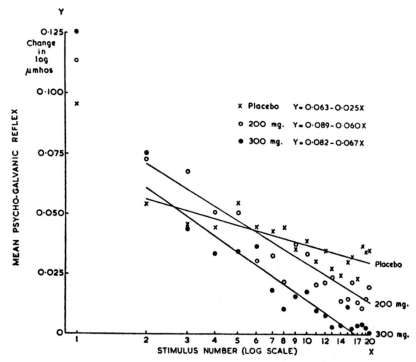

Figure 110. The effect of cyclobarbitone on the habituation regression line of the psychogalvanic reflex. Reprinted with permission from M. H. Lader: *Brain,* 87:321-340, 1964.

performance which is so characteristic of control and placebo performance. Depressant drugs, on the other hand, tend to accelerate the decline (Treadwell, 1960). Studies such as those of Bakan (1961), Uhr *et al.* (1964), and Haward (1965) are representative of many others. Prevention of decline in time of motor performance by stimulant drugs has also been demonstrated in a long series of studies by Payne and Hauty (1955, 1957) and Hauty and Payne (1955, 1958). In some experiments drug action could only be demonstrated when subjects were in a fatigued condition (Townsend and Mirsky, 1960; Kornetsky *et al.*, 1959). Good reviews of this work are given by Plotnikoff *et al.* (1960) and by Weiss and Laties (1962). On the whole these studies of vigilance and associated phenomena support the theoretical point of view here advocated, linking stimulant drugs with introverted behaviour and

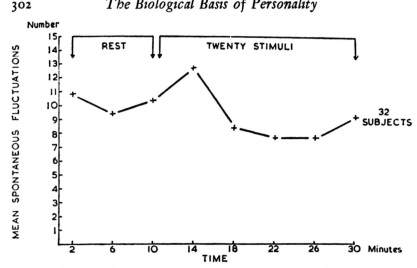

Figure 111. The effect of 20 auditory stimuli on the number of spontaneous skin conductance fluctuations. Each point represents the mean number of fluctuations counted for four periods of forty seconds. Reprinted with permission from M. H. Lader: *Brain,* 87:321-340, 1964.

depressant drugs with extraverted behaviour.

The effects of stimulant and depressant drugs on electrodermal and other related activities have been widely studied, and again only the most closely relevant studies can be reviewed. We will begin with a study of adaptation (habituation) carried out by Lader (1964), to which reference has already been made in Chapter III. Figure 109 shows the results of this study, in which skin conductance was measured during rest and in response to twenty identical auditory stimuli. It will be seen that the depressant drug used (cyclobarbitone) depresses the level of skin conductance and leads to a greater habituation effect. This is even more obvious in Figure 110, which shows the regression lines for the three conditions against a log scale of stimulus numbers. Spontaneous fluctuations in skin conductance were also reduced by the drug, as shown in Figure 111. Martin (1960) has also reported quicker adaptation-habituation under depressant drugs; her results on increase in skin resistance during twenty tone stimuli are reported in Figure 112. She also found that the drugs raised the level of skin resistance. Additional material relating to spontaneous fluctuation of autonomic activity (pulse rate) has been reported by Lader

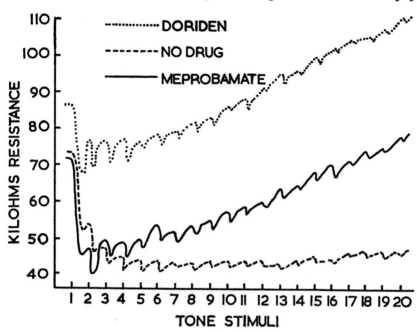

Figure 112. Measurements of palmar skin resistance during 20 tonal stimuli under three conditions—Doriden®, no drug, and meprobamate. Reprinted with permission from I. Martin, in H. J. Eysenck, 1960.

(1965); he found that cyclobarbitone increased pulse rate fluctuations, a result directly opposite to that found with skin conductance. As he points out, "in our present state of knowledge, prediction from one physiological measure to another must be done with the utmost caution . . . at present, the simplest physiological system available for study as the concomitant of physiological experiments is the skin conductance." It would be interesting to study the correlation between personality and spontaneous fluctuation in pulse rate; Lader's results suggest an inverse relationship with introversion rather than a direct one, as with sudomotor activity.

A similar paradox, also involving cardiovascular reactions, was demonstrated in another study by Lader (1965). Using the same experimental paradigm, he found that cyclobarbitone decreased mean integrated electromyogram responses, both during rest and during stimulation (Figure 113). This result is of course very much

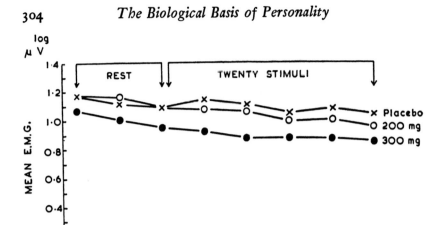

Figure 113. The effect of cyclobarbitone on the integrated electromyogram. Each point represents the mean of four readings averaged for 32 subjects. Reprinted with permission from M. H. Lader: *J. Psychosom. Res.*, 8:385-398, 1965.

as expected. However, he also found that pulse volume was increased in magnitude by the drug and that pulse rate too was increased. A possible explanation of these contradictory findings is suggested in terms of the concept of "secondary vigilance" (Fischgold and Schwartz, 1961). It is suggested that the "second-degree vigilance" mechanism "monitors incoming stimuli during drowsiness and sleep. If the stimulus is 'irrelevant' large cardiovascular responses occur without psycho-galvanic reflexes; if the stimulus is relevant, e.g., the subject's name, widespread activation occurs including a psycho-galvanic reflex. During normal wakefulness, stimuli cause psycho-galvanic reflexes but the cardiovascular responses are partially inhibited." Whether this be the true explanation or not, clearly predictions linking cardiovascular responses to personality cannot at the moment be made with great confidence; sudomotor and electromyographic responses are more likely to behave in predictable ways.

The studies quoted were carried out on normal subjects; in another experiment Wing and Lader (1965) used instead twenty neurotic patients suffering with anxiety. Figure 114 shows the re-

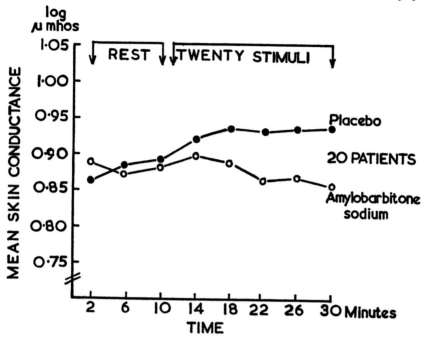

Figure 114. The effects of 20 auditory stimuli on skin conductance. Each point represents the mean of four log conductance readings. Reprinted with permission from L. Wing and M. H. Lader: *J. Neurol., Neurosurg. and Psychiat.*, 28:78-87, 1965.

sults of applying twenty identical auditory stimuli under placebo and amylobarbitone sodium administration respectively on skin conductance; it will be seen that the main differentiation is with respect to habituation—under placebo there is if anything an increase in reactivity, while under the drug there is a marked adaptation. Spontaneous skin conductance fluctuations were lower throughout under drug conditions. Results with patients are therefore similar to those with normal subjects.

A somewhat different study is reported by Lienert and Traxel (1959). An emotion-arousing word-association test was used as the stimulus, and galvanic skin responses recorded. Three groups of ten subjects each were equated on a pretest and then given either placebo, meprobamate, or alcohol. The results are shown in Figure 115; clearly the drugs have depressed GSR activity. Similar results have been reported with respect to palmar sweating by

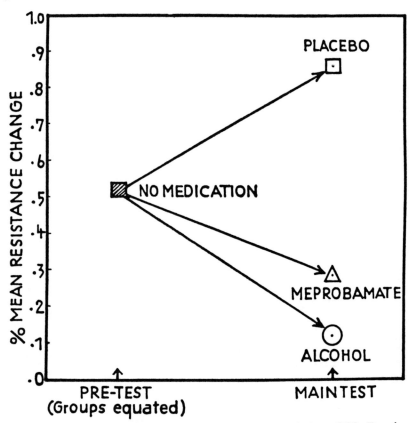

Figure 115. Effects of placebo, meprobamate, and alcohol on GSR. Reprinted with permission from G. A. Lienert and W. Traxel: *J. Psychol.*, 48:329-334, 1959.

Laties (1959), who used a short ride on a ferris wheel as the emotional stimulus. Jones *et al.* (1965) report on the effects of pentobarbital on basal conductance, the effect being one of reduction; morphine did not produce this effect.

The same authors also report on the results of experiments with the conditioned electrodermal response. Tone-shock sequences were used to produce the conditioned responses, and Figure 116 shows the results; the four groups studied were given placebo, two different doses of morphine, and pentobarbital. The depression of reactions to the tones under both conditioned and unconditioned trials will be apparent. Other authors who have shown that

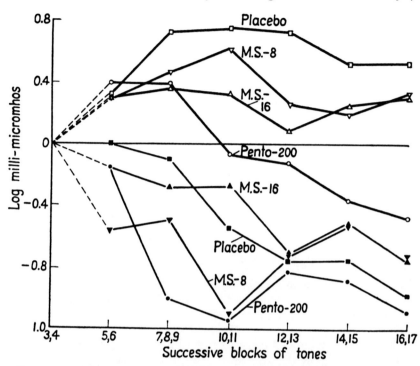

Figure 116. Effects of placebo, pentobarbital, and morphine on conditioned and unconditioned electrodermal responses. Reprinted with permission from B. E. Jones *et al.*: *Psychopharmacol.*, 7:159-174, 1965.

on the whole depressant drugs decrease and stimulant drugs increase autonomic conditioning are Dureman (1959), Rutledge and Doty (1957), Schneider and Costiloe (1957) and Mitchell and Zax (1959). Uhr *et al.* (1961) report largely negative results.

Work in our own department has concentrated rather on eyelid conditioning (Franks and Laverty, 1955; Franks and Trouton, 1958; Willett, 1960). Franks and Laverty showed that intravenous Sodium Amytal® reduced the number of conditioned eyeblink responses during acquisition and also increased the rate of extinction. Placebos did not produce any effects as compared with no-drug treatment. Willett found that Doriden® depressed the rate of conditioning significantly, while meprobamate did so at a level which was not statistically significant. Franks and Trouton used both a stimulant drug (dexamphetamine sulfate), and a depressant drug

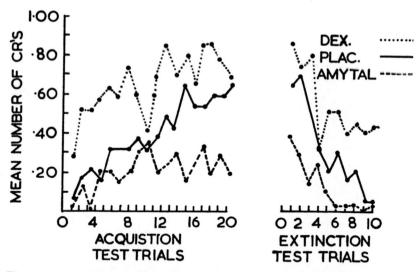

Figure 117. Eyelid conditioning and extinction under stimulant and depressant drugs. Reprinted with permission from C. M. Franks and D. Trouton: *J. Comp. Physiol., Psychol.,* 51:220-222, 1958.

(amobarbital sodium) and obtained the results shown in Figure 117. The results of the Amytal® group look very much like those obtained by Franks for extraverted subjects, while the results of the Dexedrine® group look very much like his results for introverted subjects. This study is the closest to those mentioned in Chapter III and the most important and relevant of all the conditioning studies for our theory.[6]

One further conditioning study is of some interest because the writer failed to obtain any notable drug effects (Ludvigson, 1964). In this experiment the method of partial reinforcement used by Franks was replaced with that of total reinforcement, and as explained in Chapter III this method does not allow inhibition to grow sufficiently to reduce the conditioning rate of the extra-

[6]Alcohol had also been predicted by Eysenck to have the effect of depressing rate of acquisition of conditioned eyeblink responses. Franks (1963) failed to support this prediction, but recently Hobson (1966), in a methodologically superior and better controlled experiment, studied "the effects of three ethanol doses and three adaptation levels upon the acquisition and resistance to extinction of the conditioned eyeblink response . . . in 135 men. Regardless of dosage, the action of ethanol was shown to interfere with the learning of new response patterns, confirming Eysenck's depressant drug postulate."

DRUG AND PERSONALITY

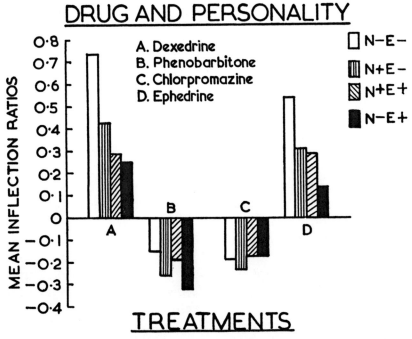

Figure 118. Effects of stimulant and depressant drugs on verbal conditioning. Reprinted with permission from J. S. Jawanda, 1966.

verted group. It is therefore quite in accord with theory that under these conditions no differences should be observed in response to extraverting and introverting drugs, just as under these conditions no differences were observed between extraverts and introverts.

One study only has come to hand relating to verbal conditioning. Jawanda (1966) used the same procedure as in his verbal conditioning experiments described in an earlier chapter to study the effect of stimulant and depressant drugs on subjects chosen on the basis of extreme scores on N and E. The four resulting subject groups, and the five drug treatments (placebo, phenobarbitone, chlorpromazine, ephedrine and Dexedrine®) resulted in a 4 x 5 design which was replicated five times, thus requiring 100 subjects in all. Both personality and drug effects were found to be significant (p < .01) by analysis of variance, but the interaction was not. As already mentioned, the personality correlations are in the direction of associating high conditioning with introversion and lack of neuroticism. The drug effects are shown in Figure 118; for all personality groups the stimulant drugs produce a greater amount of verbal conditioning, the depressant drugs a lesser amount, as compared with the placebo group.

There are a number of interesting experiments on learning which have some indirect bearing at least on our theoretical formulation of differences in consolidation as being responsible for differences in learning between extraverts and introverts. The actual experiments unfortunately are not identical with those reported in Chapter III, and consequently the evidence is purely circumstantial; it is to be hoped that more direct studies will be carried out soon in order to provide more clear-cut evidence. Nevertheless a brief look at the published work may not be amiss. Margolis (1966) has published a very interesting paper on the effects of meprobamate on associative interference. The law of associative inhibition (Müller-Schümann law) states, in brief, that when any two items, *a* and *b*, have been associated in the past, then it is more difficult to form an association between *a* and a third item, *c*. Margolis constructed lists of paired-associate letters embodying this principle, and showed that meprobamate produced a significant lessening of the interfering effects of the learning of the first list upon the learning of the second list.

Along similar lines is an experiment by Summerfield and Steinberg (1957) in which nitrous oxide was used as the depressant drug. The experiment required a learning period for attainment of partial mastery of the material (nonsense syllable anticipation learning), followed by an interval before retention was tested with air on nitrous oxide administered during this interval. In addition to the air/drug and air/air groups so constituted, there was also a control drug/drug group, i.e., one receiving nitrous oxide both during learning and during rest. Results are shown in Figure 119, and it seems clear that the depressant drug does indeed reduce forgetting, presumably through the reduction of interference.

McPeake and DiMascio (1964) have reported a particularly interesting study in which they demonstrate that drug reactions are partly dependent upon the personality of the subject. They used a simple three letter consonant nonsense syllable learning task and

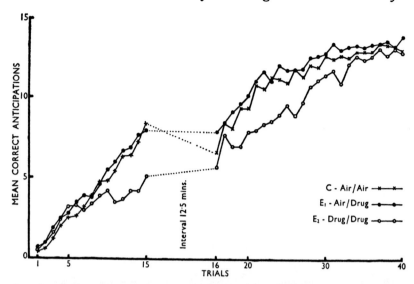

Figure 119. Learning curves for the Air/Air, Air/Drug and Drug/Drug groups, plotted in terms of mean number of syllables correctly anticipated per trial. Reprinted with permission from A. Summerfield and H. Steinberg: *Quart. J. Exp. Psychol., 9*:146-154, 1957.

found that depressant drugs produced an impairment in the extraverted subjects, but an improvement in the introverts. It would be difficult to derive this result rigourously from the theoretical preconceptions outlined in preceding chapters, but the person-drug effect interaction found is clearly in line with the general line of reasoning here followed. Much more detailed work is of course required before the intricacies of this particular experiment will be unravelled. (Another interaction effect is reported by DiMascio, 1963.) No interaction effects were observed by Willett (1960) or by Quarton and Talland (1962), who reported significant effects (positive and negative) of amphetamine and pentobarbital on running memory span.

In the work discussed so far we have taken for granted the use of placebo groups to afford a proper control for drug effects. There are two difficulties here, however, which are not always realized. In the first place this method does not make provision for what Gottschalk (1961) has called the *silent administration* of the drug, i.e., its administration unbeknown to the subject. The ef-

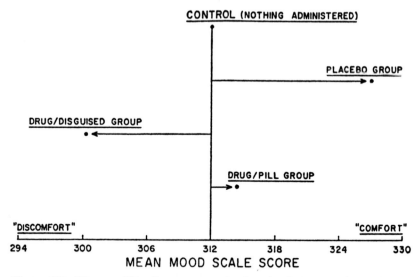

Figure 120. The specific effects on mood of each of the experimental conditions. Reprinted with permission from S. Ross *et al.*: Psychol. *Rep.*, *10*:383-392, 1962.

fects of drugs given under conditions of knowledge and ignorance respectively can be very different, as shown for instance in a study by Ross *et al.* (1962); Figure 120 shows the results for three groups (placebo, drug given in pill form, and drug given disguised in orange juice) as compared with a no-drug control. It will be seen that the simple knowledge that a drug was administered has altered the direction of the effect. This would of course not matter so much if placebo reactions could be used to counteract this effect in a quantitative manner. But, as Klerman *et al.* (1959) have shown, introverts (called type B by them) and extraverts (called type A by them) react rather differently to placebos. Figure 121 shows this quite clearly, suggesting that here is an unresolved problem which again requires for its solution the incorporation of personality measures into every psychopharmacological investigation. The differences in placebo reactions found between extraverts and introverts are every bit as large as those found in reaction to reserpine administration; for the sake of comparison these are shown in Figure 122.

The handful of researches discussed in this chapter constitute

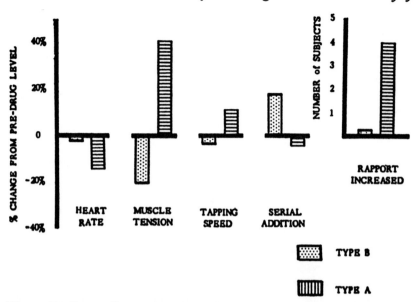

Figure 121. Personality types and reactions to placebo. Reprinted with permission from G. L. Klerman *et al.: Biological Psychiatry.* New York, Grune, 1959.

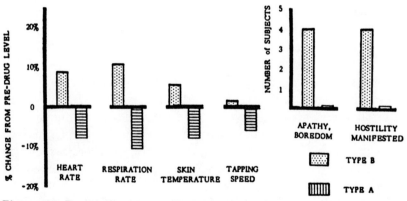

Figure 122. Personality types and reactions to reserpine. Reprinted with permission from G. L. Klerman *et al.,* 1959.

only a small portion of the vast number of psychopharmacological investigations reported in the literature; they have been singled out because they are perhaps the most relevant to our theory. Nevertheless it is recognized that there are many hundreds of peripheral studies which might have been discussed but whose bearing on our theory would have been only marginal. Does the evidence enable us to say that our theory has been supported, or are we forced to a contrary conclusion? No simple answer is possible, but we may perhaps argue that the following statements are in line with the evidence.

(a) Some of the most crucial areas give rather unambiguous evidence in favour of our theory. Thus with respect to vigilance, eyelid conditioning, verbal conditioning, C.F.F. and auditory flutter fusion, sudomotor activity and adaptation, sedation and sleep thresholds, visual masking and length of visual image duration, and spiral aftereffects, results are on the whole pretty much as predicted; even the personality interactions are usually in line whenever they have been included in the experimental design. This general agreement can hardly be regarded as accidental, particularly as many of these findings have been duplicated time after time (e.g., sedation threshold experiments). If we look at only these studies, then, the outlook would seem to be promising.

(b) In some areas, particularly that of perception, results are not so much counter to theory as they are difficult to predict in any quantitative fashion. Consider for instance the studies carried out on figural aftereffects; as long as the relationships between tests of this function and personality are not clarified to a much greater degree than is possible at present, so long will it be difficult or impossible to make precise and testable predictions on drug effects. Findings such as those of McPeake and DiMascio (1964) referred to on a previous page are obviously relevant to our theoretical system, but they cannot with any degree of rigour be derived from it. Much further theoretical clarification is therefore clearly needed before definitive experimental support can be claimed for our theory.

(c) One result of the work reported here which threatens to make the elaboration of such a quantitative theory very difficult is the frequency with which curvilinear regressions are found (or suspected). This is probably a function of the universal application of the Yerkes-Dodson law (inverted-U relation between drive and performance). If a drug increases drive (either through its action on the arousal or the activation system) then the effects may be facilitatory or inhibitory depending on the precise position on this inverted-U curve of the group tested for the task in question, and the same is true for the action of depressant drugs. This law may also account for the apparently confusing fact that small doses of a drug may have different effects from large doses; to take but one example, Haward (1965) found that a stimulant drug in small doses increased vigilance, but that it had the opposite effect in large doses. If the performance of the group in question is conceived as lying on the rising limb of the inverted-U, and if we conceive of the drug as increasing drive, then a small dose may push performance to the top of the curve (optimal performance), while a larger dose may push it onto the descending limb of the curve (super-optimal drive, leading to deterioration of performance).

(d) The prevalence of such curvilinear relations is complicated by the clearly demonstrated personality interaction with drug effects. When a drug is administered to a group of people, then it is clear that these do not all cluster round the same position on the inverted-U curve relating drive to performance. Individuals differ greatly with respect to their position on this curve; some may be below the peak, others on it, and others still beyond it. These three types of subjects would be expected to be affected quite differently by drugs affecting their standing on this curve—the first group would be improved by stimulant and impaired by depressant drugs, while the third would be impaired by stimulant and improved by depressant drugs. (Those already on the peak would of course be impaired by both.) Such a cat's cradle of curvilinear relations does not present an easy target for theoretical predictions, and the fact that so many of our predictions have in fact been found to have gained some factual support suggests that with respect to these tasks linear regressions may be found over the range of parameters used in the tests.

(e) While most of the studies reported in this chapter have taken into account relations between extraversion and drug effect only, it is clear from our discussion in Chapter I that some form of zone analysis is really required to obtain maximum information. As one example of such analysis we may quote the work of Bartholomew and Marley (1959); they were concerned with the effects of methylpentynol on fifty-four patients. All patients were

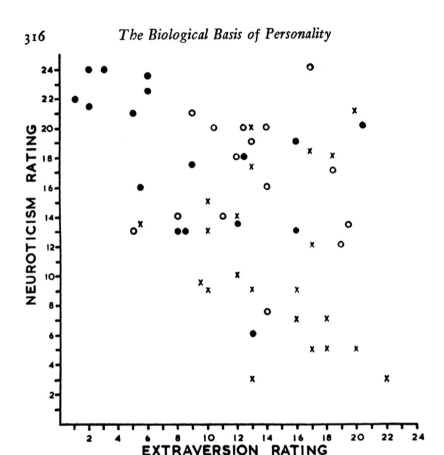

Figure 123. Scatter diagram of individual raw scores for extraversion and neuroticism in relation to response of 54 subjects to methylpentynol.
● = Clinical Grading 3 or maximal toxicity.
O = Clinical Grading 2 or minimal toxicity.
X = Clinical Grading 1 or normal response.
Reprinted with permission from A. A. Bartholomew and G. Marley: *J. Ment. Sci., 105:*957-970, 1959.

tested on the M.P.I., and the resulting picture is given in Figure 123. It will be seen that there is a marked interaction between drug effect and both personality variables, such that maximal toxicity is observed in the dysthymic quadrant (high N, low E), while least effect is observed in stable extraverts (low N, high E). These effects would have been totally obscured if only one personality dimension had been taken into account, or if straight correlations had been run with both dimensions in isolation. The absence of such a complete zone analysis in many of the reported investigations lessens the evidential value of these studies considerably.

It may be argued that the situation suggested to prevail is too complex to allow of proper hypothetico-deductive methods being used at all, and it is very obvious that most of the work done in psychopharmacology in recent years has been purely empirical. It may be suggested that if the evidence is agreed to support the hypothesis that complex relations of the kind postulated do in fact exist, then we have little choice but to accept the facts and try to improve our methods of measuring the crucial variables involved. The main claim the writer would make for the theory here presented is not that it is correct, or even that its main contentions will in future be shown to have been along the right lines, but rather that it points the way towards experimental designs and measurement more adequate to deal with the complexities obviously existing in this field. Psychopharmacologists tend to underestimate the complexity of their chosen field—indeed, the writer cannot himself plead innocence on this account; if their achievements are to come closer to their hopes, they must take into account in the design of their experiments such obviously important variables as personality interactions and curvilinear regressions. Without taking such a step, confusion will only get worse confounded as pure empiricism continues to run riot in the absence of guidance from theory.[7]

Any final estimate must run a careful course between the in-

[7]One rather curious difficulty which has not been touched on in this chapter (primarily because no work seems to have been done on bringing it into relation with personality) is the observation that decrement in performance which follows the administration of depressant drugs is not a monotonic function of the amount of drug administered. As Düker (1963, 1964), Forth (1966), Ideström and Cadenius (1963), and others have shown, very small amounts produce a slight *decrement* in performance, slightly larger (but still small) amounts produce an increment, and large and very large doses produce a decrement which is a monotonic function of the dose. Düker has given what is probably the correct interpretation of this phenomenon; he explains that with very small doses the subject is unaware of behavioural effects, while with slightly larger doses he becomes aware of performance deterioration and this awareness produces what he calls "reaktive Anspannungssteigerung," i.e., cortical arousal. This arousal more than counteracts the deleterious effects of the drug. With large doses the drug is more potent than the arousing reaction (which itself is of course weakened through the drug), and performance decrement takes place. The interaction of these phases with personality would constitute a most interesting study.

spissated gloom which decorum requires of the investigator when his own theories are being discussed and the enthusiasm which he cannot help feeling when experimental research verifies so many of the predictions which he has derived from his theory. Probably the most suitable comment is that not sufficient data exist at the moment to come to any definitive decision, and that while a beginning has been made in the hypothetico-deductive study of drug effects in the behavioural field, the major effort still lies ahead.

CHAPTER VII

PERSONALITY AND BRAIN DAMAGE

C. B. Blakemore

THE PRINCIPAL AIM of this book has been to demonstrate that personality, the organization and functional relationships existing within individual differences in behaviour not accounted for by a general factor of intelligence, has a biological basis. The contents of the book have been largely concerned with attempts to substantiate this hypothesis and to outline some of the relationships between the actual content of individual behaviour and its biological determinants. Within such a conceptual framework it would seem appropriate and reasonable to expect that further evidence concerning the biological correlates of personality might be found in the study of naturally occurring changes within the central nervous system, and in particular from those changes in behaviour which occur following injury to the brain. That pathology or injury of the brain, with its highly developed role in the organization of behaviour, should produce changes in the personality of the affected individual would seem to be a wholly reasonable hypothesis, for such impairment of the nervous system must result in changes in the organization of the biological determinants of both cognitive and noncognitive behaviour.

In clinical neurology we find that the concept of "personality change" is frequently associated with impairment of brain function, and is accorded a significance in certain cases comparable to that of the more generally observed deficits of intellectual and cognitive abilities. We might expect to find, therefore, a sizeable body of experimental data concerning brain damage in humans which would support and extend the basic hypothesis on the role of biological factors underlying personality organization. In fact one finds on examining the literature of general and clinical experimental psychology that there are very few data upon which to base firm generalizations concerning the relation of personality to brain function. This state of affairs exists despite the fact that many hundreds of studies have been reported which seek, in one way or another, to investigate behavioural changes associated with impairment of the brain, and which examine not only intellectual and cognitive changes but also those occurring in such areas as those of learning capacity, perceptual processes, and the acquisition and execution of motor skills. In this chapter an attempt will be made to show how limited are the generalizations which can be drawn from such studies in relation to the operation of personality functions, and how these limitations are due, in part, to conceptual, theoretical, and methodological difficulties which exist within the field of the behavioural study of brain injury.

A number of attempts have been made to relate individual differences in behaviour to neural processes theoretically, and in each of these the basic assumption has been that inter-individual behavioural variation is dependent to some extent upon the state or nature of the nervous system which each individual possesses. Observed behaviour in a given situation is thus dependent upon the efficiency with which the central nervous system functions, and hypothesized differences in the theoretical constructs equated with neurological efficiency are called upon to account for observed individual differences in performance. In the case of injury or pathology of the brain such neurological efficiency will be reduced, and corresponding changes and impairments of behaviour will be observed. There is, then, from such a theoretical position, the possibility of accounting for the behavioural effects of brain injury or pathology in terms of the operation of biological variables hypothesized to account for inter-individual variation in the non-brain-damaged population. Predictions can be made concerning the expected direction of behavioural changes following brain damage on the basis of the concept of reduced neurological efficiency, and it follows that empirical verification of such predictions can contribute to the status and validity of the theoretical constructs related to neurological efficiency upon which they were based.

One example of how injury to the brain invariably produces

some degree of impairment of behaviour is found in intellectual deterioration. From reviews such as those of Meyer (1960) and Yates (1966), we see that there is ample evidence in the literature to suggest that the disorganization of brain function through damage or pathology leads to some form of lowered efficiency in intellectual and cognitive abilities, which themselves differ with respect to efficiency within the general population. For a given brain-damaged individual, his present level of intellectual functioning will be dependent upon the extent of the disorganization of brain function and his level of ability prior to brain damage. That intellectual performance should be impaired to some degree by brain damage is not surprising, for the range of individual differences observed in intellectual and cognitive abilities is clearly related to a considerable extent to the general organization, efficiency, and integrity of cortico-neural processes. Considerations of this nature, in relation to intellectual functions, have tended to provide the model for subsequent attempts to demonstrate the interrelationship of all forms of inter-individual behavioural variation, the effects of brain damage, and hypothesized neurological processes, thus extending the generalizations to areas of personality and its biological basis.

It is possible to outline a number of further examples of the way in which a theoretical relationship has been postulated between the role of neural processes in individual differences in behaviour and the effects of brain damage. In these examples the type of behaviour under consideration has not been restricted to intellectual functions, which Lashley (1929) related to a theoretical construct of "cerebral efficiency"; therefore they seek to extend the model referred to above to such areas of behaviour as perception, conditioning, and learning. The concept of "satiation" proposed by Koehler and Wallach (1944) to account for the perceived displacement of the contours of a figure following prolonged inspection is one theoretical construct equated with neurological efficiency which has received much attention as a possible contributor to individual differences in perception. This hypothesized satiation of neural process has been related to such areas of perception as apparent movement, reversible figures, and visual, auditory, and kinesthetic aftereffects in general. In relation to the concept of neurological efficiency and the effects of brain injury, one might expect a more rapid build-up and persistence of satiation in the brain-damaged individual.

Support for this hypothesis comes from a number of studies investigating the effects of brain damage on perceptual processes. Bender and Teuber (1949) and Saucer and Deabler (1956) have reported that the perception of apparent movement is impaired after injury to the brain. Werner and Thuma (1942) have also shown that this is the case with brain-damaged children. Teuber and Bender (1950) have extended these findings by demonstrating that in certain instances the brain-injured individual can perceive apparent movement, even across injured regions of the occipital lobes, but that this requires a far greater rate of alternation than normally.

A further demonstration of the possible relationship between the concept of neural satiation and the effects of brain damage is found in the study of flicker-fusion thresholds. In his extensive review of the CFF, Landis (1954) concludes that there is a direct relationship of threshold to his concept of "neurological efficiency," which he postulates to account for individual differences in CFF in the general population. Many workers have shown that brain injury tends to lower CFF (Halstead, 1947; Teuber and Bender, 1949; Battersby, Bender, and Teuber, 1951; Chandler, Parsons, and Haase, 1964). The range of thresholds observed among brain-damaged subjects tends to overlap to a considerable extent that found in the general population, however; and Young (1949) has found in her study of frontal lobotomized schizophrenics that the observation of lowered CFF occurred most frequently in those individuals with high CFF prior to operation, suggesting that changes in threshold might be related to pre-injury level of neurological efficiency.

Brain damage has also been shown to produce changes in aftereffects in the expected direction on the basis of hypothesized increases in neural satiation. The review by Holland (1965) of the literature relating to the spiral aftereffect shows that the perception of this phenomenon is impaired by injury of the brain, and that when it is perceived by the brain-damaged subject it tends to persist for a shorter duration than normally found. Again we

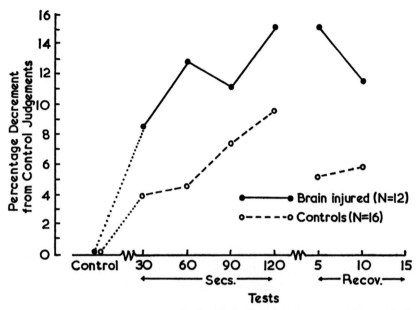

Figure 124. Mean size of kinesthetic aftereffect following varying periods of inspection of a standard wooden block, together with retest after 5 and 10 mins., of a group of 12 patients with known brain lesions and a group of 16 patients suffering from physical illnesses not involving the brain. The differences between the groups in magnitude of the aftereffect, its rate of development, and its persistance are quite apparent. Reprinted with permission from G. S. Klein and D. Krech: *J. Personality, 21*:118-148, 1952.

find that the kinesthetic aftereffect is reported to be affected by brain damage in the study by Klein and Krech (1952); as we see from Figure 124, they found greater rapidity of onset and greater magnitude and persistance of this aftereffect in twelve patients with brain tumours and encephalopathies when they were compared with control subjects. This would be predicted on the basis of the hypothesis that brain damage lowers neurological efficiency by generating an increase in the satiability of cortico-neural processes. It is worth mentioning in this contest, however, that Wertheimer (1954, 1955) has argued, from the study of individual differences in the kinesthetic aftereffect among normal and schizophrenic subjects, that the magnitude of the aftereffect is related to cortico-neural processes through a factor of "metabolic efficiency" and that decreases in such efficiency will lead to reduction of the magnitude of the aftereffect. From the standpoint of such a theoretical position the finding of Klein and Krech becomes difficult to interpret, for the conclusion would be that brain damage produces kinesthetic aftereffects of greater magnitude, and hence that "metabolic efficiency" must be increased by such conditions. On the other hand, not all workers have found increased kinesthetic aftereffects after brain injury; for example, Jaffe (1954) was unable to demonstrate aftereffects different from normal in a group of twenty subjects with known localized brain injuries, which is a finding wholly inconsistent with the neural satiation hypothesis of Koehler and Wallach (1944).

Klein and Krech (1952) proposed a concept of "cortical conductivity" to account for the rapid onset and magnitude of kinesthetic aftereffects found in brain-damaged subjects. This concept is related by them to the ease of transmission of patterns of excitation through the cortex, and with a lowering of cortical conductivity as a consequence of brain damage there is predicted to be an increase in resistance to such transmissions. In many respects this concept is similar to that of "cortical inhibition" put forward by Eysenck (1955) within the context of explaining individual differences in kinesthetic aftereffects in the non-brain-damaged population, and related in turn to the personality dimension of introversion-extraversion. The theoretical position of Eysenck, with regard to the relationships existing between the personality dimension of introversion-extraversion, the behavioural concepts of reactive and conditioned inhibition, and the states of inhibition and excitation within brain structures and their relation to the suppression and facilitating mechanisms within the reticular formation of the brain, does not require further elaboration. Throughout the chapters of this book he has attempted to show how these constructs, which were developed from his own empirical research in association with ideas derived largely from Pavlov (1927) and Hull (1943), operate in the determination of the biological basis of personality. We need only concern ourselves here, then, with the hypotheses concerning the effects of brain damage which follow from this theory.

In terms of Eysenck's theory it would follow that injury of the brain would interfere with the reciprocal exchange of neural impulses between the cortex and the reticular activating system, thus increasing the effects of suppressor mechanism. The results of brain damage would therefore be related to increased cortical inhibition, leading behaviourally to such effects as slow formation of conditioned responses, swift accumulation of reactive inhibition, and extraversion. Evidence in favour of such an hypothesis does exist, but it is by no means extensive. That the cortico-neural processes of brain-damaged subjects are characterized by states of excessive inhibition is suggested in a recent study by Birch, Belmont, and Karp (1965). In a series of experiments these workers show that when two auditory stimuli are presented with an interval between them, normal subjects tend to estimate them as equal or to overestimate the intensity of the second tone, whereas brain-damaged subjects tend to underestimate the intensity of the second tone unless the length of interval is extensive, as we can see from Figure 125. It might be argued that after the presentation of the first stimulus there is a period of neural inhibition, which in the brain-damaged subjects is of such magnitude and persists for such a time as to affect their perception of the second stimulus.

On the basis of such states of neural inhibition following brain

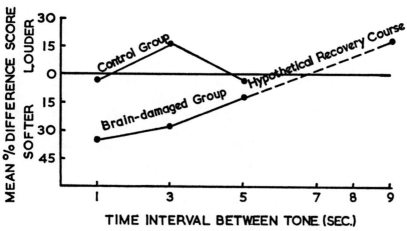

Figure 125. Judgments of the relative intensity of the second of two identical tones presented successively, but with varying time intervals, made by a group of 20 patients with evidence of unilateral brain injury and a group of 20 nonneurological patients. From H. G. Birch, I. Belmont, and E. Karp: *Cortex,* 1:397-409, 1965.

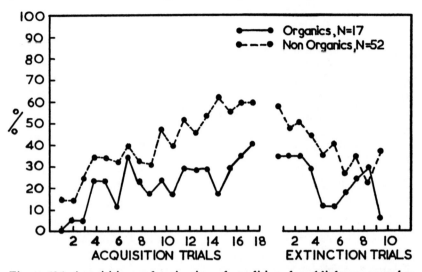

Figure 126. Acquisition and extinction of conditioned eyeblink responses by groups of mental defectives with ("organic") and without ("nonorganic") evidence of brain pathology. The curve for the "organic" group differs significantly from that of the "nonorganic" group, which in turn does not differ from normal. From Franks, 1959.

injury, it might also be expected that conditionability would be impaired in subjects suffering from such conditions. The evidence in favour of the validity of this prediction is small, but where it does exist it tends to be in favour of the hypothesis (Reese, Doss, and Gantt, 1953). The findings of V. Franks (1959) are representative of such studies. She found a significant difference on a classical eyeblink conditioning task between a group of mental defectives manifesting clear evidence of an organic impairment and a group of defectives without such diagnostic signs (Figure 126). There was no evidence that the latter group performed differently from normal in either the acquisition or extinction of this conditioned response. That the little evidence which exists is in the predicted direction is the conclusion which might also be said to apply to the direct evidence on increases in extraversion following brain damage; a few attempts have been made to evaluate changes on this dimension, but these have been restricted mainly to pre- and postoperative studies of patients undergoing a frontal leucotomy. In reviewing the evidence on this topic Willett (1960) cites a number of studies, and in particular those of Petrie (1952) and Tow 1955), which together provide partial support for some relationship between extraversion and brain damage.

The hypothesis that performance in brain-damaged subjects is associated with the rapid build-up of reactive inhibition has been investigated, but again without any firm conclusion regarding its validity being possible. Several investigations have been concerned with performance during the acquisition of motor skills. Meier (1964) examined learning and reminiscence on an inverted alphabet printing task in two groups of epileptics with differing severity of EEG abnormality and in a normal control group. He found that there was a significant difference between the course of learning in the organic and control groups (Figure 127), of a type which

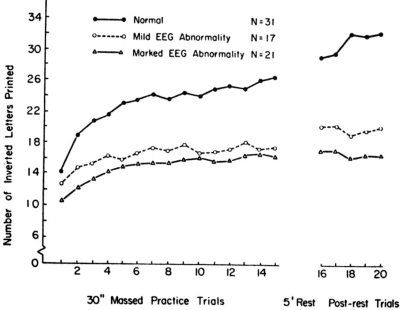

Figure 127. Performance on an inverted alphabet printing task, showing a significant impairment compared with normal control subjects, in learning during the massed practice trials of groups of epileptics with "mild" and "marked" EEG abnormality. Reminiscence after the 5-minute rest period is not significantly different for the normal controls and patients with "mild" EEG abnormality, but the reminiscence scores of the "marked" EEG abnormality group is significantly smaller than those of either of the other groups. From M. J. Meier: *Percept. Motor Skills, 19*:219-225, 1964.

would suggest excessive build-up of reactive inhibition in the subjects suffering from neuropathological conditions. On measures of reminiscence the groups of organic subjects were significantly different, with the least impaired group exhibiting greater reminiscence; and in this respect there was no difference between this group and the normal controls.

These findings are similar to those reported by Huse and Parsons (1965), who studied pursuit rotor performance in forty brain-damaged subjects and forty controls. As can be seen from inspection of their graph (Figure 128), they found significant differences between their groups for massed and spaced practice on both level of performance and improvement rate. The shapes of the curves, as we see from the "fitted spaced-practice curve" of each group, were essentially the same, however, and a significant difference did

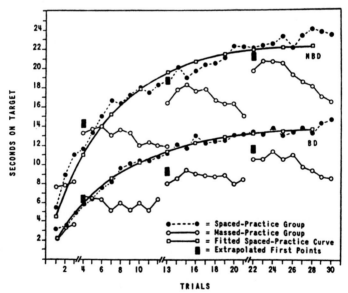

Figure 128. Learning curves for performance on the pursuit rotor under conditions of massed and spaced practice during 30 sec. trials of 40 brain-damaged patients (BD) and 40 non-brain-damaged control subjects (NBD). Although the groups differ significantly from each other under both massed and spaced practice, the curves fitted to the spaced-practice data do not differ in shape. The relationship of performance under spaced and massed practice conditions is also the same for each group. From M. M. Huse and O. A. Parsons: *J. Abnorm. Psychol.,* 70:350-359, 1965.

not exist between the groups when a comparison was made in terms of massed as opposed to spaced practice. They computed measures from these data of a number of aspects of performance which might reflect the generation of reactive and conditioned inhibition, and no significant differences between the less severely brain-injured and the control subjects were found on these measures. The massed practice curves of the severely brain-damaged subjects were markedly different from those of the normal controls or less severely damaged subjects, however, but Huse and Parsons conclude that this was due to impairment of new learning capacity and sensory-motor dysfunction in this group rather than to the build-up of reactive or conditioned inhibition.

Blakemore and Bohlen (1966) examined reminiscence on the pursuit rotor in thirty patients with known localized lesions and a control group of similar size. They too found significantly less reminiscence in the brain-damaged group, but this was found to be due to the poor rate of improvement and to the impairment of performance of the more acute cases, whilst no significant differences in performance were found between the longer standing lesion patients and the controls. In view of Eysenck's (1965) suggestion that reminiscence, to explain individual differences, requires a multiple factor theory based on the differential development of reactive inhibition during performance and the consolidation of neural traces during the rest period, each of these findings concerning reminiscence in motor learning might be attributed, in part, to poor or retarded neural consolidation in brain-damaged individuals. Studies such as that of May, Lynd, and Ley (1963), who investigated verbal learning, have shown that brain-damaged subjects tend to learn far better and more quickly under conditions of spaced rather than massed practice, and this has been attributed to retardation of the growth of reactive inhibition by spaced practice. But it might also be argued that the spacing of practice provides a greater opportunity for neural consolidation, which may be slower after brain damage, and that it is impairment in respect of this process which accounts for the general finding that injury to the brain affects the acquisition of new habits.

So far we have seen how theoretical constructs such as "satiation," "cortical conductivity," and "cortical inhibition" have been used to account for the behavioural effects of injury or pathology of the brain. Each of these constructs has been put forward originally as part of a theory which attempts to relate inter-individual behavioural variations to cortico-neural determinants. In many respects the constructs used are very similar, each being related to a concept of neurological efficiency, and the findings derived in support of one construct can usually be interpreted as support for the others. We can see, therefore, that the findings regarding the nature of certain perceptual disorders following brain damage and their relation to neural "satiation" could also be called upon to support predictions about the effects of brain damage derived from Eysenck's general personality theory, with their emphasis on increased "cortical inhibition."

When we examine the effects of brain injury and their possible relationship to variation in hypothesized central neural processes, we see that it is difficult to arrive at firm generalizations. This may be due to limitations or to a lack of unity in the theoretical constructs themselves, as the work of Honigfeld (1962) and Becker (1960) suggests, but it could also reflect theoretical and methodological problems involved in the concept of "brain damage." In theories which involve postulates regarding the relation of the effects of "brain damage" to other variables, there is usually an assumption, either explicit or implicit, within the formulation of hypotheses that one is dealing with a unitary concept. That this assumption has been readily made in the past by psychologists is largely due to the influence of Lashley (1929, 1930) and of Gestalt theorists such as Koehler (1940) and Goldstein (1939) upon the study of brain and behaviour relationships. The influence of this acceptance that injury to the brain produces unitary effects is seen very clearly in the field of clinical psychology, where for many years research and thinking have tended to be dominated by the quest for a single variable diagnostic test which will successfully differentiate all patients with brain damage from non-brain-damaged patients (Haynes and Sells, 1963).

There is now a considerable body of evidence to show that the behavioural effects of injury or pathology of the brain are far from homogeneous. This is not to say that there are no behavioural changes which are common to all cases of brain injury, but rather that the observed effects on behaviour are principally dependent upon the locus of injury and the nature of the neuropathology. Peircy's (1964) review of intellectual impairments associated with brain lesions demonstrates this very clearly. The extensive research programme of Reitan and his associates (Reitan, 1959) also clearly demonstrates this same point, but in this case the type of behaviour being sampled covers not only intellectual and cognitive functions, but also perceptual processes and psychomotor functions. These studies show that behaviour can be differentially impaired after brain injury, and Reitan (1962) points out that preliminary findings suggest that the nature of the impairment might be related to variables such as whether the injury is focal or diffuse, whether there is predominantly left, right, or bilateral hemisphere involvement, the particular lobular structures affected, whether the lesion is static or progressive, the chronicity of the lesion, and the neuropathological nature of the lesion (trauma, degenerative disease, cerebral vascular disease, tumor, etc.).

These findings are supported by many other studies carried out by research workers in the field of neuropsychology, each study usually being concerned with the detailed analysis of only one or two of the variables outlined above. Lansdell (1962) and Lansdell and Urback (1965) have added to the list of variables by suggesting on the basis of their research that cortico-neural processes and their behavioural correlates are differentially organized on the basis of sex, at least in so far as the temporal lobes are concerned, while Coppinger, Bortner, and Saucer (1963) have drawn attention to the fact that differential patterns of deficits are related to the age of the subject. In addition to the variables referred to above as determining differential patterns of impairment, in many of these studies evidence was also found, of course, of some general impairment in behaviour associated with brain damage as such, particularly in terms of some form of lowered intellectual efficiency.

The fact that different types or loci of brain injury can produce different behavioural effects does emphasize the need for care in the selection of subjects for the study of hypotheses pertaining to the *general* effects on behaviour of "brain damage." This has all too frequently been ignored, and groups which are in all probability heterogeneous with respect to the nature of their behavioural impairments have been employed. The use of groups of patients suffering from diffuse or generalized cortical involvement does not overcome the difficulty, for although the general effects of injury are likely to be more readily observable, the range of possible specific behavioural impairments will be greater. It is not surprising, in view of each of these considerations, that the most frequent observation made upon groups of "brain-damaged" subjects is that the variance of behaviour on any given task tends to be much greater than that found within the non-brain-damaged population. What is required in studies involving groups of subjects classified as "brain-damaged" is selection based on type of injury together with a detailed assessment of the behavioural deficits which each subject suffers, and in particular of deficits which might be related to variables possibly involved in performance on the tasks to be employed. One example of how important differentially distributed deficits can be in the study of the performance of brain-injured subjects is found in the work of Shapiro (1951, 1952, 1953). From a series of experiments he concluded that "rotation" in the performance of the Block Design test by brain-injured subjects could be accounted for in terms of the Pavlovian concepts of exaggerated states of inhibition and negative induction. Shapiro *et al.* (1962) were forced to conclude that such a theoretical proposition was unnecessary, for all of the findings could be accounted for on the basis of visual field and ocular motor deficits in Block Design "rotating" subjects. Another example is to be found in the work of Homskaya (1964). He investigated the effects of anterior and posterior cerebral lesions on the orienting reflex. Having demonstrated that in normal subjects the vegetative components of the orienting reflex in both its phasic and tonic forms can be activated or inhibited by verbal instructions, he then went on to show that such verbal regulation is disturbed by anterior cerebral lesions but not by posterior lesions. He suggests that this possibly indicates the importance of frontal areas of the brain in orienting reflexes determined by verbal instructions. The exact interpretation of this finding remains difficult, however, because of the possible influence of dysphasic symptoms which might occur to varying degrees as a consequence of anterior lesions, and which could therefore be directly affecting performance in the experimental situation. The possible effects of variable intellectual and cognitive deficits, and particularly those related to language and communication, should always be carefully examined by research workers examining the performance of brain-injured subjects on any task.

Theoretical and methodological difficulties similar to those dealt with previously are also encountered when attempts are made to relate clinical assessments of personality to a unitary concept of "brain damage." In the literature of clinical psychology and clinical neurology, many hundreds of studies have appeared which attempt to demonstrate the correlation of a particular personality characteristic or group of traits with brain damage. These studies have tended to concentrate upon traits frequently associated with psychiatric disorders and have concerned themselves with attempts to demonstrate changes after brain injury in the manifestation of personality characteristics such as depression, anxiety, aggression, rigidity, obsessionality, social awareness, impulsiveness, psychopathy, etc. A large number of these studies have employed global techniques of assessment and have depended upon unreliable and unvalidated instruments, such as the Rorschach and T.A.T. projective tests. As one would expect, such studies almost invariably produce inconclusive, inconsistent, or nonreplicable results. The failure of such a global approach, irrespective of the techniques of assessment employed, is typified by the clinical concept of an "epileptic personality," for which Tizard (1962) found no support in her review of the literature, partly due to the lack of agreement concerning the definition of such a concept.

A number of studies have been carried out employing more reliable and valid techniques, such as questionnaires or objective personality measures, but for the most part very few of these have produced consistent or replicable results. One finding which stems from a clinical assessment approach is worthy of some attention, however, for it demonstrates, once again, the possible lack of unity in the concept of brain damage. Anderson and Hanvik (1950) compared the M.M.P.I. profiles of patients with frontal and parietal lobe involvements. They found that a clinical picture of "hysteroid reaction type" was associated with frontal involvement, while the parietal cases tended towards "anxiety neurosis." If we extend this finding to Eysenck's general theory, then the frontal lobe cases should be extraverted while the parietal lobe cases would be introverted, and thus cortical inhibition would be increased by anterior cerebral lesions but decreased by posterior cerebral lesions. On the basis of such a hypothesis a number of predictions could be made about differential changes in such aspects of behaviour as conditioning, learning, and perception as a consequence of brain lesions of different locus; for example, one might predict that the acquisition of a conditioned response would be more rapid in patients with posterior lesions than in those with anterior lesions. From the testing of such predictions it should be possible, according to Eysenck's general theoretical position, to introduce hypotheses concerning possible differential relations between cortical areas of the inhibitory and facilitatory mechanisms of the reticular formation and their role in behaviour. Support for the suggestion that patients with anterior or posterior cerebral disease respond differently on the M.M.P.I. comes also from Williams (1952), while Pawlik and Cattell (1965) related EEG alpha indices to certain of Cattell's objective personality measures in a group of normal subjects and reported that there was some evidence to suggest that at least one personality trait shows anterior-posterior EEG correlates.

So far in this chapter we have not dealt explicitly with impairments of attention and distractability, although these variables are frequently described as characterizing the behaviour of brain-damaged subjects. These impairments could influence the brain-injured subjects' performance and the interpretation of results on most tasks employed in experimental research; as such the importance of evaluating their influence is obvious, for different degrees of impairment of attention and distractability among subjects could possibly account for many inconsistent or unpredicted research findings. In relation to a general theory of the effects of brain damage these variables could be directly related to individual differences in vigilance, and it should be remembered that attempts have been made to relate the performance of normal subjects on vigilance tasks to build-up of central inhibition (Mackworth, 1950), reactive inhibition (Adams, 1956), and extraversion-introversion (Bakan, 1959).

The possibility that impairment of attention and increased distractability are behavioural deficits found generally in brain-damaged subjects is supported by a number of studies investigating reaction times (Blackburn and Benton, 1955; Benton and Blackburn, 1957; Benton and Joynt, 1959; Benton, Kennedy, Sutton, and Brockaw, 1962; Costa, 1962; McDonald, 1964). The major conclusions that can be drawn from these studies are that brain damage does tend to produce slower reaction times on all tasks, but that different degrees of impairment on a given task are related to the locus and nature of the damage. This general conclusion is well illustrated by the graph (Figure 129) presented by Benton and Joynt (1959). Here we see that although patients with predominantly left to right hemisphere cerebral disease are differentially impaired on a simple reaction-time task in respect of their performances with the left to right hands, all aspects of their performance are nevertheless inferior to that of non-brain-injured control subjects.

Variables such as length and variation of preparatory interval between trials have been demonstrated to be significantly more important in brain-injured subjects than in normals (Costa, 1962; McDonald, 1964), but Blackburn and Benton (1955) were unable to demonstrate greater differentiation than normal on the basis of complexity of the task when simple and choice reaction times were compared in subjects with cerebral disease. One further finding which has emerged from many of these studies is that brain-damaged subjects tend not to show practice effects on reaction-time tasks, and that their performance is characterized by increased intra-individual variability with continued practice. This finding, and the known relation of reaction time to vigilance (Buck, 1966), would suggest that brain injury should produce impaired performance when compared with that of normal behaviour or vigilance tasks. McDonald and Burns (1964) investigated this possibility, using a visual vigilance task under two conditions of signal rate, and found that the performance of brain-damaged subjects was poorer than that of control subjects under all conditions. This finding has been confirmed by De Renzi and Faglioni (1965), who also produced evidence to suggest that degree of impairment on vigilance tasks is related to the site of lesion. That cortico-neural processes contribute to efficiency of normal subjects' performance on vigilance tasks is clearly shown in a recent study by Davies and

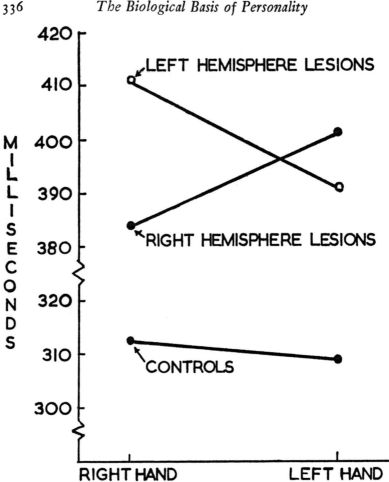

Figure 129. The performance of 20 patients with lesions in the left hemisphere of the brain, 20 patients with lesions in the right hemisphere, and 20 control subjects without history of cerebral disease on a simple visual reaction time task. Comparison of performance with the right or the left hand reveals a differential pattern of behaviour for the left and right hemisphere brain lesion groups. There is also a significant difference between the overall performance of all brain-injured subjects and the control subjects. From A. L. Benton and R. J. Joynt: *Confinia Neurol., 19*:247-256, 1959.

Krkovic (1965); they investigated the relationship of skin conductance measures, EEG alpha indices, and performance on a vigilance task over a 90-minute period. Their graphic presentation of the findings clearly reveals an association in the trends of these three variables (Figure 65).

From the evidence which has been reviewed here it does seem that further investigation of the effects of brain damage on attention and vigilance, in relation to possible cortico-neural processes associated with or determining inter-individual behaviour variation, would prove to be valuable. Such an approach could possibly contribute enormously to our understanding of both the general effects of brain injury and the clearer definition of theoretical constructs developed to account for the biological basis of individual differences and personality.

Throughout this chapter we have seen repeatedly that no conclusions can be firmly made concerning the effects of brain damage and its relation to the cortico-neural determinants of individual behaviour. Certain findings from studies on the effects of brain injury on aspects of behaviour such as the perception of apparent movement, perceptual after effects, conditioning, and learning are capable of being interpreted in terms of the operation of hypothesized neuro-cortical processes determining inter-individual behavioural variations. In each case the difficulty which always presents itself when we attempt to evaluate such interpretations is our lack of knowledge concerning the generality of these findings for a given task as representative of the behaviour of all individuals suffering from injury or pathology of the brain. All too frequently the studies under review have demonstrated only a difference on some particular task between an experimental group of brain-injured subjects and a control group of non-brain-injured subjects. But once we challenge the unitary nature of the concept of "brain damage," as a substantial amount of evidence now does, then we have to face the fact that in terms of behavioural impairments our experimental group may be heterogeneous, and in the absence of evidence to the contrary we must acknowledge that its mean performance on the task may be significantly affected by a number of individuals with some specific deficit determined by the site and/ or nature of their lesions. We have seen, for example, that such evidence as exists tends to suggest that groups of brain-damaged subjects are slow to acquire a conditioned response when compared with control subjects, but we might question whether this means that all brain-injured subjects are impaired in this respect, or that some are impaired because of specific deficits associated with the nature of their injury while others perform as normal. The value of studies of conditionability of brain-injured subjects in relation to a general theoretical postulate concerning neuro-cortical processes could depend upon the answer to this question. Of the many aspects of behaviour discussed in this chapter which might have direct relevance to the study of the biological basis of personality variables, only in the studies of reaction time and vigilance is there clear evidence that one is dealing with an area of behaviour which is generally impaired by brain injury, irrespective of differentiation in severity between subgroups within the brain-injured population. It is for this reason that further research in this area might hold perhaps the greatest immediate hope.

We need to bear in mind always the fact that behavioural deficits following injury in different areas of the brain can be highly specific and need not be limited to broad categories of behaviour such as learning or perception. We see this clearly in the variety of impairments of language and speech which can occur in dysphasic conditions. We see it also, for example, in the effects of injury to the temporal lobes. Milner (1958) and Meyer (1959) have both shown that after anterior temporal lobectomy, carried out for the relief of epilepsy in humans, impairments of learning occur, but that the nature of these deficits is dependent upon which hemisphere of the brain is operated upon. After operation on the temporal lobe of the hemisphere dominant with respect to speech, the patient will suffer for some time an impairment in his ability to learn new verbal material but will be unimpaired with respect to other forms of learning, while after operation on the temporal lobe of the nondominant hemisphere there is little impairment of any form of learning. Similar evidence in the field of perception and its relation to the problem of general deficits in behaviour following brain injury has been discussed by Teuber (1955) and Teuber and Weinstein (1956).

Although some useful data exist already, many more studies

of the specific and general effects of brain injury are required before we can establish with confidence firm generalizations about the effects of such conditions in relation to personality variables and their biological determinants. Indeed, the only final comment which can be made concerning the many aspects of research which have been reviewed is to stress the one conclusion which can be clearly and firmly stated—that further research in this area is needed.

EPILOGUE

It may be useful to pull together some of the arguments and discussions arising from various points of this book. What has been presented is a *model* of certain aspects of personality and a *theory* to explain the working of that model. Clearly the model does not attempt to deal with the whole of personality; we have restricted ourselves to those aspects for which there was sufficient evidence to posit a biological basis, and where there was also some evidence as regards the nature of that biological basis. In doing so there was no intention to deny the existence or importance of environmental influences and social factors; the futile battle between "environmentalists" and "hereditarians," with its undesirable political overtones, has taught us that what is needed is not some pseudo-scientific battle-cry but detailed evidence and specific theories. An attempt has been made to supply both, if only in a limited field; it should need no excuse that the temptation to cover a much wider field has been resisted. Personality theories have much to lose by pretending to greater coverage or rigour than they in fact possess; in following this time-honoured primrose path to damnation they easily leave the field of science altogether.

Any theory in this perplexing field is almost by definition a "weak" theory (Eysenck, 1960); its purpose is to guide research along promising and fruitful lines rather than to fulfill the function of a "strong" theory, which is to provide universally accepted laws from which rigourous deductions can with safety be made. All "strong" theories started out as "weak" theories; the heliocentric view of the universe, as advocated by Aristarchus or even by Copernicus, was weak in this sense and was rejected by such men as Archimedes for what at the time were excellent reasons (e.g., the failure to observe stellar parallax). The theory here put forward will have to earn its bread and butter rather by giving rise to in-

340

teresting and important experiments than by being "right" in some absolute sense; it may in due course grow into a strong theory, but much detailed work along more precise and quantitative lines will have to be done before this happy state can be approached, let alone achieved.

Regardless of the detailed findings, the writer feels certain that one fundamental view underlying this whole approach is likely to prove correct, namely the need for a marriage between the experimental and the "individual differences" approach. The neglect of one line of investigation by those engaged upon the other is one of the great weakness of modern psychology, and it seems likely that many of the troubles of our science arise from this cause. In this book stress has been placed on the value of the contribution which experimental psychology can make to personality study, but the inverse of this proposition is equally true. Perhaps it may be useful to illustrate this proposition by reference to the development of the theory of superconductivity in physics.

This phenomenon was discovered in 1911 by Heike Kamerlingh Onnes, a Dutch physicist who cooled a sample of mercury below its superconducting transition temperature and found that all resistance to the flow of electric current vanished. Superconductivity has since been demonstrated in hundreds of metallic elements and alloys, and even a few semiconductors; for all of these the transition temperatures lie below $20°$ Kelvin, and for most even lower than that (below $5°K$). There are thus "individual differences" between conductors (and semiconductors), and these extend even to the very existence of superconductivity; such metals as copper and silver, which are usually considered the best conductors, have never been found to display superconductivity, while poor conductors such as lead and tin do. This "typological" finding requires an explanation, which was given in terms of the Bardeen, Cooper, and Schrieffer theory. They related superconductivity to the existence of an attractive force between electrons in a metal, due to the existence of a lattice of positively charged ions. The negatively charged electrons attract the ions, distort the lattice, and create an excess positive charge to which other electrons can be attracted. This attractive force has to overcome the repulsive force existing between the negatively charged electrons, and a metal can only become a superconductor if the attractive force is in fact stronger than the repulsive force. But the good conducting properties of such metals as copper and silver are due to the fact that there is a comparatively *weak* interaction between electrons and lattice in these metals, reducing the scattering of single electrons which impairs conductivity in the normal state. This weak interaction, while thus favourable to good conductivity in the nonsuperconducting state, fails to generate the attractive force which alone can overcome the repulsive interactions between electrons; consequently good conductors do not develop superconductivity, while poor conductors do. Thus the "typological" study of the reactions of hundreds of different elements and alloys generate facts and information which lead to a general theory of superconductivity, which at the same time explains the peculiar general observation derived from the individual elements and alloys.

In the same way it would seem that any general theory of vigilance, or of arousal, or of memory, or of conditioning, must incorporate the systematic individual differences which have been demonstrated and which relate to the personality dimension of extraversion-introversion. The specific hypotheses put forward in this book are quite likely to prove wrong in the long run, or at least to require extensive emendation; the general view that a *rapprochement* between personality theory and experimental psychology is overdue is not likely to be found erroneous.

Another view which may with some confidence be put forward relates to the existence of two independent personality dimensions or factors, here called extraversion-introversion and emotionality-stability. It has been a recurring theme of lamentation in this book that so many otherwise well-planned and well-designed studies proved to give uninterpretable results because experimenters failed to keep apart these two dimensions. To compare dysthymic neurotics with normals, or subjects high on the Taylor Manifest Anxiety Scale with subjects low on this scale, makes it impossible to attribute differences to either emotionality or to introversion, because the high anxious, dysthymic individual is characterised by *both* introversion and emotionality; differences might be due to one or the other or both of these factors, and it is impossible to sort out the contribution made *ex post facto*. It is suggested that in future all investigations of this type should take great care to keep apart these two personality dimensions and thus make possible the proper attribution of observed differences.

When we turn to the large body of experimental studies designed to test specific hypotheses within the general theory here considered, we may again put forward a view which is not likely to be contested, although it too has been largely disregarded in the past. In any experimental study of a general proposition it is of the utmost importance that a proper choice of parameters be made, and in any replication of an experimental study it is essential that paramenters should be preserved unchanged. We have shown in the case of eyeblink conditioning, for instance, that short CS-UCS intervals, strong UCS, and 100 per cent reinforcement favour extraverts; these parametric differences are all deducible from theory. Yet the experimental literature shows an almost complete disregard of the need to decide carefully about the precise choice made in each case; different investigators show little awareness that they are not in fact testing a particular theory if they fail to relate choice of paramenter to the predictions made by that theory. Time and time again we had to decide that a given study could not be meaningfully related to theoretical predictions because choice of paramenters had been made on an arbitrary basis. Inadvertently such studies may add to our knowledge because they tell us what happens when hitherto unused variable-values are employed, but this is a small gain when we consider how much more useful such studies would have been if they had employed a carefully considered set of parameter values. Even the minimal usefulness which such studies may have is more than offset when authors draw far-reaching and unjustified conclusions regarding some major prediction from such irrelevant data.

A further point clearly brought out by the data is the need to take into account experimental conditions not normally controlled or even noted. Diurnal variation in performance is one example; we have noted studies showing reversal in the respective performance of extraverts and introverts during morning and afternoon testing. Another example, more easily understandable, is the difference in performance when introverts and extraverts are tested under conditions of group or individual testing. Along the same lines of argument, the reinforcing values of different types of stimuli, and even of different strengths of identical stimuli, cannot be assumed to be identical for extraverts and introverts. Predictions and test design have to take careful account of these and many other complications if useful results are to be obtained.

Another source of considerable difficulty is likely to be the choice of subjects. Identical tests, applied under experimentally identical conditions, may give quite different results because of differences in the population tested. A problem-solving test may be anxiety arousing for a dull group, not so for a bright one. A mechanical test may be stressful for an American student group, not so for an English student group. A suggestibility test may produce tension in educated people, none in poorly educated ones who may not see possible implications. Ideally one would like to monitor every test in every group by polygraph recordings of EMG, GSR, and EEG; only in this way could levels of arousal be specified and meaningful comparisons between one experiment and another be made. All this would not be so essential if only regressions between performance and arousal and activation were linear; as we have seen, nonlinearity is the rule rather than the exception, and some version of the Yerkes-Dodson law is absolutely fundamental for the proper understanding and design of experiments in this field.

Clearly we are still very far from a proper quantitative theory of personality, even in the limited field with which we have dealt in this book. A qualitative understanding is a beginning for the scientific study of a given area, but it is only a beginning, and the great need is for properly controlled and designed quantitative experiments, with suitable variation in parameter values. Most needed of all would be a proper quantification of measures of arousal and activation, but it will be clear from our discussion of the physiological basis of these concepts that this will be no easy task, and that quite likely no single figure will be truly representative of the complex interactions taking place within the organism when some external or internal stimulus impinges on the cortex and the brain stem structures. If in spite of all these complications, difficulties, and adumbrations of impending disaster, reasonably consistent findings have in fact been found to support some such generalizations as those put forward in this book, we may perhaps conclude that the causal factors involved are strong and robust enough to overcome minor departures from correct design, and that in due course most of the complexities here pointed out will yield to a determined experimental onslaught, properly directed by a consistent theory.

REFERENCES

(Page reference numbers appear in *boldface* type.)

ACKNER, B., AND PAMPIGLIONE, G.: An evaluation of the sedation threshold test. *J. Psychosom. Res.*, *3*:271-281, 1959; **275, 280.**

ADAMS, J. A.: Vigilance in the detection of low intensity visual stimuli. *J. Exp. Psychol.*, *52*:204-208, 1956; **334.**

ADEY, W. R.; SEJUNDO, J. P., AND LIVINGSTON, R. B.: Corticifugal influences on intrinsic brain stem conduction in cat and monkey. *J. Neurophysiol.*, *20*:1-16, 1957; **239.**

AIBA, S. The suppression of the primary visual stimulus. In: H. J. Eysenck (Ed.), *Experiments with Drugs*. New York, Pergamon, 1963; **291, 294.**

ALLEN, R. M.; RICHER, H. M. AND PLOTNIK, R. J.: A Study of introversion-extraversion as a personality dimension. *Genet. Psychol. Monogr.*, *69*:297-322, 1964; **178.**

ALLPORT, F. H.: *Social Psychology*. New York, Houghton, 1924; **237.**

ALTSCHULE, M. D.: *Bodily Physiology in Mental and Emotional Disorders*. New York, Grune, 1953; **59, 65, 66.**

ANDERSON, A. L., AND HANVIK, L. J.: The psychometric localization of brain lesions: the differential effect of frontal and parietal lesions on M.M.P.I. profiles. *J. Clin. Psychol.*, *6*:177-180, 1950; **333.**

ANDREASSI, J. L.: Skin-conductance and reaction-time in a continuous auditory monitoring task. *Amer. J. Psychol.*, *79*:470-474, 1966; **177.**

ANTHONY, S.: Anxiety as a function of psychomotor and social behaviour. *Brit. J. Psychol.*, *51*:141-152, 1960; **154.**

ARDIS, J. A., AND FRASER, B.: Personality and perception: the constancy effect and introversion. *Brit. J. Psychol.*, *48*:48-54, 1957; **178.**

ARMSTRONG, H. G.: The blood pressure and pulse rate as an index of emotional stability. *Amer. J. Med. Sci.*, *195*:211-220, 1938; **65.**

ATKINSON, J. W.: *An Introduction to Motivation*. London, Van Nostrand, 1964; **166.**

BAKAN, P.: Extraversion-introversion and improvement in an auditory vigilance task. *Brit. J. Psychol.*, *50*:325-332, 1959; **91, 334.**

BAKAN, P.: Effect of meprobamate on auditory vigilance. *Percept. Motor Skills*, *12*:26, 1961; **301.**

BAKAN, P.: Time-of-day preference, vigilance, and extraversion-introversion. In: D. N. Buckner, and J. J. McGrath, (Eds.): *Vigilance: A Symposium*. New York, McGraw, 1963; **93.**

BAKAN, P.; BELTON, J. A., AND TOTH, J. C.: Extraversion-introversion and decrement in an auditory vigilance task. In: D. N. Buckner and J. J. McGrath, (Eds.): *Vigilance: A Symposium.* New York, McGraw, 1963; 88.

BAKER, W. W.: Pharmacology of the central nervous system. *Progress in Neurol. Psychiat.*, *16*:95-123, 1961; 270.

BAKR, A. A.: Eperimenteller Nachweis der typologischen Bedeutung der Ranschburgschen homogenen Hemmung. Mainz, Unpublished Ph.D. thesis, 1963; 76.

BARTENWERFER, H.: Uber die Auswirkung einförmiger Arbeitsvorgänge; Untersuchungen zum Monotieproblem. Sitzungsber. *Gesellsch. z. Beförd. d. ges. Naturwiss. zu Marburg,* 80:1-70, 1957; 88.

BARTENWERFER, H.: Uber die Auswirkungen einföruniger Arbeitsvorgänge. *Sitzungsberichte der Ges. z. Bef. d. ges. Naturwiss. zu Marburg.,* 80:1-70, 1957; 88.

BARTHOLOMEW, A. A.: Extraversion-introversion and neuroticism in first offenders and recidivists. *Brit. J. Delinqu.,* *10*:120-129,1959; 38.

BARTHOLOMEW, A. A., AND MARLEY, E.: Susceptibility to methylpentynol: personality and other variables. *J. Ment. Sci.,* *105*:955-970, 1959; 315.

BASOWITZ, H.; PERSKY, H.; KORCHIN, S. J., AND GRINKER, R. R.: *Anxiety and Stress: An Interdisciplinary Study of a Life Situation.* New York, McGraw, 1955; 59.

BATTERSBY, W. S.; BENDER, M., AND TEUBER, H. L.: Effects of total light flux on critical flicker frequency after frontal lobe lesion. *J. Exp. Psychol.,* *42*:135-142, 1951; 322.

BECKER, W. C.: Cortical inhibition and extraversion-introversion. *J. Abnorm. Soc. Psychol.,* *61*:52-66, 1960; 145, 179, 330.

BEECH, H. R., AND ADLER, F.: Some aspects of verbal conditioning in psychiatric patients. *Behav. Res. Ther.,* *1*:273-282, 1963; 123.

BEECHER, H. K.: *Measurement of subjective responses.* New York, Oxford, 1959; 109, 291.

BENDER, M., AND TEUBER, H. L.: Disturbances in visual perception following cerebral lesions. *J. Psychol.,* *28*:223-233, 1949; 322.

BENDIG, A. W.: College norms for, and concurrent validity of, the Pittsburgh revision of the Maudsley Personality Inventory. *J. Psychol. Stud.,* *11*:12-17, 1959; 38.

BENTON, A. L., AND BLACKBURN, H. L.: Practice effects in reaction-time tasks in brain-injured patients. *J. abnorm. soc. Psychol.,* *54*:109-113, 1957; 335.

BENTON, A. L., AND JOYNT, R. J.: Reaction-time in unilateral cerebral disease. *Confin. Neurol.,* *19*:247-256, 1959; 335.

BENTON, A. L.; SUTTON, S.; KENNEDY, J. A., AND BROKAW, J. R.: The crossmodal retardation in reaction time of patients with cerebral disease. *J. Nerv. Ment. Dis.,* *135*:413-418, 1962; 335.

BERGUM, B. O.: A taxonomic analysis of continuous performance. *Percept. Motor Skills,* *23*:47-54, 1966; 99.

BERLYNE, D. E.: *Conflict, Arousal and Curiosity*. New York, McGraw, 1960; 110, 245.

BERNHAUT, M.; GELLHORN, E., AND RASMUSSEN, A. T.: Experimental contributions to the problem of consciousness. *J. Neurophysiol.*, 16:21-36, 1953; 232.

BESSER, G. M.: Centrally acting drugs and auditory flutter. In: *Proc. Sympos. on Drugs and Sensory Functions*, Roy. Coll. Physicians, 1966; 923.

BESSER, G. M., DUNCAN, C., AND QUILLIAM, J. P.: Modification of the auditory flutter fusion threshold by centrally acting drugs in man. *Nature*, 211 (No. 5050):751, 1966; 293.

BIESHEUVEL, S.: The measurement of threshold for flicker and its value as a preservation test. *Brit. J. Psychol.*, 29:27-38, 1938; 106.

BIESHEUVEL, S.: The Heymans-Wiersma theory of temperament. *Bull. Nat. Inst. Personnel Res.*, 3:30-40, 1952; 106.

BIESHEUVEL, S., AND PITT, D. R.: Some tests of speed and tempo of behaviour as predictors of the primary-secondary function temperament variable. *J. Nat. Inst. Personnel Res.*, 6:87-94, 1955; 177.

BILLS, A. G.: Blocking: a new principle of mental fatigue. *Amer. J. Psychol.*, 43:230-245, 1931; 83.

BINDER, A., AND SALOP, P.: Reinforcement and personality factors in verbal conditioning. *J. Psychol.*, 52:379-402, 1961; 123.

BINDRA, D., AND THOMPSON, W. R.: An evaluation of defecation and urination as measures of fearfulness. *J. Comp. Physiol. Psychol.*, 46:43-45, 1953; 31.

BIRCH, H. G.; BELMONT, I., AND KARP, E.: The prolongation of inhibition in brain-damaged patients. *Cortex*, 1:397-409, 1965; 325.

BITTERMAN, M. E.: Phyletic differences in learning. *Amer. Psychologists*, 20:396-410, 1965; 23, 23.

BITTERMAN, M. E., WODINSKY, J., AND CANDLAND, D. K.: Some comparative psychology. *Amer. J. Psychol.*, 71:94-110, 1958; 23.

BLACKBURN, H. L., AND BENTON, A. L.: Simple and choice reaction time in cerebral disease. *Confin. Neurol.*, 15:327-338, 1955; 335.

BLACKWELL, H. R.: Psychophysical thresholds—experimental studies of measurement. *Engin. Res. Bull.*, No. 36, 1953; 101.

BLAKEMORE, C.: *Brit. J. Psychol.*, in press; 136.

BLAKEMORE, C. B., and BOHLEN, H.: Pursuit-rotor performance and reminiscence as a function of chronicity of brain lesions, in press; 329.

BLITZ, B.; DINNERSTEIN, A. J., AND LOWENTHAL, M.: Relationship between pain tolerance and kinesthetic size judgment. *Percept. Motor Skills*, 22:463-469, 1966; 115.

BÖCHER, W.: Zur Frage der Extraversions-Introversions-Polarität. *Diagnostica*, 11:28-38, 1965; 178.

BONVALLET, M., AND HUGELIN, A.: Influence de la formation réticulaire et du

350   The Biological Basis of Personality

cortex cérébral sur l'excitabilité motrice au cours de l'hypoxie. *Electroenceph. Clin. Neurophysiol.*, *13*:270-284, 1961; **246**.

BRADLEY, P. B., AND KEY, B. J.: The effects of drugs on arousal responses produced by electrical stimulation of the reticular formation of the brain. *Electroenceph. Clin. Neurophysiol.*, *10*:97-110, 1958; **235**.

BREMER, F., AND STOUPEL, N.: De la modificatiin des réponses semorielles cortical's dans l'éveil reticulaire. *Acta Neurol. Belg.*, *58*:401-403,1958; **243**.

BREMER, F. AND STOUPEL, N.: Facilitation et inhibition des potentiels évoques corticaux dans l'éveil cérébral. *Arch. Int. Physiol.*, *67*:240-275, 1959; **243**.

BRENGELMANN, J. C.: The effects of exposure time on immediate recall. *J. Ment. Sci.*, *104*:436-444, 1958; **128**.

BRIERLEY, H.: The speed and accuracy characteristics of neurotics. *Brit. J. Psychol.*, *52*:273-280, 1961; **160**.

BROADBENT, D. E.: Neglect of the surroundings in relation to fatigue decrements in output. In: W. F. Floyd and A. T. Welford, (Eds.): *Fatigue*. London, Lewis, 1953; **91**.

BROADBENT, D. E.: *Perception and Communication*. London, Pergamon, 1958; **127, 165**.

BROADBENT, D. E.: Psychophysical methods and individual differences in the kinesthetic figural after-effects. *Brit. J. Psychol.*, *52*:97-104, 1961; **135**.

BROADHURST, P. L.: The interaction of task difficulty and motivation: The Yerkes-Dodson Law revived. *Acta Psychol.*, *16*:321-338, 1959; **8**.

BROADHURST, P. L.: Application of biometrical genetics to the inheritance of behaviour. In: H. J. Eysenck, (Ed.): *Experiments in Personality*, Vol. 1. London, Routledge; New York, Praeger, 1960; **19, 30, 31, 188, 211**.

BROADHURST, P. L., AND BIGNAMI, G.: Correlative effects of psychogenetic selection: a study of the Roman high and low avoidance strains of rats. *Behav. Res. Ther.*, *2*:273-280, 1965; **213**.

BROADHURST, P. L., AND EYSENCK, H. J.: Emotionality in the rat: A problem of response specificity. In: C. Banks and P. L. Broadhurst, (Eds.): *Studies in Psychology*. London, Univ. of London Press, 1965; **31, 71**.

BROCKWAY, A. L.; GLESER, G.; WINOKUR, G., AND ULETT, A. A.: The use of a control population in neuropsychiatric research. *Amer. J. Psychiat.*, *111*:248-262, 1954; **67**.

BRONZAFT, A.; HAYES, R.; WELCH, L., AND KOLTUR, M.: Relationship between P.G.R. and measures of extraversion, ascendance, and neuroticism. *J. Psychol.*, *50*:193-195, 1960; **171**.

BROWN, F. W.: Heredity in psychoneuroses. *Proc. Roy. Soc. Med.*, *35*:785-796, 1942; **208**.

BROWN, W. P.: Conceptions of perceptual defence. *Brit. J. Psychol., Mon. Suppl.*, 1961; **148**.

BRUNER, J. S., AND POSTMAN, L.: Perception, cognition and behavior. *J. Personality*, *18*:14-31, 1949; **148**.

Buck, L.: Reaction time as a measure of perceptual vigilance. *Psychol. Bull.*, 65:291-304, 1966; **335**.

Buckner, D. N., and McGrath, J. J.: *Vigilance: A symposium.* New York, McGraw, 1963; **87**.

Burch, W. R., and Greiner, T. H.: A bioelectric scale of human alertness: concurrent recordings of the EEG and GSR. *Psychiat. Res. Rep.*, No. 12: 183-193, 1960; **173**.

Burdick, J. A.: Spontaneous autonomic nervous system activity and the M.P.I. New York, Brooklyn Coll., Unpublished M.A. thesis, 1965; **171**.

Burns, B. D; Robson, J. G., and Welt, R. J. L.: The effects of nitrous oxide upon sensory thresholds. *Canad. Anaesth. Soc. J.*, 7:411-422, 1960; **290**.

Burt, C.: Factorial studies of personality and their bearing on the work of the teacher. *Brit. J. Educ. Psychol.*, 35:368-378, 1965; **39**.

Burt, C., and Howard, M.: The multifactorial theory of inheritance and its application to intelligence. *Brit. J. Statist. Psychol.*, 9:95-131, 1956; **187, 207**.

Byrne, D.: Regression-sensitization as a dimension of personality. In B. A. Maher (Ed.): *Progress in Experimental Personality Research.* New York, Academic Press, 1964; **149**.

Cameron, B., and Myers, J. L.: Some personality correlates of risk taking. *J. Gen. Psychol.*, 74:51-60, 1966; **101**.

Carment, D. W.; Miles, C. G., and Cervin, W. B.: Persuasiveness and personality as related to intelligence and extraversion. *Brit. J. Soc. Clin. Psychol.*, 4:1-7, 1965; **178**.

Carter, H. D.: Twin similarities in personality traits. *J. Genet. Psychol.*, 43: 312-321, 1933; **194**.

Cattell, R. B.: Research designs in psychological genetics with special reference to the multiple variance method. *Amer. J. Hum. Genet.*, 5:76-91, 1953; **207**.

Cattell, R. B.: The multiple abstract variance analysis equations and solutions for nature-nurture research on continuous variables. *Psychol. Rev.*, 67:353-372, 1960; **207**.

Cattell, R. B.: The interaction of hereditary and environmental influences. *Brit. J. Statist. Psychol.*, 16:191-210, 1963; **207**.

Cattell, R. B.; Blewett, D. B., and Beloff, J. R.: The inheritance of personality. *Amer. J. Hum. Genetics*, 7:122-146, 1955; **207**.

Cattell, R. B.; Stice, G. F., and Kristy, N. F.: A first approximation to nature-nurture ratios for eleven primary personality factors in objective tests. *J. Abnorm. Soc. Psychol.*, 54:143-159, 1957; **207**.

Cattell, R. B., and Tatro, D. F.: The personality factors, objectively measured, which distinguish psychotics from normals. *Behav. Res. Ther.*, 4:39-52, 1966; **223**.

Cattell, R. B.; Young, H. B., and Hundleby, J. B.: Blood groups and personality traits. *Amer. J. Genet.*, 18:397-402, 1964; **219**.

CHANDLER, P. J.; PARSONS, O. A., AND HAASE, G. R.: Identification of brain damage by flicker perimetry: A second cross-validation. *Percept. Motor Skills,* 19:217-219, 1964; **322.**

CHILD, D.: The relationships between introversion-extraversion, neuroticism and performance in school examinations. *Brit. J. Educ. Psychol.,* 34:187-196, 1964; **98, 99.**

CHILD, I. L.: Personality. *Ann. Rev. Psychol.,* 5:149-170, 1954; **42.**

CLARIDGE, G. S.: The excitation-inhibition balance in neurotics. In: H. J. Eysenck, (Ed.): *Experiments in Personality,* Vol. 2. New York, Praeger, 1960; **88, 145.**

CLARIDGE, G. S.: Arousal and inhibition as determinants of the performance of neurotics. *Brit. J. Psychol.,* 52:53-63, 1961; **284.**

CLARIDGE, G. S.: The effects of meprobamate on the performance of a five-choice serial reaction time task. *J. Ment. Sci.,* 107:590-601, 1961; **284.**

CLARIDGE, G. S.: *Personality and Arousal.* London, Pergamon, 1967; **286.**

CLARIDGE, G. S., AND HERRINGTON, R. N.: Sedation threshold, personality, and the theory of neurosis. *J. Ment. Sci.,* 106:1568-1583, 1960; **281.**

CLARIDGE, G. S., AND HERRINGTON, R. N.: An E. E. G. correlate of the Archimedes spiral after-effect and its relationship with personality. *Behav. Res. Ther.,* 1:217-230, 1963; **144.**

CLARIDGE, G. S., AND HERRINGTON, R. N.: Excitation-inhibition and the theory of neurosis: A study of the sedation threshold. In: H. J. Eysenck, (Ed.): *Experiments with Drugs.* New York, Pergamon, 1963; **286.**

CLARIDGE, G. S.; WAWMAN, R. J., AND DAVIES, M. H.: Sedation threshold, autonomic lability and excitation-inhibition theory of personality. I. The cold pressor test. *Brit. J. Psychiat.,* 109:548-552, 1963; **284.**

CLARK, J. W., AND BINDRA, D.: Individual differences in pain thresholds. *Canad. J. Psychol.,* 10:69-76, 1956; **113.**

COFER, C. N., AND APPLEY, M. H.: *Motivation: Theory and Research.* London, Wiley, 1964; **227.**

COHEN, S., AND SILVERMAN, A. J.: Body and field perceptual dimensions and altered sensory environment. Durham, Duke, 1963. (Annual Rep., Dept. of Psychol.) **117.**

CONRAD, K.: *Der Konstitutionstypus.* (2nd Ed.) Berlin, Springer, 1963; **214.**

COLQUHOUN, W. P.: Temperament, inspection efficiency and time of day. *Ergonomics,* 3:377-378, 1960; **93.**

COLQUHOUN, W. P., AND CORCORAN, D. W. J.: The effects of time of day and social isolation on the relationship between temperament and performance. *Brit. J. Soc. Clin. Psychol.,* 3:226-231, 1964; **93.**

COPPEN, A.; COWIE, V., AND SLATER, E.: Familial aspects of "neuroticism" and "extraversion." *Brit. J. Psychiat.,* 111:70-83, 1965; **208.**

COPPINGER, N. W.; BORTNER, R. W., AND SAUCER, R. T.: A factor analysis of psychological deficit. *J. Genet. Psychol.,* 103:23-43, 1963; **331.**

CORCORAN, D. W. J.: The relation between introversion and salivation.

Amer. J. Psychol., 77:298-300, 1964; **107.**

CORCORAN, D. W. J.: Personality and the inverted-U relation. *Brit. J. Psychol.*, 56:267-274, 1965; **95.**

COSTA, L. D.: Visual reaction time of patients with cerebral disease as a function of length and constancy of preparatory interval. *Percept. Motor Skills*, 14:391-397, 1962; **335.**

COSTELLO, C. G.: The effects of meprobamate on time perception. *J. Ment. Sci.*, 107:63-73, 1961; **194.**

COSTELLO, C. G.: The effects of meprobamate on kinesthetic figural after-effects. *Brit. J. Psychol.*, 53:17-26, 1962; **294.**

COSTELLO, C. G.: The effects of meprobamate on apparent movement. In: H. J. Eysenck (Ed.): *Experiments with Drugs*. New York, Pergamon, 1963; **294.**

COSTELLO, C. G.: The effects of meprobamate on the spiral after-effect. In: H. J. Eysenck, (Ed.): *Experiments with Drugs*. New York, Pergamon, 1963; **294.**

COSTELLO, C. G.: The effects of meprobamate on the visual after-effect. In: H. J. Eysenck, (Ed.): *Experiments with Drugs*. New York, Pergamon, 1963; **294.**

COSTELLO, C. G., AND EYSENCK, H. J.: Persistence, personality and motivation. *Percept. Motor Skills*, 12:169-170, 1961; **111.**

COWIE, V.: The incidence of neurosis in the children of psychotics. *Acta Psychiat. Scand.*, 37:37-87, 1961; **223.**

CRAWFORD, P. L., AND SNYDER, W. U.: Differentiating the psychopath and psychoneurotic with the LAIS. *J. Consult. Psychol.*, 30:178, 1966; **131.**

CRONBACH, L. J.: The two disciplines of scientific psychology. *Amer. Psychologist*, 12:671-684, 1957; **26.**

CROOK, M. N.: Intra-family relationship in personality test performance. *Psychol. Rec.*, 1: 479-502, 1937; **208.**

CROOK, M. N., AND THOMAS, M.: Family relationships in ascendance-submission. Publ. Univ. Calif. *Educ. Philos. & Psychol.*, 1:189-192, 1939; **208.**

CROOKES, T. G., AND HUTT, S. J.: Scores of psychotic patients on the Maudsley Personality Inventory. *J. Consult. Psychol.*, 27:243-247, 1963; **38.**

CURRY, E. T., AND KURTZROCK, A. H.: A preliminary investigation of the ear-choice technique in threshold audiometry. *J. Speech Hearing Dis.*, 16:340-345, 1951; **101.**

DANIEL, R. S.: Electroencephalographic pattern quantification and the arousal continuum. *Psychophysiology*, 2:146-160, 1966; **256.**

DARLING, R. P.: Autonomic action in relation to personality traits in children. *J. Abnorm. Soc. Psychol.*, 35:246-260, 1940; **69.**

DARLINGTON, C. D.: Heredity and environment. Proc. IX Internat. Congress of Genetics. *Caryologia*, 370-381, 1954; **190.**

DARLINGTON, C. D.: Psychology, genetics and the process of history. *Brit. J. Psychol.*, 54:293-298, 1963; **192.**

DARROW, C. W., AND HEATH, L. L.: Reaction tendencies relating to personality. In: K. S. Lashley, (Ed.): *Studies in the dynamics of behavior*. Chicago, U. of Chicago, 1932; **69**.

DARROW, C. W., AND SOLOMON, A. P.: Galvanic skin reflex and blood pressure reactions in psychotic states. *Arch. Neurol. Psychiat.*, *32*:273-299, 1934; **171**.

DAS, J. P.: Hypnosis, verbal satiation, vigilance, and personality factors. *J. Abnorm. Soc. Psychol.*, *68*:72-78, 1964; **91**.

DAVIDSON, P. O.; PAYNE, R. W., AND SLOANE, R. B.: Introversion, neuroticism and conditioning. *J. Abnorm. Soc. Psychol.*, *68*:136-143, 1964; **125**.

DAVIES, D. R., AND KRKOVIC, A.: Skin-conductance, alpha-activity, and vigilance. *Amer. J. Psychol.*, *78*:304-306, 1965; **168, 337**.

DAVIES, M. H.; CLARIDGE, G. S., AND WAWMAN, R. J.: III. The blood pressure response to an adrenaline antagonist as a measure of autonomic lability. *Brit. J. Psychiat.*, *109*:558-567, 1963; **284**.

DAVIS, D. R.: Neurotic predisposition and the disorganization observed in experiments with the Cambridge cockpit. *J. Neurol. Psychiat.*, *9*:119-124, 1946; **153**.

DAVIS, D. R.: Disorders of skill: an experimental approach to some problems of neurosis. *Proc. Roy. Soc. Med.*, *40*:583-584, 1947; **153**.

DAVIS, D. R.: *Pilot Error—Some Laboratory Experiments*. London, H.M.-S.O., 1948; **153**.

DAVIS, D. R.: The disorder of skill responsible for accidents. *Quart. J. Exp. Psychol.*, *1*:136-142, 1949; **153**.

DAWSON, G. D.: A summation technique for the detection of small evoked potentials. *Electroenceph. Clin. Neurophysiol.*, *6*:65-84, 1954; **256**.

DAWSON, G. D.: The relative excitability and conduction velocity of sensory and motor nerve fibres in man. *J. Physiol.*, *131*:436-451, 1956; **256**.

DE FRIES, J. C.: Prenatal maternal stress in mice. *Heredit.*, *55*:289-295, 1964; **18**.

DE RENZI, E., AND FAGLIONI, P.: The comparative efficiency of intelligence and vigilance tests in detecting hemispheric cerebral damage. *Cortex*, *1*:410-433, 1965; **335**.

DELL, P.; BONVALLET, M., AND HUGELIN, A.: Mechanisms of reticular deactivation. In: G. G. W. Wolstenholme and M. O'Connor, (Eds.): *The Nature of Sleep*. London, Churchill, 1961; **246**.

DEWHURST, W. G.: On the chemical basis of mood. *J. Psychosomat. Res.*, *9*:115-127, 1965; **268**.

DEWHURST, W. G., AND MARLEY, E.: Action of sympathomimetic and allied amines on the central nervous system of the chicken. *Brit. J. Pharmacol.*, *25*:705-727, 1965; **268**.

DIAMOND, S.; BALVIN, R. S., AND DIAMOND, F. R.: *Inhibition and Choice*. New York, Harper, 1963; **75, 248**.

DIMASCIO, A.: Drug effects on competitive paired associate learning: Relationship to and implications for the Taylor Manifest Anxiety Scale. *J. Psychol.*, 56:89-97, 1963; **311**.

DINNERSTEIN, A. J.; LOWENTHAL, M.; MARION, R. B., AND OLIVO, J.: Pain tolerance and kinesthetic after-effect. *Percept. Motor Skills*, 15:247-250, 1962; **114**.

DODT, E.: Centrifugal impulses in rabbit's retina. *J. Neurophysiol.*, 19:301-307, 1956; **239**.

DODWELL, P. C.: Some factors affecting the hearing of words presented dichotically. *Canad. J. Psychol.*, 18:72-91, 1964; **148, 150**.

DOERR, H. O., AND HOKANSON, J. E.: The relation between heart rate and performance in children. *J. Person. Soc. Psychol.*, 2:70-77, 1965; **8, 31**.

DOMINO, E. F., FOX, K. E., AND BRODY, T. M.: Pharmacological actions of a convulsant barbiturate. I. Stimulant and depressant effects. *J. Pharmacol.*, 114:473-483, 1955; **268**.

DOUCHIN, G., AND LINDSLEY, D. B.: Visually evoked response correlates of perceptual masking and enhancement. *Electroenceph. Clin. Neurophysiol.*, 19:325-335, 1965; **259**.

DUFFY, G.: Tensions and emotional factors in reaction. *Genet. Psychol. Monogr.*, 7:1-79, 1930; **62, 226**.

DUFFY, G.: *Activation and Behaviour.* London, Wiley, 1962; **55, 59, 65, 66, 67, 68, 167, 226, 228**.

DÜKER, H.: Uber reaktive Anspannungssteigerung. *Ztschr. F. Exp. Angew. Psychol.*, 10:46-72, 1963; **317**.

DÜKER, H.: Die reaktive Anspannungssteigerung als Störfaktor bei der Wirkungsprüfung von Schlafmitteln. *Neuro-Psychopharmacology*, 3:172-175, 1964; **317**.

DUNCAN, C. P.: On the similarity between reactive inhibition and neural satiation. *Amer. J. Psychol.*, 69:227-235, 1956; **79**.

DUNN, S.; BLISS, J., AND SIIPOLA, S.: Effects of impulsivity, introversion, and individual values upon association under free conditions. *J. Personality*, 26:61-76, 1958; **178**.

DUNSTONE, J. J., DZENDOLET, G., AND HENCKERUTH, O.: Effect of some personality variables on electrical vestibular stimulation. *Percept. Motor Skills*, 18:689-695, 1964; **103**.

DU PREEZ, P. D.: Judgment of time and aspects of personality. *J. Abnorm. Soc. Psychol.*, 69:228-233, 1964; **148**.

DUREMAN, I.: Drugs and autonomic conditioning. *Acta Acad. Reg. Sci. Upsaliensis*, 4:1-162, 1959; **307**.

DUREMAN, I.: Relationships between flicker-fusion threshold and two parameters of visual motion after-effect. *Scand. J. Psychol.*, 6:254-256, 1965; **145**.

DZENDOLET, E.: Sinusoidal electrical stimulation of the human vestibular apparatus. *Percept. Motor Skills*, 17:171-185, 1963; **103**.

EASON, R. G.; BEARDSHALL, A., AND JAFFEE, S.: Performance and physiological indicants in a vigilance situation. *Percept. Motor Skills*, 20:3-13, 1965; **95**.

EHLERS, B.: Eine experimentelle Untersuchung der Wahrnehmungshemmung und ihre Beziehung zur Extraversion. Marburg, Unpublished Ph.D. thesis, 1963; **149.**

EKMAN, G.: On the number and definition of dimensions in Kretschmer's and Sheldon's constitutional system. In: *Essays in Psychology Dedicated to David Katz.* Uppsala, Elmquist and Wiknells, 1951. **214.**

ELLINGSON, R. J.: The incidence of EEG abnormality among patients with mental disorders of apparently nonorganic origin: a critical review. *Amer. J. Psychiat., 111*:263-275, 1954; **67.**

ERICKSEN, C. W., AND BROWNE, C. T.: An experimental and theoretical analysis of perceptual defence. *J. Abnorm. Soc. Psychol., 52*:224-230, 1956; **149.**

EVANS, F. J.: Field dependence and the Maudsley Personality Inventory. *Percept. Motor Skills,* 1967. To appear; **117.**

EVANS, J. T., AND HUNT, S. McV.: The "emotionality" of rats. *Amer. J. Psychol., 55*:528-545, 1942; **31.**

EYSENCK, H. J.: *Dimensions of Personality.* New York, Praeger, 1947; **36, 164, 218.**

EYSENCK, H. J.: Schizothymia-Cyclothymia as a dimension of personality. II. Experimental. *J. Personality, 20*:345-384, 1952a; **223.**

EYSENCK, H. J.: *The Scientific Study of Personality.* New York, Praeger, 1952b; **223.**

EYSENCK, H. J.: The psychology of Politics. London, Routledge and Kegan Paul, 1954.

EYSENCK, H. J.: Cortical inhibition, figural after-effect, and the theory of personality. *J. Abnorm. Soc. Psychol., 51*:94-106, 1955a; **114, 135, 324.**

EYSENCK, H. J.: A dynamic theory of anxiety and hysteria. *J. Ment. Sci., 101*:28-51, 1955b; **179.**

EYSENCK, H. J.: Psychiatric diagnosis as a psychological and statistical problem. *Psychol. Rep., 1*:3-17, 1955c; **223.**

EYSENCK, H. J.: The inheritance of extraversion-introversion. Acta Psychol., *12*:95-110, 1956a; **199, 202.**

EYSENCK, H. J.: Reminiscence, drive and personality theory. *J. Abnorm. Soc. Psychol., 53*:328-333, 1956b; **133.**

EYSENCK, H. J.: *The Dynamics of Anxiety and Hysteria.* New York, Praeger, 1957; **78, 79, 106, 117, 121, 135, 142, 178, 264.**

EYSENCK, H. J.: *Maudsley Personality Inventory.* London, U. of London, 1959a. San Diego, Educ. Indust. Testing Service, 1962; **6, 39, 102, 233.**

EYSENCK, H. J.: Personality and the estimation of time. *Percept. Motor Skills, 9*:405-406, 1959b; **146.**

EYSENCK, H. J.: Personality and problem solving. *Psychol. Rep., 5*:592, 1959c; **98.**

EYSENCK, H. J.: Personality and verbal conditioning. *Psychol. Rep., 5*:570, 1959d; **123.**

EYSENCK, H. J.: Scientific methodology and the dynamics of anxiety and hysteria. *Brit. J. Med. Psychol.*, *32*:56-63, 1959e; **120.**

EYSENCK, H. J.: Serial position effects in nonsense syllable learning as a function of interlist rest pauses. *Brit. J. Psychol.*, *50*:360-362, 1959f; **179.**

EYSENCK, H. J. (Ed.): *Experiments in Personality.* New York, Praeger, 1960a; **104.**

EYSENCK, H. J.: A factor analysis of selected tests. In: H. J. Eysenck, (Ed.): *Experiments in Personality.* New York, Praeger, 1960b; **181, 196.**

EYSENCK, H. J.: Objective psychological tests and the assessment of drug effects. *Internat. Rev. Neurobiol.*, *2*:333-384, 1960c; **272.**

EYSENCK, H. J.: *The place of theory in psychology.* In: H. J. Eysenck, (Ed.): *Experiments in Personality,* Vol. 2. New York, Praeger, 1960d; **340.**

EYSENCK, H. J.: *The Structure of Human Personality.* London, Methuen, 1960e; **34, 36, 69, 106, 209, 213, 229, 275.**

EYSENCK, H. J.: Conditioning and personality. *Brit. J. Psychol.*, *53*:299-305, 1962a; **121.**

EYSENCK, H. J.: Figural after-effects, personality and intersensory comparisons. *Percept. Motor Skills, 15*:405-406, 1962b; **135.**

EYSENCK, H. J.: Reminiscence, drive and personality—revision and extension of a theory. *Brit. J. Soc. Clin. Psychol.*, *1*:127-140, 1962c; **132, 133.**

EYSENCK, H. J.: Emotion as a determinant of integrated learning: An experimental study. *Behav. Res. Ther.*, *1*:197-211, 1963a; **212.**

EYSENCK, H. J.: *Experiments with Drugs.* New York, Pergamon, 1963b; **10, 108, 272, 275, 286.**

EYSENCK, H. J.: *Crime and Personality.* Boston, Houghton, 1964a; **25, 53, 55, 164, 184, 205, 290.**

EYSENCK, H. J. (Ed.): *Experiments in Behavior Therapy.* New York, Pergamon, 1964b; **XIII.**

EYSENCK, H. J. (Ed.): *Experiments in Motivation.* New York, Pergamon, 1964c; **11.**

EYSENCK, H. J.: Involuntary rest pauses in tapping as a function of drive and personality. *Percept. Motor Skills, 18*:173-174, 1964d; **87.**

EYSENCK, H. J.: Personality and reminiscence—an experimental study of the "reactive inhibition" and the "conditioned inhibition" theories. *Life Sci., 3*:189-198, 1964e; **134.**

EYSENCK, H. J.: Extraversion and the acquisition of eyeblink and GSR conditioned responses. *Psychol. Bull.*, *63*:258-270, 1965a; **44, 120, 165.**

EYSENCK, H. J.: *Smoking, Health and Personality.* New York, Basic Books, 1965b; **58.**

EYSENCK, H. J.: A three-factor theory of reminiscence. *Brit. J. Psychol.*, *56*:163-181, 1965c; **50, 130, 329.**

EYSENCK, H. J.: Conditioning, introversion-extraversion, and the strength of the nervous system. *Proc. XVIIth Int. Cong. Exper. Psychol.*, Moscow, 9th Symp., 33-34, 1966a; **121, 123.**

EYSENCK, H. J.: On the dual nature of consolidation. *Percept. Motor Skills,* 22:273-274, 1966b; **134.**

EYSENCK, H. J.: Personality and experimental psychology. *Bull. Brit. Psychol. Soc.,* 62: 1-28, 1966c; **130.**

EYSENCK, H. J.: Personality and extra-sensory perception. *Proc. (Brit.) Soc. Psychic. Res.,* 1967. To appear; **178.**

EYSENCK, H. J., AND AIBA, S.: Drugs and personality. V. The Effects of stimulant and depressant drugs on the suppression of the primary visual stimulus. *J. Ment. Sci.,* 103:661-665, 1957; **294.**

EYSENCK, H. J., AND BROADHURST, P. L.: Experiments with animals. In: H. J. Eysenck, (Ed.): *Experiments in Motivation.* New York, Pergamon, 1964; **19, 31, 70, 211.**

EYSENCK, H. J., AND CLARIDGE, G.: The position of hysterics and dysthymics in a two-dimensional framework of personality description. *J. Abnorm. Soc. Psychol.,* 64:46-55, 1962; **142, 180.**

EYSENCK, H. J., AND EASTERBROOK, J. A.: Drugs and personality. VIII. The effects of stimulant and depressant drugs on visual after-effects of a rotating spiral. *J. Ment. Sci.,* 106:842-844, 1960a; **294.**

EYSENCK, H. J., AND EASTERBROOK, J. A.: Drugs and personality. IX. The effects of stimulant and depressant drugs upon visual figural after-effects. *J. Ment. Sci.,* 106:845-851, 1960b; **294.**

EYSENCK, H. J., AND EASTERBROOK, J. A.: Drugs and personality. X. The effects of stimulant and depressant drugs upon kinaesthetic figural after-effects. *J. Ment. Sci.* 106:852-854, 1960c; **294.**

EYSENCK, H. J., AND EASTERBROOK, J. A.: Drugs and personality. XI. The effects of stimulant and depressant drugs upon auditory flutter fusion. *J. Ment. Sci.,* 106:855-857, 1960d; **293.**

EYSENCK, H. J., AND EYSENCK, S. B. G.: The classification of drugs according to their behavioural effects: A new method. In: H. J. Eysenck, (Ed.): *Experiments in Personality,* Vol. 1. New York, Praeger, 1960a; **270.**

EYSENCK, H. J., AND EYSENCK, S. B. G.: Reminiscence on the spiral after-effect as a function of length of rest and number of pre-rest trials. *Percept. Motor Skills,* 10:93-94, 1960b; **142.**

EYSENCK, H. J., AND EYSENCK, S. B. G.: *Eysenck Personality Inventory.* San Diego, Educ. Indust. Testing Service, 1964; **39.**

EYSENCK, H. J., AND EYSENCK, S. B. G.: *Personality Structure and Measurement.* San Diego, R. R. Knapp, 1967; **6, 34, 39, 41, 104, 208, 229.**

EYSENCK, H. J., AND HIMMELWEIT, H. T.: An experimental study of the reactions of neurotics to experiences of success and failure. *J. Gen. Psychol.,* 35:59-75, 1946; **164.**

EYSENCK, H. J.; HOLLAND, H. C., AND TROUTON, D. S.: Drugs and personality. III. The effects of stimulant and depressant drugs on visual after-effect. *J. Ment. Sci.,* 103:650-655, 1957a; **294.**

EYSENCK, H. J.; HOLLAND, H. C., AND TROUTON, D. S.: Drugs and personality. IV. The effects of stimulant and depressant drugs on the rate of fluctuation of a reversible perspective figure. *J. Ment. Sci.*, 103:656-659, 1957b; **294.**

EYSENCK, H. J., AND LEVEY, A.: Alternation in choice behaviour and extraversion. *Life Sci.*, 4:115-119, 1965; **178, 274.**

EYSENCK, H. J., AND PRELL, D.: The inheritance of neuroticism: An experimental study. *J. Ment. Sci.*, 97:441-465, 1951; **200.**

EYSENCK, H. J., AND PRELL, D.: A note on the differentiation of normal and neurotic children by means of objective tests. *J. Clin. Psychol.*, 8:202-204, 1952; **201.**

EYSENCK, H. J., AND RACHMAN, S.: *The Causes and Cures of Neurosis.* San Diego, R. R. Knapp, 1965; **25, 53, 55, 223.**

EYSENCK, H. J., AND SLATER, P.: Effects of practice and rest on fluctuations in the Müller-Lyer illusion. *Brit. J. Psychol.*, 49:246-256, 1958; **3.**

EYSENCK, H. J., AND WHITE, P. O.: Personality and the measurement of intelligence. *Brit. J. Educ. Psychol.*, 34:197-202, 1964; **26.**

EYSENCK, H. J.; WILLETT, R. A., AND SLATER, P.: Drive, direction—rotation, and massing of practice as determinants of the duration of the after-effect from the rotating spiral. *Amer. J. Psychol.*, 75:127-133, 1962; **142.**

EYSENCK, S. B. G.: An experimental study of psychogalvanic reflex responses of normal, neurotic and psychotic subjects. *J. Psychosom, Res.*, 1:258-272, 1956; **59, 223.**

EYSENCK, S. B. G.: Neurosis and psychosis: An experimental analysis. *J. Ment. Sci.*, 102:517-529, 1956; **223.**

EYSENCK, S. B. G.: *Manual of the Junior E.P.I.* San Diego, Educ. Indust. Test. Service, 1965; **39, 193.**

EYSENCK, S. B. G., AND EYSENCK, H. J.: On the dual nature of extraversion. *Brit. J. Soc. Clin. Psychol.*, 2:46-55, 1963; **196, 214.**

FAHRENBERG, J., AND DELIUS, L.: Eine Faktoren analyse psychischer und vegetativer Regulationsdaten. *Nervenarzt*, 34:437-443, 1963; **69.**

FARBER, I. E.: Anxiety as a drive state. In: M. R. Jones (Ed.), *Nebraska Symposium on Motivation.* Lincoln U. of Nebr., 1954; **42.**

FARLEY, F. H.: Individual differences in free response speed. *Percept. Motor Skills*, 22:551-558, 1966a; **161.**

FARLEY, F. H.: Individual differences in solution time in error-free problem solving. *Brit. J. Soc. Clin. Psychol.*, 5:306-309, 1966b; **161, 162.**

FARLEY, F. H.: Introversion and achievement motivation. *Psychol. Rep.*, 19:112, 1966c; **167.**

FARLEY, F. H.: Reminiscence and post-rest performance as a function of length of rest, drive and personality. London, unpublished Ph.D. thesis, 1966d; **133.**

FAURE, J. A une approche bio-electrique des emotions. *J. Physiol.* (Paris), 42:589-590, 1950; **67.**

FINESINGER, J. E.: The effect of pleasant and unpleasant ideas on the respiratory patterns (spirogram) of psychoneurotic patients. *Amer. J. Psychiat.* 100:659-667, 1944; **66.**

FINLEY, K. H.: On the occurrence of rapid frequency potential changes in the human electroencephalogram. *Amer. J. Psychol.*, 101:194-200, 1944; **67.**

FISCHER, R., GRIFFIN, F., AND ROCKEY, M. L.: Gustatory chemoreception in man: multi-disciplinary aspects and perspectives. *Persp. Biol. Med.*, 9:549-577, 1966; **104.**

FISCHGOLD, H., AND SCHWARTZ, B. A.: A Clinical, electroencephalographic and polygraphic study of sleep in the human adult. In G. E. W. Wolstenholme and M. O'Connor (Eds.): *The Nature of Sleep.* Boston, Brown, 1961; **304.**

FISHER, R. A.: The correlation between relatives on the supposition of Mendelian inheritance. *Trans. Roy. Soc. Edin.*, 52:399-433, 1918; **187.**

FLECHTNER, G.: Uber die Monotonie, zugleich ein Beitrag zur Persönlichkeitsforschung. *Unters. Psych. Phil. Päd.*, 12 (No. 2), 1937; **88.**

FORREST, R. W.: Relationship between sharpening and extraversion. *Psychol. Rep.*, 13:564, 1963; **178.**

FORTH, H.: Uber die Wirkung vershiedener Dosen eines Schlafmittels auf einige psychische Leistungen. *Psychol. Beitrage*, 9:3-46, 1966; **317.**

FOULDS, G. A.: Temperamental differences in maze performance. I. Characteristic differences among psychoneurotics. *Brit. J. Psychol.*, 42:209-217, 1951. II. The effect of distraction and electroconvulsive therapy on psychomotor retardation. *Brit. J. Psychol.*, 43:33-41, 1952; **160.**

FOULDS, G. A.: A method of scoring the TAT applied to psychoneurotics. *J. Ment. Sci.*, 99:235-246, 1953; **160, 178.**

FOULDS, G. A.: *Personality and Personal Illness.* London, Tavistock, 1965; **280.**

FOULDS, G. A., AND CAINE, T. M.: Psychoneurotic symptom clusters, trait clusters and psychological tests. *J. Ment. Sci.*, 104:722-731, 1958; **160.**

FOX, R., AND LIPPERT, W.: Spontaneous GSR and anxiety level in sociopathic delinquents. *J. Consult. Psychol.*, 27:368, 1963; **173.**

FRANKENHAEUSER, M., AND PATKAI, P.: Interindividual differences in catecholamine excretion during stress. Rep. Psychol. Lab. Univ. Stockholm, p. 178, 1964; **59.**

FRANKS, C. M.: Conditioning and personality: A study of normal and neurotic subjects. *J. Abnorm. Soc. Psychol.*, 52:143-150, 1956; **118.**

FRANKS, C. M.: Differences determinées par la personalité dans la perceptions visuelle de la verticalité. *Rev. de psychol. appl.*, 6:235-246, 1956; **117.**

FRANKS, C. M.: Personality factors and the rate of conditioning. *Brit. J. Psychol.*, 48:119-126, 1957; **118.**

FRANKS, C. M.: The apparent failure of ethyl alcohol to inhibit the formation of conditioned eyeblink responses in man. *Psychopharmacologia*, 4:433-440, 1963a; **308.**

FRANKS, C. M.: Ocular movements and spontaneous blink rate as functions of personality. *Percept. Motor Skills, 16*:178, 1963b; **87, 119, 142.**

FRANKS, C. M., AND LAVERTY, S. G.: Sodium amytal and eyelid conditioning. *J. Ment. Sci.*: *101*:654-663, 1955; **307.**

FRANKS, C. M., AND LINDAHL, L. E. H.: Extraversion and rated fluctuation of the Necker cube. *Percept. Motor Skills, 16*:131-137, 1963; **108.**

FRANKS, C. M., AND TROUTON, D.: Effects of amobarbital sodium and dexamphetamine sulphate on the conditioning of the eyelid response. *J. Comp. Physiol. Psychol., 51*:220-222, 1958; **307.**

FRANKS, V.: An experimental study of conditioning and learning in mental defectives. Unpublished Ph.D. Thesis, Univ. of London; **326.**

FRASER, D. C.: Vigilance stress. Med. Res. Coun., A.P.U. Rep. 174/52, 1952; **93.**

FORSSMAN, H., AND FREY, T. S.: Electroencephalogram of boys with behavior disorders. *Acta Psychiat. Scand., 28*:61-73, 1953; **67.**

FREEDMAN, N. L.; HAFER, B. M., AND DANIELS, R. S.: EEG arousal decrement during paired-associate learning. *J. Comp. Psychol., 61*:15-19, 1966; **247.**

FREEMAN, A. L.: *The Energetics of Human Behavior.* Ithaca, Cornell, 1948; **68, 226.**

FREEMAN, A. L., AND KATZOFF, E. G.: Muscular tension and irritability. *Amer. J. Psychol., 44*:789-792, 1932; **62.**

FREMMING, K. H.: *Morbid Risks of Mental Disease and other Mental Abnormalities in an Average Danish Population.* Copenhagen, Munksgaard, 1947; **209.**

FRENCH, J. D.: Corticifugal connections with the reticular formation. In: H. H. Jasper, *et al.*, (Eds.), *Reticular Formation of the Brain.* London, Churchill, 1957; **251.**

FRENCH, J. D.; VERZEANA, M., AND MAGOUN, K. V.: Contrasting features of corticopetal conduction in direct and indirect sensory systems. *Trans. Amer. Neurol. Ass., 77*:44-47, 1952; **239.**

FULLER, J. L., AND THOMPSON, W. R.: *Behavior Genetics.* London, Wiley, 1960; **208, 209, 211.**

FURNEAUX, W. D.: The Nufferno tests. *Bull. Nat. Found. Educ. Res. England and Wales, 6*:32-36, 1955; **162.**

FURNEAUX, W. D.: Neuroticism, extraversion, drive and suggestibility. *Internat. J. Clin. Exper. Hypnosis, 9*:195-214, 1961; **182.**

FURNEAUX, W. D.: The psychologist and the university. Universities Quart., Dec. 1962. Reprinted in *Research and experiment in education.* Newcastle, Dept. Educ., King's College; **98.**

FURNEAUX, W. D.: Neuroticism, extraversion and suggestibility: A comment. *Internat. J. Clin. Exper. Hypnosis, 11*:201-202, 1963; **183.**

FURNEAUX, W. D., AND GIBSON, H. B.: The Maudsley Personality Inventory as a predictor of susceptibility to hypnosis. *J. Clin. Exper. Hypnosis,*

362 The Biological Basis of Personality

9:167-177, 1961; **183.**

FUSTER, J. M.: Effects of stimulation of brain stem on tachistoscopic perception. *Science*, *127*:150, 1958; **243.**

GALAMBOS, R.: Suppression of auditory nerve activity by stimulation of efferent fibres to cochlea. *J. Neurophysiol.*, *19*:438-445, 1956; **239.**

GANZ, L.: Mechanism of the figural after-effects. *Psychol. Rev.*, *73*:128-150, 1966; **138.**

GARNER, W. R.; HAKE, H. W., AND ERIKSEN, C. W.: Operationism and the concept of perception. *Psychol. Rev.*, *63*:149-159, 1956; **78.**

GASTAUT, H.: The brain stem and cerebral electrogenesis in relation to consciousness. In: F. Delafesnaye, (Ed.): *Brain Mechanism and Consciousness*. Springfied, Thomas, 1954; **66.**

GASTAUT, H.: Confrontations entre les données de l'électroencéphalogramme et des examens psychologiques chez 522 sujets repartis en trois groupes differents. In: H. Fishgold and H. Gastaut, (Eds.): *Conditionnement et Reactivité en Électroencéphalographie*. Paris, Masson, 1957; **66.**

GASTAUT, H., AND ROGER, A.: Les mécanismes de l'activité nerveuse supérieure envisagés au niveau des grands structures fonctionnelles du cerveau. The Moscow Coll. Electroencephal. of higher nervous activity. *Electroenceph. Clin. Neurophysiol. Supp.*, *13*:13-38, 1960; **244.**

GAUTHIER, C.; PARMA, M., AND ZANCHETTI, A.: Effect of electrocortical arousal upon development and configuration of specific evoked potentials. *Electroenceph. Clin. Neurophysiol.*, *8*:237-244, 1956; **238.**

GEBHARDT, R.: Düsseldorf, Psychol. Inst., Unpublished work, 1966; **126.**

GELLHORN, E.: Prolegomena to a theory of emotions. In: *Perspectives in biology and medicine*, Vol. 4. Chicago, U. of Chicago, 1961; **232.**

GELLHORN, E.; KOELLA, W. P., AND BALLIN, H. H.: Interaction on cerebral cortex of acoustic or optic with nociceptive impulses: the problem of consciousness. *J. Neurophysiol.*, *17*:14-21, 1954; **238.**

GELLHORN, E., AND LOOFBOURROW, G. N.: *Emotions and Emotional Disorders*. New York, Harper, 1963; **55, 230, 235, 236.**

GHISELLI, E. E.: Differentiation of individuals in terms of their predictability. *J. Appl. Psychol.*, *40*:374-377, 1956; **183.**

GHISELLI, E. E.: Moderating effects and differential reliability and validity. *J. Appl. Psychol.*, *47*:81-86, 1963; **182, 183.**

GIBSON, H. B.: Furneaux's discussion of extraversion and neuroticism with regard to suggestibility. A criticism. *Internat. J. Clin. Exper. Hypnosis*, *10*:281-287, 1962; **183.**

GIBSON, H. B.: *Manual of the Gibson Spiral Maze*. London, U. of London, 1965; **161, 162.**

GLUCK, H., AND ROWLAND, V.: Defensive conditioning of electrographic arousal with delayed and differentiated auditory stimuli. *Electroenceph. Clin. Neurophysiol.*, *11*:485-496, 1959; **248.**

GOFF, W. R.; ROSNER, B. S., AND ALLISON, T.: Distribution of cerebral somato-sensory evoked responses in normal man. *Electroenceph. Clin. Neurophysiol.*, *14*:697-713, 1962; **261**.

GOLDMAN-EISLER, F.; SHARBECK, A., AND HENDERSON, A.: Breath rate and the selective action of chlorpromazine on speech behaviour. *Psychopharmacologia*, *8*:415-427, 1965; **14**.

GOLDSTEIN, K.: *The Organism.* New York, American Book Co., 1939; **330**.

GOLDSTONE, S.; BOARDMAN, W. K., AND LHAMON, W. T.: Effect of quinal barbitone, dextro-amphetamine and placebo on apparent time. *Brit. J. Psychol.*, *49*:324-328, 1958; **294**.

GOODMAN, L., AND GILMAN, A.: *The Pharmacological Basis of Therapeutics.* New York, Macmillan, 1955; **266**.

GOTTESMAN, I. I.: Heritability of personality: A demonstration. *Psychol. Monogr.*, 77: No. 9, 1963; **194**.

GOTTESMAN, I. I.: Genetic variance in adaptive personality traits. Paper, A.P.A. meeting, Division of Developmental Psychology, 1965; **195**.

GOTTESMAN, I. I.: Personality and natural selection. In: S. G. Vandenberg, (Ed.): *Methods and Goals in Human Behavior Genetics.* London, Academic Press, 1965; **199, 222**.

GOTTESMAN, I. I., AND SHIELDS, J.: Schizophrenia in twins: sixteen years consecutive admission to a psychiatric clinic. *Brit. J. Psychiat.*, in press; **223**.

GOTTLEIB, J. S.; KNOTT, J. R., AND ASHLAY, M. C.: Electroencephalographic evaluation of primary behavior disorders in children. *A.M.A. Arch. Neurol. Psychiat.*, *53*:138-143, 1945; **67**.

GOTTLOBER, A. B.: The relationship between brain potentials and personality. *J. Exp. Psychol.*, *22*:67-74, 1938; **177**.

GOTTSCHALK, L. A.: The use of drugs in interrogation. In: A. B. Biderman and H. Zimmer, (Eds.): *The Manipulation of Human Behavior.* New York, Wiley, 1961; **311**.

GRANGER, G. W.: Abnormalities of sensory perception. In H. J. Eysenck (Ed.): *Handbook of Abnormal Psychology.* London, Pitman, 1960; **291**.

GRANGER, G. W.: Eysenck's theory of anxiety and hysteria and the results of visual adaptation experiments. *Acta Psychol.*, *13*:98-126, 1957; **178**.

GRANIT, R.: Centrifugal and antidromic effects on ganglion cells of the retina. *J. Neurophysiol.*, *18*:388-411, 1955; **239**.

GRASTYAN, E.: The hippocampus and higher nervous activity. In: M. A. Brazier, (Ed.): *The Central Nervous System and Behavior;* **251**.

GRAY, J. A.: *Pavlov's Typology.* New York, Pergamon, 1965; **80, 100, 103, 106, 180, 220, 241, 244, 245, 252, 289**.

GREBE, H.: Diskordanzursachen bei erbgleichen Zwillingen. *Acta Genet. Med. Gemell.*, *1*:89-102, 1952; **191**.

GROSS, O.: *Die Cerebrale Sekundärfunktion.* Leipzig, 1902; **106**.

HAGBARTH, K. E., AND KERR, D. I. B.: Central influences on spinal afferent conduction. *J. Neurophysiol.*, *17*:295-307, 1954; **239**.

HALCOMB, C. G., AND KIRK, R. E.: Organismic variables as predictors of vigilance behavior. *Percept. Motor Skills*, 21:547-552, 1965; **91**.

HALL, C. S.: The genetics of behavior: In: S. S. Stevens, (Ed.): *Handbook of Experimental Psychology*. New York, Wiley, 1951; **30**.

HALSTEAD, W. C.: *Brain and Intelligence*. Chicago, U. of Chicago, 1947; **322**.

HANLEY, W. B.: Hereditary aspects of duodenal ulceration: Serum-pepsinogen level in relation to +BO blood groups and salivary ABH secretor status. *Brit. Med. J.*, 1:936-940, 1964; **219**.

HARDY, J. D.; WOLFF, H. G., AND GOODELL, H.: Studies of pain. *J. Clin. Invest.*, 19:649-657, 1940; **102**.

HARDY, J. D.; WOLFF, H. G., AND GOODELL, H.: *Pain Sensations and Reactions*. Baltimore, Williams & Wilkins, 1952; **201**.

HARE, R. D.: Temporal gradient of fear arousal in psychopaths. *J. Abnorm. Psychol.*, 70:442-445, 1965; **173**.

HARE, R. D.: Psychopathy and choice of immediate versus delayed punishment. *J. Abnorm. Psychol.*, 71:25-29, 1966; **173**.

HASLAM, D. R.: Individual differences in pain threshold and the concept of arousal. Bristol, Unpublished Ph.D. thesis, 1966; **102, 291**.

HAUGEN, F. P., AND MELZAK, R.: The effects of nitrous oxide on responses evoked in the brain stem by tooth stimulation. *Anesthesiology*, 18:183-195, 1957; **286**.

HAUTY, G. T., AND PAYNE, R. B.: Effects of analeptic and depressant drugs upon psychological behavior. *Amer. J. Pub. Health*, 48:571-577, 1958; **301**.

HAUTY, G. T., AND PAYNE, R. B.: Mitigation of work decrement. *J. Exp. Psychol.*, 49:60-67, 1955; **301**.

HAWARD, L. R. C.: Drug-induced fatigue decrement in air traffic control. *Percept. Motor Skills*, 20:952, 1965; **301, 315**.

HAYNES, J. R., AND SELLS, S. B.: Assessment of organic brain damage by psychological tests. *Psychol. Bull.*, 60:316-325, 1963; **330**.

HEBB, D. O.: Drives and the c.n.s. (conceptual nervous system). *Psychol. Rev.*, 62:243-254, 1955; **8, 227, 245**.

HEBB, D. O.: *A Textbook of Psychology*. Philadelphia, Saunders, 1958; **50, 227**.

HECKENMUELLER, E. G.: Stabilization of the retinal image: A review of method, effects, and theory. *Psychol. Bull.*, 63:157-169, 1965; **83**.

HELSON, H.: *Adaptation-level Theory*. New York, Harper, 1964; **250**.

HENDRICKSON, A., AND WHITE, P. O.: Promax: A quick method for rotation to oblique simple structure. *Brit. J. Stat. Psychol.*, 17:65-70, 1964; **180**.

HENRY, C. E., AND KNOTT, J. R.: A note on the relationship between "personality" and alpha rhythm of the electroencephalogram. *J. Exp. Psychol.*, 28:363-366, 1941; **177**.

HERNANDEZ-PEÓN, R.: Neurophysiological correlates of habituation and other manifestations of plastic inhibition (internal inhibition). In: H. H. Jasper and G. D. Smirnov, (Ed.): Moscow Colloquium on EEG of Higher Nervous Activity. *Electroenceph. Clin. Neurophysiol.*, Suppl.

13:101-114, 1960; **248, 251.**

HERNANDEZ-PEÓN, R.: Reticular mechanisms of sensory control. In: W. Rosenblith, (Ed.): *Sensory Communication.* New York, Wiley, 1961; **240.**

HERNANDEZ-PEÓN, R., AND DONOSO, M.: Subcortical photically evoked electric activity in the human waking brain. *First Internat. Congress Neurol. Sci., 1957;* Quoted by Samuels, 1959; **240.**

HERNANDEZ-PEÓN, R; GUZMAN-FLORES, C.; ALCARAZ, M., AND FERNANDEZ-GUARDIOLA, A.: Sensory transmission in visual pathway during attention in unanesthetized cats. *Acta. Neurol. Lat. Amer., 3*:1-8, 1957. Quoted by Samuels, 1959; **239.**

HERNANDEZ-PEÓN, R., AND HAGBARTH, K. E.: Interaction between afferent and cortically induced reticular responses. *J. Neurophysiol., 18*:44-55, 1955; **238.**

HERNANDEZ-PEÓN, R.; SCHERRER, H., AND JOUVET, M.: Modification of electric activity in cochlear nucleus during attention in unanesthetized cats. *Science, 123*:331-332, 1956; **239.**

HERRICK, C. J.: *The Evolution of Human Nature.* Austin, U. of Texas, 1956; **234.**

HERZ, A.: Drugs and the conditioned avoidance response. *Internat. Rev. Neurobiol., 2*:229-277, 1960; **272.**

HEYMANS, A.: *Inleiding tot de Speciale Psychologie.* Haarlem, Bohn, 1929; **106.**

HILDEBRAND, H. P.: A factorial study of introversion-extraversion. *Brit. J. Psychol., 49*:1-11, 1958; **180, 275.**

HILGARD, E. R.: *Hypnotic Susceptibility.* New York, Harcourt, 1965; **183.**

HILL, D., AND PARR, G. (Eds.): *Electroencephalography* (2nd Ed.). London, Macdonald, 1964: **66, 67.**

HIMMELWEIT, H. T.: Speed and accuracy of work as related to temperament. *Brit. J. Psychol., 36*:132-144, 1946; **160.**

HIMMELWEIT, H. T.: A comparative study of the level of aspiration of normal and neurotic persons. *Brit. J. Psychol. 37*:41-59, 1947; **165.**

HOBSON, G. N.: Ethanol inhibition of formation of conditioned eyeblink responses in man. *Psychopharmacologia, 9*:93-100, 1966; **308.**

HOCH, P.; KUBIS, J. F., AND ROUKE, F. L.: Psychogalvanometric investigations in psychoses and other abnormal mental states. *Psychosom. Med., 6*:237-243; **59.**

HODGKIN, A. L.: The local electric changes associated with repetitive action in a non-medullated axon. *J. Physiol., 107*:165-181, 1948; **50.**

HOFFEDITZ, E. L.: Family resemblances in personality traits. *J. Soc. Psychol., 5*:214-227, 1934; **208.**

HOGAN, M. J.: Influence of motivation on reactive inhibition in extraversion-introversion. *Percept. Motor Skills, 22*:187-192, 1966; **92.**

HOLLAND, H. C.: Measures of perceptual functions. In: H. J. Eysenck, (Ed.): *Experiments in Personality,* Vol. 2. New York, Praeger, 1960. **142.**

HOLLAND, H. C.: A note on differences in the duration of the spiral after-effect following continuous and intermittent stimulation. *Acta Psychol.,* 20:304-307, 1962; **142.**

HOLLAND, H. C.: The spiral after-effect and extraversion. *Acta Psychol.,* 20:29-35, 1962; **142.**

HOLLAND, H. C.: Massed practice and reactive inhibition, reminiscence and disinhibition in the spiral after-effect. *Brit. J. Psychol.,* 54:261-272, 1963; **142.**

HOLLAND, H. C.: "Visual masking" and the effects of stimulant and depressant drugs. In: H. J. Eysenck, (Ed.): *Experiments with Drugs.* New York, Pergamon, 1963; **254, 294, 296.**

HOLLAND, H. C.: *The Spiral After-effect.* London, Pergamon, 1965; **87, 142, 322.**

HOLLAND, H. C., AND GOMEZ, B. H.: The effects of stimulant and depressant drugs upon visual figural after-effects. In: H. J. Eysenck, (Ed.): *Experiments with Drugs.* New York, Pergamon, 1963; **294.**

HOMSKAYA, E. D.: Verbal regulation of the vegetative components of the orienting reflex in focal brain lesions. *Cortex,* 1:63-76, 1964; **322.**

HONIGFELD, G.: Cortical inhibition, perceptual satiation, and introversion-extraversion. *J. Abnorm. Soc. Psychol.,* 65:278-280, 1962; **179, 330.**

HONIGFELD, G.: "Neurological efficiency", perception, and personality. *Percept. Motor Skills,* 15:531-553, 1962; **179, 300.**

HORD, D. J.; JOHNSON, L. C., AND LUBIN, A.: Differential effect of the law of initial value (LIV) on autonomic variables. *Psychophysiol.,* 1:79-87, 1964; **57.**

HOVLAND, C. I.: Experimental studies in rote-learning. V. Comparison of distribution of practice in serial and paired-associate learning. *J. Exp. Psychol.,* 25:622-633, 1939; **4.**

HOWARTH, E.: Some laboratory measures of extraversion-introversion. *Percept. Motor Skills,* 17:55-60, 1963; **98, 126, 135, 146, 178.**

HOWARTH, E.: Differences between extraverts and introverts on a button-pressing task. *Psychol. Rep.,* 14:949-950, 1964; **157.**

HUGELIN, A.: Analyse de l'inhibition d'un reflexe nociceptif los de l'activation du système reticulo-spinal dit "facilateur." *C. R. Soc. Biol. (Paris),* 149:1893-1898, 1955; **241.**

HUGELIN, A.: Étude comparée de l'activation du système réticulaire activateur ascendant et du système réticulaire facilitateur descendant. *C.R. Soc. Biol. (Paris),* 149:1963-1965, 1955; **241.**

HUGELIN, A.; BONVALLET, M., AND DELL, P.: Activation réticulaire et corticale d'origine chémoceptive au cours d'hypoxie. *Electroenceph. Clin. Neurophysiol.,* 11:325-340, 1959; **246.**

HUGELIN, A., AND DUMONT, S.: Controle réticulaire du réflexe linguo-maxillaire et des afférences somesthesiques. *J. Physio. (Paris),* 52:119-120, 1960; **241.**

HULL, C. L.: *Principles of Behaviour*. New York, Appleton, 1943; **77, 179, 324**.

HUSE, M. M., AND PARSONS, O. A.: Pursuit-rotor performance in the brain-damaged. *J. Abnorm. Psychol.*, 70:350-359, 1965; **328**.

IDESTRÖM, C. M., AND CADENIUS, B.: Chlordiazepoxide, Dipiperon and Amo-barbital. Dose effect studies in human beings. *Psychopharmacologia*, 4:235-246, 1963; **317**.

ILTIS, H.: *The Life of Mendel*. London, Allen & Unwin, 1966; **188**.

INGHAM, J. G.: Changes in M.P.I. scores in neurotic patients: A three year follow-up. *Brit. J. Psychiat.*, 112:931-939, 1966; **221**.

INGLIS, J.: Abnormalities of motivation and "ego functions". In: H. J. Eysenck, (Ed.): *Handbook of Abnormal Psychology*. New York, Basic Books, 1960; **148**.

INGVAR, D. H. AND HUNTER, J.: Influence of visual cortex on light impulses in the brain stem of the unanesthetized cat. *Acta Physiol. Scand.*, 33:194-218, 1955; **239**.

IPPOLITOV, F. V.: The strengths and sensitivity of the nervous system when comparing three analyzers. Proc. 18th Int. Congress Exp. Psychol., 9th Symposium, 175-177, 1966; **103**.

JACOBSON, E.: Differential relaxation during reading, writing, and other activities as tested by the knee-jerks. *Amer. J. Physiol.*, 86:675-693, 1928; **64**.

JACOBSON, E.: *Progressive Relaxation*. Chicago, U. of Chicago, 1938; **64**.

JAFFE, R.: Kinesthetic aftereffects and stroboscopic movement. *Amer. J. Psychol.*, 67:668-676, 1954; **324**.

JANKE, W.: *Experimentelle Untersuchungen zur Abhängigkeit der Wirkung psychotroper Substanzen von Persönlichkeitsmerkmalen*. Frankfurt, Aka-demische Verlagsgesellschaft, 1964; **14**.

JASPER, H. H.; NAQUET, R., AND KING, E.: Thalamo-cortical recruiting re-sponses in sensory receiving areas in the cat. *Electroenceph. Clin. Neuro-physiol.*, 7:99-114, 1955; **238**.

JASPER, H. H.; SOLOMON, P., AND BRADLEY, C.: Electroencephalographic analogues of behavior problem children. *Amer. J. Psychiat.*, 95:641-658, 1938; **67**.

JAWANDA, J. S.: Age, sex and personality variables in verbal conditioning and its modification by drugs. Punjab Univ., Unpublished Ph.D. thesis, 1966; **123, 309**.

JENKINS, J. J., AND LYKKEN, D. T.: Individual differences. *Ann. Rev. Psychol.*, 9:79-112, 1958; **119**.

JENSEN, A. R.: The Maudsley Personality Inventory. *Acta Psychol.*, 14:314-325, 1958; **38**.

JENSEN, A. R.: An empirical theory of the serial-position effect. *J. Phychol.*, 53:127-142, 1962; **6, 126, 132, 179**.

JENSEN, A.: Extraversion, neuroticism and serial learning. *Acta Psychol.*,

20:69-77, 1962; **6.**

JENSEN, A.: Individual differences in learning: Interference factor. *U.S. Dept. Health, Educ. & Welf., Project Rep. 1867,* 1964; **127, 131, 160.**

JENSEN, A. R.: The measurement of reactive inhibition in humans. *J. gen. Psychol.,* 75:85-94, 1966; **158.**

JINKS, J. L.: Behaviour is a phenotype: The biometrical approach. *Bull. Brit. Psychol. Soc,* 18:25-30, 1965; **188.**

JOFFE, J. M.: The effects of prenatal maternal stress on emotionality and learning ability in rats selected for emotional reactivity. Unpublished Ph.D. thesis, Univ. of London, 1965; **16.**

JOHNS, J. M., AND QUAY, H. C.: The effect of social reward on verbal conditioning in psychopathic and neurotic military offenders. *J. Consult. Psychol.,* 26:217-220, 1962; **125.**

JONES, B. E.; AYRES, J. J. B.; FLANARY, H. G., AND CLEMENTS, T. H.: Effects of morphine and pentobarbital on conditioned electrodermal responses and basal conductance in man. *Psychopharmacologia,* 7:159-174, 1965; **306.**

JONES, H. E.: Perceived differences among twins. *Eugenics Quart.,* 5:98-102, 1955; **202.**

JONES, H. G.: The study of patterns of emotional expression. In: M. L. Reymert, (Ed.): *Feelings and Emotions.* London, McGraw, 1950; **170.**

JONES, H. GWYNNE: Learning and abnormal behaviour. In: H. J. Eysenck, (Ed.): *Handbook of Abnormal Psychology.* New York, Basic Books, 1960; **41, 42, 43.**

JONES, M. B. AND FENNELL, R. S.: Runway performance by two strains of rats. *Quart. J. Florida Acad. Sci.,* 28:289-296, 1965; **20.**

JOST, H.: Some physiological changes during frustration. *Child Develop.,* 12:9-15, 1941; **69.**

JOUVET, M.: Récherches sur les mécanismes neurophysiologiques du sommeil et de l'apprentissage négatif. In: A. Fressard *et al.,* (Eds.): *Brain Mechanisms and Learning.* Oxford, Blackwell, 1961; **251.**

JUNG, R.: Co-ordination of specific and non-specific afferent impulses of single neurons of the visual cortex. In: H. H. Jasper *et al.,* (Eds.): *Reticular Formation of the Brain.* Henry Ford Hospital Internat. Symp. London, Churchill, 1957; **244.**

JUNG, R., AND HASSLER, R.: The extrapyramidal motor system. In: *Handbook of Physiology,* Vol. 1. Washington, Amer. Physiol. Soc., 1959; **241.**

JUNKO, M.; JOST, H., AND HILL, T. S.: Pathology of the energy system. *J. Psychol.,* 33:183-198, 1952; **66.**

KAGAN, J.: Body build and conceptual impulsivity in children. *J. Personality,* 34:118-128, 1966; **219.**

KAMANO, D. K.; MARTIN, L. K.; OGLE, M. E., AND POWELL, B. J.: Effects of amobarbital on the conditioned emotional response and conditioned avoidance response. *Psychol. Rec.,* 16:13-16, 1966; **307.**

KATKIN, E. S.: The relationship between a measure of transitory anxiety and spontaneous autonomic activity. *J. Abnorm. Psychol.,* 71:142-146, 1966; 59.

KELLY, D. H. W.: Measurement of anxiety by forearm blood flow. *Brit. J. Psychiat.,* 112:789-798, 1966; 56.

KELLY, D. H. W.; WALTER, C. J. S., AND SARGANT, W.: Modified leucotomy assessed by forearm blood flow and other measurements. *Brit. J. Psychiat.,* 112:871-881, 1966; 57.

KEMPF, E.: The autonomic functions and the personality. New York and Washington, Nerv. Ment. Dis. Publ. Co., 1921; 168.

KENNARD, M. A.; RABINOWITCH, M. S., AND FISTER, W. P.: The use of frequency analysis in the interpretation of the EEGs of patients with psychological disorders. *Electroenceph. Clin. Neurophysiol.,* 7:29-38, 1955; 67.

KERR, D. I. B., AND HAGBARTH, K. E.: An investigation of olfactory centrifugal fiber system. *J. Neurophysiol.,* 18:363-374, 1955; 239.

KILLAM, E. K.: Drug action on the brain-stem reticular formation. *Pharmacol. Rev.,* 14:175-224, 1962; 270, 271.

KIMBLE, G. A.: An experimental test of a two-factor theory of inhibition. *J. Exp. Psychol.,* 39:15-23, 1949; 84, 132.

KISSIN, B.; GOTTESFELD, H., AND DICKES, R.: Inhibitions and tachistoscopic thresholds for sexually charged words. *J. Psychol.,* 43:333-339, 1957; 149.

KLEBAN, M. H.: Strain differences recurring in an experimental study of punishment. *Psychol. Rep.* 16:531-536, 1965; 18.

KLEIN, G. S., AND KRECH, D.: Cortical conductivity in the brain-injured. *J. Personality,* 21:118-148, 1952; 323.

KLEINSMITH, L. J., AND KAPLAN, S.: Paired-associate learning as a function of arousal and interpolated interval. *J. Exp. Psychol.,* 65:190-193, 1963; 50.

KLEINSMITH, L. J., AND KAPLAN, S.: Interaction of arousal and recall interval in nonsense-syllable paired-associate learning. *J. Exp. Psychol.,* 67:124-126, 1964; 129.

KLEITMAN, N.: *Sleep and Wakefulness.* Chicago, U. of Chicago, 1939; 95.

KLERMAN, G. L.; DiMASCIO, A.; GREENBLATT, M., AND RINKEL, M.: The influence of specific personality patterns on the reactions to phrenotropic agents. In: *Biological Psychiatry.* New York, Grune, 1959; 312.

KNOTT, J. R.: Electroencephalography and physiological psychology: evaluation and statement of problem. *Psychol. Bull.,* 38:144-175, 1941; 177.

KNOWLES, J. B., AND KRASNER, L.: Extraversion and duration of the Archimedes spiral after-effect. *Percept. Motor Skills,* 20:997-1000, 1965; 142.

KOGAN, A. B.: The manifestations of processes of higher nervous activity in the electrical potentials of the cortex during free behavior animals. In: H. H. Jasper and G. D. Smirnov, (Eds.): *Moscow Colloquium on EEG of Higher Nervous Activity. Electroenceph. Clin. Neurophysiol., Suppl.* 13:51-64, 1960; 248.

KOGAN, A. B.: The physiological nature of the electrical correlates of reaction attention. Proceedings 18th Internat. Congress Exp. Psychol., Symposium 5:11-14, 1966; 158.

KOGAN, N., AND WALLACH, M. A.: The effect of anxiety on relations between objective age and caution in an older sample: In: P. H. Hoch and J. Zubin, (Eds.): *Psychopathology of Ageing*. New York, Grune, 1961; 184.

KOGAN, N., AND WALLACH, M. A.: *Risk Taking: A Study in Cognition and Personality*. London, Holt, Rinehart & Winston, 1964; 53, 184.

KÖHLER, W.: *Dynamics in Psychology*. New York, Liveright, 1940; 78, 330.

KÖHLER, W., AND FISHBACK, J.: The destruction of the Müller-Lyer illusion in repeated trials. I. An examination of two theories. *J. Exp. Psychol.*, 40:267-281, 1950; 3, 78.

KÖHLER, W., AND WALLACH, H.: Figural after-effects. *Proc. Amer. Phil. Soc.*, 88:265-357, 1944; 321, 324.

KOHLMAN, T.: *Die Psychologie der motorischen Begabung*. Wien, Baumüller, 1958; 157.

KORNETSKY, C.; MIRSKY, A. F.; KESSLER, E. R., AND DROFT, J. A.: The effects of dextro-amphetamine on behavioral deficits produced by sleep loss in humans. *J. Pharmacol. Exp. Therap.*, 127:46-50, 1959; 301.

KRISHNAMOORTI, S. R., AND SHAGASS, C.: Some psychological test correlates of sedation threshold. In: J. Wortis. (Ed.): *Recent Advances in Biological Psychiatry*. New York, Plenum Press, 1963; 282.

LACEY, J. I.: Individual differences in somatic response patterns. *J. Comp. Physiol. Psychol.*, 43:338-350, 1950; 68.

LACEY, J. I.; BATEMAN, D. E., AND LEHN, R. V.: Autonomic response specificity: An experimental study. *Psychosom. Med.* 15:8-21, 1953; 68.

LACEY, J. I., AND LACEY, B. C.: Verification and extension of the principle of autonomic response stereotypy. *Amer. J. Psychol.*, 71:50-73, 1958; 68.

LACEY, J. I., AND LEHN, R. V.: Differential emphasis on somatic response to stress. *Psychosom. Med.*, 14:71-81, 1952; 68.

LADER, M.: The effect of cyclobarbitone on the habituation of the psychogalvanic reflex. *Brain*, 87:321-340, 1964; 302.

LADER, M.: The effects of cyclobarbitone on the pulse volume, pulse rate and electromyogram. *J. Psychosom. Res.*, 8:385-398, 1965; 303.

LADER, M.: The effects of cyclobarbitone on spontaneous autonomic activity. *J. Psychosom. Res.*, 9:201-207, 1965; 303.

LADER, M., AND WING, L.: Habituation of the psycho-galvanic reflex in patients with anxiety states and in normal subjects. *J. Neurol. Neurosurg. Psychiat.*, 27:210-218, 1964; 174.

LADER, M., AND WING, L.: *Physiological Measures, Sedative Drugs and Morbid Anxiety*. Maudsley Monograph, No. 14. Oxford, 1966; 303.

LAGUTINA, N. I.: Proc. All-Union Congr. Psychologists, Biochemists and Pharmacologists, Moscow, 1955. Quoted by Lynn, R., 1965; 251.

References 371

LANDAUER, A. A.; SINGER, G., AND DAN, R. H.: Correlation between visual and Kinesthetic spatial aftereffects. *J. Exper. Psychol.*, 72:892-894, 1966; **138.**

LANDIS, C.: *An Attempt to Measure Emotional Traits in Juvenile Delinquency.* Chicago, Univ. of Chicago, 1932; **171.**

LANDIS, C.: Determinants of the critical flicker fusion threshold. *Physiol. Rev.*, 34:259-286, 1954; **322.**

LANDIS, C., AND ZUBIN, J.: Effect of thonzylamine hydrochloride and phenobarbital sodium on certain psychological functions. *J. Psychol.*, 31:181-200, 1951; **291.**

LANSDELL, H.: A sex difference in effect of temporal-lobe neurosurgery on design preference. *Nature*, 194:852-854, 1962; **331.**

LANSDELL, H., AND URBACK, N.: Sex differences in personality measures related to size and side of temporal lobe ablations. Distributed from National Institute of Neurological Diseases and Blindness, N.I.H., Bethesda, U.S.A. (1965); **331.**

LASHLEY, K. S.: *Brain Mechanisms and Intelligence.* Chicago, U. of Chicago, 1929; **321, 330.**

LASHLEY, K. S.: Basic neural mechanisms in behaviour. *Psychol. Rev.*, 37:1-24, 1930; **330.**

LATIES, V.: Effects of meprobamate on fears and palmar sweating. *J. Abnorm. Soc. Psychol.*, 59:156-161, 1959; **306.**

LAVERTY, S. A.: Sodium amytal and extraversion. *J. Neurol. Neurosurg. Psychiat.*, 21:50-54, 1958; **280.**

LEGGE, D.: Analysis of visual and proprioceptive components of motor skill by means of a drug. *Brit. J. Psychol.*, 56:243-254, 1965; **300.**

LEPLEY, W. M.: Serial reactions considered as conditioned reactions. *Psychol. Monogr.*, 46: (No. 205) 1934; **179.**

LEVEY, A.: Eyelid conditioning, extraversion and drive: An experimental test of two theories. Univ. of London, Unpublished Ph.D. thesis, 1967; **121.**

LEVI, D.: Life stress and urinary excretion of adrenaline and noradrenaline. In: W. Raab, (Ed.): *Preventive Cardiology.* Springfield, Thomas, 1965; **59.**

LEVINE, F. M., TURSKY, B., AND NICHOLS, D. C. Tolerance for pain, extraversion and neuroticism: failure to replicate results. *Percept. Mot. Skills*, 23:847-850, 1966; **111.**

LEVY, P., AND LANG, P. J.: Activation, control, and the spiral after movement. *J. Person. Soc. Psychol.*, 3:105-112, 1966; **143.**

LIEBENAM, L.: Zwillingspathologische Untersuchungen. *Z. Verer. u. Konstl.*, 22:373-417, 1938; **191.**

LIENERT, G. A., AND HUBERT, H. P.: Strukturwandel der Intelligenzfaktoren unter der Wirkung von Amphetamin. *Arzneimittelforschung.*, 16:304-305, 1966; **16.**

LIENERT, G. A., AND REISSE, H.: Ein korrelationsanalytischer Beitrag zur genetischen Determination des Neurotizismus. *Psychol. Beitr.*, 7:121-130, 1961; 207.

LIENERT, G. A., AND TRAXEL, W.: The effects of meprobamate and alcohol on galvanic skin response. *J. Psychol.*, 48:329-334, 1959; 305.

LINDNER, R. M.: Experimental studies in constitutional psychopathic inferiority. *J. Crim. Psychopath.*, 3:252-276, 1942; 173.

LINDSLEY, D. B.: Emotion. In: S. S. Stevens, (Ed.): *Handbook of Experimental Psychology*. New York, Wiley, 1951; 227.

LINDSLEY, D. B.: Physiological psychology. *Ann. Rev. Psychol.*, 7:323-348, 1956; 239.

LINDSLEY, D. B.: The reticular system and perceptual discrimination. In: H. H. Jasper *et al.*, (Eds.): *Reticular Formation of the Brain*. Henry Ford Hosp. Internat. Symp. London, Churchill, 1957; 244.

LINDSLEY, D. B.: Attention, consciousness, sleep and wakefulness. *Handbook of Physiology*. Washington, Amer. Physiol. Soc., 1960; 237.

LINDSLEY, D. B., AND CUTTS, K.: The electroencephalograms of "constitutionally inferior" and behaviour problem children: comparisons with normal children and adults. *A.M.A. Arch. Neurol. Psychiat.*, 44:1199-1212, 1940; 67.

LIPPERT, H.: *Einführung in die Pharmako-psychologie*. Bern, H. Huber, 1959; 272.

LLEWELLYN-THOMAS, E.: Successive time estimation during automatic positive feedback. *Percept. Motor Skills*, 9:219-224, 1959; 146.

LOEHLIN, J. C.: A heredity-environment analysis of personality inventory data. In: S. G. Vandenberg, (Ed.): *Methods and Goals in Human Behavior Genetics*. London, Academic Press, 1965; 210.

LUDLUM, S. D. W.: Physiologic psychiatry. *Med. Clin. N. Amer.*, 2:895, 1918. Quoted by Duffy, 1962; original not seen; 58.

LUDVIGSON, H. W.: Chlorpromazine and D-amphetamine in eyelid conditioning. *Psychol. Rep.*, 14:402, 1964; 308.

LUNDERVOLD, A.: Electro-mygraphy as a test for pilot aspirants. *J. Aviation Med.*, 21:147-149, 1950; 64.

LYNN, R.: Personality factors in reading achievement. *Proc. Roy. Soc. Med.*, 48:996-998, 1955; 98.

LYNN, R.: Two personality characteristics related to academic achievement. *Brit. J. Educ. Psychol.*, 29:213-216, 1959; 98.

LYNN, R.: Extraversion, reminiscence and satiation effects. *Brit. J. Psychol.*, 51:319-324, 1960; 142.

LYNN, R.: Introversion-extraversion differences in judgments of time. *J. Abnorm. Soc. Psychol.*, 63:457-458, 1961; 146.

LYNN, R.: Reversible perspective as a function of stimulus intensity. *Amer. J. Psychol.*, 74:131-133, 1961; 107.

LYNN, R.: *Attention, Arousal and the Orientation Reaction*. New York,

Pergamon, 1965; 243, 250, 251.

LYNN, R., AND BUTLER, J.: Introversion and the arousal jag. *Brit. J. Soc. Clin. Psychol.*, 1:150-151, 1962; 101.

LYNN, R., AND EYSENCK, H. J.: Tolerance for pain, extraversion and neuroticism. *Percept. Motor Skills*, 12:161-162, 1961; 113.

LYNN, R., AND GORDON, I. E.: The relation of neuroticism and extraversion to intelligence and educational attainment. *Brit. J. Educ. Psychol.*, 31:194-203, 1961; 99.

MacLEAN, P. D.: Contrasting functions of limbic and neocortical system of the brain and their relevance to psychophysiological aspects of medicine. *Amer. J. Med.*, 25:611-626, 1958; 230, 234.

MacLEAN, P. D.: Psychomatics. In: *Handbook of Physiology*. Washington, Amer. Physiol. Soc., 1960; 234.

MACKWORTH, H.: Researches in the measurement of human performance. M.R.C. Special Rep. No. 268. London, H.M.S.O., 1948; 300, 334.

MADLUNG, K.: Uber den Einfluss der typologischen Verauflagung auf die Flimmergrenzen. *Untersuch. Psychol. Phil, Päd.*, 10:70-78, 1935; 105.

MAGOUN, H.: The Waking Brain. Springfield, Thomas, 1963; 76, 248.

MALMO, R. B.: Measurement of drive: An unsolved problem. In: M. R. Jones, (Ed.): *Nebraska Symposium on Motivation*. Lincoln, U. of Neb., 1958; 227.

MALMO, R. B.: Activation: A neurophysiological dimension. *Psychol. Rev.*, 66:367-386, 1959; 8, 227.

MALMO, R. B., AND SHAGASS, C.: Physiologic study of symptom mechanisms in psychiatric patients under stress. *Psychosom. Med.*, 11:25-29, 1949; 64, 66.

MALMO, R. B., AND SHAGASS, C.: Studies of blood pressure in psychiatric patients under stress. *Psychosom. Med.*, 14:82-93, 1952; 65.

MALMO, R. B.; SHAGASS, C.; BELANGER, D. J., AND SMITH, A. A.: Motor control in psychiatric patients under experimental stress. *J. Abnorm. Soc. Psychol.*, 46:539-547, 1951; 64, 65.

MALMO, R. B.; SHAGASS, C., AND DAVIS, F. H.: Symptom specificity and bodily reactions during psychiatric interview. *Psychosom. Med.*, 12:362-376, 1950; 64.

MALMO, R. B.; SHAGASS, C., AND DAVIS, J. F.: Electromyographic studies of muscular tension in psychiatric patients under stress. *J. Clin. Exp. Psychopath.*, 12:45-66, 1951; 64.

MALMO, R. B.; SHAGASS, C., AND HESLAM, R. M.: Blood pressure response to repeated brief stress in psychoneurosis: A study of adaptation. *Canad. J. Psychol.*, 5:167-179, 1951; 65.

MALMO, R. B., AND SMITH, A. A.: Forehead tension and motor irregularities in psychoneurotic patients under stress. *J. Personality*, 23:391-406, 1955; 64.

MALTZMAN, I., AND RASKIN, D. S.: Effects of individual differences in the orienting reflex on conditioning and complex processes. *J. Exp. Res. Person.*, 1:1-16, 1965; 252.

MANDELBAUM, J.: Dark adaptation, some physiologic and clinical considerations. *Arch. Opthal.*, 26:203-239, 1941; 291.

MANDLER, C., AND SARASON, S. B.: A study of anxiety and learning. *J. Abnorm. Soc. Psychol.*, 47:166-173, 1952; 42.

MANGAN, G. L.: A factorial study of speed, power and related temperamental variables. *Brit. J. Educ. Psychol.*, 29:144-154, 1959; 160.

MARGOLIS, H. J.: Associative interference: effects of meprobamate on normal adult's performance on a Müller-Schümann type learning task. *Psychopharmacologia*, 8:379-388, 1966; 310.

MARTIN, I.: Personality and muscle activity. *Canad. J. Psychol.*, 12:23-30, 1958; 64.

MARTIN, I.: The effects of depressant drugs on palmar skin resistance and adaptation. In: H. J. Eysenck, (Ed.): *Experiments in Personality*. New York, Praeger, 1960; 302.

MARTIN, I., AND DAVIES, B. M.: Sleep thresholds in depression. *J. Ment. Sci.*, 108:466-473, 1962; 281.

MARTIN, I., AND LEVEY, A. B.: Efficiency of the conditioned eyelid response. *Science*, 150:781-783, 1965; 123.

MARTIN, I., AND LEVEY, A. B.: Latency of the eyelid UCR during conditioning. *Life Sci.*, 5:17-26, 1966; 123.

MARTON, M., AND URBAN, I.: An electroencephalographic investigation of individual differences in the process of conditioning. *Proc. 18th Internat. Congress Exp. Psychol.*, 9th Symposium, 106-109, 1966; 178.

MATHER, K.: *Biometrical Genetics*. London, Methuen, 1949; 187.

MATTOON, P. F.: After-contraction as a function of extraversion and central inhibition. *Acta Psychol.*, 20:121-127, 1962; 142.

MAY, A. E.; LYND, B. R., AND LEY, P.: The effects of distributed practice on the learning performance of brain-damaged patients. *Brit. J. Soc. Clin. Psychol.*, 3:139-140, 1963; 329.

MAY, J.: Note on the assumptions underlying Holzinger's h^2 statistic. *J. Ment. Sci.*, 67:466-467, 1951; 190.

MCADAM, W., AND ORME, J. E.: Personality traits and the normal electroencephalograph. *J. Ment. Sci.*, 100:913, 1954; 177.

MCCLEARN, G. E.: Genetic differences in the effect of alcohol upon behaviour of mice. *Proc. Third Internat. Conf. Alcohol and Road Traffic*, London, 1962; 16.

MCDONALD, D. G.; JOHNSON, L. C., AND HORD, D. J.: Habituation of the orienting response in alert and drowsy subjects. *Psychophysiology*, 1:163-173, 1964; 171.

MCDONALD, R. D.: Effect of brain damage on adaptability. *J. Nerv. Ment. Dis.*, 138:241-247, 1964; 335.

MCDONALD, R. D., AND BURNS, S. B.: Visual vigilance and brain damage:

an empirical study. *J. Neurol. Neurosurg. Psychiat.*, 27:206-209, 1964; 335.

McDougall, W.: The chemical theory of temperament applied to introversion and extraversion. *J. Abnorm. Soc. Psychol.*, 24:293-309, 1929; 108.

McDowell, C. R., and Inglis, J.: Verbal conditioning and personality. *Psychol. Rep.*, 10:374, 1962; 123.

McEwen, P., and Rodger, R. S.: Some individual differences in figural after-effects. *Brit. J. Psychol.*, 51:1-8, 1960; 135.

McLaughlin, R. J., and Eysenck, H. J.: Visual masking as a function of personality. *Brit. J. Psychol.*, 57:393-396, 1966; 254.

McLaughlin, R. J., and Eysenck, H. J.: Extraversion, neuroticism and paired associate learning. *J. exper. Res. in Person.* 1967. To appear; 132.

McPeake, J. D., and DiMascio, A.: Drug-personality interaction in the learning of a nonsense syllable task. *Psychol. Rep.*, 15:405-406, 1964; 310, 314.

McReynolds, P., Acker, M., and Brackhill, G.: On the assessment of anxiety: IV. By measures of basal conductance and palmar sweat. *Psychol. Rep.*, 19:347-354, 1966; 176.

Mefferd, R. B., and Wieland, B. A.: Modification in autonomicaly mediated physiological responses to cold pressor by word associations. *Psychophysiology*, 2:1-9, 1965; 57.

Meier, M. J.: Interrelationships among personality variables, kinesthetic figural after effect, and reminiscence in motor learning. *J. Abnorm. Soc. Psychol.*, 63:87-94, 1961; 135.

Meier, M. J.: Reminiscence in inverted alphabet printing as a function of degree of EEG abnormality. *Percept. Motor Skills, 19*:219-225, 1964; 327.

Mendel, G.: Versuche über Pflanzenhybriden. *Verh. des naturf. Vereins in Brünn, 4,* 1866; 188.

Meredith, G. M.: Contending hypotheses of autogenesis for the exuberance-restraint personality factor, U.I. 21. *J. Genet. Psychol., 108*:89-104, 1966; 129.

Meyer, V.: Cognitive changes following temporal lobectomy for the relief of temporal lobe epilepsy. *A.M.A. Arch. Neurol. Psychiat., 81*:299-309, 1959; 338.

Meyer, V.: Psychological effects of brain damage. In: H. J. Eysenck, (Ed.): *Handbook of Abnormal Psychology.* London, Pitman, 1960; 321.

Miller, D. R.: Responses of psychiatric patients to threat of failure. *J. Abnorm. Soc. Psychol., 46*:378-387, 1951; 165.

Milner, B.: Psychological defects produced by temporal lobe excision. In: *The Brain and Human Behaviour,* A.R.M.N.D. Research Publication 36. Baltimore, Williams & Wilkins, 1958; 338.

Mitchell, L. E., and Zax, M: The effects of chlorpromazine on GSR conditioning. *J. Abnorm. Soc. Psychol., 59*:246-249, 1959; 307.

Moffat, J., and Levine, S.: The sedation threshold of psychoneurotic and alcoholic patients. *Brit. J. Med. Psychol., 37*:313-317, 1964; 280.

MORGAN, C. T.: *Physiological Psychology.* New York, McGraw, 1965; 55, 234, 236, 239.

MORUZZI, G.: Synchronizing influences of the brain stem and the inhibiting mechanisms underlying the production of sleep by sensory stimulation. In: H. H. Jasper and G. D. Smirnov, (Eds.): Moscow Colloquium on Electroencephalography of Higher Nervous Activity. *Electroenceph. Clin. Neurophysiol.,* Suppl. 13, 1960; 251.

MUCKER, H., AND WENDT, H. W.: Gruppenversuch zur Bestimmung der kritischen Verschmelzungsfrequenz beim binokularen Sehen. Anderung unter Koffein und nach normaler Tagearbeit. *Arch. Exper. Path. Pharmakol.,* 214:29-37, 1951; 291.

MUNDY-CASTLE, A. C., AND McKIEVER, B. L.: The psychophysiological significance of the galvanic skin response. *J. Exper. Psychol.,* 46:15-24, 1953; 171.

MUNDY-CASTLE, A. C.: Theta and beta rhythm in the electro-encephalogram of normal adults. *Electroenceph. Clin. Neurophysiol.,* 3:477-486, 1951; 248.

MUNDY-CASTLE, A. C.: The relationship between primary-secondary function and the alpha rhythm of the electroencephalogram. *J. Nat. Inst. Personnel Res.,* 6:95-102, 1955; 177.

MUNKELT, P.: Personlichkeitsmerkmale als Bedingungsfaktoren der psychotropen Arzneimittelwirkung. *Psychol. Beiträge,* 8:98-183, 1965; 10.

MUNSTERBERG, H.: *Psychological and Industrial Efficiency.* Boston: Houghton, Mifflin Co., 1913; 88.

MURAWSKI, B. J.: Flicker fusion thresholds in control subjects and identical twins. *J. Appl. Physiol.,* 15:246-248, 1960; 105.

MURRAY, H. A.: *Explorations in Personality.* New York, Oxford, 1938; 163.

NAGEL, R. F.: Evaluation of ear-choice technique. *Dissert. Abstr.,* 17:435, 1957; 101.

NEBYLITSYN, V. D.; ROZHDESTVENSKANA, V. I., AND TEPLOV, B. M: Concerning the interrelation between absolute sensitivity and strength of the nervous system. *Quart. J. Exper. Psychol.,* 12:17-25, 1960; 100.

NEWMAN, H. H.; FREEMAN, F. N., AND HOLZINGER, K. J.: *Twins.* Chicago, U. of Chicago, 1937; 190, 192.

NORROSS, K. J.; LIPMA, R. S., AND SPITZ, H. H.: The relationship of extraversion-introversion to visual and kinesthetic after-effects. *J. Abnorm. Soc. Pyschol.,* 63:210-211, 1961; 135.

O'HANLON, J. F.: Adrenaline and noradrenaline: relation to performance in a visual vigilance task. *Science,* 150 (No. 3695): 507-509, 1965; 255.

OLLEY, M.: Motivation in relation to temperament. Paper read at Brit. Psychol. Soc., Ann. Conf., 1964; 166.

OMINSKY, M., AND KIMBLE, G. A.: Anxiety and eyelid conditioning. *J. Exp. Psychol.,* 71:471-472, 1966; 46.

ORME, J. E.: Time estimation and personality. *J. Ment. Sci.,* 108:213-216,

1962; **148.**

OSLER, S. F., AND LEVINSOHN, P. M.: The relation between manifest anxiety and perceptual defence. *Amer. Psychologist, 9:*466, 1954 (Abstract); **149.**

OTTO, W.: Inhibition potential in good and poor achievers. *J. Educ. Psychol., 56:*200-207, 1965; **99.**

OTTO, W., AND FREDRICKS, R. C.: Relationship of reactive inhibition to reading skill attainment. *Educ. Psychol., 54:*227-230, 1963; **99.**

PAPEZ, J. V.: A proposed mechanism of emotion. *Arch. Neurol. Psychiat., 38:*725-743, 1937; **234.**

PARÉ, W.: The effect of caffeine and seconal on a visual discrimination task. *J. Comp. Physiol. Psychol., 54:*506-509, 1961; **50.**

PARKER, N. I., AND NEWBIGGING, P. L.: Decrement of the Müller-Lyer illusion as a function of psychophysical procedure. *Amer. J. Psychol., 18:*603-608, 1965; **4.**

PARTANEN, J., BRUUN, K., AND MARKKANEN, T.: Inheritance of drinking behaviour. *Finnish Foundation for Alcohol Study.* Vol. 14, 1966; **197.**

PAUL, S. K.: Figural after-effects, intermodality correlation and personality. *Ind. J. Psychol., 39:*1-6, 1964; **135.**

PAVLOV, I. P.: *Conditioned reflexes.* (Trans. by G. V. Anrep). London, Oxford, 1927; **324.**

PAWLIK, K., AND CATTELL, R. B.: The relationship between certain personality factors and measures of cortical arousal. *Neuropsychologia, 3:*129-151, 1965; **334.**

PAYNE, R. B., AND HAUTY, G. T.: Factors affecting the endurance of psychomotor skill. *J. Amat. Med., 25:*382-389, 1955; **301.**

PAYNE, R. B., AND HAUTY, G. T.: Restoration of tracking proficiency as a function of amount and delay of analeptic medication. *J. Comp. Physiol. 50:*146-149, 1957; **301.**

PAYNE, R. W., AND HEWLETT, J. H. G.: Thought disorder in psychotic patients. In: H. J. Eysenck, (Ed.): *Experiments in Personality,* Vol. 2. New York, Praeger, 1960; **223.**

PERSKY, H.; GAMM, S. R., AND GRINKER, R. R.: Correlation between fluctuation of free anxiety and quantity of hippuric acid excretion. *Psychosom. Med., 14:*34-40, 1952; **59.**

PETRIE, A.: The study of experimental methods of assessing personality. London: Unpublished Ph.D. thesis, 1945; **160.**

PETRIE, A.: *Personality and the Frontal Lobes.* London, Routledge & Kegan Paul, 1952; **327.**

PETRIE, A.: Some psychological aspects of pain and the relief of suffering. *Am. N. Y. Acad. Sci., 86:*13-27, 1960; **114, 139.**

PETRIE, A.: *Individuality in Pain and Suffering: The Reducer and Augmenter.* Chicago, U. of Chicago, 1967; **138, 140.**

PETRIE, A.; COLLINS, W., AND SOLOMON, P.: Pain sensitivity, sensory deprivation and susceptibility to satiation. *Science, 128:*1431-1433, 1958; **114, 139.**

378   *The Biological Basis of Personality*

PETRIE, A.; COLLINS, W., AND SOLOMON, P.: The tolerance for pain and for sensory deprivation. *Amer. J. Psychol.*, *123*:80-90, 1960; 114.

PETRIE, A.; HOLLAND, T., AND WOLK, I.: Perceptual indicators of basic algeric types—a new look. Proc. 1st Internat. Congr. Psychosom. Med. & Maternity, Paris. 1965; 138, 140.

PETRIE, A.; McCULLOCH, R., AND KAZDIN, P.: The perceptual characteristics of juvenile delinquents. *J. Nerv. Ment. Dis.*, *134*:415-421, 1962; 140.

PICKERSGILL, M. J., AND JEEVES, M. A.: After-effect of movement produced by a rotating spiral. *Nature*, *182*:1820, 1958; 142.

PIERCY, M.: The effects of cerebral lesions on intellectual functions: a review of current research trends. *Brit. J. Psychiat.*, *110*:310-352, 1964; 331.

PLOTNIKOFF, N.; BIRZIS, L., AND MITOMA, C.: *Drug Enhancement of Performance.* Stanford Res. Institute, 1960; 301.

POSER, E.: Der figurale After-effect als Persönlichkeitsmerkmal. Paper read at XVth Int. Congress Exper. Psychol., Bonn, 1960; 114.

PUROHIT, A. P.: Personality variables, sex difference, G.S.R. responsiveness and G.S.R. conditioning. *J. Exper. Res. Person.* 1:166-173, 1966; 126.

QUARTON, G. C., AND TALLAND, G. A.: The effects of methamphetamine and pentobarbital on two measures of attention. *Psychopharmacologia*, *3*:66-71, 1962; 311.

QUAY, H. C.: Psychopathic personality as pathological stimulation seeking. *Amer. J. Psychiat.*, *122*:180-183, 1965; 125.

QUAY, H. C., AND HUNT, W. A.: Psychopathy, neuroticism and verbal conditioning: a replication and extension. *J. Consult. Psychol.*, *29*:283, 1965; 125.

RACHMAN, S.: Effect of a stimulant drug on extent of motor responses. *Percept. Motor Skills*, *12*:186, 1961; 297.

RACHMAN, S.: Psychomotor behaviour and personality with special reference to conflict. London, Unpublished Ph.D. thesis, 1961; 155.

RAMSAY, R. W.: Personality and speech. Univ. of London. Unpublished Ph.D. thesis, 1966; 157, 162.

RAMSAY, R. W.; UBRECHT, L. C., AND ALHEMA, D.: The effect of massed versus spaced practice on auditory threshold. In press; 104.

RANKIN, E. F.: Reading test performance of introverts and extraverts. 12th Yearbook, Nat. Reading Conf., 1963; 98.

RANKIN, E. F.: Reading test reliability and validity as function of introversion-extraversion. *J. Developm. Reading*, *6*:106-117, 1963; 98.

RANSCHBURG, P.: Uber Hemmung gleichzeitiger Reizwirkungen. *Ztschr. f. Psychol.*, *30*:39-85, 1902; 76.

RANSCHBURG, P.: Über die Bedeutung der Ahnlichkeit beim Erlernen, Behalten und bei der Reproduktion. *J. Psychol. Neurol.*, *5*:113-288, 1905; 76.

RECHTSCHAFFEN, A.: Neural satiation, reactive inhibition and introversion-extraversion. *J. Abnorm. Soc. Psychol.*, *57*:283-291, 1958; 135.

RECHTSCHAFFEN, A., AND BOOKBINDER, L. J.: Introversion-extraversion and kinesthetic after-effects. *J. Abnorm. Soc. Psychol.*, *61*:459-466, 1960; **135**.

REED, G. F.: Audiometer response consistency, auditory fatigue and personality. *Percept. Motor Skills*, *12*:126, 1961; **98**.

REED, G. F.: Psychogenic deafness, perceptual defence, and personality variables in children. *J. Abnorm. Soc. Psychol.*, *63*:663-665, 1961; **152**.

REED, G. F., AND FRANCIS, T. R.: Drive, personality, and audiometric response consistency. *Percept. Motor Skills*, *15*:681-682, 1962; **98**.

REED, G. F., AND KENNA, J. C.: Personality and time estimation in sensory deprivation. *Percept. Motor Skills*, *18*:182, 1964; **115**.

REED, G. F., AND SEDMAN, G.: Personality and depersonalization under sensory deprivation conditions. *Percept. Motor Skills*, *18*:659-660, 1964; **115**.

REES, L.: Constitutional factors and abnormal behaviour. In: H. J. Eysenck, (Ed.): *Handbook of Abnormal Psychology*. New York, Basic Books, 1960, **213**.

REES, L., AND EYSENCK, H. J.: A factorial study of some morphological and psychological aspects of human constitution. *J. Ment. Sci.*, *91*:8-21, 1945; **213**.

REESE, W.; DOSS, R., AND GANTT, W. H.: Autonomic responses in differential diagnosis of organic and psychogenic psychoses. *A.M.A. Arch. Neurol. Psychiat.*, *70*:778-793, 1953; **326**.

REITAN, R.: *The Effects of Brain Lesions on Adaptive Abilities in Human Beings.* Indianapolis, Indiana University Medical Center. (Mimeo.) 1959; **331**.

REITAN, R. N.: Psychological deficit. *Ann. Rev. Psychol.*, *13*:415-444, 1962; **331**.

REUNING, H.: A new flicker apparatus for measuring individual differences. *J. Nat. Inst. Personnel Res.*, *6*:44-54, 1955; **106**.

RENSSEN, W.: A case of discordant ptosis in monozygotic twins. *Genetica*, *23*:247-256, 1943; **191**.

REYMERT, M. L.: *Feelings and Emotions.* London, McGraw, 1950; **167**.

RICH, G. I.: A biochemical approach to the study of personality. *J. Abnorm. Soc. Psychol.* *23*:158-175, 1928; **58**.

RIM, Y.: Personality and group decisions involving risks. Psychol. Rec., *14*:37-45, 1964; **178**.

ROBACK, G. S.; KRASNER, L. R., AND IVY, A. C.: Drug effects on flicker fusion threshold. *J. Appl. Physiol.*, *4*:566-574, 1952; **291**.

RODNIGHT, E., AND GOOCH, R. N.: A new method for the determination of individual differences in susceptibility to a depressant drug. In: H. J. Eysenck, (Ed.): *Experiments with Drugs.* New York, Pergamon, 1963; **286**.

ROITBACK, A. I.: Concerning the mechanism of extinction of orientation and conditioned reflexes. *Physiol. Brhemoslovenica*, *7*:152-134, 1958; **248, 251**.

ROSENBAUM, R.: Stimulus generalization as a function of level of experimentally induced anxiety. *J. Exp. Psychol.*, 45:35-43, 1953; 31.

ROSENBAUM, G.: Stimulus generalization as a function of clinical anxiety. *J. Abnorm. Soc. Psychol.*, 53:281-285, 1956; 31.

ROSS, L. E., AND SPENCE, K. W.: Eyelid conditioning performance under partial reinforcement as a function of UCS intensity. *J. Exper. Psychol.*, 59:379-382, 1960; 118.

ROSS, S.; KRUGMAN, A. D.; LYERLY, S. B., AND CLYDE, D. J.: Drugs and placebos: A model design. *Psychol. Rep.*, 10:383-392, 1962; 312.

ROSSI, A. F., AND ZANCHETTI, A.: The brain stem reticular formation: anatomy and physiology. *Arch. Nat. Biol.*, 95:199-435, 1957; 244.

ROSVOLD, H. R.; MIRSKY, A. F.; SARASON, I.; BRANSOME, R. D., AND BECK, L. H.: A continuous performance test of brain damage. *J. Consult. Psychol.*, 20:343-350, 1956; 91.

RUBIN, L. S.: Autonomic dysfunction as a concomitant of neurotic behavior. *J. Nerv. Ment. Dis.*, 138:558-574, 1964; 59, 62.

RUESCH, J., AND FINESINGER, J. E.: Muscular tension in psychiatric patients. *A.M.A. Arch. Neurol. Psychiat.*, 50:439-449, 1943; 64.

RUNQUIST, W. N., AND ROSS, L.: The relation between physiological measures of emotionality and performance in eyelid conditioning. *J. Exper. Psychol.*, 57:329-332, 1959; 120.

RUNQUIST, W. N., AND SPENCE, K.: Performance in eyelid conditioning as a function of UCS duration. *J. Exper. Psychol.*, 57:249-252, 1959; 120.

RUNQUIST, W. N., AND TOWART, E.: Further evidence for introversion decrements in eyelid conditioning. *Psychol. Rep.*, 17:891-897, 1965; 118.

RUTLEDGE, L. T., AND DOTY, R. W.: Differential action of chlorpromazine on reflexes conditioned to central and peripheral stimulation. *Amer. J. Physiol.*, 191:189-192, 1957; 307.

RUTTER, M.; KORN, S., AND BIRCH, H. G.: Genetic and environmental factors in the development of primary reaction patterns. *Brit. J. Clin. Soc. Psychol.*, In press; 219.

SAINSBURY, P.: Psychosomatic disorders and neurosis in outpatients attending a general hospital. *J. Psychosom. Res.*, 4:261-273, 1960; 38.

SAINSBURY, P., AND GIBSON, J. G.: Symptoms of anxiety and tension and the accompanying physiological changes in the muscular system. *J. Neurol. Neurosurg. Psychiat.*, 17:216-224, 1954; 64.

SAMUELS, I.: Reticular mechanisms and behavior. *Psychol. Bull.*, 56:1-25, 1959; 238, 239, 240, 252.

SANFORD, R. N.; ADKINS, H. M.; MILLER, R. B., AND COBB, E.: Physique, personality and scholarship. *Mon. Soc. Res. Child Develop.*, 7 (No. 34), 1943; 69.

SAUCER, R. T., AND DEABLER, H. L.: Apparent movement in organic and schizophrenic patients. *J. Consult. Psychol.*, 20:385-389, 1956; 322.

SAUNDERS, D. R.: Moderator variables in prediction. *Educ. Psychol. Measmt.*,

16:209-222, 1956; **183.**

SAVAGE, R. D.: Electro-cerebral activity, extraversion and neuroticism. *Brit. J. Psychiat., 110*:98-100, 1964; **177.**

SAVAGE, R. D.: An analysis of learning curves: inherited strain and environmental determinants. *Behav. Res. Ther., 2*:281-284, 1965; **213.**

SAVAGE, R. D., AND EYSENCK, H. J.: The definition and measurement of emotionality. In: H. J. Eysenck, (Ed.): *Experiments in Motivation.* New York, Pergamon, 1964; **27, 42.**

SCARR, S.: Genetics and human motivation. Unpublished Ph.D. thesis, Harvard Univ., 1964. Quoted in Scarr, 1965; **202.**

SCARR, S.: The inheritance of sociability. Paper read at Meeting of the Amer. Psychol. Ass., 1965; **204.**

SCARR, S.: Environmental bias in twins studies. Unpublished report from Inst. Child. Study, Univ. Maryland, 1966; **203.**

SCHACHTER, S., AND LATANE, B.: Crime, cognition and the autonomic nervous system. In: D. Levine, (Ed.): *Nebraska Symposium on Motivation.* Lincoln, U. of Nebr., 1964; **173.**

SCHALLING, D., AND LEVANDER, S.: Ratings of anxiety-proneness and responses to electrical pain stimulation. *Scand. J. Psychol., 5*:1-19, 1964; **114.**

SCHEIBEL, M. E., AND SCHEIBEL, A. B.: On circuit patterns of the brain stem reticular core. *Ann. N. Y. Acad. Sci., 89*:857-865, 1961; **239.**

SCHERRER, H., AND HERNANDEZ-PEÓN, R.: Inhibitory influence of the reticular formation upon synaptic transmission in pracilis nucleus. *Fed. Proc., 14*:132, 1955. Quoted by Samuels, 1959; **239.**

SCHLOSBERG, H.: Three dimensions of emotion. *Psychol. Rev.,* 61:81-88, 1954; **227.**

SCHMIDTKE, H.: Uber die Messung der psychischen Ermüdung mit Hilfe des Flimmertests. *Psychol. Forsch., 23*:409-463, 1951; **291.**

SCHMIDTKE, H.: *Die Ermüdung.* Bern, H. Huber, 1965; **82, 95, 105, 160.**

SCHNEIDER, R. A., AND COSTILOE, J. P.: Effects of centrally active drugs on conditioning in man. *Amer. J. Med. Sci., 233*:418-423, 1957; **307.**

SCHWARTZ, M., AND SHAGASS, C.: Note on the relation between autokinesis and psychiatric diagnosis. *Percept. Motor Skills, 11*:253-257, 1960; **178.**

SCOTT, E. D., AND WILKINSON, D.: Adaptation as related to the introversion-extraversion dimension. U.S. Public Health Service, N.I.M.H. Report, Grant MH 06956-01, 1962; **171.**

SCOTT, J. P., AND FULLER, J. L.: *Genetics and the Social Behavior of the Dog.* Chicago, U. of Chicago, 1965; **71.**

SEVRANSKY, C. New York, Columbia Univ. Unpublished thesis. 1965; **165.**

SHAGASS, C.: The sedation threshold. A method for estimating tension in psychiatric patients. *Electroenceph. Clin. Neurophysiol., 6*:221-233, 1954; **274.**

SHAGASS, C.: Anxiety, depression, and the photically driven EEG. *A.M.A. Arch. Neurol. Psychiat., 74*:3-10, 1955; **67, 256.**

SHAGASS, C.: Sedation threshold. *Psychomt. Med.*, *18*:410-419, 1956; **274**.

SHAGASS, C.: A measurable neurophysiological factor of psychiatric significance. *Electroenceph. Clin. Neurophysiol.*, *9*:101-108, 1957; **274**.

SHAGASS, C.: Neurophysiological studies of anxiety and depression. *Psychiat.
Res. Rep.*, *8*:100-117, 1958; **274**.

SHAGASS, C.: A neurophysiological approach to perceptual psychopathology.
Psychopathology of Perception. New York, Grune, 1965, pp. 41-61; **256,
259**.

SHAGASS, C., AND JONES, A. L.: A neurophysiological test for psychiatric diagnosis: Results in 750 patients. *Amer. J. Psychiat.*, *114*:1002-1009, 1958; **274**.

SHAGASS, C., AND KERENYI, A. B.: Neurophysiologic studies of personality.
J. Nerv. Ment. Dis., *126*:141-147, 1958; **274, 280**.

SHAGASS, C., AND KERENYI, A. B.: The "sleep" threshold. A simple form of
the sedation threshold for clinical use. *Canad. Psychiat. J.*, *3*:101-109, 1958;
279.

SHAGASS, C., AND LIPOWSKI, F. J.: Effects of methedrine on critical flicker
fusion and its relation to personality and affect. *J. Nerv. Ment. Dis.*,
127:407-416, 1958; **291**.

SHAGASS, C., AND NAIMAN, J.: The sedation threshold, manifest anxiety, and
some aspects of ego function. *A.M.A. Arch. Neurol. Psychiat.*, *74*:397-406,
1955; **274**.

SHAGASS, C., AND NAIMAN, J.: The sedation threshold as an objective index
of manifest anxiety in psychoneurosis. *J. Psychosomat. Res.*, *1*:49-57, 1956;
274.

SHAGASS, C.; NAIMAN, J., AND MIKALIK, J.: An objective test which differentiates between neurotic and psychotic depression. *A.M.A. Arch. Neurol.
Psychiat.*, *75*:461-471, 1956; **274, 275**.

SHAGASS, C., AND SCHWARTZ, M.: Cerebral responsiveness in psychiatric patients. *A.M.A. Arch. Gen. Psychiat.*, *8*:177-189, 1963; **259**.

SHAGASS, C., AND SCHWARTZ, M.: Neurophysiological dysfunction associated
with some psychiatric disorders. *Psychiat. Res. Rep.*, *17*:130-152, 1963;
256.

SHAGASS, C., AND SCHWARTZ, M.: Age, personality, and somatosensory
cerebral evoked responses. *Science*, *148*:1359-1361, 1965; **260**.

SHAGASS, C.; SCHWARTZ, M., AND KRISHNAMOORTI, S. R.: Some psychologic
correlates of cerebral responses evoked by light flashes. *J. Psychosom. Res.*,
9:223-231, 1965; **260**.

SHANMUGAM, T. E.: Personality, severity of conflict and decision time. *J.
Ind. Acad. Appl. Psychol.*, *2*:13-23, 1965; **162**.

SHANMUGAM, T. E., AND SANTHANAM, M. L.: Personality differences in serial
learning when interference is presented at the marginal visual level. *J. Ind.
Acad. Appl. Psychol.*, *1*:25-28, 1964; **127, 132**.

SHAPIRO, M. B.: Experimental studies of a perceptual anomaly: I. Initial
experiments. *J. Ment. Sci.*, *97*:90-110, 1951; **332**.

SHAPIRO, M. B.: Experimental studies of a perceptual anomaly: II. Confirmatory and explanatory experiments. *J. Ment. Sci.*, *98*:605-617, 1952; **332.**

SHAPIRO, M. B.: Experimental studies of a perceptual anomaly: III. The testing of an explanatory theory. *J. Ment. Sci.*, *99*:394-409, 1953; **332.**

SHAPIRO, M. B.; BRIERLEY, J.; SLATER, P., AND BEECH, H. R.: Experimental studies of a perceptual anomaly: VII. A new explanation. *J. Ment. Sci.*, *108*:655-668, 1962; **332.**

SHARPLESS, S., AND JASPER, H. H.: Habituation of the arousal reaction. *Brain*, *79*:655-680, 1956; **238.**

SHELDON, W. H.: *The Varieties of Human Physique*. New York, Harper, 1940; **214.**

SHELDON, W. H.: *The Varieties of Temperament*. New York, Harper, 1942; **214.**

SHERMAN, L. J.: Retention in psychopathic, neurotic, and normal subjects. *J. Personality*, *25*:721-729, 1957; **131.**

SHIELDS, J.: Personality differences and neurotic traits in normal twin school children. A study in psychiatric genetics. *Eugen. Rev.*, *45*:213-246, 1954; **205.**

SHIELDS, J.: *Monozygotic Twins*. Oxford, Oxford, 1962; **198.**

SHIELDS, J., AND SLATER, E.: Heredity and psychological abnormality. In: H. J. Eysenck, (Ed.): *Handbook of Abnormal Psychology*. New York, Basic Books, 1960; **222.**

SHIELDS, J., AND SLATER, E.: La similarité du diagnostic chez les jumeaux. *L'Evolution Psychiat.*, *2*:441-451, 1966; **2, 441, 451.**

SHOCK, N. W.: Physiological factors in behavior. In: J. McV. Hunt, (Ed.): *Personality and the Behavior Disorders*. New York, Ronald, 1944; **58.**

SHOUL, S. M., AND RENUING, H.: Speed and variability components in Paul's test, CFF and alpha rhythm. *J. Nat. Inst. Personnel Res.*, *7*:28-44, 1957; **106.**

SIEGMAN, A. W., AND PAPE, B.: Personality variables associated with productivity and verbal fluency in the initial interview. Proc. 73rd. Ann. Conv. A.P.A., 273-274, 1965; **178.**

SIGAL, J. J.; STAR, K. H., AND FRANKS, C. M.: Hysterics and dysthymics as criterion groups in the study of introversion-extraversion. *J. Abnorm. Soc. Psychol.*, *57*:143-148, 1958; **38.**

SIMONSON, E., AND BROZEK, J.: Flicker fusion frequency. *Physiol. Rev.*, *32*:349-378, 1952; **105.**

SIMONSON, E., AND ENZER, N.: Effect of perritin (desoxyephedrine) on fatigue of the central nervous system. *J. Indust. Hyg. Toxicol.*, *24*:205-209, 1952; **291.**

SIMONSON, E.; ENZER, N., AND BLANKSTEIN, S. S.: Effect of amphetamine (Benzedrine) on fatigue of the central nervous system. *War Med.*, *1*:690-695, 1941; **291.**

SINGH, S. D.; GUPTA, V. P., AND MANOCHA, S. N.: Physical persistence, personality and drugs. *Indian J. appl. Psychol.*, 3:92-95, 1966; 112.

SINHA, S. N.: Effects of GABA and metrazol on alternation of response. *Amer. Psychologist, 534*: (Abstract), 1964; 274.

SINHA, S. N.; FRANKS, C. M., AND BROADHURST, P. L.: The effect of a stimulant and depressant drug on a measure of reactive inhibition. *J. Exp. Psychol.*, 56:349-354, 1958; 272.

SKANTHAKUMARI, S. K.: Personality differences in the rate of forgetting. *J. Ind. Acad. Appl. Psychol.*, 2:39-47, 1965; 128.

SKAWRAN, P. R.: Heyman's concept of primary and secondary function as a means of classifying temperaments. *Psychol. Afric.*, 9:119-132, 1962; 106.

SLOANE, R. B.; DAVIDSON, P. O., AND PAYNE, R. W.: Anxiety and arousal in psychoneurotic patients. *Arch. Gen. Psychiat.*, 13:19-23, 1965; 118, 280.

SMITH, P. C.: The prediction of individual differences in susceptibility to industrial monotony. *J. appl. Psychol.*, 39:322-329, 1955; 88.

SMITH, R. T.: A comparison of socioenvironmental factors in monozygotic and dizygotic twins. In Vandenberg, S. G., (Ed.): *Methods and goals in Human Behavior Genetics.* New York, Academic Press, 1965; 202.

SMITH, S. L.: The effect of personality and drugs on auditory threshold when risk-taking factors are controlled. In press; 100.

SOKOLOV, E. N.: Neuronal models and the orienting reflex. In: M. A. Brazier, (Ed.): *The Central Nervous System and Behavior.* New York, J. Moon, 1960; 249, 250.

SOLOMON, C. I.; BROWN, W. T., AND DEUTSCHER, M.: Electroencephalography in behavior problem children. *Amer. J. Psychiat.*, 101:51-61, 1944; 67.

SOLOMON, P.; KUBZANSKY, P. E.; LEIDERMAN, P. H.; MENDELSON, J. H.; TRUMBULL, R., AND WEXLER, D.,(Eds.): *Sensory Deprivation.* Cambridge, Harvard, 1967; 109.

SPAIN, B.: Eyelid conditioning and arousal in schizophrenic and normal subjects. *J. Abnorm. Psychol.*, 71:260-266, 1966; 120.

SPEARMAN, C: *Abilities of Man.* London, Macmillan, 1927; 79.

SPENCE, K. W.: *Behavior Theory and Conditioning.* New Haven, Yale, 1956; 8, 42.

SPENCE, K. W.: Anxiety (drive) level and performance in eyelid conditioning. *Psychol. Bull.*, 61:129-139, 1964; 44, 120.

SPENCE, K. W., AND SPENCE, J. T.: Sex and anxiety differences in eyelid conditioning. *Psychol. Bull.*, 65:137-142, 1966; 46.

SPENCE, K. W., AND TAYLOR, J. A.: Anxiety and strength of UCS as determinants of amount of eyelid conditioning. *J. Exp. Psychol.*, 42:183-188, 1951; 44.

SPIELMAN, J.: The relation between personality and the frequency and duration of involuntary rest pauses during massed practice. London: Unpublished Ph.D. thesis, 1963; 84.

STANDISH, R. R., AND CHAMPION, R. A.: Task difficulty and drive in verbal learning. *J. Exp. Psychol.*, *59*:361-365, 1960; **46.**

STARR, H. E.: The concentration of the mixed saliva considered as an index of fatigue and of emotional excitation, and applied to a study of the metabolic etiology of stammering. *Amer. J. Psychol.*, *33*:394-418, 1922; **58.**

STARZL, T. E.; TAYLOR, C., AND MAGOUN, H. W.: Ascending conduction in reticular activating system with special reference to the diencephalon. *J. Neurophysiol.*, *14*:461-477, 1951a; **236.**

STARZL, T. E.; TAYLOR, C., AND MAGOUN, H. W.: Collateral afferent excitation of reticular formation of brain stem. *J. Neurophysiol.*, *14*:479-496, 1951b; **236.**

STERN, J. A.; DAS, K. C.; ANDERSON, J. M.; BIDDY, R. L., AND SURPHLIS, W.: "Conditioned" alpha desynchronization. *Science*, *134*:388-389, 1961; **246.**

STERIADE, M., AND DEMETRESCU, M.: Reticular facilitation of responses to acoustic stimuli. *Electroenceph. Clin. Neurophysiol.*, *14*:21-36, 1962; **244.**

STORMS, L. H.; BOROCZI, G., AND BROEN, W. E.: Effects of punishment as a function of strain of rat and duration of shock. *J. Comp. Physiol, Psychol.*, *56*:1022-1026, 1963; **18.**

STORMS, L. H., AND SIGAL, J. J.: Eysenck's personality theory with special reference to *The Dynamics of Anxiety and Hysteria*. *Brit. J. Med. Psychol.*, *31*:228-248, 1958; **120.**

SUMMERFIELD, A., AND STEINBERG, H.: Reducing interference in forgetting. *Quart. J. Exper. Psychol.*, *9*:146-154, 1957; **310.**

SWARD, K., AND FRIEDMAN, M. B.: Jewish temperament. *J. Appl. Psychol.*, *19*:70-84, 1935; **208.**

SWEENEY, D. R., AND FINE, B. J.: Pain reactivity and field dependence. *Percept. Motor Skills*, *21*:757-758, 1965; **117.**

SWETS, J. A.: Indices of signal detectability obtained with various psychophysical procedures. *J. Acoust. Soc. Amer.*, *31*:511-513, 1959; **101.**

SYLVESTER, J.: Depressant-stimulant drugs, inhibition and the visual constancies. In: H. J. Eysenck, (Ed.): *Experiments with Drugs*. New York, Pergamon, 1963; **294.**

TAYLOR, J.: Drive theory and manifest anxiety. *Psychol. Bull.*, *53*:303-320, 1956; **42.**

TERRY, P. G.: Autonomic balance and temperament. *J. Comp. Physiol. Psychol.*, *46*:454-460, 1953; **69.**

TEUBER, H. L.: Physiological psychology. *Ann. Rev. Psychol.*, *6*:267-296, 1955; **322.**

TEUBER, H. L., AND BENDER, M.: Alterations in pattern vision following trauma of the occiptal lobes in man. *J. Gen. Psychol.*, *40*:35-57, 1949; **322.**

TEUBER, H. L., AND BENDER, M.: Perception of apparent movement across acquired scotomata in the visual field. *Amer. Psychologist*, *5*:271, 1950. (Abstract); **322.**

TEUBER, H. L., AND WEINSTEIN, S.: General and specific effects of cerebral lesions. *Amer. Psychologist*, *10*:408-409, 1955. (Abstract); **338.**

TEUBER, H. L., AND WEINSTEIN, S.: Ability to discover hidden figures after cerebral lesions. *A.M.A. Arch. Neurol. Psychiat.*, 76:369-377, 1956; **338**.

THERON, P. A.: Peripheral vasomotor reactions as indices of basic emotional tension and lability. *Psychosom. Med.*, 10:335-346, 1948; **167**.

THIESEN, J. W., AND MEISTER, R. K.: A laboratory investigation of measures of frustration tolerance of pre-adolescent children. *J. Genet. Psychol.*, 75:277-291, 1949; **68**.

THOMAS, A.; CHESS, S.; BIRCH, H. G.; HERTZIG, M. E., AND KORN, S.: *Behavioral Individuality in Early Childhood.* London; U. of London, 1964; **219**.

THOMPSON, G. C., AND HUNNICUTT, C. W.: The effect of repeated praise or blame on the work achievement of "introverts" and "extraverts". *J. Educ. Psychol.*, 35:257-266, 1944; **25**.

THOMPSON, L. A.: Measuring susceptibility to monotony. *Personnel J.*, 8: 172-197, 1929; **88**.

THOMPSON, L. W., AND OBRIST, W. D.: EEG correlates of verbal learning and overlearning. *Electroenceph. Clin. Neurophysiol.*, 16:332-342, 1964; **246, 247**.

THOMPSON, L. W., AND THOMPSON, V. D.: Comparison of EEG changes in learning and overlearning of nonsense syllables. *Psychol. Rep.*, 16:339-344, 1965; **247**.

THOMPSON, R. F., AND WELKER, W. I.: Role of auditory cortex in reflex head orientation by cats to auditory stimuli. *J. Comp. Physiol. Psychol.*, 56:996-1002, 1963; **251**.

THOMPSON, V. R., AND OLIAN, S.: Some effects on offspring behavior of maternal adrenalin injection during pregnancy in three inbred mouse strains. *Psychol. Rep.*, 8:87-90, 1961; **18**.

THORNDIKE, E. L.: *Animal Intelligence.* New York, Macmillan, 1911; **23**.

THORPE, J. G., AND BAKER, J. C.: Objectivity of the sedation threshold. *Arch. Neurol. Psychiat.*, 78:194-196, 1957; **280**.

TIZARD, B.: The personality of epileptics: a discussion of the evidence. *Psychol. Bull.*, 59:196-210, 1962; **333**.

TOMAN, J. E. P.: Neuropharmacology of peripheral nerves. *Pharmacol. Rev.*, 4:168-218, 1952; **266**.

TOW, P. M.: *Personality Changes Following Frontal Leucotomy.* London, Oxford Medical Publications, 1955; **327**.

TOWNSEND, A. M., AND MIRSKY, A. F.: A comparison of the effects of meprobamate, phenobarbital and d-amphetamine on two psychological tests. *J. Nerv. Ment. Dis.*, 130:212-216, 1960; **301**.

TRAUEL, N. N.: The effects of perceptual isolation on introverts and extraverts. Washington State Univ; Unpublished Ph.D. thesis, 1961; **116**.

TREADWELL, E.: The effects of depressant drugs on vigilance and psychomotor performance. In: H. J. Eysenck, (Ed.): *Experiments in Personality.* New York, Praeger, 1960; **301**.

TROUTON, D. S., AND EYSENCK, H. J.: The effects of drugs on behaviour. In: H. J. Eysenck, (Ed.): *Handbook of Abnormal Psychology*. New York, Basic Books, 1960; **266, 268, 271, 272**.

TROUTON, D. S., AND MAXWELL, A. E.: The relation between neurosis and psychosis. *J. Ment. Sci., 102*: 1-21, 1956; **223**.

UHR, L.; CLAY, M.; PLATZ, A.; MILLER, J., AND KELLY, E. L.: Effects of meprobamate and of prochlorperazine on positive and negative conditioning. *J. Abnorm. Soc. Psychol., 63*:546-551, 1961; **307**.

UHR, L.; PLATZ, A.; FOX, S. S., AND MILLER, J. G.: Effects of meprobamate on continuous attention behavior. *J. Gen. Psychol., 70*:51-57, 1964; **301**.

ULETT, G. A.; GLESER, G.; WINOKUR, G., AND LAWLER, A: The EEG and reaction to photic stimulation as an index of anxiety-proneness. *Electroenceph. Clin. Neurophysiol., 5*:23-32, 1953; **66, 67**.

VAN DER MERWE, A. B.: The diagnostic value of peripheral vasemotor reactions in the psychoneuroses. *Psychosom. Med., 10*:347-354, 1948; **167**.

VAN DER MERWE, A. B., AND THERON, D. A.: A new method of measuring emotional stability. *J. Gen. Psychol., 37*:109-123, 1947; **68**.

VENABLES, P. H.: Change in motor response with increase and decrease in task difficulty in normal industrial and psychiatric patient subjects. *Brit. J. Psychol., 46*:101-110, 1955; **154**.

VENABLES, P. H.: The relationship between level of skin potential and fusion of paired light flashes in schizophrenic and normal subjects. *J. Psychiat. Res., 1*:279-287, 1963; **26, 120**.

VENABLES, P. H.: Selectivity of attention, withdrawal and cortical activation. *Arch. Gen. Psychiat., 9*:74-78, 1963.

VENABLES, P. H., AND MARTIN, I.: *Manual of Psychophysical Methods*. Amsterdam, North Holland Publishing Co., 1967; **57**.

VERSCHUER, O. V.: Beiträge zum Konstitutionsproblem an den Ergebnissen der Zwillingsforschung. *Z. menschl. Vererb.-u. Konstit-Lehre, 30*:646-661, 1952; **213**.

VOGEL, F., AND WENDT, G. G.: Zwillingsuntersuchung über die Erblichkeit einiger anthropologischer Masse und Indices. *Z. menschl. Vererb. Konstit.-Lehre, 33*:425-446, 1956; **213**.

VORONIN, L. G., AND SOKOLOV, Y. N.: Cortical mechanisms of the orienting reflex and its relation to the conditioned reflex. The Moscow Coll. on Electroencephalography of higher nervous activity. *Electroenceph. Clin. Neurophysiol., Suppl. 13*, 335-346, 1960; **243, 249**.

VOSS, G.v.: Über die Schwankungen der geistigen Arbeitsleistung. *Psychol. Arb., 2*:399-453, 1899; **83**.

VOTH, A. C.: Individual differences in the autokinetic phenomenon. *J. Exper. Psychol., 29*:306-322, 1941; **178**.

VOTH, A. C.: An experimental study of mental patients through the autokinetic phenomenon. *Amer. J. Psychiat., 103*:793-805, 1947; **178**.

WAGONER, R. A.: Differences in response latency and response variability between high and low anxiety subjects in a flicker fusion task. *J. Abnorm. Soc. Psychol.*, *61*:355-359, 1960; **106.**

WALKER, R. N.: Body build and behavior in young children. *Monogr. Soc. Res. Child Developm.*, 27 (No. 84), 1962; **219.**

WALLACH, M. A., AND GAHM, R. C.: Effects of anxiety level and extraversion-introversion in probability learning. *Psychol. Rep.*, 7:387-398, 1960; **178.**

WALLACH, M. A., AND GAHM, R. C.: Personality functions of graphic constriction and expansiveness. *J. Personality*, *28*:73-88, 1960; **157.**

WALLACH, M. A., AND THOMAS, H. L.: Graphic constriction and expansiveness as a function of induced social isolation and social interaction: experimental manipulations and personality effects. *J. Personality*, *31*:491-509, 1963; **157.**

WALSH, J. F., AND MISIAK, H.: Diurnal variation of critical flicker frequency. *J. Gen. Psychol.*, *75*:167-175, 1966; **95.**

WALTER, W. G. Spontaneous oscillatory system and alteration in stability. In: R. G. Genell, (Ed.): *Neural Physiopathology*. New York, Hoeber, 1962; **256.**

WASHBURN, M. F.; HUGHES, G.; STEWARD, C., AND SLIGH, G.: Reaction time, flicker, and affective sensitiveness as tests of extraversion and introversion. *Amer. J. Psychol.*, *42*:412-413, 1930; **104.**

WASSENAAR, G. M. C.: Labiliteit as temperaments-faktor. *J. Soc. Res.* (S. Africa), *9*:23-35, 1958; **69.**

WATSON, D.: Introversion, neuroticism, rigidity and dogmatism. *J. Consult. Psychol.*, in press.

WAWMAN, R. J.; CLARIDGE, G. S., AND DAVIES, M. H.: II. The mecholyl test. *Brit. J. Psychiat.*, *109*:553-557, 1963; **284.**

WEIR, M. W., AND DE FRIES, J. C.: Prenatal maternal influence on behavior in mice. *J. Comp. Physiol. Psychol.*, *58*:412-417, 1964; **18.**

WEISEN, A.: Differential reinforcing effects of onset and offset of stimulation on the operant behavior of normals, neurotics, and psychopaths. Univ. of Florida: Unpublished Ph.D. Thesis, 1965; **110.**

WEISS, B., AND LATIES, V. G.: Enhancement of human performance by caffeine and the amphetamines. *Pharmacol. Rev.*, *14*:1-36, 1962; **272, 301.**

WELLEK, A.: Ranschburg-Hemmung und absolutes Gehör in der Persönlichkeitsdiagnose. *Arch. f. d. Ges. Psychol.*, *115*:61-82, 1963; **77.**

WENGER, M. A.: The measurement of individual differences in autonomic balance. *Psychosom. Med.*, *3*:427-434, 1941; **69.**

WENGER, M. A.: The stability of measurement of autonomic balance. *Psychosom. Med.*, *4*:94-95, 1942; **69.**

WENGER, M. A.: Studies of autonomic balance in Army Air Forces personnel. *Comp. Psychol. Monogr.*, *19*:1-111, 1948; **65, 66, 69.**

WENGER, M. A.: Patterns analysis of autonomic variables during rest. *Psychosom. Med.*, *19*:240-244, 1957; **69.**

WENGER, M. A.: Studies of autonomic balance. *Psychophysiology*, 2:173-186, 1966; **69.**

WERRE, P. F.: *The relationship between electroencephalographic and psychological data in normal adults.* Leiden, Univ. Press, 1957; **66.**

WERNER, H., AND THUMA, B. D.: A deficiency in the perception of apparent motion in children with brain injury. *Amer. J. Psychol.,* 55:58-67, 1942; **322.**

WERTHEIMER, M.: The differential satiability of schizophrenic and normal subjects: A test of a deduction from the theory of figural aftereffects. *J. Gen. Psychol.,* 51:291-299, 1954; **323.**

WERTHEIMER, M.: Figural aftereffects as a measure of metabolic efficiency. *J. Personality,* 24:56-73, 1955; **323.**

WHYTT, R.: Observations on the nature, causes and cure of those disorders which have been commonly called nervous, hypochrondriac, or hysteric. Edinburgh, 1765; **37.**

WIKLER, A.: Sites and mechanisms of action of morphine and related drugs in the central nervous system. *Pharmacol. Rev.,* 2:435-506, 1950; **269.**

WIKLER, A.: Pharmacological dissociation of behavior and EEG "sleep patterns" in dogs. *Proc. Soc. Exp. Biol.,* 79:261-265, 1952; **235, 269.**

WIKLER, A.: *The Relation of Psychiatry to Pharmacology.* Baltimore, Williams & Wilkins, 1957; **270.**

WILDE, G. J. S.: Inheritance of personality traits. *Acta Psychol.,* 22:37-51, 1964; **196.**

WILDER, J.: The law of initial value in neurology and psychiatry: facts and problems. *J. Nerv. Ment. Dis.,* 125:73-86, 1957; **57.**

WILDER, J.: Basimetric approach (law of initial value) to biological rhythms. *Ann. N. Y. Acad. Sci.,* 98:1211-1219, 1962; **57.**

WILLETT, R. A.: The effects of depressant drugs on learning and conditioning. In: H. J. Eysenck, (Ed.): *Experiments in personality.* New York, Praeger, 1960; **307, 311.**

WILLETT, R. A.: The effects of surgical procedures on behaviour. In: H. J. Eysenck, (Ed.): *Handbook of Abnormal Psychology.* London, Pitman, 1960; **326.**

WILLETT, R. A.: Measures of learning and conditioning. In: H. J. Eysenck, (Ed.): *Experiments in Personality,* Vol. 2. New York, Praeger, 1960; **125, 326.**

WILLETT, R. A.: Eyeblink conditioning and situation-induced anxiety drive. In: H. J. Eysenck, (Ed.): *Experiments in Motivation.* New York, Pergamon, 1964; **44.**

WILLETT, R. A.: Situation-induced drive and paired associate learning. In: H. J. Eysenck, (Ed.): *Experiments in Motivation.* New York, Pergamon, 1964; **48.**

WILLETT, R. A., AND EYSENCK, H. J.: Experimentally induced drive and difficulty level in serial rote learning. *Brit. J. Psychol.,* 53:35-39, 1962; **49.**

WILLIAMS, H. L.: The development of a caudality scale for the M.M.P.I. *J. Clin. Psychol.*, 8:293-297, 1952; **334.**

WILLIAMS, R. J.: *Biochemical Individuality*. London, Wiley, 1956; **73.**

WILSON, J. W. D., AND DYKMAN, R. A.: Background autonomic activity in medical students. *J. Comp. Physiol. Psychol.*, 53:405-411, 1960; **173.**

WING, L.: Studies on the physiological effects of performing a difficult task in patients with anxiety states and normal control subjects. London, Unpublished Ph.D. thesis, 1965; **61.**

WING, L., AND LADER, M. H.: Physiological and clinical effects of amylobarbitone sodium therapy in patients with anxiety states. *J. Neurol. Neurosurg. Psychiat.*, 28:78-87, 1965; **304.**

WITKIN, H. A.; DYKE, R. B.; GOODENOUGH, D. R., AND KARP, S. A.: *Psychological Differentiation.* New York, Wiley, 1962; **117.**

WOLFF, H. G.; HARDY, J. D., AND GOODELL, H.: Measurement of the effect on the pain threshold of acetylsalicylate acid, acetanilid, acetophenetidine, aminopyrine, ethyl alcohol, trichlorethylene, a barbiturate, quinine, ergotamine tartrate and caffeine; and analysis of their relation to the pain experience. *J. Clin. Invest.*, 20:63-80, 1941; **290.**

YATES, A.: Abnormalities of psychomotor functions. In: H. J. Eysenck, (Ed.): *Handbook of Abnormal Psychology.* New York, Basic Books, 1960; **153, 163.**

YATES, A.: *Frustration and Conflict.* London, Methuen, 1962; **54.**

YATES, A. J.: Psychological deficit. In: P. R. Farnsworth *et al*, (Eds.): *Annual Review of Psychology.* Palo Alto, Annual Reviews Inc., 17:111-144, 1966; **321.**

YOUNG, K. M.: Critical flicker frequency. In: F. A. Mettler, (Ed.): *Selective Partial Ablation of the Frontal Cortex.* New York, Hoeber, 1949, pp. 257-263; **322.**

ZERSSEN, D. V.: Dimensionen der morphologischen Habitusvariationen und ihre biometrische Erfassung. *Z. menschl. Vererb-u. Konstit.-Lehre,* 37:611-625, 1964; **214.**

ZUBECKI, J. P.: Effects of prolonged sensory and perceptual deprivation. *Brit. Med. Bull.,* 20:38-42, 1964; **109.**

ZUBIN, J.; ERON, L. D., AND SCHUMER, F.: *An Experimental Approach to Projective Techniques.* New York, Wiley, 1965; **59.**

ZWISLOCKI, J. et al.: Effects of practice and motivation on threshold of audibility. *J. Acoust. Soc. Amer.,* 30:254-259, 1958; **101.**

SUBJECT INDEX

A

Abnormality, 37
Achievement, 91, 99, 163, 166
Activation, 9, 55, 173, 226, 227, 228, 233, 314
Activity, 16, 37
Adaptation, 171, 248, 250, 302, 314
Adrenal glands, 71
Adrenaline, 59, 255, 268
Adrenergic, 61
Afferant pathways, 238, 239
Affiliation, 163, 204
Aftercontraction effect, 142
After-images, 294
Age, 260
Aggressiveness, 197
Alcohol, 12, 13, 308
Alcoholic fumes, 16
Alcoholism, 205
Alertness, 235
Alkaline saliva, 58
Alpha activity, 168, 170
Alpha frequencies, 67, 106, 171, 244
Alternation behaviour, 178, 272, 273
Ambiverts, 121
Ambulation, 17, 30, 212
Amobarbital sodium, 308
Amphetamine, 16, 102, 268, 271, 289, 293, 311
Amygdala, 230
Amylobarbitone sodium, 268, 293, 296, 305
Amytal, 273, 295
Anaesthetics, 266
Analgesics, 266
Analytic type, 77
Anatomy, 76
Annulus, 253
Anticipation of shock, 173
Anti-epileptics, 266

Antipyretics, 266
Anthropologie, 34
Anxiety, 36, 44, 50, 52, 53, 56, 58, 66, 67, 104, 120, 157, 168, 171, 173, 176, 184, 229, 233, 304
Anxiety neurosis, 152, 209, 275, 333
Apparent movement, 294, 322
Arousability, 242, 245
Arousal, 14, 50, 51, 95, 97, 129, 173, 175, 226, 231, 233, 235, 239, 240, 243, 245, 265, 269, 286, 314
Arousal thresholds, 248, 289, 290
Ascendance, 220
Ascorbic acid depletion, 71
Association value, 46
Asymmetry, 190
Astropine sulfate, 235, 236
Attention, 4, 241, 282, 334
Audioanalgesia, 140
Audiometric response consistency, 98
Auditory flutter fusion, 292, 314
Auditory stimuli, 239
Auditory thresholds, 104
Augmenters, 138, 139
Autokinesis, 178
Autonomic activity, 202
Automic conditioning, 307
Autonomic nervous system, 55
Autonomic Reactivity, 69, 167
Autonomic system, 19, 68

B

Barbiturates, 271
Basal skin conductance, 173
Base line, 56
Basic emotional tension, 168
Behaviour pathology, 228
Behaviour problem, 67, 257
Benzedrine, 299
Bernreuter's Personality Inventory, 194

391